The New History of England

General Editors
A. G. Dickens and Norman Gash

5

The New History of England

*Already published
† Publication 1984

Country and Court

England 1658–1714

J. R. Jones

Edward Arnold

© J. R. Jones 1978

First published 1978
by Edward Arnold (Publishers) Ltd
41 Bedford Square, London WC1B 3DQ

Reprinted, with corrections 1980
Reprinted, with corrections and additions 1983

British Library Cataloguing in Publication Data

Jones, J. R.
    Country and court—(The new history of England).
    1. Great Britain—History—Commonwealth
    and Protectorate, 1649–1660 2. Great Britain
    —History—1660–1714
    I. Title II. Series
    942.06   DA425

ISBN 0—7131—6103—5
ISBN 0—7131—6104—3   Pbk

Filmset in 'Monophoto' Baskerville 11 on 12 pt and
printed in Great Britain by
Richard Clay (The Chaucer Press) Ltd,
Bungay, Suffolk

Contents

Preface

The plan of the book is that the first four chapters are analytical and cover their subjects through the whole period; foreign policy is treated separately in two chapters, covering the periods before and after 1688; the other chapters are chronological.

Those to whom I wish to acknowledge my gratitude and obligations fall into four categories. First, there are my colleagues, and particularly Professor Robert Ashton, Dr Hassell Smith, Mr Victor Morgan and Dr Bill Speck, who have given suggestions and advice, and more generally encouragement and intellectual stimulation. Then there are my students over the years and particularly those in special subject classes from whom I have learnt a great deal, and who have often untidied the over-neat packages I was presenting to them; I would particularly like to thank Kris Milne, David Sharp, Steve Terry, Dermot Smowton, Gina Saussehrd and Frances Noble. Thirdly Professor Dickens, the general editor, has helped greatly to improve this study, mitigating some idiosyncrasies that would baffle most readers. Finally, but most of all, I must express my gratitude to my wife and family who have kept twentieth-century life going, while I inhabited the strange world of late-Stuart Britain.

1 Introduction

The Restoration of 1660, at first rapturously welcomed, failed to satisfy for long the almost universal desire for a settled order and political stability, for government by legal, known and constitutional rather than arbitrary methods. After two decades of civil war, social upheaval and military government, the nation pitched its expectations at unattainably high levels, and some degree of disillusionment was probably inevitable. But it is not too much to say that within a short time a prolonged malaise came to affect the nation; its political life was chronically unhealthy during almost the whole period between 1660 and 1688. A nation that had suffered so severely in the recent past from intestine strife was again repeatedly convulsed by a succession of acute crises. On three occasions—in 1681 at the height of the struggle for Exclusion, in 1685 with Monmouth's rebellion, and when William invaded in 1688—England stood on the brink of another disastrous civil war with incalculable effects. It was as if a whole generation of Englishmen had been subjected to the traditional Chinese curse, that they should 'live in interesting times'. Politically, they inhabited a world of change and uncertainty, of sensational plots and conspiracies, of endless personal intrigue and manoeuvring, of widespread corruption and almost universal cynicism.

Constitutionally and politically, neither the so-called English Revolution of the 1640s nor the Restoration had settled any fundamental issues—primarily those concerning the distribution of power between the monarchy, the two houses of parliament and the electorate, and the functioning of these institutions, together with the judiciary, corporations and magistrates. It is quite inappropriate to talk of a structure of politics in Restoration England, of the kind that Sir Lewis Namier used to evaluate eighteenth-century politics; during this period the character of politics was constantly changing, and in unpredictable ways. Consequently, it is easy to condemn ministers and politicians for lack of principles and consistency, but they operated in a world of flux and uncertainty, in which appearances were often deceptive and the penalties for miscalculation severe.

The fluidity of politics, the lack of constitutional definition and the absence of any consensus made the period between 1660 and 1689 unique in one extraordinary respect: it was an age of major projects and sweeping political adventures—the Second Dutch War of 1665–7; the policies of the Cabal including the secret Treaty of Dover with Louis xiv and the Declaration of Indulgence; the raising of an army by Danby in 1678 ostensibly for a war against Louis; the campaign to pass an Exclusion bill removing James from the succession in 1679–81; Monmouth's rebellion in 1685; Tyrconnel's remodelling of Irish government and society in 1687–90; James ii's religious policies in favour of the catholics and toleration; his campaign in 1687–8 to pack a compliant parliament; and finally William's invasion in 1688. The common factor in these projects is that, with the single exception of the last, all ended in absolute and complete failure, with disastrous consequences for many of those involved. Clarendon was banished (1667); Clifford driven into retirement and premature death (1673); Danby spent five years in the Tower; Shaftesbury died a fugitive in Amsterdam (1683); Russell, Sydney, Monmouth and nearly a thousand victims of Jeffreys's western circuit of 1685 were executed for treason. Tyrconnel died as the last jacobite strongholds in Ireland were being overrun, and his master James was twice driven into exile (1688 and 1690).

These personal failures contrast with the successful advances in status and wealth achieved by other politicians, and this difference underlines the fact that politics during the Restoration period were a form of gambling. Many of the most prominent politicians were little better than gamesters, some were nothing but sharpers or cheats. All the major projects listed above involved an element of deliberate deception. Besides their openly declared aims there were concealed objectives and unavowed aspirations: the Second Dutch War was intended to destroy Clarendon as chief minister, and set up a new system controlled by those who supplanted him; the Cabal planned to legalize catholicism and establish effective absolutism; in 1678 Danby was trying to perpetuate his hold on office, and probably dispense with parliament; James intended to entrench catholicism, and use a subordinate parliament to establish permanent royal absolutism. On their side, Shaftesbury, Monmouth and the other whig leaders encouraged a mass following, but their ultimate aim was to concentrate power in an exclusive oligarchy. Finally, William declared that he was invading in 1688 to save the liberties and religion of the nation, but his primary aim was to embroil England in war against France.

Deceit and double-dealing on the part of kings, ministers and politicians, cynicism on the part of the people, produced an appalling debasement of politics. Nothing was taken on trust or at its stated face-value. Self-interest, hypocrisy and corruption were taken for granted. Politicians, like revellers in a carnival, were assumed to be wearing masks in order to conceal their true features, and to aid them in the seduction of their victims. Indeed, Charles's most effective political attribute was his skill in the art of dissimulation; like Cardinal Richelieu, he was a master at concealing his own feelings and views, while penetrating the thoughts and intentions of others. It was no accident that the word 'sham' was coined during this period, when there was a succession of sensational revelations—of the number of catholics in high places in 1673, during the Popish Plot in 1678–9, the whig Rye House Plot of 1683, and perhaps the most monstrously successful lie in the whole of English history, the story that James passed off as a newborn prince of Wales a suppositious child, who was smuggled into the queen's bed in the celebrated warming pan.

Few ministers or politicians were given credit for any measure of integrity. Altruism and a sense of duty and responsibility were apparently obsolete virtues. Within the world of high politics, there was cut-throat competition for power, wealth and advancement; it was a world closely resembling Hobbes's state of nature, with every man fearing, but also wishing to dominate or destroy, his fellows. Rankling envy of the successful, a readiness to attribute base motives for every action, vicious vendettas (such as those between Buckingham and William Coventry, Halifax and Rochester, Shaftesbury and Danby), vituperative lampoons and character assassination (the best example is Dryden's memorable study of Shaftesbury in *Absalom and Achitophel*), a willingness to collaborate with foreign powers even against the national interest, all complete an ugly picture of Restoration politics.

Almost everyone in Restoration England felt insecure. The people were repeatedly gripped by panic fears of popery. Charles and his ministers came to fear, after 1673, that the monarchy was again threatened by rebellion and republicanism, or that at the very least the sovereign would be stripped of all effective power. The 'country' opposition and the whigs saw a different danger just as vividly: they suspected that Charles and his court were actually engaged in a 'design' to introduce absolutism or arbitrary government. The political nation was divided over which was the more acute danger: in 1672–3 and 1678–80 it seemed to most that it was the combined threat from absolutism and catholicism; in 1681, 1683 and 1685 the fear of another ruinous civil war predominated. James's achievement during his brief reign was to confirm by actual policies the worst apprehensions of absolutism and catholicism, to the point where a

significant majority of the political nation was ready to take the risk
of another civil war by supporting those leaders who had invited
William to intervene in England with an army. James performed the
feat of uniting most of the nation—against himself. Nevertheless, in
intervening, William (a believer in predestination) took the biggest
risks of all: he relied on the word of Englishmen who had almost all
behaved deviously and discreditably in the recent past. He promised
to be guided by a free parliament, but most sessions of the last five
parliaments had been characterized by faction fighting, obstruction
of the administration and rampant corruption. William's winter invasion was itself risky, but the impediments and difficulties in the
way of its success being followed and consolidated by a lasting constitutional settlement were even more considerable.

It may be a cliché, but it cannot be emphasized too strongly that
the distinctive character of English politics in the seventeenth century derived from the part played by parliament in national life.
Although far from democratic, parliament was genuinely representative of all regions and most interests, it was the one institution that
could embody national unity—something of which the monarchy was
incapable after the brief raptures of 1660. But in practice successive
developments had distorted its position, jeopardizing its capacity to
contribute constructively to good government. First, the 'standing'
Cavalier Parliament inevitably and progressively lost much of its
representative character during its long life from 1661 to 1679, and
its integrity and independence were undermined by the creation
(through the distribution of pensions and other inducements) of a
bloc of ministerial dependants. Then, in complete contrast, there
followed three short-lived and disputatious parliaments in 1679–81,
each totally dominated by the issue of Exclusion, and consequently
legislatively sterile, with a whig-controlled Commons locked into
confrontation with the king and the Lords. Charles regarded these
parliaments as constituting a threat to the monarchy and the peace
of the kingdom, and so dispensed with parliament during his last
four years. His brother James set out in 1687–8 to enslave parliament. Systematically organized intervention in most of the constituencies, in order to rig general elections and pack a parliament
that would enact whatever legislation he required, was the most
subversive and dangerous of all the royal policies that provoked the
Revolution of 1688. First and foremost the architects of the
Revolution Settlement were concerned to prevent any repetition of
such an attempt.

The success of the Revolution Settlement was due to the guarantees which it provided to ensure that parliament would hencefor-

ward be a permanent partner in government, as well as a part of the constitution. Although the relation between parliament and the administration had to be worked out in a process of trial and error and in the difficult conditions of two long wars against France, government could never again be attempted without reference to the views of parliament and the interests that it represented.

After 1688 there was a consensus over basic constitutional principles that was embodied in the Bill of Rights (1689) and the Act of Settlement (1701), and accepted by almost all, whig and tory alike, court and country, anglican and dissenter. The exiled James claimed that, after infringing his royal right, the usurping government would certainly proceed to invade and destroy the rights and properties of the nation. This is what had happened in the 1650s, confirming Charles 1's predictions; but the Revolution Settlement, by safeguarding individual and corporate rights, refuted jacobite claims. In England (though not in Scotland and Ireland) the jacobites were insignificant, a residual and declining minority without the ability to influence events.

Post-Revolutionary politics centered on the continuous struggle to control parliament. Ministers disposed of an official court interest of royal servants and dependants, but this always fell far short of even a working majority in either house. Ultimately any administration had to seek support from one of the two parties. Competition between whigs and tories, the 'rage of parties' in a contemporary phrase, was the dominant characteristic of politics in the years 1689–1714. Robert Walcott, in a revisionist study published in 1956, argued that interest groups and connections were more important than parties, and that a two-party system did not exist. Few historians have agreed with this claim, that a political structure basically similar to that uncovered by Namier for the 1760s was in existence during Anne's reign. Recent research by Geoffrey Holmes, W. A. Speck, Henry Horwitz, B. W. Hill and H. T. Dickinson has reaffirmed the importance of party, and shown that every aspect of life (social, religious, intellectual, artistic and economic was well as political) was heavily influenced by party considerations. Every section, region, class and community was divided (although in varying proportions) between whig and tory.

Paradoxically, the often bitter division of the nation into warring whig and tory camps contributed to the success of the Revolution Settlement. Although the whigs tried to monopolize 'Revolution principles', claiming them as their property, all whigs and almost all tories operated within the system laid down in 1689, and had no desire to change it. Both parties were led by individuals and groups belonging to the aristocracy and gentry. Militant activists in both parties—popular radicals and semi-republicans on the whig side, high-flying clerics and London populists in the tory camp—were confined to the role of auxiliaries. They and such journalistic moulders of opinion as Swift, Defoe and Dyer served the party, but they could not directly influence, or share in the making of, actual policy. More generally the rival parties crystallized opinions. They provided a framework within which worked interests, enmities, prejudices, passions and ambitions. Extra-parliamentary politics hardly existed, except for ineffectual jacobite plotting.

In international affairs the period 1688–1714 saw a transformation of England's place in Europe and the world. Before the Revolution, apart from the Dutch wars, England played a very minor and only intermittently active role. Direct intervention by foreign powers in English domestic politics was more important, and productive of results, than English diplomatic activity in Europe. The Cabal's policies, including the Third Dutch War, depended on the assurance of French support and subsidies; they were wrecked by Dutch counter-intervention in English affairs. Louis was the instigator of Danby's fall in 1678, and it was his reluctant decision to renew financial support for Charles and James in 1681 that enabled the king to dispense with parliament after the dissolution of the Oxford session. William failed in his attempts to resolve (and exploit) the Exclusion Crisis, and Monmouth's rebellion collapsed before he could intervene, but in 1688 he decided the destiny of England and Scotland. By comparison most English diplomatic moves during these two decades were mere shadow boxing; the European states took Charles and James no more seriously than they had their father.

The Revolution of 1688 spelled the end of this state of isolation and impotence. Under William's firm (and often resented) guidance, England was educated in the realities of European affairs, and committed to policies that were to continue through much of the eighteenth century. A European balance of power must be maintained, which meant containing, and if possible reducing, French power. Naval supremacy was essential—to prevent invasion of the British Isles, ensure the safe continuance of overseas trade on which the economy depended, and foil French control of the Mediterranean. But if French power was to be checked, it was necessary to oppose Louis's main instrument of power, his army, with a large British contingent, and with troops obtained from subsidized allies and neutrals. Moreover, in addition to becoming for the first time a major European military power, England had also to become a major partner in a succession of alliances, and to establish regular diplomatic relations with virtually all important European states.

Whereas Charles and James had been subsidized by France, and many of their ministers and diplomats had received 'gifts' and pensions, it now became necessary to imitate these techniques, by buying up minor rulers and building pro-English and anti-French parties in European courts.

The novelty and expense of an active foreign policy, the likelihood that once England became a major participant in European affairs it would become impossible to withdraw from commitments and treaty obligations, naturally provoked opposition. In particular there was intense hostility to the raising of large armies for continental warfare, and in 1697 an absolute refusal to maintain large forces in peacetime. A standing army was still seen as a threat to constitutional liberties. But in the last resort England had no choice; active participation in the European wars against France was necessary to protect the most vital of all Revolution principles—the Protestant Succession. With Louis supporting James at St Germain, threatening invasions that were to be coordinated with jacobite risings (1692, 1696 and 1708), and recognizing James III in 1701, the independence of England or, after 1707, of Great Britain was dependent on unity with her European allies.

Although in theory most tories were as committed to the Protestant Succession as were all whigs, in practice many had reservations about close relations with European allies and were suspicious of the intentions of the court of Hanover. In the Act of Settlement they attempted to put strict limitations on the exercise of power by future Hanoverian sovereigns. By their conduct of foreign policy in the years 1710–14 the tory ministers alienated George, creating the impression both at Hanover and in Britain that they and many of their supporters were crypto-jacobites. This had far-reaching and lasting consequences. The overall results of elections during the period 1697–1713 showed that the tories represented a natural majority of the political nation. Their whig rivals were not only a minority, but also an artificial combination of various sections and interests, although they were far more effectively led and more efficiently organized. During Anne's last years the whigs were forced on to the defensive, until the mistakes of the tory ministers gave them the issue of the Protestant Succession on which to capitalize. Only in the final months of the reign can one see the first signs of their party leaders establishing the basis of the ascendancy that was to be the chief political characteristic of the early Hanoverian period.

2 The Working of Politics

It would be historically incorrect to call this chapter 'the structure of politics in the late-Stuart period' for the reason that, during this period, there was no settled system of politics such as that which existed at the accession of George III. Obviously, the Revolution of 1688 produced profound changes in the constitutional and political relationships between crown, ministers, parliament and the law, but there were other major changes occurring throughout the period in the ways that politics actually worked, and at all levels. It was necessary for sovereigns, ministers, officials, peers and MPs, candidates for election to parliament, municipal and local office-holders, to adapt themselves to frequent, drastic and unpredictable changes. The later seventeenth century appears superficially to be a period of politics without much in the way of principle, of politicians largely devoid of honesty and consistency, with a nation frequently bewildered and often demoralized, taken up with sectional interests and pervaded by cynicism. The primary explanation is that people lived in conditions of abnormal uncertainty, of changes which could not be generally understood, still less controlled or prevented. Developments in late-Stuart England were less destructive and turbulent than had been the events of the so-called English Revolution of the 1640s and 1650s, but they were unsettling and confusing to those who lived through them, and no one at such times of crisis as 1659, 1679 and 1688 could have been confident that in the near future the nation would achieve political stability, administrative competence and international power.

The purpose of this chapter is to examine, over the whole period, the way in which politics actually worked, with an emphasis on the changes that were constantly occurring. The first section looks at the changing characteristics of parliament, the different styles adopted by sovereigns, their consorts and heirs to the throne. The second briefly analyses the influences exerted by public opinion at home and intervention by foreign states. The position of the court as an institution is then examined, and the careers of leading political figures are sketched in a series of short, linked biographies. Then the functioning of the Commons, its procedures and the activities of MPs are discussed, with a similar examination of the upper house. Finally, a description of politics at the grass-roots level looks at the different types of constituencies and patterns of voting, and relates local conditions to the general struggle between whig and tory.

The basic character of parliament repeatedly changed. The prolongation of the Cavalier Parliament from 1661 until early in 1679 meant the suspension of electoral political activity, apart from the lottery of by-elections. Political power, it came to be recognized, depended on organizing the Lords and Commons. New techniques were developed of using influence, patronage and management within what was criticized as a 'standing parliament'. But its dissolution was followed by three very short-lived parliaments, in 1679, 1680–81 and at Oxford (for a week) in 1681, which meant three general elections within two years, and a continuously high level of popular excitement and political consciousness. During these years of the Exclusion Crisis, electoral, not parliamentary, management and organization became the keys to power. But popular agitation and systematic propaganda were abnormal features of politics, and were suppressed as subversive after 1681. Changes in public attitudes and opinions played a comparatively minor part in the crown's success in obtaining the 'loyal' parliament of 1685, from which the previously dominant whigs were almost totally excluded. The change in the composition of the Commons was a valuable by-product of the legal action taken against the municipal charters in 1682–5, but James was to use the enhanced powers of the crown in 1687–8 to try to produce a reliably subservient parliament.

The Revolution of 1688 ended this threat of permanent royal subjection of parliament; but the dependence of the administration on parliament voting sufficient money and passing the necessary legislation to maintain the war against France, meant that inevitably ministers would again try systematically to build a strong court interest in both houses. The 1690–95 parliament was labelled 'the Officers' Parliament' because of the increased number of court dependants who sat in the Commons, and it was in order to counter the revival of techniques formerly used in the Cavalier Parliament that the country opposition forced through the crucial Triennial Act of 1694. This statute transformed the whole character of politics by limiting the life of all future parliaments (until the Septennial Act was passed in 1716) to a maximum of three years. However, it had some quite unexpected and certainly unintended results. The object was to make it unprofitable for ministers to use patronage or corrupt inducements to build a court interest among MPs. A three-year limit to the life of any parliament would make investment in managerial methods doubtfully worthwhile, or at best a short-term gain. The country was assuming (wrongly) that, as in 1679, proven pensioners and dependants would be pilloried and find it difficult to get re-elected, since the crown had comparatively few safe seats to offer them. But the main effect of the Triennial Act was to institute regular and frequent general elections. These intensified and perpetuated political animosities and divisions, contributing directly to the 'rage of parties' that was to be the chief characteristic of politics down to the 1720s. They also priced the ordinary gentry out of this intensified electoral competition, and hastened the establishment of a permanent oligarchical control over the mechanism of elections which changed the composition of the Commons.

There was no uniformity or consistency in the ways in which ministries were composed or in which they operated. There were periods when administration was controlled, and effective power exerted, by a single predominant minister—Clarendon in 1660–67, with Southampton as sleeping partner; Danby as lord treasurer in 1673–9; and again more tentatively in 1690–93; Rochester in 1685–6; Godolphin from 1702 until 1710; finally Harley (Oxford) from 1710 to 1714. Secondly, there were several collective ministries, in which no single minister predominated, but their duration, cohesion and unity of purpose varied considerably. The Cabal (1669–73), although formidable and feared as an absolutist confederacy, was throughout its life an uneasy combination of competitive and mutually distrustful rivals for influence and primacy. By contrast, the whig Junto (1693–9) was a settled and effective group-ministry of virtual equals, who were basically agreed on their objectives and principles. Other combinations were largely interim arrangements, following the fall of a long entrenched minister or ministry; the Chits (Hyde, Godolphin, Sunderland and Seymour), all junior and relatively inexperienced ministers, came after the fall of Danby in 1679, and the collapse of the Junto in 1699 led to a weak formation of tory stop-gap ministers.

For the historian, the most difficult and confusing periods are those in a third category, when there was neither a chief minister nor a predominant group, but a divided court of separate, competitive groups and individuals, none possessing full and assured power to make major policy decisions, or confident that their advice would be accepted and followed by the sovereign. On occasion this was a matter of deliberate royal policy, with the object of preserving a balance within the court so that no group would be preponderant: Charles kept Halifax in office after 1681 as a counterweight to James, Hyde and Sunderland; William's first appointments in 1689 were a calculated mixture of whig and tory—Halifax and Danby, Nottingham and Shrewsbury, Godolphin and Delamere, Hampden,

Mordaunt. Although this arrangement quickly broke down, William in the last months of his reign reverted to the same principle, bringing in whigs to form an uneasy partnership with tory ministers.

One of the reasons for establishing mixed ministries was that it left the final decisions and power in the hands of the sovereign. Despite wide and obvious differences in personality, methods and style, all late-Stuart rulers (Mary alone being the exception) were determined to have and exercise the final authority.

Charles, unlike his cousin Louis xiv, was never a regular participant in the routine business of government, but after 1667 he became active as a working politician, and his activity was of a character that created almost insoluble problems for all subsequent ministers. This was because Charles followed, or at least created for himself the option of doing so in the future, alternative and indeed contradictory lines of policy. A master of dissimulation and intrigue, he often simultaneously committed himself publicly to one policy, while secretly engaging in another that was entirely incompatible, and not even his closest servants and intimates could rely on being able to penetrate his real intentions. Charles consciously mystified his ministers as well as his opponents and the public. Concealing his real intentions behind a mask of cynicism and habitual indolence, he constantly deceived even the most astute and unscrupulous politicians. So far from being malleable and easily led, Charles originated all the unscrupulous, subtle and cleverly disguised moves that led to the decisive royal victory during the Exclusion Crisis over the first whigs. Yet when he finally achieved security and a monopoly of power, Charles had no ambitions to fulfil, no dynamic or long-term policy; in cricketing parlance, during his last years he calmly played out time.

By contrast, James was devoted and publicly committed to long-term policies that were designed to transform the political and religious (and eventually the commercial) state of the nation. James was frank and open in proclaiming his intentions, obstinate and single-minded in adhering to them and refusing to compromise (until it was too late). While Charles was cynically and indifferently aware of the duplicities, dishonesties and disloyalties of his ministers, but correctly confident that he could always outwit them, James expected loyalty and obedience. He failed to detect or prevent self-seeking, factional behaviour and outright treachery. He never realized how his commitment to advancing the interests of catholicism was being exploited by courtiers and fair-weather opportunists (notably Sunderland), and even more by Louis xiv.

James's rigidity of mind, his distaste for scheming and personal intrigue, his espousal of ambitious long-term policies to increase the powers and prestige of the monarchy, his belief in a personal mission or destiny, were all attributes which he shared with his nephew and supplanter, William. The key to the latter's tenure of the crown, as to his whole life, lay in his literal belief in predestination, which alone gave him the psychological strength and physical stamina to assume the crushing burden of his mission to curb and reduce the power of France. His absorption in this task led William to treat English politics as a difficult and distasteful but inescapably necessary means to that end. William could never trust English ministers as he did his Dutch servants, but paradoxically he was obliged to leave the kingdom in the hands of his wife Mary (and he did not believe that women were capable of a political or governmental role) and his ministers, acting as lords justices, while he was fighting overseas. Because of the war, William was for eight years virtually an absentee king. The resulting aggrandizement of ministerial influence was anathema to the country politicians who legislated, in the 1701 Act of Settlement, to prevent a repetition when the Hanoverians succeeded: they were not to leave the kingdom and so leave government in ministerial hands, unless parliament gave permission—a provision that was repealed before it ever went into effect.

In his last three years, 1699–1702, after being forced to disband nearly all his army and discard his whig ministers, William tried to regain control over parliament. But his activities as a politician and his dissolutions in 1700 and 1701 did not prove effective. Anne did not imitate him in trying to take an active political role, but she could never be taken for granted. Anne had strong personal preferences, for causes as well as for persons, and these had considerable political relevance. Her firm loyalty to the anglican church, tested by her father's persistent attempts to convert her to catholicism, was the abiding principle, but after 1706 she came to desire peace, and to blame as warmongers those who were failing to bring about the end of hostilities. The jacobites believed that her conscience also disturbed her for she had helped to dethrone her father, and was keeping her half-brother (the Pretender) off the throne; but there is no evidence to substantiate their assertions that, if free to do so, she would have nominated him as her successor.

The role and influence of heirs to the throne varied a great deal. In particular James's position during Charles's reign fluctuated like a barometer in unsettled weather. As lord high admiral he was the principal sponsor of the Second Dutch War, but he very nearly went down with his father-in-law, Clarendon, in 1667 when schemes were discussed for a royal divorce to enable Charles by remarrying to get legitimate heirs. Yet in 1669–73 James was second only to Charles in pressing for another Dutch war, a French alliance, religious toleration and an end to dependence on parliament. With the failure of these policies and the growing suspicion that he had become a catholic, James became the symbol of an alleged court design to over-throw the protestant religion and subvert the constitution. When the Popish Plot apparently confirmed this suspicion and the whigs con-centrated on the bill to exclude him from the succession, James's fortunes reached their nadir. His exile in March 1679 was univer-sally interpreted as the preliminary to his being abandoned, but after returning in August James emerged as a leader of the tories and courtiers who resisted the first whigs. During Charles's last years a reversionary interest formed around James, with several ministers (especially Hyde and Sunderland) staking their future on his out-living Charles. Yet the latter never allowed James to become pre-dominant, keeping Halifax in office to balance him, and even playing with the idea of rehabilitating the bastard duke of Monmouth in order to keep James under control.

Opposition to James's policies and openly asserted principles quickly produced an entirely new reversionary interest from the end of 1685, as discontented politicians began to look to Mary and William. The opposition could not halt James, but the known disap-proval of William and Mary gave the promise that royal policies would be reversed after his death. Similarly, those who became dis-illusioned with William began in the 1690s to form an alternative court around Anne—it was his persistence in associating with them that led to Marlborough's disgrace in January 1692. William re-cognized the possible dangers of friction, accentuated after Mary's death in December 1694, and in his last years tried to conciliate Anne; it was as part of this operation that he took back into office Marlborough and Godolphin.

Although the Act of Settlement in 1701 named the Hanoverians as heirs to Anne, the court at Hanover took surprisingly little interest in English politics and did little to foster its own prospects, until anta-gonized in 1711–12 by the foreign policy of the tory ministry. But thereafter, as Anne's health weakened and political tensions moun-ted, the succession issue became crucial, and whig percipience in recognizing this and winning George's confidence prepared the way for their supremacy after 1714.

Of the wives and husbands of ruling monarchs, only Mary of Modena, James's second wife, was of any importance. Catherine of Braganza and George of Denmark had neither abilities nor in-fluence, but Mary of Modena was an enthusiast for her husband's catholicizing policies, the centre of the *camarilla*, an inner group of catholic and francophile ministers, and the key figure at court in 1688 as potential regent for her newborn son. Mary II was in a dif-ferent category. Nominally co-sovereign with William she deferred to him in all political matters, and was diffident in making decisions in his absence.

Politics were not altogether and always a matter for those established within the system, at court or in parliament. However, the scope for popular activity, the possibility and permissibility of having, expressing and disseminating political opinions, varied enormously. The Restoration was followed by repressive statutes to restrict petitioning, tighten up the treason laws and suppress unauthorized printing (Licensing Act, 1662), and the restoration of episcopal authority led to close supervision of preaching. In the 1660s there was a substantial fall in the number of all types of publications, but official censorship through the agency of the Stationers Company began to lose some of its effectiveness during the 1670s, and after the first Licensing Act expired in 1679, it virtually collapsed during the Exclusion Crisis. There then occurred an explosion of polemical pamphleteering and journalism comparable to that of the 1640s, with the lead being taken by a conspicuously radical group of London printers and booksellers. Public opinion again became a major political factor. The first whigs organized mass petitions, the tories countered with abhorrences, and Charles had to appeal to the nation in declarations. However, once the whigs had been defeated, a tight censorship was reimposed, any open attempts at opposition activity were punished as seditious, and the penal laws against the dissenters were systematically enforced for nearly four years. Under James there was an abrupt reversal of policy. While continuing to restrict expressions of political opinions, he positively encouraged religious publications as part of his campaign to establish religious toleration, with catholics being able to publicize their doctrines and practices.

The Revolution of 1688 was preceded by a fierce propaganda war, in which James's professional writers tried to counteract the effects of large-scale imports of William's propaganda-machine material. It was followed by a continuing duel for over two decades between whig and tory journalists and publishers. Although the new Licensing Act expired in 1693 and was not renewed, the judges were to adopt a consistently harsh and restrictive line in interpreting the law in press cases, reserving to themselves the usually crucial decision as to whether the publication in question was seditious. They justified this severity as being necessary to prevent the unlimited evils of an uncontrolled press, in disturbing the internal peace of the nation, defaming ministers and bringing the government into contempt, and arousing the unstable and only partly educated (though often literate) urban masses. Consequently, each party had to try to protect its own writers and publishers, while using the law to harass its opponents. The position of independents without such protection was virtually untenable, but at each general election a journalistic war flared up between the parties.

At times of exceptional political excitement the parties mobilized opinion in the form of mass petitions—for Exclusion in 1679–81, against the standing army in 1697–9, for a strong foreign policy in 1700–1701. But most petitions to parliament were concerned with local, economic and commercial issues—in the 1690s, for example. against the import of oriental cotton textiles, and in 1713 against the proposed commercial treaty with France. Some of these petitions genuinely reflected local and sectional interests, but a substantial proportion were the work of paid lobbyists or of organized pressure groups manipulating opinion for their own advantage.

Not all the pressures on king, ministers and parliament came from internal sources. Systematic efforts by foreign powers to influence policy decisions, or to neutralize those already made, were not confined to intervention at court, but extended to building up and using support at Westminster, and appealing by propaganda to the mass of the people. Some of the most important developments of this period were the direct consequence of foreign intervention, in different forms. The policies of the Cabal could never have been launched without the assurance of French financial support, but they were wrecked in 1673 by a Dutch campaign of propaganda and subversion. In 1678 the French ambassador instigated the parliamentary attacks that brought down Lord Treasurer Danby and produced the Exclusion Crisis, but in 1681 Charles was finally able to dispense with the whig-dominated parliaments only because Louis had decided to give him renewed financial aid. The Revolution of 1688 was the culmination of two decades of foreign intervention, but for the following two reigns Louis kept to the same pattern by giving asylum and (except in 1697–1700) intermittent support to the jacobite exiles, and trying to exploit their scattered partisans in Scotland, Ireland and England. Finally in Anne's last two years it became increasingly evident that the key to future political power lay in the hands of the Hanoverian court, even though George's agents and associates had failed (together with the diplomatic agents of the other allies) to sabotage the conclusion of the tory peace with France, in what was the most blatant of all foreign attempts to influence policy.

All ministers and aspirants for office and influence operated primarily within the court at Whitehall. As the unrivalled centre of upper-class society, frequented by all the fashionable and most of the influential, its political importance derived from royal control over, and ministerial disposal of, all major patronage. Moreover, the court

functioned continuously as a centre of politics, whereas parliamentary sessions were relatively short, and up to 1689 extremely irregular in timing and duration.

Ministers and courtiers lived, intrigued, competed and also actually carried on administrative duties in a court environment that
was largely determined by the sovereign's own style. The first essen-
tials were to guide and influence kings or queens, to be able to
predict accurately their reactions to proposals, to detect instantly
changes in their preferences and dislikes, and to have the ability to
prejudice their minds or feelings for or against policies, individuals
and supplicants for favours. Exclusive control over access to the
sovereign could never be entirely achieved (even by the duchess of
Marlborough during Anne's reign). Ministers and serious politicians
had to reckon with the occult influence that could be exerted by the
'little people'—mistresses, favourites, adventurers, menial body servants, physicians, priests, foreign visitors and diplomats on unofficial
missions—who had the advantage of personal contact with the
sovereign. They could never be completely controlled and, if they were
most in evidence at Charles's particularly informal court, they were
also important in the other reigns.

A second major difficulty for established ministers, but one that
offered glittering opportunities for the unscrupulous and ambitious,
stemmed from the absence of any convention of collective ministerial
responsibility. Juniors worked to supplant their superiors, and even
their patrons (Clifford displaced Arlington, Danby Buckingham).
Factions and splinter groups existed in almost all administrations,
from Arlington's formation of a young men's group within
Clarendon's ministry in the early 1660s (with the king's approval), to
Bolingbroke's belatedly successful moves against Oxford in 1713–
14. Furthermore, there was no uniformity in the way that ministers
treated their offices and responsibilities. Some concentrated on
the politics of the court itself (Sunderland under Charles and James),
others devoted themselves to parliamentary management (Danby,
Wharton), while a few (Buckingham in 1667–9 and Mordaunt in
1689–90) affected a popular image. With a few exceptions they were
all intent on making or improving a fortune, or establishing a great
family. Insatiable ambitions working in a period of uncertainty and
constant change produced a political world of cut-throat competition,
in which the private virtues of constancy and openness could lead to
ruin. The fluidity of politics and modes of government are reflected
in an extraordinary variety of ministerial and political careers.

Two early failures were Clarendon and Sir William Coventry.
Edward Hyde was created earl of Clarendon and appointed lord
chancellor, effectively chief minister, in 1660 in recognition of his

services to Charles I and Charles II in exile. Even in the worst of times he had never despaired of the cause of constitutional monarchy, and in 1660 he was able to achieve his objective of a restoration of the rule of law. But he believed in the literal restoration of the former order, censoriously disapproving of all political, administrative and social innovations, even when experience made it apparent that some changes were needed. An obstinate adherence to tradition in practice as well as theory meant that Clarendon failed to adapt himself to the changing nature of politics after 1662. Principles together with inertia prevented him from developing a parliamentary following, he failed (for complicated personal and psychological reasons) to take full advantage of his daughter's marriage to the duke of York, and he retained the faithful and honest but totally ineffective Southampton in the key post of lord treasurer. Additionally, Clarendon's health broke down. Elderly, with friends almost exclusively in the older generation, he was hopelessly lost in the raffish, cynical and mercilessly competitive court of Charles's first years. It is surprising that he survived so long as an outwardly imposing, but crumbling, ministerial edifice. He resembled the grand mansion that he built in St James's—ironically but symbolically with materials so riddled with dry-rot that the house had soon to be demolished. But his determined refusal to resign meant that he remained to serve as scapegoat for the failures of the Dutch war and general disillusionment. He was dismissed on 30 August 1667, but in October when an impeachment was launched against him Charles ostentatiously withdrew his protection. Clarendon was forced into lifelong exile, spending his time revising his *History of the Rebellion*, and justifying his conduct of affairs since 1660 in the *Continuation*.

Quite wrongly, Clarendon blamed Coventry as one of the chief agents of his fall. The latter, younger son of a lord keeper, was very much a new man of the Restoration era. Shrewdly, he found in 1660 an express route to office and influence and became private secretary to James. But like his colleague and friend, Pepys, who occupied a much humbler station, Coventry secured his position and made his mark by industrious and efficient administrative service. He opposed Clarendon's pedantic obstruction of all proposals for administrative reforms, but he also deplored and disassociated himself from the blatant self-aggrandizement of those who impeached Clarendon and drove him into exile. In 1667 Coventry became a privy councillor and reforming treasury commissioner, and was generally recognized as a coming great man. But in March 1669 he fell from office abruptly and irrevocably, ostensibly because of a farcical quarrel with Buckingham involving a challenge to a duel. The common cause of these two failures was that both ministers incurred Charles's

hostility. The king saw Clarendon as a liability and brutally discarded
a minister to whom he was greatly indebted. The reasons for his intense dislike of Coventry are more obscure, but it was implacable;
Coventry was spoken of as possible lord treasurer in 1673 and 1675,
he achieved an almost unique reputation as a constructive parliamentarian over the years down to 1681, but Charles would never
let him hold office again.

Clarendon also blamed Henry Bennet, created a baron in 1665
and earl of Arlington in 1672, for his fall. He had behaved as the
most thrusting of the younger group of aspirants for high office. A
former ambassador in Madrid and a specialist in foreign affairs, he
was not only appointed secretary of state but in 1663 Charles
installed him as court manager in the Commons, overriding
Clarendon's objections. After the latter's fall he was the prime aspirant for chief ministerial power. He was a signatory of the secret Treaty
of Dover. But he failed to achieve primacy, first being balanced
by the demagogic duke of Buckingham, and then humiliatingly
outstripped by his own protégé, Clifford, who became lord treasurer
in 1672. A cool and reserved courtier, Arlington repulsed an attempt
at impeachment and reconciled himself after 1674 to comparative
powerlessness, settling for the lucrative office of lord chamberlain.

Shaftesbury's reaction to the loss of power was dramatically different. During the whole of the 1660s he was a minor minister as
chancellor of the exchequer under his third wife's uncle,
Southampton, and the least important of the 1667 treasury commissioners and later of the Cabal ministers. He fell in with Charles's
policies, being rewarded with the prestigious and lucrative, but
politically secondary, office of lord chancellor in 1672. However
when he realized that Charles had been cynically deceiving him,
and when he was loaded with the blame in 1673 for a court
stratagem that had gone wrong (an unauthorized issue of writs for
by-elections) he abandoned a decade's service to the court, and invited
dismissal. He then went calculatingly into systematic opposition,
openly proclaiming that he would return to office only on his own
terms, setting himself, in contemporary language, to 'force the king's
closet'. Again on returning in 1679 as lord president of a recon-
stituted privy council, when he found that office was an inducement
to abandon opposition activity and principles, and that he had no
control over policy, he publicized his intransigence and so provoked
dismissal. For his last three years his opposition leadership was characterized by increasingly virulent extremism.

The black and white marquesses, Halifax and Carmarthen, so-called
because of their contrasting complexions, were lifelong rivals.

Throughout their careers, these two north-country men operated on diametrically opposed principles, using totally different methods. Thomas Osborne (successively earl of Danby, marquess of Carmarthen and duke of Leeds) was *par excellence* the political technician and a man of immense stamina and resilience, staying in politics for over forty years, riding out three attempted impeachments and recovering after spending the years 1679–84 in the Tower under threat of trial. Originally, he acted as Buckingham's organizer. A surprising and probably stop-gap choice as lord treasurer in 1673, he quickly entrenched himself in office, not so much because of his financial competence but because of his skill in managing patronage, manipulating the court, Lords, Commons and commission of the peace to build a political machine that enabled him to dominate politics from 1673 to 1679. Later he played the most important role (for an Englishman) in the Revolution of 1688, and happily and profitably resumed his managerial activities under William. Even the revelation in 1693 that he had been involved in massive corruption did not lead to his exclusion from official life; he continued as a dispenser of minor patronage until 1699. With a shrewd eye to political advantage he also assumed the role of champion of the anglican church, and by negotiating Mary's marriage to William in 1677 he sought to secure his own future. Thomas Osborne left a lasting mark on English politics in another respect; it was he who pioneered the techniques that were to be developed further by Godolphin, Walpole and the duke of Newcastle to form the basis of eighteenth-century politics.

George Savile, viscount Halifax from 1668 (earl in 1679, marquess in 1682) had too fine a mind and too much sensitivity to immerse himself in the rough and tumble of politics. He prided himself on his independence. Called the 'Trimmer' after his celebrated pamphlet, he consciously sought to balance administrations with the purpose of preventing any single individual or group having a damaging predominance; but he was comparatively uninterested in routine business and never tried systematically to build up a following. Consequently, his career alternated between periods of importance and others of virtual retirement, and paradoxically he played an active role mainly during times of the maximum crisis and tension, when the risks and unpopularity of being a minister were greatest, only to fade into the background in times of peace and relative stability. He incurred genuine hatred by helping Charles defeat Shaftesbury and Exclusion in 1680–81, but got little compensatory credit for trying to check an ascendant James over the last years of the reign. Having warily declined to have anything to do with William's invasion and its preparation, he was sent in late

November 1688 by the desperate James to try to mediate with the victorious William, and emerged from the crisis as the latter's lord privy seal, and a counterbalance to Danby in the mixed ministry. However, he could not endure the virulent attacks made on him, resigning in February 1690 and retiring like an ancient Roman to his place in the country.

Clifford and the second earl of Sunderland were the two men who were more closely associated with James, at different times, than any other ministers, but no pair could be more dissimilar in all respects. Clifford, like James, was an enthusiast in everything he did: both men became fervent catholic converts, although they knew the risks. Clifford remained unflinchingly constant to his principles, energetically and blindly pursuing the causes on which he had set his heart—the Second and Third Dutch Wars, the French alliance and the catholicizing policies of 1672–3. Resolute, energetic but inclined to adopt simplistic attitudes and administrative short-cuts, invariably rejecting any advice to act cautiously or compromise, Clifford was the one minister in the Cabal who really believed that it was practicable to introduce royal absolutism and toleration for the catholics. Alone, he would have persisted in 1673 in the face of opposition in parliament, which he would have dissolved, and indiscreetly but forthrightly he would have tried in the Lords to justify unpopular policies which his colleagues and king were hastily abandoning. The Test Act forced him to resign, and he did not survive his fall for many months.

Sunderland philosophically survived three equally abject failures: in 1680 he deserted James and voted for Exclusion in the incorrect belief that Charles was about to capitulate to the whigs. In 1688, after acting as chief minister and cynically becoming a catholic to win the favour of the queen, he was dismissed by James on the eve of William's invasion, in an attempt to propitiate public opinion which had become incensed against Sunderland as the instigator of James's most detestable policies. An anglican again within a few months, he easily gained William's confidence, but in 1697 his appointment as lord chamberlain provoked a storm and led to his early resignation. Only a consummate courtier could have retrieved so many disastrous mistakes. Sunderland had an unrivalled knowledge of Whitehall, its inhabitants and workings. He was never burdened by scruples, and his one principle was to serve and please the sovereign, whoever he was.

Favourites, that is courtiers without public office or holding one of honorific status, and those best described as mere hangers-on, could have considerable influence through their personal contact with the sovereign, although no one during this period rose to supremacy entirely through personal favour as had Somerset and Buckingham under James I. Charles Berkeley, created earl of Falmouth, probably would have done so had he not been killed at sea during the Second Dutch War (1665). Nevertheless, the public readily believed largely mythical stories of the power and influence secretly exerted by those said to be close to the sovereign. Father Petre, the bogey man of 1688, had far less influence than was believed, and similarly anti-Dutch critics greatly exaggerated the power in English (as distinct from foreign) affairs of William's successive confidants, Portland and Albemarle. Anne's intimates—the duchess of Marlborough, the duchess of Somerset and Lady Masham —had considerable influence in turn over her, and were invaluable allies for a ministry or minister, but on their own they could achieve little.

The last working lord treasurers were Godolphin and Oxford who, as ministers in Anne's reign, successively enjoyed the queen's personal confidence. Both faced the herculean and increasingly complex tasks of financing the War of the Spanish Succession, and of getting official business through parliaments which became polarized between the whig and tory parties, both demanding a high price in return for votes and support. They arrived at the highest office by very different routes. Godolphin acquired the reputation of being an efficient, reliable and unobtrusive administrator, 'never in the way or out of the way' in Charles II's words. Quietly ambitious, undramatic, a skilful political manager, he was also greatly assisted by a partnership with the Marlboroughs; but like them he developed a tendency after 1708 to hang on to office at all costs, which meant giving continuous concessions to the whigs, and eventually lost him virtually all freedom of action and antagonized Anne.

Before he was elevated to the Lords as earl of Oxford, Robert Harley was the most skilful and experienced parliamentarian of his age, achieving influence and prominence first as chairman of the public accounts committee and then as Speaker. He knew more about parliamentary procedures and tactics, and about MPs individually, than any rival in his generation. His other great asset was that he won Anne's trust through his loyalty to her and to the anglican church. He also suffered from one major defect: by the time he effectively became chief minister in 1710 he had come to love and engage in intrigue and manoeuvres for their own sake. From being a master of short-term tactics and opportunist policies, who could have used the infamous phrase of a twentieth-century prime minister that a week was a long time in politics, he became a procrastinator, putting off decisions and refusing to delegate authority. But his deviousness did enable him to keep his ruthless and ambitious subordinate Bolingbroke at bay until the last week of the reign.

Oxford's colleague and eventual rival, Henry St John, first made his mark by a combination of competent administrative services and careerist attachment to rising ministers, first Marlborough, then Harley; but after 1712 he aimed at displacing the latter as chief minister. Contrary to his later theories on government (in the *Idea of a Patriot King*) and apologetic explanations (*Letter to Sir William Wyndham*), Bolingbroke's motivating force was an insatiable desire for power, which he saw could be seized from his superior, Oxford, only by courting the tory-party enthusiasts and adopting their prejudices and policies. It took him over a year to force the closet of an ailing queen, and even in July 1714 when he obtained Oxford's dismissal he was not assured of ministerial primacy.

Bolingbroke's political disadvantage arose from the basic characteristics of the tory party. It was the more difficult party to lead because of the undisciplined independence, often sheer irresponsibility and perversity, of its gentry and clerical activist members, their comparative lack of interest in constructive legislation and routine administration. Although (or perhaps because) it constituted a permanent majority of the political nation, the tory party was less cohesive and manageable than its whig adversary, and Bolingbroke never achieved either the political mastery over his followers or the disciplined effectiveness that the whig Junto ministers possessed. This formidable group combined many talents. Thomas, earl of Wharton, was a parliamentary pugilist and an outstandingly industrious electoral organizer. Somers combined the most capable legal ability of the age with an acute political sensitivity; only Anne seems to have been immune to his celebrated charm. Orford absorbed political attacks; he specialized in two perilous areas, the conduct of the navy and patronage. Two other leading Junto men suffered from serious defects. Charles Montagu, the financial expert, was too thin-skinned and easily intimidated by intense pressure, on occasions wavering in his loyalty to the party in attempts to reach the mirage of an accommodation with the moderates in the other party camp. The third earl of Sunderland, by contrast, was a total partisan. No son could have been more different from his father (the courtier): he was brusque, direct, aggressive, self-confident and zealous, and naturally attracted storms of hostility.

The Junto ministers and politicians had the important political gift of being able to attract the most promising men of the younger generation, partly by their astute talent-spotting, partly by their appealing social conviviality (for example in the celebrated Kit-Kat drinking club). Although they underestimated and snubbed Jonathan Swift (to their great loss), the whigs won and retained the services of the most practical politician England has ever known, Robert Walpole, of able writers like Maynwaring, Addison and Steele, and of soldiers, of whom Stanhope was the most important. Finally, and most decisive of all, the Junto whigs impressed with their sincerity and efficiency George's diplomatic advisers, Bothmer and Robethon, as the men who should be trusted to ensure the Protestant Succession.

The Anglican champions, Rochester and Nottingham, both inherited a special relationship with the anglican church and clergy from their fathers, Clarendon and Lord Chancellor Finch. Rochester was certainly motivated by the desire to vindicate the principles of his father, whose *History of the Rebellion* he was editing. With a reputation for consistency and sincerity, their services were in demand. The bishops were conscious of their dependence on temporal authority, and aware of the unreliability of Charles, James, William and the opportunistic or indifferent majority of ministers and aspirants to high office. In return for protection, the leaders of the church could materially help their champions, especially with the votes of the episcopal bloc in the Lords, and the wide if often provocative influence of the parochial clergy. However, before 1688 such an alliance with the bishops carried the risk of conflicting with the royal tendencies in favour of toleration (and catholicism), and this particularly affected Rochester, who had another asset in being James's brother-in-law and uncle to Mary and Anne. At the end of 1686, he had to choose between retaining his anglican faith or retaining office by conversion to catholicism; his eventual refusal to change, which led to his dismissal (January 1687) as lord treasurer gave him a stamp of integrity that few contemporaries possessed.

Rochester tended to work with the more conservatively minded clergy, Nottingham with the younger generation who were influenced by the new scientific and philosophical developments. Both men were also tory-party stalwarts, attached to the traditional principles of legitimacy, and active and aggressive parliamentarians. Nottingham did not accept William and Mary as *de jure* sovereigns but nevertheless accepted office as secretary of state; under Anne he was consistently excluded from office and, embittered against the tory ministers who rejected him after 1710, he attempted to regain office by an alliance with the whigs. This led to his finally emerging as the leading tory partisan of the Hanoverian succession when his concern for protestantism outweighed any remaining constitutional doubts about parliament disposing of the crown by statute. Rochester's career also underwent contrasting changes. He was deeply distrusted as a trouble-maker by William, who snubbed him

after the Revolution, and accepted him in office with reluctance in
1700. Rochester confirmed his reputation in the first years of Anne's
reign, when he used the anglican policy of a bill against occasional
conformity to embarrass Marlborough and Godolphin. Eased out of
office by them in February 1703, he reacted with vehement irresponsibility, which made it all the more surprising that in 1710 he behaved as a mature elder statesman, assisting Harley with constructive advice.

It is clear that there were fundamental differences in the position of
parliament and the ways in which it worked in the two periods—
before and after 1688. In the earlier, there was no regularity or
certainty whatever about the times at which it met, or for how long,
since the calling and dissolving of parliament, the length and frequency of sessions were all entirely at the king's arbitrary discretion.
There were only two legal constraints. By the 1641 Triennial Act
(which was shorn of its sanctions in 1664), there was to be a parliamentary session at least once every three years—although Charles
ignored this in 1684; and secondly, parliament would be automatically dissolved by a sovereign's death. Otherwise there were no
maximum or minimum limits to the length of a parliament's life:
Charles kept the Cavalier Parliament from 1661 to 1679, but then
allowed the three Exclusion parliaments very limited lives—just over
two months in 1679, three in 1680–81, and a bare week in 1681.
William seems to have expected to keep the Officers' Parliament,
elected in 1690, for the duration of the war against France, but the
whigs and country opposition forced him to assent to the Triennial
Act in 1694 which enforced its dissolution. This also imposed a
maximum of three years to the life of parliament, but it did not
prevent earlier dissolutions: William dissolved in December 1700 a
parliament with six months to run, and in November 1701 one that
had met for only one session. In 1710 dissolution of the only whig-
dominated parliament of Anne's reign, which could have continued
for another session, was the crucial power given to Harley to aid him
in dismantling the Marlborough–Godolphin administration and
constructing an alternative.

There was no restriction at any time on the royal power of prorogation—that is of bringing a session to an end and of fixing the
date for its reconvening—but again there was in practice a clear
contrast between the periods before and after 1688. Over the long
life of the Cavalier Parliament sessions were extremely irregular;
there were sixteen, meeting for sixty-three months in all, but there
was no uniform length. The first lasted over eight months, the shortest
(late 1673) only a week, but there was a tendency to shorten

sessions in the 1670s to about two months, and eleven were of this length or less. There were no sessions at all in 1672 and 1676. The timing of sessions also followed no pattern; they began in every month except August, and many were discontinuous with interruptions caused by frequent adjournments at the king's order. For example, the session starting in February 1677 sat until 16 April, then for a week in late May, but was then adjourned to January 1678, sat until March, and again for a fortnight in April and then finally, after another adjournment, from 29 April to 13 May. Interruptions like these dislocated business, and left the opposition in a state of constant uncertainty. Charles was playing a cat-and-mouse game with parliament on this occasion, and he later used this power of allowing or postponing a session with great effect. The parliament elected in August and September 1679 should have met in October, but it was successively prorogued to January, April, May, June, July and August 1680 and met only on 22 October, by which time Charles hoped that the ferment of political excitement would have subsided. James's only parliament was prorogued after reconvening for ten days in November 1685, and then kept in suspended animation by prorogations in February, May and November 1686, and February and April 1687; on any of these dates it could have begun a session with the result that many MPs came up to London, but it was dissolved in July without ever sitting again.

This irregularity, and the uncertainties it caused, had important consequences. Independent or country MPs never knew whether a session would actually begin on the appointed day, whereas officials (who were mainly London-based) and court dependants could be instructed to attend, or tipped off on the king's intentions by circular letters. Consequently the court was always well represented at the beginning of sessions, with independent and opposition MPs drifting in casually later, especially those from remote constituencies; in 1664 they arrived too late to defeat or obstruct amendment of the 1641 Triennial Act. At the other end sessions were artificially prolonged, so that with the advent of Christmas or the heat of summer the opposition ranks would thin as the less committed went home. Secondly a prorogation meant that all bills that had not passed all their stages lapsed, and would have to start all over again in the next session. Before 1688 many prorogations were snap ones that killed several bills, and dislocated sessions meant that sufficient time and continuous attention could not be given to most proposed legislation, so that many bills were introduced in one session after another but never passed into law.

The Revolution produced no formal restriction on the prerogative power of prorogation, but the pressure of business connected with

the French wars imposed a rhythm and routine down to 1712.
Parliament met every year, with sessions beginning in the autumn
(except in 1700); eight started in October, nine in November and
five in December. The primary business was to pass supply bills to
finance the next year's campaign, so that a regular duration became
conventional, of just over five months in both reigns, with no session
lasting less than four. This gave independent and opposition MPs
much better opportunities to get legislation through, and adequate
advance notice of prorogations was usually given, in order that bills
could be pushed through their final stages and presented for the
royal assent on the last day. Regular sessions of fairly uniform length
also facilitated party organization at Westminster, but their actual
dates were dictated by the overseas commitments and absences first
of William and then of Marlborough, both of whom spent the summers on campaign or engaged in diplomatic activities. Only at the
end of Anne's reign was the pattern broken. The 1713 session (unusually from April to July) was geared to the conclusion of peace at
Utrecht. The first meeting of the parliament elected in the autumn
of 1713 was postponed, largely by the increasing differences within
the tory administration, until February 1714. It sat until three weeks
before Anne's death, and then (under the provisions of the 1707
Regency Act, aimed at avoiding uncertainty that the jacobites might
exploit) for the first three weeks of the new reign of George I.

Sessions usually began with a speech from the throne, or a short
message which was expanded by the lord chancellor or keeper. The
response of the two houses often provided an opportunity for a trial
of strength. Court managers and opposition leaders tussled in drafting and voting an address in reply, which could either contain
thanks and promises of service, or could be in effect a remonstrance.
The sovereign also frequently intervened by sending messages, reminding the two houses of unfinished business (particularly on
supply), or threatening, promising concessions or cajoling them.

There was a variety of ways in which bills could be initiated: they
could start in either the Lords or the Commons, and be promoted by
officials (and especially privy councillors) on behalf of the crown,
when they were usually drafted in advance, or as a result of a resolution of either house, frequently instigated by opposition peers or
MPs. In the latter case the house had to give leave for a bill to be
introduced, and a committee was then appointed to draft it. Often
such resolutions were carefully prepared, or the stage set for them,
by the presentation of petitions to the house, although these were
more common at a later point when the details of a bill were being
discussed. This possession of the legislative initiative by both houses

was, of course, of the first importance, but the enactment of measures
demanded industry and careful management (especially of time) by
sponsors of bills. A bill almost invariably received a first reading, and
was then referred for detailed examination and revision to a committee appointed by the house. In the case of the Commons the size
of committees varied: many were small, ten MPs or fewer, but some
contained as many as forty. The chairman played a crucial part, not
only in presiding over and convening its proceedings, but also in
making recommendatory reports to the house which could set the
tone for a debate. The major debate and the decisive stage in the
legislative process was usually on the second reading; if it was given
the bill would then be recommitted. After further examination by
the committee, and amendments in the light of the full debate which
were sometimes in the form of actual instructions, the revised bills
were engrossed, that is put into a fair and final form, and after the
third reading were sent to the other house, where all the same stages
had to be passed. Differences between the two houses could be resolved by a conference, attended by nominated panels of peers and
MPs, but neither house could force the other to give attention to a
bill. Most often it was the Commons who reminded the upper house
of bills sent up to them, but the peers frequently ignored them and
let bills lapse untouched.

The primary task of court managers throughout the period was to
ensure the passage of supply bills, while their leading opponents
tried either to defeat them or reduce the sums of money provided.
More ambitiously, the latter could try to insist on the court accepting some controversial measure as the price of obtaining supply (the
Test Act of 1673 was the most important example), but this pay-off
was difficult to achieve—paradoxically because of a major advance
in the Commons' powers. In 1671 and 1678 the Commons resolved
that the Lords had no power or right to amend or reject supply bills,
and although this was merely a convention until as late as 1909–10,
in practice supply bills normally passed through the upper house
quickly and without change. This created a formidable problem of
timing for the opposition, since the measures which it wanted as a
quid pro quo for supply could be held up or amended in the upper
house, or rejected after the royal assent had been given to the supply
bills. On occasion (as in 1704 over occasional conformity) the opposition considered the exceptional tactic of 'tacking': by this method it
attached to a supply bill a proposal that had no natural connection
with it, in order either to inhibit the Lords from touching it, or to
force the court to accept the measure as the only way to obtain
money.

Before 1688 the court managers normally enjoyed the assistance of the Speaker in the Commons. Nominated by the latter (although the king could disallow his election, as in 1679 when Seymour was vetoed) nevertheless the Speaker was effectively a royal agent, entrusted with the tasks of controlling proceedings by allowing or disallowing resolutions, seeing or not seeing those who wanted to speak in debates, and above all obeying royal orders to adjourn, or accept a prorogation without delay. The Speaker was also the king's main source of information about men, measures and movements of opinion within the lower house, and in return Charles's Speakers were usually paid £1,000 a session. Similarly, Trevor in 1690–95 regarded himself as an agent, or even a member, of the ministry, but after his unparalleled disgrace—he was dismissed and expelled the house for taking bribes—most Speakers followed the example of Williams, the partisan whig Speaker in 1680 and 1681, and saw themselves as primarily servants of the Commons in relation to the king and ministers. The election of a new Speaker at the start of a new parliament became a practical as well as symbolic contest between court and country, and under Anne, between whig and tory; Foley (1695) and Harley (1701) were country Speakers, Littleton (1698) a court servant; John Smith (1705) and Richard Onslow (1708) were whigs, Bromley (1710) and Hanmer (1714) tories.

The Speaker could not always control proceedings, since many members equalled him in procedural experience and expertise, particularly through their personal work in committees. He could be by-passed altogether by the Commons going into committee of the whole house, which it invariably did on supply matters and could decide to do on other types of business; this was the full house but presided over by an elected chairman. Court managers and opposition leaders made use of a large repertoire of procedural tactics—motions that the question be put (to foreclose debate), for candles (to prolong one), to recommit bills so as to stifle them, to rearrange the order of business, to provoke disputes with the Lords. The timing of divisions created difficult problems. There were no lobbies for voting; astute managers ensured that the noes withdrew and were counted as they left the chamber, while the other pair of tellers counted those who remained as ayes. This gave the latter a general advantage, but the procedure also meant that MPs in the house could not abstain when a division was called. The earliest examples of whips are members who were stationed at the door to stop their own supporters leaving (particularly at dinner time), while letting others go; this required a wide knowledge of the faces and opinions of several hundred MPs. Divisions, however, were less frequent (especially before 1688) than might be thought.

Table: Commons' divisions

Session	Supply	General issues	Private, economic	Procedural, privilege	War	Election cases	Total	300 + voting
October–December 1678	—	13	—	2	—	—	15	6
March–June 1679	1	1	4	1	—	5	12	7
October 1680–January 1681	—	3	2	2	—	2	9	2
1685	1	2	5	—	—	3	11	6
November 1693–April 1694	27	4	18	17	9	10	85	15
December 1706–April 1707	10	7	10	3	—	6	36	10
November 1708–April 1709	3	13	18	10	2	40	86	27

Unless personally given leave by the house, and this was often witheld, all MPs had a duty to attend. If numbers were low, the house could be called, and absentees sent for in custody, which apart from the humiliation meant paying heavy fees. But then, as now, a high proportion of MPs were virtual passengers, making little impact on proceedings. Most remained silent in debates, which were largely monopolized by a regular group of the more aggressive and articulate, although the surviving reports have to be treated with caution, since they were unofficial and subjective, and are incomplete. Furthermore, a number of this group who dominated debates also virtually controlled committees, and they were usually opposition spokesmen since the court managers held offices (as secretaries of state and treasury commissioners) which left them no time to attend committee meetings as well as parliamentary debates. In both the 1670s and the 1690s the court was desperately short of capable and active supporters; most dependants were serviceable only as marshalled voters. There were many debates dominated by well informed opposition speakers who had clearly prearranged their speeches and tactics and pinned back isolated court spokesmen on the defensive, but which ended with divisions in which a literally silent court majority swamped the opposition. Two consequences followed. First, arguing that persuasion by speeches and logical argument was less effective than that by pensions, places and promises, the country feared that parliament itself was in process of being enslaved, and responded with a series of bills to exclude all placemen. Secondly, the court had no option but to enlist the services of some of its critics; in the 1670s a succession of country MPs were bought, in the 1690s the Junto whigs had to be won over.

A few MPs specialized in committee work concerned with the drafting and examination of private bills, and those on regional and commercial matters, which took up a considerable proportion of time. Then, as now, lawyer MPs had an advantage in this field, and

more generally because they could combine professional appearances in the law-courts in neighbouring Westminster Hall with
their parliamentary duties. Courtiers with their base in Whitehall,
London financiers and merchants (several of whom were always to
be found representing provincial boroughs) could also combine their
duties with their normal domestic and business routines, but for the
permanent majority of MPs who were country gentlemen and landowners the sessions at Westminster involved a complete break with
their customary way of life. They had to live, for unpredictable
periods before 1688, away from their homes in an alien and expensive metropolitan environment, irked by the sophisticated and
mocking cockney cabmen, watermen, servants and landlords on
whose services they were forced to rely, but who rooked them of their
money while conspicuously failing to give them the respect which
they expected as of right from their social inferiors in their own
'countries'. To maintain their morale and combat home-sickness,
members clubbed together to eat and (especially) drink in regional
groups—from Yorkshire, Wales, Herefordshire—and feelings of
isolation and inadequacy led many MPs to join for social reasons a
series of clubs organized for party political purposes, from the Green
Ribbon during the Exclusion Crisis to the whig Kit-Kat and the
October and March clubs of Anne's reign.

Changes in the upper house were fewer than in the Commons.
Although there was no legal restriction on the exercise of the prerogative power of creating peers, this power was used with caution
since existing peers would be antagonized by the cheapening of
noble status that would result from a repetition of the mass creations
of James I's time. Charles II created sixty-four new peerages, but these
were counterbalanced by fifty-three dying out, and by the exclusion
of catholic peers by the second Test Act (1678). James created eight
peerages but eight lapsed, and his post-Revolutionary creations were
invalid. In 1688 there were 153 peers. William added twelve supporters in 1689–90, creating thirty altogether, but twenty-one peerages disappeared. Anne also created thirty, but fifteen of these were
given to men who would inherit peerages in time, so that the size of
the house was not inflated. However, it was during her reign that the
question of new peerages became a major issue. First, in 1707 sixteen Scottish representative peers were added under the terms of the
Union; they were chosen from their own number by Scottish peers (a
separate order of nobility from the English and Irish) at the beginning of each parliament for its duration. This was the largest ever
single addition and caused disquiet. Consequently, when the
Scottish duke of Hamilton was created a British duke (1711), so that
he could sit of right, the lords refused to accept him, resolving that

Scottish peers at the time of the Union could sit only as one of the fixed number of sixteen representatives. The other mass creation was more directly a party matter—the creation of twelve peers to ensure the ratification of the preliminaries to the Treaty of Utrecht in December 1711 and January 1712. Eight of the new peers were heirs to existing peerages, which limited the long-term effects, but this move was seen as a dangerous precedent that later ministries might follow. In 1719 a bill was unsuccessfully promoted to fix in perpetuity the size of the upper house: sovereigns would be limited to granting new peerages to replace those that lapsed.

Many peers were senior ministers, or held high posts at court, but some were relatively poor and were as eager in their quest for sinecures and minor posts as placemen in the Commons. With some exceptions the bishops occupied the same position as ministerial clients after their restoration to the Lords in 1661. Bishops were nominated by the sovereign. They usually went first to a minor see with a relatively modest stipend, but knew that translation to one of the ecclesiastical plums (Worcester, Salisbury, Exeter, Ely, Durham and Winchester in ascending order of income) was more easily earned by faithful service of the administration in the Lords than by performance of duties in their dioceses. The one exception was the see of London, the most important after the two archbishoprics, since control over the clergy and population of the capital was recognized (after Charles I's experiences in 1640–42) as the key to internal order and security.

Royal appointments determined the character of the episcopal bench: under Charles the bishops proved to be the crown's most reliable supporters, but only one of the seven bishops who petitioned James in 1688 and were put on trial subsequently recognized William and Mary. To replace those who were deprived, William and Mary took care to appoint men who were not extreme partisans, but during the reign the bench of bishops assumed a whig character that Anne did not have the opportunity to reverse.

The other category of recruits to the peerage consisted of successful politicians who achieved high office. For reasons of prestige they expected promotion to a peerage: Clarendon, Arlington, Clifford, Shaftesbury, Danby, Halifax, Rochester, Somers, Godolphin, Marlborough, Oxford and Bolingbroke all received grants of peerages; fewer leading ministers inherited them—the two Sunderlands, Buckingham, Essex, Shrewsbury and Wharton (and only the two last were old peerages). By moving to the upper house they left gaps in the leadership and management of the Commons that were often difficult to fill, but a minister had a more comfortable life in the

Lords: he was less isolated, far less under daily criticism and pressure from the opposition and had a much lighter parliamentary work-load. He also enjoyed the benefits of his legal privileges as a peer, of which the most notable was the right to be tried only by his fellow peers. This gave virtual immunity from effective punishment to such murderous reprobates as Mohun and Cornwallis, but politically it was an advantage to ministers, in that the verdict in any impeach-ment against them was by a vote of the house to which they belonged.

In addition to legislative functions, the Lords had judicial duties. It acted as court of appeal in civil cases. In impeachments it acted as judge and jury; these were legal processes voted against a named person by the Commons, which drafted the articles containing the charges and named 'managers' to conduct the prosecution before the upper house. The Lords tried the case, giving the verdict by majority vote and, in cases of guilt, similarly determining the penalties to be imposed. All late Stuart ministers worked under the threat of im-peachment, but actual cases were few. The procedure was time-consuming and clumsy: it involved the suspension of all other par-liamentary business, and the Lords were never prepared to rush a hearing. It was really on this point that the Sacheverell impeach-ment foundered in 1710 as a political demonstration. Impeachments were more often threatened than undertaken and Danby survived three attempts without being brought to trial. When the Junto ex-ministers were impeached in 1701 the Commons lacked sufficient confidence in their charges to proceed with the trial, but protested vehemently when the Lords would not delay proceedings and acquitted the accused.

The character of politics at the local level, and especially the ways in which elections were organized and fought, varied considerably at different times. The 1660 elections were unusual in that identifiable cavaliers were barred from standing, and many returning officers were new in their posts, following Monk's recent purges of repub-licans. The 1661 elections followed the traditional pattern in all respects, but there was no further general election until 1679, and during this interval most electoral interests in the constituencies withered. There were by-elections, spaced out accidentally over the years, but in 1675 there were fourteen English and three Welsh counties where there had been none since 1661; seventy-three two-member and thirteen single-member boroughs were in the same position. At the start of the last session in October 1678 ten English counties and one Welsh, fifty-one double and ten single boroughs still had their original members. The Exclusion Crisis, and

Shaftesbury, changed all this. It was his achievement to politicize opinion, to 'turn citizens into statesmen', that is to make them politically conscious. The second general elections of 1679 were largely fought on party lines, and in the 1681 elections whig organization played a significant role in defeating the tories.

Parties and their domination of elections were abnormal and suspect, and were officially and effectively discouraged in the 1685 elections. But in his last year James himself imitated Shaftesbury in intervening systematically in the constituencies (particularly the boroughs) in a massive attempt to pack parliament. The Revolution was necessary to check this, but it was followed by a transformation of electoral politics. The Triennial Act (1694) required regular and frequent elections. There were eleven of these (1689, 1690, 1695, 1698, 1700, 1701, 1702, 1705, 1708, 1710 and 1713) which produced a permanent 'rage of party' in the constituencies. Divisions within communities, partisan bitterness and recrimination, violent press propaganda, became normal. Because of the three-year maximum to the life of a parliament, candidates needed after 1694 to maintain an electoral organization in the intervals between, as well as at, elections. More money had to be paid out for a shorter tenure of a seat, but this did not reduce competition, and already by 1714 many gentry families were having for financial reasons to drop out of electoral contests.

All English counties had two members, the Welsh only one. There was a standard franchise of forty-shilling freeholders, which produced electorates of several hundred in the smallest counties, and in Middlesex and Yorkshire of over ten thousand. The number was generally too large for candidates at this time to attempt to buy a county seat by corrupt practices, but unavoidably high electoral expenses had to be incurred, reinforcing the social convention by which county seats were reserved for members of great aristocratic and substantial gentry families. Candidates had to bear the costs of the poll, if there was one, and in any event had to take responsibility for giving food, drink, shelter and sometimes transport to at least two or three thousand voters who assembled at the county town, often far from their homes; in the event of a poll they had to be maintained throughout its duration, and in a large county this could be for up to a week. Candidates also had to meet the costs of canvassing, which was a technically difficult operation in large counties such as Devon and Lincolnshire with distinct sub-regions, and in counties like Suffolk where there were few large blocs of property but a large number of small landlords.

The political structure of individual counties depended on the social structure, particularly on whether there was a great magnate with extensive and well-managed estates (like the duke of Newcastle in Nottinghamshire), whether the county was divided like Leicestershire into rival aristocratic-led camps, or whether it was a gentry county without dominant families. There was a possibility for a time that the lord lieutenant, the king's chief representative, might assume control or direction of county elections. Lords lieutenant were nominated because (except in 1687–8) they possessed local influence in their own right. Their control over the militia gave them a network of authority throughout the county, and the sheriff (who was the returning officer) was usually their nominee. In 1685 a systematic campaign was launched to prearrange elections, with the lords lieutenant convening county meetings to which most of the leading gentry were invited. These discussed and arranged officially backed candidates for the counties; those present who possessed borough patronage and influence were asked to find places for those who agreed to stand down as county candidates, in order to avoid contests. This technique worked well—there were few county contests—but there were obvious dangers in elections being predetermined by a clique, who in 1685 also made use of the sheriffs to deny independent candidates a poll, or ended it prematurely before everyone present had voted, or in Surrey moved the election from its customary place without giving notice. These fraudulent techniques would all have been used by James in the elections he planned for November 1688, and malpractices by sheriffs continued to be a feature of county elections after the Revolution, despite a series of legislative attempts to prevent them.

County elections after 1688 provided a test for the strength of the whig and tory parties. Landlords mobilized their tenants (who were often also small freeholders and so had the vote), canvassed their neighbours and appeared in blocs to countenance their candidates. Although they were active behind the scenes it became inadvisable for peers to participate in person (as they had often done during the Exclusion elections); the Commons resolved that for peers to do so would be a breach of privilege—a convention that continued until the twentieth century—and enforced this resolution by invalidating elections which peers openly influenced. County polls continued for several days, with voters getting more and more drunk at the candidates' expense. They usually voted in blocs, as men from a parish or neighbourhood or estate were marshalled unsteadily by parish officers or estate stewards to the hustings from the whig or tory public houses (there was seldom much difficulty in locating voters). The degree of party or personal control over voters varied: some were, or had no choice but to be, plumpers, casting both votes as they were directed, but many freeholders even of modest status and means would promise only one certain vote, using the other at their discretion. Candidates had to keep agents at the hustings, to check on the honesty and accuracy of the clerks of the polls, and to ensure that promises made by voters were honoured; all voting was open.

The patterns of elections and voting in urban constituencies varied according to the different franchises, and also reflected the size and particular social, economic and religious composition of the electorate. In corporation boroughs the governing body provided all the electors. These included many small market towns (Thetford, Tamworth, Devizes) where relatively modest tradesmen filled municipal offices and could be easily overawed or controlled by a magnate and the local gentry. But they also included comparatively large towns whose wealthy and independent office-holders resisted outside influences, bargaining with candidates from a position of strength; Bath was the most conspicuous example. Secondly, in burgage tenure boroughs, the franchise was attached to specified pieces of property—usually houses, although uniquely at Droitwich, brine-pits. Such properties were systematically purchased for electoral purposes as they came on the market, at steadily increasing prices, and most burgage tenure boroughs were, or were on the way to becoming, pocket constituencies during this period; Appleby which fell into the Lowthers' hands is a good example. In the case of the third franchise category, freemen boroughs, everything depended on the regulations or conventions governing the creation of freemen. In large towns with a strong tradition of municipal independence, freemen normally had to be residents, and were mostly themselves the sons of freemen, but in many smaller places they could be non-residents and the mayor could create freemen without having to obtain the formal and open consent of the governing body. Such places generally fell under the influence of the neighbouring country gentry; Dunwich is such a case. Fourthly, there were many boroughs with scot and lot franchises, where all who paid poor rates had the vote. Finally there were boroughs where all male inhabitants possessed the franchise; at Preston this was unconditional and lodgers could vote, but in other cases the voter had to be a potwalloper, that is he had to have a hearth.

This variety of franchises and the haphazard distribution of representation to include large, small and totally decayed towns made for a complex electoral situation which, during the first part of the period, was still further confused by the basic uncertainty as to what franchise should apply in individual boroughs. Repeatedly, petitions against election returns claimed that the franchise being used was not the legal or customary one, and it was not uncommon for rival polls to take place, each on a different franchise. The Commons had the exclusive power to decide disputed elections, and it could declare (either arbitrarily for party reasons, or on the basis of a thorough examination of the case and precedents) on the franchise, deciding who had the right to vote. Even the Last Determinations Act of 1696 did not abolish this power; this act made returns invalid that were not in accordance with the last determination of the franchise by the Commons, but it was still possible to petition against a return on the existing franchise, arguing that it was incorrect, and persuade the Commons to change it. This was so until an act of 1729 declared the last determination to be permanently binding on the Commons. The decisive factors in most elections were local rather than national, and returns in many were always such a foregone conclusion that a poll was never, or very seldom, challenged.

Pocket boroughs were those absolutely controlled by a political interest, usually that of a great landowner. Proprietorship of virtually all local property conferred irresistible influence, whatever the franchise; the Russells controlled Tavistock (freemen), the Howards Castle Rising (burgage tenure), the Turgises Gatton (scot and lot). The number of pocket boroughs steadily increased as an inevitable by-product of the rise of a dominant social and economically powerful oligarchy.

Venal boroughs, where money was the main argument, provided opportunities for political adventurers and *nouveaux riches* to bribe their way into the Commons, although few could afford to maintain for a political lifetime the rate of expenditure that was usually necessary, and was steadily increasing as competition for seats grew. By their nature, seats bought in a corrupt competition were insecure; the voters in such degraded places as Stockbridge, drunken Ludgershall and popular Southwark were always encouraging fresh candidates, for their appearance meant more money being expended, and the sitting members would be forced to increase their expenditure. Consequently, those who were intent on establishing a new but hopefully permanent interest were better advised to purchase a pocket borough—as Thomas Pitt did on returning from India, when he bought the classic pocket borough of Old Sarum.

Most boroughs were of no uniform character, with a wide variety of competitive influences and socio-economic conditions which were often changing. A crude but useful categorization is to separate interests and influences that were external to boroughs from those that were basically municipal and urban. The most common external interests were those of magnates or country gentry whose power derived primarily from the ownership of urban property; tradesmen also depended on their commercial patronage, and they often employed urban labour on a considerable scale. Furthermore, smaller towns were subject to the jurisdiction of the county JPs, whose help-ful or obstructive attitudes and decisions could materially affect in-dividual livelihoods and the prosperity of the community. Medium-sized towns, although they often had their own bench of magistrates, also needed cooperation with the county commission and only large cities with exclusive jurisdictional rights could disregard it. Secondly, although most clergy were resident, they were effectively agents of external forces—the bishop and the tory country gentry to whom the clergy looked for support and encouragement. The church was often an important ground landlord, especially in cathedral cities, but even more pervasive and influential was clerical control over the dispensing and administration of charitable funds. This led to the formation in most places of groups of anglican clients. Private chari-ties also preserved votes—they saved poor electors from being dis-franchised for receiving parochial relief—and because of clerical activity the tories often had a larger urban tail of indigent voters than their whig rivals. The clergy also controlled a certain amount of local patronage, including school posts, and the influence of preach-ing on opinion was still considerable, although now less influential than the press at times of crisis.

By contrast with the anglican, the dissenting interest often became identified with the cause of urban independence. Crown interven-tion in municipal affairs, designed to eliminate dissenting influences, started with the Corporation Act (1661) which ejected republicans, dissenters and their sympathizers. Under the act commissioners, who were invariably country gentry, acted as the agents of the purges and naturally installed their own associates and protégés as replacements. In most places these dependants of the gentry proved to be less influential and determined than those who had been ejected, so that by the late 1660s and 1670s the latter (or their sons) were beginning to recover local influence and regain office, and they provided the first whigs in 1679–81 with the basis of their electoral support. Consequently, after 1681 they were again the target for royal and magisterial intervention, and were again ejected *en masse*. But in 1687–8, in a reversal of policy that was an admission of the local superiority and effectiveness of the dissenting interest, James made a bid for their support, discarding in the process the tory and anglican townsmen associated with the gentry who were trying to obstruct his policies. After 1688, with the establishment of religious toleration, the dissenters remained politically influential in both municipal and parliamentary elections. They were a cohesive force, strongly en-trenched in medium-sized and larger towns, where they were well represented among the class of tradesmen, retailers and artisans. A grudging tribute to their strength and persistence can be found in the series of tory occasional conformity bills, which finally passed in 1711, penalizing officeholders who attended dissenting places of worship; the purpose was either to eliminate dissenters from town offices, or to force those with local ambitions to conform to the anglican church.

The tories also sponsored from 1696, and eventually passed in 1710, a measure imposing property qualifications on all MPs, to the value of £600 per annum for county members, £300 for boroughs. This was deliberately intended to bar townsmen, most of whose wealth was in business stock and working capital, not landed property. The act was resented, particularly by leading families in larger towns, but it is significant that the whigs did not repeal it after 1714, as they did the Occasional Conformity Act. The Qualification Act was easily evaded by fictitious conveyances of landed property to candidates, but this device put the latter into the hands of a sponsoring magnate. An act intended to discriminate in favour of country gentry, and against urban tradesmen, manufacturers and professional men, served only in the long term to increase the influence of the new oligarchy.

Election techniques and conditions varied according to the wealth and connections of candidates, the openness and corruptibility of voters, the intensity of competition, and the attitudes of the returning officer, but the Triennial Act of 1694 marks a significant divide. Before then, elections occurred at irregular and unpredictable intervals, and consequently many electoral campaigns had to be hastily improvised, but the act provided in effect for regular elections. Thereafter, everyone knew that a maximum of three years could elapse between elections: it became essential to maintain permanent electoral interests, and was no longer enough to mobilize resources when an election was proclaimed. The Triennial Act also had the effect, and the importance of this can hardly be overstated, of dividing most constituencies into bitterly hostile party groups. Frequent elections and increasing competition meant that communities were being constantly ripped apart by what was all too often literally electoral and party warfare, leaving behind lasting vendettas and endless recriminations.

Elections were often accompanied by a great deal of ugly violence —although one need not take at face value a contemporary description of a Huntingdon election being a quiet one because only one person was killed. Moreover, many constituencies and their inhabitants in general (whatever the franchise) were degraded by the dubious or flagrantly corrupt practices of agents acting for candidates. The key men in urban constituencies were the returning officer (the mayor, head bailiff or the equivalent) and those who dispensed poor relief. The former fixed the time of the election, and by his conduct (especially of the poll) could give one party a decisive advantage—closing it before all present had voted, spinning it out while one party mustered its reserves, allowing spurious and disallowing valid votes, and finally adding up accurately or fraudulently the votes cast for each candidate. Returning officers had to be fireproof. They were subject during elections to badgering pressure by candidates, their sponsors and their agents—to whom in weakness they had often given contradictory promises. They had the thankless and frequently impossible duty of preserving some kind of order at the polls and were in danger of mob violence from frustrated or cheated voters. They had the responsibility of signing the actual return to the Commons, and if a petition was presented against the return by defeated candidates or voters (and there was an average of over forty petitions at the start of each new parliament) the returning officer was usually summoned to justify his conduct before the committee of privileges and elections at Westminster. Many were fined or imprisoned for their frauds.

By comparison the churchwardens, clergy and other dispensers of charity worked in obscurity. However, they were invaluable for their detailed knowledge of the inhabitants and their financial status, and particularly of the poor who were obvious targets for bribes. As indigent voters came to poll, a churchwarden could object on the grounds of their having received parochial relief, or remain silent, according to his and their political persuasion. Other agents organized votes in advance, mainly by opening accounts on behalf of their candidates at public houses. Most constituencies were awash with drink at election times, but after 1694 corrupt practices were often organized in semi-permanent forms such as 'loans' which were effectively retainers, and members and candidates contested mayoral elections annually so as to have a favourable returning officer. Violence was an inevitable consequence of drink. Often it was perpetrated mainly by those who did not have a vote, clamorously demanding a role and a share of the largesse being distributed, and who were used to intimidate opposing voters as they approached the hustings, or an unfavourable returning officer, or to protect supporters against coercion. It was almost impossible for effective action to be taken to prevent riotous behaviour since it became an obligatory convention after 1688 to keep troops and the militia (who alone could suppress large-scale violence) away from parliamentary boroughs during elections. Violence was preferable to the risk of official intervention, since there was every likelihood that this (as an isolated case at Grantham in 1678 had shown) would be used for partisan purposes.

Despite the increasing use of corrupt practices, public and par-

liamentary opinion was less cynical and more disapproving than was
the case a century later. Bills to curb malpractices in elections were
sponsored by the country opposition which was worried at the
prospect of being priced out of elections, but they had little effect.
A proposal permanently to disfranchise the notoriously corrupt
borough of Stockbridge came to nothing, but several constituencies
where gross corruption was proved lost their representation for the
life of a single parliament, the Commons refusing to authorize writs
for a by-election. But here again there was a gentry interest at stake:
moral considerations were reinforced by envy of, and hostility to, the
monied men who were using their new wealth to buy up voters in
such susceptible boroughs as the Cinque Ports.

Although the country as a whole was sharply divided at election
times into whig and tory camps, voters in both counties and
boroughs were (when they had an opportunity, that is when elections
were contested and went to a poll) surprisingly volatile. A hard core
voted consistently for a party or an individual; this was the case with
the clergy, and accounts for the value of their support for tory candidates. But most voters tried if possible to retain freedom of choice
for their second vote, often upsetting candidates' calculations.
However, with the growth of oligarchical influences, an increasing
number of voters were becoming dependent on a patron, or had
fewer opportunities to act independently as the number of contested
elections declined—although these were trends that were in their
early stages before 1714.

Because so many elections were corrupt, so many MPs placemen
or clients, and because such a high proportion of those elected were
drawn from a small upper class of landed proprietors, it would be
easy to conclude that parliaments during this period were totally
unrepresentative and indifferent to public opinion. This is not so.
Even if they could avoid a poll, candidates had to defer to the
populace at election times. Often there was a distinctly saturnalian
atmosphere, sometimes one of sheer anarchy in which the clergy and
gentry were treated with popular contempt and physical abuse.
More seriously, politicians knew that there were at times issues on
which an informed and politically conscious section of the electorate
had strong views which could not be ignored. Party leaders had to
guide and mould opinion, as well as managing parliament and
undertaking electoral organization.

Certain basic issues aroused feelings and prejudices of such
strength that politicians had no option but to accept them, or at least
disguise their own reservations. The prime example was anti-popery,
always just below the surface and easily aroused among the urban
masses, and especially those in London. This conferred one impor-

tant advantage on the opposition under Charles and James, for it legitimized activities which might otherwise have been much more generally condemned as factious or even rebellious. The second sentiment, xenophobia, operated before 1688 in favour of the opposition and the whigs, since the absolutist policies and aspirations of the court were associated with Louis xiv. After the Revolution it was directed against Dutch influences at William's court, and the alleged exploitation of England by her continental allies, with the tories adopting isolationist principles and trying to fix on the whigs the character of the party of war and high taxation. Connected with this there survived an acute and widespread fear of standing armies, based both on past experience of Cromwell and the Rump and on an appreciation of how absolute monarchy in France, Prussia and Denmark was made practicable by a greatly enlarged and professional army. This sentiment flared up repeatedly, in 1673, 1678, 1688, 1697–9 and 1709–11, and ministers were placed on the defensive when they tried to argue that national security and a realistic foreign policy required the maintenance of professional forces at levels that the country opposition regarded as constitutionally unsafe.

Finally there was the universal belief that parliament ought to be free, which testified to the central place that it occupied throughout the period (except, perhaps, in 1681–5). It is such a truism that historians may at times forget how important parliament was in the life of the nation, and that its survival to play an active role in government after 1688 was the most distinctive characteristic of late-Stuart England, and the one that differentiated the country from other states in Europe. The demand for a free parliament was absolutely decisive when Monk and William invaded England in 1660 and 1688, it inspired both Shaftesbury's first whigs and the post-Revolutionary country opposition, and it formed the essential conditional basis of both the Bill of Rights and the Act of Settlement.

With the growth of London and a fairly high level of male literacy, the press became the most important medium for influencing opinion. The Licensing Act of 1662 did for a time impose effective control, but during first the Exclusion crisis and then the controversies that preceded and accompanied the Revolution, the press became virtually free and extremely important as a political instrument. Shaftesbury's writers contributed substantially to his electoral successes, while James in self-defence hired several of them to work on his behalf as his policies began to unite opinion against him. After the expiration of the second Licensing Act in 1695, the rival parties gave moral and financial encouragement, but only moderately effective legal protection, to their own journalists, occasional pamphleteers, publishers and printers. The judges consistently interpreted the law of libel in a way that restricted free expression by making inaccuracies as well as reflections on the conduct of government punishable. But they could not prevent either the appearance of a continuous stream of polemical (and often virulently offensive) material or its circulation and sale. The Stamp Act of 1712, intended to restrict the influence of papers on the masses by making them prohibitively expensive, was only partially effective. The results surprised foreign visitors who remarked that a unique feature of English life was the informed if prejudiced interest in politics taken by the urban masses. There were few even of the poor who were not passionate partisans of one or other of the two rival parties, although this is not to say that they understood the issues, still less could influence party policies.

The words whig and tory coined during the Exclusion Crisis to describe the rival parties were originally words of abuse, and intended to smear opponents by associating them with detestable extremists: whiggamores were Scottish covenanting rebels and terrorists, tories were Irish papist outlaws, cattle-thieves and brigands. An element of caricature underlay the way in which the parties saw each other, and themselves. Naturally, each thought of itself as representing the best interests of the nation against the menacing and subversive policies represented by the other.

The whigs proclaimed their opposition to absolutism, popery and crypto-popery, anglican intolerance and all attempts to encroach on the liberties of the nation. Before 1688 they condemned the tories as creatures of a would-be absolutist court; after the Revolution they denounced them as crypto-jacobites and friends or unconscious instruments of Louis xiv. Positively, the whigs claimed to stand for the ancient constitutional laws and liberties, with only the uninfluential radical wing pressing for reform and political innovation, for the defence of the protestant religion and for toleration. But from the beginning their chief *raison d'être* was the paramount necessity of preserving the Protestant Succession as the guarantee of the nation's liberties, religion, properties and independence, a principle that was first formulated in the policy of Exclusion and then embodied in what were termed Revolution principles.

For their part the tories saw themselves as defenders of domestic peace and order against the spirit of faction and rebellion, allegedly active in demagogic whig politics and a continuing threat to the anglican church. After 1688 they also adopted an isolationist stand against continuous involvement in continental warfare, stigmatizing the whigs as the party of war. Tories depicted their whig opponents as the direct descendants of the rebels against Charles i, as a party led by an artful and ambitious clique of demagogues who concealed personal motives of rancour or aggrandizement under the cover of concern for public causes. The whig party was characterized as an artificial combination of sectional and separatist groups—dissenters, men of no religion, financiers and the monied interest, careerist lawyers and Scottish, Dutch and Huguenot immigrants—all engaged in pursuing their own personal, selfish interests. By contrast the tories, in their own eyes, were a national party, protecting the integrity of the church, representing the leading social and economic class of landowners, and safeguarding England from the excessive demands of its unreliable European allies.

In reality, as distinct from the propaganda picture put forward by the parties, it is clear that after the mid-1690s the tories did constitute a quite considerable and permanent majority of the political nation, and it must be emphasized that this meant a majority within a relatively large electorate, around 250,000 in Anne's reign, which amounted to approximately twenty per cent of the adult male population. In virtually every county the tories enjoyed the support of most country gentlemen, those who saw themselves as natural leaders of their own rural communities. The lower, parochial, clergy were with few exceptions fervent tory partisans, and tried to instil in their congregations the political as well as religious principles that they valued. The tories also made a sustained but only partially successful appeal to the mercantile and trading classes (as distinct from the financiers and bankers), exploiting their weariness at the losses and dislocations caused by the two long wars against France.

By comparison, because they were a distinct minority during Anne's reign, the whigs were necessarily the better organized party. Indeed, from their origins under Shaftesbury in 1679–81, the whig peers and MPs formed a better disciplined and more cohesive group than their tory opponents. Whereas the latter had the consistent support of the established landowning and clerical classes, the whigs did constitute an artificial or synthetic combination of separate groups and interests. The tories came to represent the *status quo*, and after 1700 this meant those who were becoming alarmed by evidence of social and economic as well as political change; but the whigs because of their artificial and composite character were more capable and conscious of the need of adapting themselves, of assimilating new interest groups such as those associated with the Bank of England and the new East India Company, careerist army and navy officers and the legal profession. By incorporating these new elements and representing their interests, the whigs increasingly discarded the country opposition characteristics that had given them their initial strength in 1679–81. The whigs transformed themselves from being the party of opposition into the party of power and influence, although it was only by ruthlessly and skilfully exploiting the favourable circumstances of 1714–15 that they succeeded in entrenching themselves as the party of government. On the other side the tories won the support of country elements by their opposition to the increases in governmental machinery, taxation and debt that were an unavoidable consequence of the two French wars. But the suspicions of ministerial methods which the tory leaders encouraged in the time of the whig Junto and Godolphin were to persist after the tories gained control of the administration in 1710. Most tory MPs continued to behave largely as a country opposition when their own leaders were in power. Even though they may have had reason to distrust Oxford and Bolingbroke, the tory party was unwittingly preparing itself for its post-1714 role as a permanent opposition.

3 Administration and Finance

The restoration of the monarchy inevitably involved a return to the pre-war principles and institutional forms of administration, although this meant the revival of many anomalies and causes of inefficiency. The legal position was clear: all innovations introduced since 1642 without the king's assent were automatically invalid. Understandably, traditionalists like the principal ministers, Clarendon, Southampton and Nicholas, had no sympathies for change or novelty, although they were sufficiently flexible to accept the excise on commodities as a replacement for the former feudal duties of the crown. But the restoration of the old imperfect order was popular and reassuring for the subject; there was no desire to retain institutions and changes that made for what modern historians would call efficient government. In particular the gentry and members of corporations rejoiced in their liberation from the oppressive, expensive and intrusive forms of centralization associated with the Commonwealth.

A practical obstacle to any reorganization of government existed in the enormous mass of urgent business that needed to be done in a short time. This pressure resulted in two major miscalculations that were largely to determine the character of politics until 1688. Charles was voted what soon proved to be an inadequate financial settlement, through a serious overestimate of the yield of the revenues granted to him in 1660, and the error was not rectified by the Cavalier Parliament. This was not the result of a conscious decision to keep the king dependent on parliament; indeed the whigs later criticized the Convention Parliament for having given half the excise in perpetuity and the other half for Charles's life, so reducing control over the crown. But the inadequacy of the revenue meant that financial solvency had to become the first priority of successive lord treasurers—to be achieved only after 1681; until then Charles, unlike all his predecessors, could not afford to do without parliament.

The second crucial decision, an immensely popular one, was not to attempt any revival of the prerogative courts (the Star Chamber, High Commission and Council of the North) that had been abolished by statute in 1641. This greatly strengthened the effective autonomy of those controlling administration in the localities, both counties and corporations, and it left the clergy dependent on local magistrates for enforcement of the penal laws that secured the anglican establishment. Organizationally, the disappearance of the prerogative courts provided guarantees against both the revival of Charles i's methods of personal government, and the development of the kind of absolutism that underpinned Louis XIV's authority. The prerogative courts, like the *grands courts* in Paris staffed by *maîtres de réquêtes*, had produced a class of bureaucrats who were indispensable for major extensions of government. In England there was no institution after 1660 which could train and employ professional personnel in any numbers to serve either at the centre, or as *intendants* to supervise, direct and sometimes supersede those charged with local administrative duties.

These two deficiencies meant that the policies of absolutism attempted by some of Charles's and James's ministers were really one-dimensional; they were aimed specifically at making the crown politically independent of parliament, but the relatively extensive administrative and bureaucratic developments that would have been necessary never even got under way. The weakness and inadequacies of Restoration administration had a second major effect. The history of Brandenburg–Prussia and Sweden during the seventeenth century, as well as that of France under Louis, shows that administrative efficiency and royal absolutism were largely geared to foreign policy: the chief aim was military power to support policies of external aggrandizement. Success in war was the test by which governments were judged, not prosperity or economic development. By this test Charles and James failed lamentably. Failure in the Second Dutch War was largely, in the Third partly, the result of financial weakness and progressive administrative breakdown. Danby's financial system was undermined by his war preparations in 1678. James's resources were exhausted by his organization of defences against William in 1688.

During the post-Revolution wars against France, national survival was at stake—the Nine Years War subjected every aspect of administration to previously unknown strains. Administratively as well as politically, the Revolution marks a division within the late Stuart period, and it was not until involvement in prolonged European wars demanded the mobilization of English financial resources on an unprecedented scale that significant major governmental developments occurred.

The Lord chancellor in terms of precedence held the first office, and Clarendon in 1660 regarded this appointment as crowning his career and conferring preponderant influence. This was a decisive error; experience was to show that control of the treasury was the key element in government and politics. Nevertheless, the chancellor had very great power and importance, if he chose or was free to exert himself.

The chancellor (or keeper, who had the same functions, but with inferior status) was the head of the legal profession, and personally presided at the equity court of Chancery. He recommended candidates for appointment as judges by the king; from 1668 to 1689 their commissions were 'during royal pleasure', which meant that they could be dismissed at will. This involved Finch (keeper, 1672–5, chancellor 1675–82), North (1682–5) and Jeffreys (1685–8) in constantly monitoring and increasingly manipulating the judicial bench. From 1689 William reverted to commissions 'during good behaviour', which made judges effectively independent, but supervision (and in practice manipulation) of the justices of the peace remained a major task for chancellors and keepers. The considerations were almost entirely political. Finch intervened in the counties to ensure enforcement of the laws against the dissenters; under Jeffreys the objective in 1686–8 was the reverse—to guarantee toleration. After the Revolution the remodelling of the commission of the peace became an integral part of warfare between the parties. The two outstanding partisan manipulators were the whig Somers (keeper 1693–7, chancellor 1697–1700) and Sir Nathan Wright (keeper 1700–1705) for whom historians have had little but contempt, but who earned contemporary tory applause by industriously and ruthlessly ejecting many identifiable whig JPs. Subsequently much of this work was undone by Cowper (keeper 1705–7, chancellor 1707–10), so that another mass removal of whigs had to be undertaken by Harcourt (keeper 1710–13, chancellor 1713–14).

In addition to legal patronage, the chancellor or keeper controlled valuable ecclesiastical patronage. Although the sovereign could and did act himself or herself, the chancellor generally made recommendations for appointments of bishops, deans and some professors and heads of houses at the universities. Clarendon and his successor Bridgeman (keeper 1667–72) sincerely attempted to champion anglican interests, but others reflected the abrupt changes in royal religious policies. Shaftesbury (chancellor 1672–3) was appointed to enforce toleration under the Declaration of Indulgence. While Danby was chief minister his protégé Finch reversed the policy and renewed close contact with the bishops, but from 1681 to 1684 he was superseded in his dispensing of ecclesiastical patronage by a special commission. After the Revolution patronage was at first reserved for Queen Mary, but after her death Somers controlled it for over five years. Naturally he sponsored whigs, and the paradox of the chief positions in the church being filled by a man who was at best a deist, and widely denounced by tories as an atheist, led to the anglican parochial clergy raising the cry of 'the church in danger'. Consequently, Anne followed her sister's example, leaving only the less important appointments to both the whig Cowper and the tory Harcourt, who failed to overcome her refusal to make Swift and Sacheverell bishops.

Chancellors and keepers also had the responsibility of presiding over the Lords, and representing the king in parliament. Following the king's opening speech at the start of sessions they often made more detailed propositions to the two houses, and they had to marshal the court peers, and especially the bishops. They also acted as legal advisers to the council, instructed and supervised the attorney- and solicitor-general, and formally briefed the judges each autumn before they went out on their assize circuits. A mass of routine administration prevented chancellors (except for Clarendon, whose health broke under the strain) aiming at political primacy—only Somers achieved front political leadership, and that was as a member of a whig team. However, the office was highly remunerative; Finch, North, Cowper and Harcourt founded long-lived families of aristocratic rank.

The treasury was in practice the most important office: the crown's financial weakness made the administration of royal finances absolutely crucial. Insolvency put Charles at the mercy of parliament— for example, his enforced acceptance of the Conventicle and Test Acts in 1670 and 1673 respectively. During the Exclusion Crisis he was not a free agent until the army raised for a war against France had been paid off, and only Hyde's retrenchment policies made it possible for hostile parliaments to be dispensed with. After 1689 this could never happen again; royal dependence on parliamentary supply was institutionalized by the terms of the 1689 financial settlement. In addition the Revolution was followed by a considerable expansion of government necessitated by the wars; this gave treasury ministers greater powers of patronage, but they had also to find unprecedentedly large amounts of money.

Financial administration could be organized in either of two ways —by a lord treasurer, or by a commission with a first lord and up to four other commissioners. Three of the seven lord treasurers during this period were outstandingly successful—Rochester (1685–7), Godolphin (1702–10) and Oxford (1711–14), and two were disastrous—Southampton (1660–67) and Clifford (1672–3). Each of the successful treasurers had previously served as treasury commissioners

(Rochester and Godolphin for long periods), and combined great political experience with administrative and financial competence, and application to their duties. Danby (1673–9) was also industrious and financially capable, but his interests were always primarily political and he did not attempt either financial innovations or a by then overdue reorganization. Instead he engaged in a series of improvisations that were always likely to end in a crash. Shrewsbury, the last lord treasurer in British history, was a stop-gap appointed to guarantee the Protestant Succession in 1714.

There was a variety of reasons, some of them good, for the alternative of putting the treasury into commission. Often it was a reaction to the prolonged and ultimately less than effective term of a lord treasurer—this happened in 1667, 1679 and 1710. These three commissions, and those of 1690 (headed by Godolphin) and 1697 (by Montagu) undertook reorganization. But other treasury commissions were cobbled together for political advantage of a short-term kind; in 1679 Charles included Essex as first lord in a composite commission which was intended to impress the opposition (it didn't); the 1689 commission joined four whigs incompatibly with Godolphin and this proved unworkable. Some combinations made for strength—the rough new men of 1667 for example—but two continuing causes of weakness were attempts to combine ministers with conflicting party loyalties, and the inclusion of figureheads and passengers.

Experience soon showed that it was the office of lord treasurer that carried the greatest power and influence, but it also imposed a crushing, almost intolerable, burden of responsibility and grinding, inescapable toil. An effective lord treasurer had to formulate financial policy and get the necessary supply bills through the Commons; after 1667 it was recognized that they had to be specialists in parliamentary management. Negotiations with bankers and government creditors, after 1694 the Bank of England, control of appointments and grants, supervision over spending departments, all had to be undertaken. Before 1688 a lord treasurer was faced with the almost impossible task of exerting some measure of control over what was still literally the king's expenditure, which under Charles tended to rise proportionately more rapidly when there was any perceptible improvement in the overall financial position. Only Rochester achieved effective control of this kind.

A lord treasurer or first lord needed political courage, personal resilience and stamina, more than fiscal or financial expertise. He had to be able to resist pressure and blandishments, to refuse favours and send petitioners away unsatisfied, to make invidious decisions knowing that those whom he had to disappoint would become enemies. He needed a detailed knowledge of all levels of politics and government, their workings and personnel, although the actual distribution of secret service money and negotiations with supplicants for minor offices and favours were usually delegated to subordinates, sometimes private assistants like Wiseman in the 1670s, but regularly to the secretary of the treasury and his clerks. The first treasury secretary, Sir Philip Warwick (originally appointed under Juxon in 1636, and continued under Southampton until 1667) was honest, hard-working and almost totally ineffective. He and his master lacked administrative creativity. They failed to comprehend the urgent need in new circumstances for systematic management of court, parliament and bankers. They stuck to methods of raising money by taxation and in credit operations that were becoming obsolete, mishandled an attempt at retrenchment when it became apparent that the pre-war system would have to be modified, and were then faced with the problem of financing the Second Dutch War.

When the formidably abrasive and energetic Downing became secretary to the new treasury commission in 1667, he had virtually to institute effective organization and businesslike methods. Not all the commission's reforms worked, but the reorganization enabled Downing's successors Howard (1671–3) and Bertie (1673–9) to concentrate, respectively, on furthering personal interests, and building and exploiting patronage for political management purposes. Similarly, the durable and unscrupulous Henry Guy (1680–88 and 1691–5) was a politician rather than an administrator, something that was still possible during the early stages of the Nine Years War, when short-term and short-sighted financial expedients were still being employed. But Guy's successor, William Lowndes, marked a significant change. Not only did he provide continuity in office (1695–1724), but he was a professional administrator on whom the politicians came to rely heavily as a financial technician and expert adviser. Although an MP he was one of the first who can accurately be described as a civil servant.

Finally, it is clear that the treasury led to personal wealth as well as power. Southampton, Warwick and Clifford made only modest amounts of money, although the last clearly aimed at becoming the greatest subject in England—a Strafford or a Colbert. But the rest used the treasury to enrich themselves, rising from respectable but secondary families (Danby, Godolphin, Montagu, Oxford) to wealth on a sufficiently large scale to establish a great landed family.

Next in importance were the secretaries of state. From 1660 until 1708 and the union with Scotland, there were invariably two secretaries whose primary duties were the handling of foreign affairs. The senior was responsible for southern Europe, that is the great powers

France and Spain, and also Portugal and Italy; the junior dealt with the north—Scandinavia, Germany and the United Provinces. They corresponded with diplomats abroad and maintained contact with foreign representatives in London. Some secretaries actively helped in the formulation of foreign policy at council or in cabinet, but their duties also included a wide variety of domestic duties. Like John Thurloe during the Commonwealth, they kept a watch on political refugees abroad—regicides and republicans in the 1660s, whig plotters after 1683 and jacobites after 1688. At home they maintained an intelligence network, receiving reports from agents in provincial towns about disaffected elements (especially catholics and dissenters) and commissioning, directing and interrogating spies and informers. The disappearance of the prerogative courts left them with the responsibility for supervising and licensing all printing and publishing, and the importation of books. Prosecutions for seditious libel were used systematically to silence partisan printers and publishers, and general warrants were frequently issued, empowering officials to seize bookstock and printing material without alleging reasons (and without time limit). Even if prosecutions were not launched, such seizures were calculated to drive suspects out of business.

For many secretaries the most onerous and time-consuming duty was that of representing the court in the Commons. This was not a departmental duty, since foreign affairs were exclusively a matter for the royal prerogative, but when chief ministers were almost invariably peers, the secretaries had to defend and propound ministerial policies generally, and act as managers. There were periods when, almost unsupported in debates and under constant attacks, these parliamentary duties added very heavily to the burden of office; this was true of Henry Coventry and Williamson in 1674–8, and Trenchard in 1693–5. Secretaries who sat in the Lords were less loaded with routine work—several of them were in the first rank of ministers, and aspirants for position or influence as chief minister. This was the case with Arlington (1662–74) who used the office to undermine Clarendon, and then aimed at replacing him. Similarly, Sunderland (1679–80 and 1683–8) tried to become chief minister, and Shrewsbury (1689–90 and 1694–9) could have achieved this had he possessed greater determination and better health. Harley (1704–8) was third in the triumvirate with Marlborough and Godolphin and tried to unseat the latter; ironically his own position as treasurer was undermined by his secretary Bolingbroke (1710–14) at the very end of Anne's reign.

By contrast many other secretaries were little more than administrative drudges, executing foreign policies which they had had no share in formulating. Conway (1681–3), Trumbull (1695–7), James

Vernon (1697–1702) and Hedges (1702–6) fell into this category. At times when England had no effective foreign policy, or when all the major decisions were made by William, secretaries could be employed on other important duties; the loyal Jenkins (1680–84) did most of the work in obtaining the surrender or forfeiture of municipal charters to Charles; Nottingham (1689–93) was virtually navy minister.

Clarendon believed that the privy council should be the body responsible for advising the king on all major decisions, and he blamed his own failure partly on Charles's reversion to taking private advice, the course that had led Charles I to ruin. Clarendon's preference for transaction of all important matters in the full privy council was shared by country opinion throughout the period, which condemned the use of smaller, inner groups described opprobiously as 'cabals', 'cabinets' and 'cabinet-councils'. As late as 1701 a clause in the Act of Settlement stated:

> All matters and things relating to the well governing of this kingdom which are properly cognizable in the privy council by the laws and customs of this realm shall be transacted there.

In practice the privy council fulfilled a more modest governmental function; it issued proclamations and directives to lords lieutenant and JPs, acted as a clearing house for business, but frequently overloaded itself with trivial and private matters. This lack of discrimination in taking on business, and a tendency to grow in size—twenty-seven in 1660, forty in 1664, fifty in 1675—made it inevitable that an inner group of leading ministers would emerge. At first the privy council had four standing committees (for treasury matters, Ireland, the navy and the plantations), but an informal committee for foreign affairs (which in fact meant anything secret), whose members were chosen by Charles, discussed all important business. This was institutionalized by the 1668 reorganization that followed Clarendon's fall, when the committee for foreign affairs was constituted as a committee of council; it also dealt with internal order and differed significantly from the other committees in that it was not limited to business referred to it by the council, and by Charles's regular attendances.

In 1679 the privy council was totally remodelled, being reduced to a membership of thirty. The inner group of leading ministers formed the committee of intelligence; there were also committees for Tangier, Ireland and for trade and the plantations. The startling innovation in 1679 was the inclusion of five commoners and ten peers as independents to balance the fifteen officers and courtiers.

This notion quickly proved unworkable, but the whole project of a reformed council was in reality a tactical device to split the opposition. Throughout his reign Charles invariably took the most vital decisions without consulting either the council or any formal committee—only three councillors were involved in the secret Treaty of Dover (1670), only two in the subsidy treaty with France in 1681. James consulted on sensitive issues with a *camarilla* of catholic ministers and advisers; it was to gain admission to this body that Sunderland staged his cynical conversion to catholicism in the summer of 1688.

After the Revolution, the size of the council increased to more than eighty; such an unwieldy body, although the quorum was only six, could transact only formal business. Inevitably the most crucial decisions were made in a small body; in 1689–90 when the situation in Ireland was critical, the Irish committee of the privy council became a quasi-cabinet, but from 1690 William was out of England for every compaigning season. He left Mary to preside over the government, assisted by lords justices named for the year, but he consciously tried to prevent a cohesive cabinet developing; in 1694, the last year of her life, Mary was told to consult ministers individually, but not to meet them collectively. However, a real cabinet of six ministers did meet regularly, in her absence, and this practice continued during later years while William was abroad; when he was in London the king played a leading role, and sought the advice of this body on most types of business. Although not recognized as a formal part of government, this inner group met regularly, its membership gradually increasing to nine, and ultimately to as many as fourteen.

Under Anne business was first discussed by a much smaller body, the lords of committee, averaging five or six and meeting regularly in the rooms of a minister or secretary; the queen never attended. This committee called in experts or junior ministers and consulted with allied diplomats before sending recommendations to the cabinet. The cabinet was larger (average attendance nine, with a tendency to grow—under Oxford to eleven), it met in a royal palace and in the queen's presence, but less frequently than the committee. It was the cabinet that made all final decisions, and by this time holders of the great offices were *ex officio* members—the chancellor, treasurer or first lord, president of the council, privy seal, commander in chief and secretaries.

At the local level the lieutenancy was at first of crucial importance. In many ways England was still a confederation of counties, and after 1660 there was a permanent and deep distrust of any attempt at centralization, a determination to prevent any revival of the devices used in the past—prerogative courts before 1640, major generals in Cromwell's day—or the introduction of *intendants* who in France supervised and controlled (and often superseded) the ordinary agents of local government. The lord lieutenant was (as he still is) the representative of the crown within a county. His tenure of this office gave a holder additional prestige, but he did not expect to receive direct assistance from central government, and he would resent continual and detailed directives. The court normally appointed the heads of leading territorial families, those whose influence and interests gave them a permanent leadership role—the uncrowned kings of their region such as the earls of Derby in Lancashire, the earl of Rutland in Leicestershire. The only exception came in 1687–8, when James replaced tory magnates, who would not collaborate with him in packing parliament, by a collection of inexperienced and often relatively little known catholic peers, whom he then proceded to direct; the results demonstrated the wisdom of the normal arrangements.

Technically, the lord lieutenant's main task was to organize and command the militia which, after the disbanding of most of the army in 1660–61, provided the main security against internal disaffection and foreign invasion. The deputies and militia officers were appointed by the crown on his recommendation. Each landowner had to provide men to serve, and the county paid a rate to meet expenses. This virtually autonomous system left a lord lieutenant considerable freedom of action, and there were wide variations in efficiency. However, there was one significant exception. Charles, James and their ministers maintained close and continuous supervision over the London lieutenancy and militia, ensuring that they were kept in loyal hands and efficient. But in the case of the counties the correspondence of interests between the crown and the larger landowners was assumed to make close control unnecessary.

In the 1660s the militia was used to hunt republican suspects, in 1670 to break up concerted dissenting defiance of the new Conventicle Act, in 1678 to guard London against papist conspirators and incendiaries. In 1683 under tory officers it was used to search the houses of conspicuous whigs for arms after the discovery of the Rye House Plot. Similarly, after the Revolution militia units were used to guard against the jacobites. Fortunately, the efficiency of the militia against the more formidable danger of a foreign invasion was not seriously tested. In 1667 it helped repulse the Dutch attack on Landguard fort in Suffolk, and in 1685 it performed rather ingloriously against Monmouth's hastily improvised army. Nevertheless, after 1688 the absence abroad of almost all regular troops meant that defence against a French invasion depended primarily on the militia; it was perhaps fortunate that it was never put to the test of opposing regular forces.

In practice, such was the insular confidence or complacence of Englishmen, the office of lord lieutenant was more political than military even during wartime. He was the main source of information for the court on local affairs. He sent recommendations for minor appointments on behalf of his local associates, and acted on behalf of ministers in local politics, particularly in supervising or controlling the corporations. Before 1688 most lord lieutenants could manipulate or use ministers in order to serve their own personal interests, or those of a county. But this became less possible because of the vast extension of governmental and fiscal machinery, and personnel, necessitated by the French wars. Local assessment commissioners and revenue officers multiplied in numbers, providing a new network for ministers independent of both the lieutenancy and the commission of the peace; exploitation of this new system of influence was a key factor in Godolphin's and Walpole's hold on office.

Ordinary Englishmen and women were actually ruled by the justices of the peace, who had extensive powers over their lives, and particularly those of the poor and the labouring class. They were empowered to fix wages and the prices of basic foods, they regulated apprenticeships and supervised the administration of the poor law. Before 1640 there had been periods when the council had supervised the JPs very closely (for example after 1631, enforcing the book of orders), and they in turn were required to ensure that the parish officers—the constables and overseers of the poor—obeyed instructions and performed their duties efficiently. After 1660, by comparison, the JPs were very much left to themselves in deciding how, and how far, to carry out their obligations in routine administration. Intervention by the council after the Restoration was for political rather than administrative purposes—to search for catholic priests, whig conspirators or jacobite agents, to enforce the penal laws against dissenters and recusants. Political, not social, control was the objective. Except in times of serious food shortages (for example in 1693) there is no evidence to show that either the central government or the JPs were consciously concerned to defend the social and political status quo against a popular insurrectionary threat from below. In local affairs the interest which counted was that of the individual parish, or rather of those of its residents who had to pay the poor rates. Just as England can be described as a confederation of counties, so each county was a confederation of parishes. The failure of most JPs to maintain strict and regular supervision over parish officers, as they were statutorily obliged to, meant that each parish set its own standards and these were almost invariably as low as possible, in order to reduce expenditure to an absolute minimum. Most ratepayers and many parish officers themselves subsisted uncomfortably close to the poverty line, and understandably but ruthlessly acted to reduce the burdens that they carried. The drastic Act of Settlement (1662) that confined relief for paupers to the place of his or her original settlement was used by parishes to offload as many paupers as possible; it was not a measure of social panic, to restrict mobility of population, or intended to give JPs of the gentry class absolute power over the lives of the masses. The evidence is that it was not widely or consistently enforced, and JPs did not take the initiative in such cases, but decided only settlement appeals at quarter sessions.

It is difficult to find any sense of direction in the administration of local government before the Revolution, other than the constant desire at all levels to keep expenditure at a minimum. There is little evidence of laissez-faire notions either at the centre or in the localities. JPs were given additional powers (for example an act of 1693 provided that no person was to be given relief without authorization by a JP), but it depended entirely on their own inclinations and interests as to whether they used these extra powers. However, from the late 1680s there is evidence of a new attitude to social problems and poverty that was to be characteristic of the next century. During the last quarter of the century there was a relatively modest but perceptible increase in the levels of economic activity, and particularly overseas trade. Social confidence was confirmed by the rapidity with which the country recovered from the plague, fire and war of the 1660s, and by the contrast between its resilience during the 1690s and the virtual collapse of contemporary France into famine and destitution. But men were worried by an apparent increase in the numbers of the poor in urban communities (most conspicuously in London). The total amounts being extracted from rate payers were rising, and this was reflected in a change of attitude towards the relief of the poor. In place of the compassion felt for the helpless victims of such uncontrollable catastrophes as plague and fire, with discussion during periods of distress of how means could be provided to enable the poor to earn a living and become independent, from the 1690s there was an increasing tendency to blame the poor as being largely responsible for their own predicament. They were depicted as being idle from choice. It was commonly thought that they preferred to work only the minimum that was necessary, wasting most of their time in vicious pursuits or idleness. Moral corruptions were regarded as the primary cause of poverty. Harsher attitudes designed to drive paupers to seek and continue at work became more prevalent, and low wages were seen as socially desirable, because need would compel labourers and journeymen to stay at work. Furthermore, the laws for the protection of property from theft were both strengthened and more rigorously enforced.

Administratively, the Restoration had a reactionary character since it involved the replacement of a salaried, professional bureaucracy by a very various collection of office-holders appointed through favour and connection, with little or no regard to their capacity and skill. Some held office for life, but most at the king's pleasure. Although salaries were attached to offices, the holders relied for remuneration mainly on fees, perquisites and poundage. This reduced their dependence on their superiors, and often led them to treat their offices primarily as entitling them to extract money from the public rather than as involving regular attention to their duties. Salaries were often low, sometimes nominal, and usually in arrears, all of which encouraged corrupt and semi-corrupt practices—the receipt of 'presents', the lengthy retention of revenues which could then be put out at interest for private profit, the purchase of debts owed by the crown, but unlikely to be honoured for years, which an official with inside influence could then get repaid promptly.

At the centre it is hardly possible to speak of a bureaucracy. Under-secretaries (to the secretaries of state), the secretary at war, the secretary and members of the admiralty board, the clerks at the treasury, constituted a group of officials which was only just emerging in the 1660s from having the status of personal servants to the great officers of state, responsible to and paid by them, and not to or by the king. This informality and lack of a fixed, rigid structure gave latitude and opportunities to a generation of able public servants— Pepys, Blathwayt, Vernon, Lowndes—who developed a professional and expert attitude to their duties and accepted major responsibilities. But such men were less numerous than the officers of the old model who served in the two labyrinthine departments of the household and the exchequer, both of which retained structures and methods of administration that had hardly changed since early Tudor times. However, despite the cost and inefficiencies, there could be no serious attempt at rationalization or economical reform in either; sinecures, and offices whose duties were performed by under-paid deputies, were an invaluable part of the system of patronage, and the king could not afford to pay compensation to holders of offices that he might wish to suppress.

Although there were fears of attempted moves for governmental absolutism from the early 1660s until 1688, there was never any strong financial basis for a serious attempt to imitate Louis XIV and his methods. A high proportion of the time and energies of those who directed central government had of necessity to be concentrated on an almost continuously desperate struggle for financial solvency. Before 1688 the immediate aim was to subsist, but if possible to achieve a measure of financial, and so political, independence from parliament; from 1689 it was to support the two prolonged wars against France that were in effect wars of national independence.

When the king came into his own again, he changed the poverty of exile for an accumulation of debts and obligations, some of which he had to honour. The first priority was to disband the republican army, which could be done only by satisfying arrears of pay. Much of the fleet (which was in bad material condition) had also to be paid off, and since most of the ships would have to be refitted Charles had no option but to recognize a large part of the existing navy debt. On these two accounts money had to be raised quickly; apart from the political dangers involved, the longer he retained these forces the greater the total that would have to be expended. The Convention Parliament appreciated this, voting extraordinary supply of £800,000. On the other hand it was an easy way out to fail to recognize, but never formally to repudiate, most of the debts due to private subjects—many of them devoted royalists. Those who did receive something were mainly associates of Clarendon and Monk, rather than particularly deserving cases—hence the bitter reproach that those who had served the king were rewarded with oblivion, whereas his opponents at least obtained indemnity. Altogether Charles paid just under £400,000 of his father's debts, and rather more than £100,000 of those he had incurred himself.

While the Convention was reasonably generous in voting extraordinary supply, it granted an inadequate ordinary revenue, that is sources of income for the whole of Charles's reign. Unfortunately, we know very little about the discussions that led to this absolutely crucial decision, one that plunged Charles into financial difficulties that lasted for over twenty years, but those in charge of the treasury do not seem to have provided either leadership or informed guidance; there was an over-large commission until the ineffective Southampton became lord treasurer in August. The assumption was that government would require £1,200,000 per annum. Traditional sources of revenue were estimated to produce just over £773,000, but one of them was no longer available: the Long Parliament had abolished by ordinance wardship and feudal dues attached to certain lands. As compensation the Convention continued the excise on commodities, the major fiscal innovation of the Interregnum, half in perpetuity and (after bargaining) half for Charles's life, to remedy the estimated deficit in his ordinary revenue.

Although neither far-sighted nor energetic, Southampton soon discovered that the ordinary revenue voted would not provide more than £865,000, and this was reported to the enthusiastically loyal Cavalier Parliament in June 1661. However, this parliament contained fewer MPS with financial and fiscal experience and expertise. After making facile estimates of how the revenues already voted could be improved, it granted (May 1662) an entirely new and perpetual hearth tax in the expectation that this would make up the deficit of over £300,000. This was a wild overestimate. In the first year the tax produced barely one third of the estimate, and when in 1666 the hearth tax was farmed out—that is sold for a lump sum to contractors who would do the actual collection—at £145,000 per annum, the enterprise failed, and the farm had to be abandoned in 1668.

There were also long-term reasons for the king's financial difficulties in this first phase of the reign. Bad harvests throughout western Europe in 1661–3, and therefore high prices for food, affected trade and manufactures by reducing demand, and this brought down the yield of customs and excise. Secondly, Charles and his restored court were undoubtedly extravagant, making hay while the sun shone after the poverty-stricken years of exile. Windfalls such as the dowry accompanying the Portuguese marriage and the proceeds of the sale of Dunkirk (approximately £300,000) were spent as income, and in ostentatious ways that aroused public anger. During the first four years of the reign, despite the voting of more than £2,500,000 for disbanding and the discharge of debts, the king was becoming more heavily indebted. It has been calculated that the total increased from about £925,000 to £1,250,000, and all the new debts had to be serviced by interest payments.

Against this background of a deteriorating financial position the whole policy of launching an aggressive Dutch war represented a foolish gamble. Admittedly parliament and public were at first enthusiastic, voting what by contemporary standards were prodigious sums—over £5 million in all. But war finances suffered from a basic weakness in the mercantilist calculations on which the war was planned. A sharp fall in the volume and value of foreign trade was caused by the pressing of seamen, requisitioning of ships and the siphoning off of capital in government credit operations. Combined with the accidental catastrophes of plague and fire, the effect was a reduction in the yield of the royal revenues, by around twenty-five per cent in 1665–7. By the end of the war royal debt stood at £2,500,000, and parliamentary criticism of the conduct of the war made the provision of additional extraordinary supply unlikely at a politically acceptable price. All sources of credit were exhausted.

The financial crisis of 1667 coincided with the death of

Southampton which provided an opportunity for drastic action. The
treasury was put into commission, with two figureheads (Albemarle
and Ashley), three junior but dynamic ministers (Clifford,
Duncombe and Sir William Coventry), and as secretary the exceptionally active Downing, who had personal knowledge of Dutch
financial methods. Not before time, a systematic inquiry was undertaken into every aspect of the finances. Businesslike methods were
introduced. However, in order to get these attempted reforms into
perspective it must be stressed that two major weaknesses were present from the start. For the two dominant commission members,
Clifford and Downing, the ultimate aim was a new Dutch war, not
long-term reforms, and Clifford was ready to take short cuts and
adopt short-term expedients, gambling that a victorious war would,
by obtaining an indemnity from the defeated enemy and a massively
increased share of international trade for English merchants, boost
royal revenues to the point where the king would become financially
independent of parliament. Secondly, Downing's ingenious schemes
amounted to an attempt to fund royal debts, enlarging the sources
from which credit could be obtained; but the necessary trust (both
political and financial) was lacking, and the ministry could not wait
until administrative reorganisation began to produce a financial
surplus.

Nevertheless, the achievements of the 1667 treasury commission
were impressive in the short term, taking over as it did in conditions
of virtual governmental bankruptcy and disorganization. Downing
put the office and accounts on a businesslike basis, establishing pro-
perly kept records—order, warrant, letter and minute books. The
commissioners required all receipts and expenditure to pass through
the exchequer, and on 31 January 1668 an order in council decreed
that all departmental expenditure must first be approved by the
treasury. It also ratified the principle of treasury supremacy in all
revenue matters. Downing made an important innovation in this
area; first in the case of extraordinary taxes already voted (the 1665
additional aid of £1,250,000), but later for all the ordinary revenue,
he issued treasury orders repayable 'in course'. This meant an easier
and surer way of raising money on the security of specific taxes or
duties (including customs, excise and hearth tax); the man who advanced money had his advance formally registered and numbered.
Repayments would then be made in consecutive order. The orders
carried interest at six per cent, payable half yearly, and were assign-
able, that is they could be transferred or sold. Downing hoped that
this would enable him to tap new sources of credit, freeing the
treasury from undue dependence on a particular group of financiers
(mainly farmers of customs and excise) who had been the main

source of loans but were now refusing credit. The commissioners were hard, rough men who were not to be trifled with; in 1671 after tough bargaining a new customs farm was agreed, but in September the treasury repudiated the agreement rather than accept further demands from the new farmers; instead there was a return to direct collection.

The most hard-headed move by the treasury commissioners (dominated by Clifford now) came in January 1672 with the Stop of the Exchequer. Orders had to be paid in strict sequence, but instead of attracting advances from new lenders, those that had been issued were bought by financiers (at discounts varying according to the time that would elapse before repayment), in preference to making further advances direct to the treasury. This had the effect of strengthening, rather than weakening, the influence of those who were already royal creditors, and the flow of money was being adversely affected on the eve of the war planned for 1672. Disposable royal money would be hopelessly inadequate for a war, and would probably be insufficient to meet even the ordinary costs of government. The Stop suspended payment of orders (except those on the additional aid and some duties recently imposed by statute) in an attempt to get the best of both worlds; the advances had provided a capital sum for the fitting out of the fleet, now the revenues pledged to repay those advances were coming in, but were disposable to meet recurrent expenditure, such as that on pay and victuals.

The Stop was a form of state repudiation such as was common in seventeenth-century France and Spain. If the war had succeeded, public and parliamentary reactions could have been ignored. The war was based on a confidence trick; the extraordinary supply voted in 1670 (a subsidy for the navy, additional duties on wine for eight years and an additional excise for six) had been requested for the defence of (not an attack on) the Low Countries, and had been accompanied by a spurious anglican policy. MPs realized later that they had been wilfully misled. They did vote an assessment in 1673 to finance a second summer's campaign, but only in return for the Test Act, which destroyed Clifford and the Cabal ministry. The deceptions of 1670 and the Stop had a permanent effect on parliamentary responses to all later royal requests for extraordinary supply. Distrust of Charles, and a consistent policy of keeping the king short of money, were liabilities inherited from Clifford by his successor as lord treasurer, Sir Thomas Osborne.

Osborne (later earl of Danby) was far more successful as a politician than as a financial administrator; he was the real pioneer in the arts of management and the manipulation of patronage, but although hard-working and thorough he was no financial or

administrative innovator or reformer. Inheriting a floating debt of
£1,036,000 he ended in 1679 with one of £2,400,000, and in the last
stages of his ministry he virtually lost control of expenditure. His fall
was precipitated by the Popish Plot, but financial mismanagement
was already undermining his ministerial position, and he left the
accounts of his last months in disorder.

Danby's initial success was due to his determination to cut expenditure quickly, particularly by ending the Dutch war at the
earliest moment. He suspended the payment of salaries and pensions,
an exercise that forced those who had been appointed, or given grants,
by his predecessors to come to terms with the new minister. His fiscal
policy was also concerned with patronage. He repudiated the excise
farm negotiated by Clifford, substituting a new one on better terms
that bound the farmers to himself. In what might seem a retro-
gressive step he abandoned the system of direct collection of the
hearth tax (introduced in 1670), reverting to a new farm. Danby's
preference for tax farms was due to the large advances which farmers
could be required to make—although these (with interest added)
would have to be deducted from later receipts. Advances were also
facilitated by the establishment of credit receiverships in the excise
(1674) and customs (1677).

Another advantage for Danby was that he inherited the additional taxes that had been voted in 1670 and 1671, but as these
expired in 1676–8 he was faced with a declining revenue unless these
taxes could be renewed or substitutes voted. Danby relied on two
forms of persuasion, both expensive, in trying to get parliament to
vote further extraordinary taxes. He spent heavily in secret service
money to construct and consolidate a working majority; in the years
1676–9 this absorbed between £250,000 and £300,000. Secondly, by
citing the danger from French expansionism, he obtained relatively
generous grants in 1677, a renewal of the additional excise and an
assessment for the fleet. But throughout his ministry he suffered from
a major weakness—an inability to control royal expenditure; as
revenue yields rose, royal expenditure rose even faster.

Distrust of Charles compromised Danby's anti-French policies.
In 1678 he asked for supply for a war against Louis, but the
Commons held back supply. They refused even to consider a plan to
increase the ordinary revenue by £300,000, although this was accompanied by a promise to appropriate £500,000 of the revenue for
the maintenance of the navy. Danby gambled by raising an army
and setting out the fleet before he had been voted taxes. The result
was disastrous. Only a poll tax of £300,000 was voted, but he had
already incurred over £700,000 expenditure, and costs of a year's
war would be more than £2,500,000. When in May the prospects of

a war receded, the Commons voted £619,000, appropriated for disbanding the newly raised forces. Danby took the money but did not disband. He appears to have considered ruling without parliament, using the army to suppress opposition, but it is hard to see how this could have been financed unless illegal levies of money were attempted. Expenditure on the army and navy in the two years from March 1677 amounted to £1,385,000 more than the revenues voted for them. Strenuous attempts to raise fresh advances on the strength of new hearth tax and excise farms did no more than offset the losses suffered by the customs, on account of the 1678 statutory prohibition of imports from France. By the end of the year, the king's financial position was desperate, and the Commons made it clear that extraordinary taxes would not be voted so long as Danby remained lord treasurer.

Laurence Hyde, created earl of Rochester in 1682, directed royal finances as first lord and treasurer from 1679 to 1686, except during Charles's last six months. His great success in enabling Charles to rule without parliament and extraordinary supply was directly due to his establishing more effective control over expenditure than had been achieved by his predecessors. During the Exclusion crisis the Commons were unwilling to vote money for any purpose other than the belated disbanding of Danby's army, and the extraordinary taxes of 1670–71 lapsed without possibility of renewal. Necessity at last converted Charles to principles of good housekeeping. Secret service money was drastically cut. Receipts from the secret subsidy treaty with Louis XIV (£400,000 in 1681–5) were spent on inescapable routine purposes, particularly the navy. Charles was induced to live within his income, which averaged just over £1,280,000 per annum.

Rochester established strict treasury control over all spending departments and over all forms of borrowing. This was combined with a policy of cooperation with the JPS in the counties and tories in the towns. These years of tory reaction realized many of the 'country' ideals—prudent financial administration, no direct taxes on land, a less ostentatious court, fewer pensions and grants, no foreign adventures (Tangier was abandoned in 1683) and an attempt to reduce royal indebtedness (from just over £2 million to rather less than £1,700,000). Direct collection was substituted for farming of the excise (1683) and the hearth tax (1684), with a resulting increase of a third in receipts by 1688. The end of the prohibition on imports from France resulted in an expansion of trade, and consequently of the yield from customs. Excluding subsidies from Louis, total revenue rose from £1,100,000 in 1680–81 to £1,370,000 in Charles's last year.

The financial settlement which James received in 1685 was based

on the same principles. Parliament voted extraordinary taxes to pay
Charles's debts and suppress Monmouth's Rebellion in the form of
indirect taxes on wine, tobacco, linen, silk and spirits, which produced more than the estimated yield. James was the last sovereign to
have a permanent ordinary revenue: this was identical to that which
Charles had received, but as trade and domestic consumption increased so the yield increased annually. James had no difficulty in
living within an income that rose from £1,370,000 in 1685 to an
average of £1,600,000 in his last two years. He could expand his
army and simultaneously reduce debts. Rochester's dismissal (for
politico-religious reasons unconnected with finance) appears not to
have been followed by any change of policy or decline in efficiency.
The new treasury commission containing two catholic figureheads
(Bellasis and Dover) was actually directed by Godolphin. However,
in 1688 the costs of fitting out a fleet and concentrating the army to
oppose William, together with an embargo on overseas voyages, imposed expenditure that could only be met by parliamentary votes of
extraordinary supply, since there was a general and ominous refusal
by the king's usual financiers to advance money. Had a civil war
broken out, with the calling of parliament impracticable as well as
politically dangerous, James would have had either to enter into
negotiations in a position of weakness, or try to raise forcible and
illegal financial exactions.

The financial settlement of 1689 was based on a conscious decision
by parliament never again to grant the sovereign the full ordinary
revenues for life. This was an understandable reaction to the use
which James had made of his financial independence, but William
(who voluntarily surrendered the hated, perpetual hearth tax) felt
personally aggrieved at the lack of trust. Parliament was being
harshly realistic: it was royal dependence on votes of supply, not the
necessity for annual Mutiny Acts, that made regular parliamentary
sessions necessary; never again after 1688 would a year pass without
a session. But neither ministers nor peers and MPs initially understood the implications of the desperate and long war which ensued,
producing over the next decade a real revolution in government and
finance.

At first in 1689 the totals involved in revenue and expenditure
were of an order of magnitude that was familiar and manageable.
William inherited debts of £2 million, parliament voted £600,000 to
repay the Dutch the costs of their expedition to England, and with
some reluctance (on the argument that Cromwell had done it for
less) £2 million was voted for the conquest of Ireland. Ultimately,
however, the sums involved in financing both military and naval

campaigns and subsidizing continental allies totally dwarfed all early calculations and previous patterns of expenditure. The Nine Years War is estimated to have cost £49,320,000, about £5,500,000 per annum, that is over three times the average level of government expenditure during James's reign. All forms of taxation were sharply increased, including poll taxes and a new regular direct tax, the aid or land tax (which brought in over £19 million during the war). But total revenue from all sources during the war years amounted to only £32,766,000, leaving a gap of over £16 million that had to be borrowed.

The need to expand governmental credit operations on such an unprecedented scale, and to institutionalize what at first were a series of improvisations, led to the aptly titled 'financial revolution'. In the early years short-term expedients were used, on the unfounded expectation that the war would soon be over, so that it was only from 1693 that a long-term loan policy emerged. The 'Million loan' of 1693–4 raised £108,100 by a tontine (ten per cent interest to all until 1700, then seven per cent distributed among the diminishing number of survivors), and £892,000 by annuities bearing fourteen per cent interest. There followed in 1694 a 'Million lottery loan'; in addition to ten per cent for fourteen years, prizes of up to £1000 would be drawn for. But the most significant development was the Tonnage Act (so called because the interest was charged on additional customs) by which the subscribers were to advance £1,200,000 and, in addition to receiving eight per cent interest, were to be incorporated as the Bank of England (April 1694). But not all loans succeeded; the 1697 lottery loan for £1,400,000 raised only £17,630, and the elaborate land bank scheme of 1696 proved to be an even more ignominious failure.

Long-term loans over the whole reign amounted to £8 million, but short-term borrowings during the shorter period of the war totalled over £32 million. This was the result of taking easy ways out of financial difficulties, with the same kind of ultimately dangerous and inescapable consequences that were to wreck French governmental finances during Louis's last decade. When taxes were anticipated the yield was often grossly overestimated, with the result that advances could not be repaid. Goods and services were obtained from contractors on credit, by payment in tallies, which were receipts for payments due to be made into the exchequer. By 1695–6 the treasury had lost effective control over the number being issued. When holders of existing tallies found that these were not being honoured at the time set for repayment, it became impossible to get anyone to accept new tallies, even at discounts that rose in 1696–7 to thirty-three per cent. By then, spending departments found that services and goods would be provided only for cash, and that was almost non-existent. The total deficiency in short-term borrowing was vast— over £5 million in 1697—that is of advances and loans not covered by receipts from the revenues charged for their repayment.

It was in this crisis of imminent governmental bankruptcy that the services of the Bank of England became indispensable. It had already made advances in addition to the original £1,200,000, but only an institution could have carried out the funding of the floating and effectively unsecured loans which was now necessary to prevent bankruptcy. This was done by the Bank holding a subscription for new bank stock, four fifths of it payable in tallies, with the treasury undertaking to pay eight per cent until they were repaid. This strengthened government credit until the end of the war, when expenditure fell rapidly. A second device was intended to put future short-term borrowing on a more regularized basis; from 1696 exchequer bills were issued, mostly of low denomination (£5 and £10), and as they circulated freely they had an additional advantage of being usable by those engaged in business as paper currency.

It is a cliché to say that, after the Revolution of 1688, parliament, and specifically the Commons, became a partner in the actual business of government; but detailed examination of the ways in which government functioned shows that there was no obvious or generally agreed role for the Commons to play. The financial settlement had the intended consequence that all demands for supply had to be justified in detail, and that the Commons (invariably meeting in committee of the whole house, not referring supply matters to select committees) regularly examined the details of the policies for which money was being asked, and such technical aspects as the likely yields of taxes voted. William and his ministers had to keep parliament constantly informed of the problems of government, and they also had to acquiesce when amateurs in the Commons disputed and disregarded estimates and provisions drafted by departmental experts; in 1692, for instance, MPs rejected figures for wear and tear in the navy estimates and substituted sums well below the minimum which the admiralty representatives stated was necessary. Although a great deal of the criticism directed against ministers was prejudiced and ill-informed, it could no longer be disregarded since delay or major reductions in grants of supply could impede effective prosecution of a difficult war.

While unrelenting in criticism, the Commons (with one exception) were not ready to become involved in actual governmental responsibilities. When in November 1689, after sharp attacks on mismanagement, William invited the Commons to nominate seven per-

sons to provision the army in Ireland, and another group of in-
spectors to examine the state of that army, the house warily declined.
Only in January 1696 were there serious proposals to take over
governmental functions, with the (abortive) plan for a council of trade.
Its members were to be nominated by parliament, not the king, to
represent mercantile interests; MPS were eligible for membership. This
council was directly to control the protection of merchant shipping
against the French, issuing orders to the admiralty, and reporting misbehaviour and incompetence by naval officers to the king. This scheme
would have set up two rival sets of authority, one deriving powers
from the crown, the other backed by parliament, and the likelihood of
confusion was a principal reason why it was eventually abandoned.

Generally the objective of the Commons during William's reign
was to get into a position to invigilate all aspects of government, and
to be able to interrogate and if necessary call to account all officials
and ministers. Parliament moved in the direction of a formal and
permanent separation of powers between the executive and an independent legislature, and developed during the 1690s the institutional
machinery to maintain a constant and expert watch over all actions
and proposals of the administration. A public accounts committee, of
seven MPS (with officers barred), was elected by secret ballot of the
house during every session of 1690–97. The names of the elected
members were inserted in supply bills, which gave them statutory
powers to inspect all accounts and interrogate any public servant.
They were paid an annual salary of £500 to make them independent
and resistant to official inducements, but those elected were invariably men who had made themselves conspicuous as parliamentarians – the membership during most of these years reads like a roll-
call of opposition activists.

The public accounts committee exerted continuous pressure on
the administration, and at times made the position of court managers at Westminster almost untenable. Its members and especially
those who were successively re-elected, developed as much expertise
and knowledge about the intricacies and technicalities of royal
finances as treasury spokesmen. They guided and informed the
generally inexperienced country MPS on the central issues of supply.
Debates were influenced by the committee's reports on revenue and
expenditure, to which treasury commissioners had to reply (in writing) with their answers and objections. Its investigations could not
be openly resisted; in February 1695 James Craggs, then an army
clothier, was sent to the Tower for refusing to submit his private
account books. Secret service payments had to be revealed (on oath)
to the committee in February 1694. Ministers found it wise to establish unofficial links with influential members. The committee was

most effective during the period of political realignment of the 1690s, when 'country' sentiment united former whigs and tories in resentment of the financial burdens being imposed on the nation, and suspicion of the honesty of those in charge of administration. If the country opposition could have maintained its ascendancy of 1690–93, a separation of powers might have emerged, with exclusion of all office-holders from the Commons, a politically active Speaker who had formerly served in the accounts committee (as Paul Foley, Harley and Bromley did), and the committee feeding the house with the information that would enable it to control supply, so as to keep the ministers in check. But the re-emergence of parties checked this development; in February 1697 the whigs packed the committee with members who allowed its powers to lapse, and although it was revived after the fall of the whig ministry, the tory members were more concerned to use it to attack the misdeeds of the former whig ministers than to put restrictions and limits on the current (tory) ministers. Like all other institutions, the public accounts committee became a prize (and an instrument) in warfare between the parties.

Financial and military (but not naval) administration during the Nine Years War had largely to be improvised to meet critical problems as they arose—the conquest of Ireland, the provision of a large army for Flanders, the large-scale maintenance of such specialized services as engineers, transport and artillery, the remittance of money abroad for the army, the allies and the fleet in the Mediterranean. Major policy decisions were made by William, heavily influenced by his earlier Dutch experience and Dutch advisers, but they had to be implemented by inexperienced English administrators—inevitably with uneven results. During the War of the Spanish Succession, by contrast, the administration worked systematically, and with far greater efficiency than that of any other combatant state, the Dutch included.

Godolphin proved himself the most successful of all financial administrators during the late-Stuart period, but he had the advantage of developed fiscal machinery and an elaborate network for credit operations, with the Bank, the new East India Company and individual financiers, many of whom now enjoyed extensive connections with European banking groups and firms. The Bank agreed to underwrite exchequer bills in 1707. Two years later it funded short-term debts totalling £1,750,000, and agreed to cover £2,500,000 in new bills—receiving in return an extension of the Bank's charter from 1710 until 1732. So close were relations between Godolphin and the principal figures in the Bank that in 1710 the governor, Heathcote, warned the queen against dismissing the lord treasurer.

Many of Harley's associates feared that the whole credit system would collapse after the change of ministry, but he had already taken precautionary moves, and brought into partnership a new combination of bankers and financiers—Janssen, Lambert, Hoare and Gibbon—to take the place of those exclusively connected with the whigs. Furthermore he planned to lessen the government's dependence on the Bank by establishing a second privileged company, the ultimately ill-fated South Seas Company, which from the beginning was more concerned with loan operations than with mercantile trading.

Money still furnished the sinews of war. Military and naval campaigns (with only one major engagement at sea, Malaga, 1704) made relatively small demands for material, and much of that used by the army was procured locally in overseas theatres of war. Men were obtained by various means, mostly dubious and often (such as crimping) illegal, but a series of Pressing Acts gave JPS power to conscript the unemployed and paupers. The main task of ministers was the preparation of annual estimates for the army and the navy, with occasional demands for subsidies for the allies, which were presented each winter to parliament and were scrutinized in detail.

The passage of supply bills through the Commons was facilitated by the patronage powers at Godolphin's disposal. There was a proliferation of revenue officials, varying in importance from county assessment officers and receivers for the land tax, who were often members of leading landed families and nominated by parliament, to local officials of the customs and excise who formed the earliest class of minor bureaucrats. They had to pass elementary educational tests, were not permitted to serve in their own native region but had to move frequently from one district to another, and had to enter security for the honest and efficient performance of their duties. Naturally, they were valuable as electoral agents; under Godolphin the ministry increased its influence in the constituencies by using them as sources of information, and for the communication of ministerial views and instructions. Their supervisors, for example commissioners of customs, were barred from sitting as MPS (1700), but this success of the Country party meant that all direction of the new army of minor officials was concentrated in whoever controlled the treasury.

The growth of a bureaucracy, many of whose members developed an expertise (particularly in fiscal techniques) on which the politicians had necessarily and increasingly to rely as the tasks and problems of government became more extensive and complex, made for administrative stability and continuity. The holders of politically influential posts, or of sinecures and 'jobs' that were simply inducements or rewards, were usually purged on the occasion of a change of minister or ministry. This certainly applied to offices in the localities, where minor patronage was a primary issue in party politics, but a universal spoils system did not come into existence. The wholesale sackings of all officials, and their replacement by partisans who might be totally inexperienced, such as the tory extremists clamoured for after the ministerial change of 1710, would have dislocated the administration in such vital sectors as the admiralty (dockyards, victualling and supply), ordnance, and the revenue agencies. Demands for sweeping changes ran counter to the interests of new ministers, who knew that the professional and expert administrators were not only necessary to ensure continuity and efficiency, but also would transfer to them the loyalty and service they had previously given to the out-going ministers.

Godolphin and Oxford controlled a far more efficient and reliable administration than had their predecessors, one that operated according to regular procedures, not hasty improvisations. The key expert officials served under successive ministries, achieving a status approximating to that of civil servant, and contributed significantly to the victories of the War of the Spanish Succession, during which French government and finances came close to total disorganization and collapse.

4 Social Trends

Society in the half century after the Restoration appears at first sight to display characteristics of stability and quiescence, in sharp contrast to the social turbulence of the years of the mid-century English Revolution, when the world was for a time turned upside down. However, the changes that had occurred in the two decades before 1660, although dramatic and frequent, proved to be remarkably short-lived and limited in their effects. General and severe repression was not needed in and after 1660, in order to restore the traditional social as well as political forms and values, but their relatively easy reimposition and subsequent acceptance masked the operation of forces making for long-term, structural social changes. Under the surface, the economic and social position of the middling and lesser gentry and the less well-off freeholders slowly but consistently deteriorated, while the mercantile and urban retailing interests increased in importance, and an entirely new social class, the 'monied interest', gained in prominence, wealth and influence. The number of government officials multiplied significantly, especially in the provinces. In place of the social division between a cosmopolitan court and the unfashionable country led by the rural landowners, there now emerged a new synthetic oligarchy, an upper class with the capacity to absorb and assimilate the most successful elements and individuals, and whose new values and ostentatious life-style were resented and rejected by those who lacked either the will or the resources to enjoy them.

Most articulate Englishmen (and they were a minority) welcomed the Restoration on social as well as political grounds. It brought back the forms and principles of a hierarchical social order. The landowning classes resumed their traditional dominance in the counties. Split into opposite camps during the Civil War, they had generally been displaced from offices and power after 1649, but they had already begun to recover local influence and positions under the Protectorate. In 1660 the aristocracy and gentry regained their places as leaders and governors of the counties from early February, months before the Convention recalled the king, and over a year before the anglican establishment fully regained their former positions.

Experience of the social anarchy that had existed in many areas during the recent past, notably in 1640–42 and 1647–9, made the landowning classes determined to consolidate the governmental and social positions which they recovered in 1660. Nothing in the way of fundamental social changes had happened to make this impossible. The extensive changes in the ownership of land that had taken place during the Interregnum had already proved, before 1660, to be surprisingly limited in their effects. Royalists had had to sell land (or mortgage it) in order to pay the penalties imposed by the Long Parliament's committee for compounding, and to pay high and differential taxes, but these private sales of land had not led to the emergence of a new, 'bourgeois' class of landowners. The bulk of private sales happened before 1649, and most of the purchasers were either from the section of the gentry who supported the parliamentarian cause, or lawyers and speculators interested in making quick profits by early reselling. Their customers were mainly landed gentry, and only a few 'new men' (for example, Thomas Turgis of Gatton) emerged from this process. Indeed many royalist landowners had managed to recover at least part of their alienated lands before 1660.

The significant if temporary social and economic changes of the English Revolution had come later, after 1649, with the confiscation and disposal of the estates of the crown, the church and conspicuous royalist leaders. These lands were mostly granted or sold to men who served or were closely associated with the republican regimes. At the centre they formed a new and entirely synthetic ruling class – generals, lawyers, politicians and officials, men of varied social origins. In the counties the Rump and Cromwell were mainly served by another similarly artificial combination of army officers, lawyers and (in many but not all counties) gentry of more modest status and wealth than those customarily employed to administer the counties before 1642. Intruders of this sort lost their places in 1660, and all the beneficiaries of the land grants and sales carried out by the Rump and the Protectorate lost their gains at the Restoration—except, surprisingly, in Ireland, where they were needed as part of an effective protestant ascendancy. Elsewhere the resumption of crown and church lands virtually annihilated the new interest that underpinned the Protectorate.

Despite their recovery of offices and influence in 1660–62, the unfashionable provincial gentry did not subsequently feel secure, and their continuing anxieties provide a main theme in the social history of the late seventeenth century. It was not so much that they feared that the popular disturbances of the past would recur: they took it for granted that the poor would always have to be controlled. What alarmed them was the realization that, while they were finding it increasingly difficult to maintain their standards of life, there were favoured sections of society whose wealth and influence were improving to the point where, it was believed, they would be able to supersede the gentry. The first of these intrusive (and also parasitic) rivals were the groups associated with the courts of Charles II and James II, the would-be exponents and beneficiaries of absolutism; the second was the monied interest, of bankers and financiers.

The gentry were disillusioned by the failure, as they saw it, of the Restoration settlement to give them back what they believed to be their rightful position as the main class on whom government should depend; later they regarded the Revolution of 1688, which destroyed the absolutist policies of James II, as an equally empty triumph. Because the gentry were articulate and filled the House of Commons, grand juries and the commission of the peace, their grievances received constant and prominent publicity. Jealousy and envy, feelings of relative deprivation, as well as more creditable and open sentiments, underlaid the fears of absolutism that developed during the 1670s. For decades the 'country' gentry took pride in their independence, and maintained constant vigilance against official corruption and malfeasance, demanded public frugality and defended the traditional virtues and values. But personal and political frustration increasingly soured these country attitudes; they all too frequently degenerated into a consistent and sullen suspicion of all in office, blind but effective obstruction of all administration, and eventually a retreat into the corrosive prejudices and totally unreal fantasies of the October Club and the post-1714 tories. This embitterment of many of the gentry was due to the increasingly obvious, and apparently irreversible, discrepancy between the political and social dominance which they claimed as of right, as the largest and soundest part of the landowning classes, and the economic and governmental changes which were altering the overall situation to their obvious disadvantage.

Underlying the decline of the lesser gentry was the long economic recession which, in the half century after 1660, affected especially the two basic industries, agriculture and the associated manufacture of textiles, mostly situated in rural areas. With some isolated exceptions, this was not a period of technical inventiveness, enterprise or higher productivity in either industry. A technologically primitive agricultural system could normally provide what the nation required, but it remained frighteningly vulnerable to adverse climatic conditions. It should be remembered that the background to all aspects of life at this time was the 'little ice age', the trough in a major downturn in the climate, a period of frequent wet summers and autumns, and markedly shorter growing seasons. This depopulated whole areas of Scotland, but in England the effects were serious rather than catastrophic. Shortages and high prices for food reduced demand for consumer goods. High unemployment and increased pauperism raised the burden of poor rates at precisely the time that rural communities were least able to bear them.

The second disruptive economic factor was war. The Dutch wars closed the Baltic to English exports, the French wars seriously affected all overseas trade (and especially that to the Levant which took large quantities of textiles). Land taxes affected the gentry and freeholders disproportionately, and produced a stagnant market in land itself. After 1694 it was safer, easier and more profitable to invest in government stock, so that the demand for land as an investment fell away. This was a significant change from the situation in the century before 1640. No major redistribution of land ownership occurred, but although the gentry still held on to their property this was no longer crucial; the proportion of land which they owned was to remain constant, or nearly so, but the proportion of national wealth which this represented was steadily falling. Depression of the market in land made it extremely difficult to realize wealth invested in land, either in order to supplement inadequate incomes or for investment purposes. Only a comparatively few landowners (great magnates, the most substantial gentry and a few larger tenant farmers) possessed wealth in forms that could be easily realized, and so were in a position to take advantage of, or at least to adapt to, the frequent and unpredictable fluctuations in the prices of and demands for agricultural products.

Throughout this period the gentry and their spokesmen in the Commons constantly complained that a steady fall in the level of rents was impoverishing them. Generally, the lesser gentry let out the bulk of their estates rather than farmed them on their own account and now, in contrast to the period before 1640, they had limited opportunities to increase their incomes by trying to raise rents. Lack of working capital meant that they could not follow the example of a few progressive (and mainly substantial) landowners in systematically improving their estates and developing efficient home farms—and this is also why there were comparatively few enclosures. There was neither the capital nor the incentive to justify the costs and trouble of obtaining Enclosure Acts, which did not become common again until the mid-eighteenth century. A persistent shortage of tenants was the factor that weakened the position of the smaller gentry. Frequently, this meant that rents had actually to be reduced, or arrears remitted, since otherwise tenants would abandon their farms, and tenancies would remain unfilled. Attempts to increase the landlord's income by rack-renting would be self-defeating. The un-improved estates of many minor gentry, with dilapidated buildings, neglected drains and overrun with destructive game birds and animals for the squire to hunt, were difficult to let. Successful and enterprising tenant farmers preferred to rent at higher rates from the minority of substantial landowners who had been able and willing to spend on improvements, and were beginning to take a direct and informed interest in estate management and agricultural innovation.

An identity of interests between the substantial landowners, key elements in the new oligarchy, and the monied tenant farmers, who often also owned some freehold land and so possessed the vote in parliamentary elections, operated to the disadvantage of the minor gentry. But small owner-occupiers without capital were in a pre-carious state, and as a class their position deteriorated steadily: it was not relative but absolute poverty and deprivation that many of these descendants or successors of the old yeoman class suffered. Many had to sell their land or were sold up by creditors; the shrinking pro-portion of land owned by small occupiers represents the one major shift in land ownership during the period. Many emigrated overseas, more to London and other towns, and large numbers were reduced to the level of small tenants or even to that of day labourer. The very appreciable increase in electoral corruption, notably in county elec-tions where it had been rare, was a direct consequence of this im-poverishment of the small owner-occupier.

They seldom possessed any reserve assets, unlike most of the minor gentry; a single disastrous harvest, floods or an outbreak of cattle disease could quickly and irretrievably ruin them. But although the decline of the fortunes of the minor gentry caused far less suffering, it was much more important in social and political terms. With stag-nant or falling incomes they were seriously affected by the land tax which, especially in the more accurately assessed counties of the south and east, meant a tax of twenty-five per cent for most of the war years, 1689–97 and 1702–13. This meant that they could not possibly match the patterns of conspicuous expenditure that deter-mined the status of members of the upper classes—building, keeping carriages, renting a London house for the season, sending sons on the Grand Tour abroad, contracting good marriages for daughters in-volving generous dowries, contesting parliamentary elections. These desirable activities were increasingly out of reach because, apart from limited incomes, it became more difficult to realize capital by selling land.

The legally sophisticated and elaborate device of the strict settlement was being developed during this period. By imposing restrictions on their powers and rights, this turned heads of landowning families into tenants for life, who enjoyed the income but could not sell the estate. For richer families it provided guarantees against personal extravagance or bad management in one generation, and made it practicable to plan over long periods with assurance. Legal settlements prevented the less affluent landowner realizing his capital, except by the expensive and uncertain process of a private parliamentary act. He could not raise loans on the security of his lands because he was not free to sell them. In any case there were fewer purchasers in the market than there had been in the early seventeenth century, and in real terms prices were lower. Comparatively few wanted land in order to improve it; lawyers, merchants, officials and others who wished for reasons of social prestige to obtain landowning status preferred to buy estates that had already been improved, and they were increasingly influenced in their choice of estates by non-commercial factors, by such amenity values as nearness to London, good air, a pleasant prospect and established gardens. For them landed estates were not seen as attractive propositions for large-scale investment. Earlier in the century land had been the only really secure form of investment which also gave a reasonable return. After the establishment of the Bank of England in 1694, investment in government stock was equally secure, provided an attractive return (tax-free, unlike land), and could be quickly realized—with, after the first years, an element of capital appreciation. The only active sector of the land market was concerned with real estate development in and around London, where spectacular profits and lucrative leasing and renting operations enriched ground landlords (for example the Russells and Grosvenors) and speculators.

Although the minor gentry blamed the court and the monied interest, war taxation and high wages for labourers for their own misfortunes, they also directed consistently vitriolic and revealing attacks against another prime target, the inordinate growth and excessive wealth and influence of London. The capital continued to grow, to a population of over 550,000 in 1700; this compared with perhaps 60,000 in 1500 and 225,000 in 1600, and was larger than that of any other European city except perhaps Constantinople. The fact that the capital contained around ten per cent of the total population of England and Wales was generally considered to be unhealthy and undesirable. Attempts by Elizabeth and Charles 1 to curb its growth were praised by Restoration MPs, but the repeopling after the Plague of 1665–6, and the rebuilding of the City after the Great Fire of 1666, showed how futile any legal checks were likely to be. In the second half of the seventeenth century a new form of expansion began in the West End, with large estates laid out for the well-off, and in pleasant and healthy residential villages further west (Kensington and Chelsea) and north (Highgate). Commercial and industrial suburbs also grew rapidly, especially Southwark on the south bank of the Thames.

London's role in national life was even more dominant than it is in the twentieth century. It was the seat of the court, parliament, the law courts (all major civil actions had to go to Westminster Hall), the base for the great overseas trading companies (the East India, Levant, Muscovy, African and South Seas). It possessed more deep-water shipping than all other English ports combined. It was the one great financial centre, uniquely linked to such other centres as Amsterdam, Frankfurt and Geneva. London totally dwarfed all other cities. Even major provincial capitals—Bristol, Norwich, York and Newcastle—each contained barely one twentieth of the population of the capital, and an even smaller proportion in terms of wealth. In the 1660s Graunt and Petty demonstrated scientifically what contemporary critics suspected—that the population of London was increasing only because of a constant inflow of people from the provinces: the constant excess of deaths over births showed that it would quickly diminish without this immigration. London therefore appeared to be causing a haemorrhage in both economic and demographic terms: it was draining away the wealth and population of the counties, and corrupting all classes by the peculiar temptations of metropolitan life.

As the centre of fashion and luxury, London was denounced by economists and moralists as an entirely parasitical, or even cancerous, growth. The quality of life certainly differed in most respects from that of the provinces. High fashion was concentrated there, around the court and during the London season, apart from the periodical migrations to its satellite establishments—Bath and Tunbridge Wells as health resorts, Newmarket for racing. No other city contained comparable theatres or the amusement parks that were the ancestors of Vauxhall and Ranelagh. There were more, and more varied, clubs, coffee houses and eating places. Women were attracted by the abundance of specialized shops with the widest stocks to be found anywhere. London was the privileged centre of the publishing trade; elsewhere only the two universities had their own presses, and none was allowed in provincial towns for the sake of securer enforcement of the Licensing Acts. So it was not until the 1700s that provincial newspapers began to appear, and then on a

small scale. London was until then the sole centre, and provided the
one mass market, of journalism and more scholarly literary activities.
Political pamphlets, works of literature and criticism, religious works
(especially sermons by popular preachers), almanacs, pornography—
anything and everything that would sell—poured from the presses.
The earliest series of subscription concerts was being organized, and
the opera was being introduced. London began to attract musicians
with European reputations, and foreign artists like Lely and Kneller
in portraiture, and Hollar and Loggan in engraving, found plenty of
commissions. The intellectual activities of the Royal Society earned
for its founding members an international reputation such as no
English writer or poet possessed, and it relegated the universities to
comparative obscurity and insularity.

For those with lower tastes, London offered unrivalled opportunities for indulgence in every form of vice. Gaming was being organized commercially (and illegally). Cock-fighting was as popular as
in rural areas, and there can be found the earliest stages of professional pugilism. Commercialized sex was available in great
variety. Brothel quarters were to be found in each part of London—
some were the target for the presumably frustrated apprentice
rioters in 1668. At the top of the scale were actresses, several of
whom found their way into Charles II's bed, and 'misses', girls
whose services were exclusively at the disposal of their protectors.
Lower down there were masses of street-walkers, of whom Pepys
wisely fought shy, as well as the amateur shop-girls and barmaids
whom he patronized. Indulgence in vice carried serious dangers, as
contemporary moralists never tired of demonstrating. Specialists,
who were often unqualified quacks, were in great demand to treat
venereal disease, and there were even more dubious and obscure
characters who claimed to be able to procure abortions by means
largely of noxious chemical and herbal potions. In close proximity to
the brothels, and in a fashion functionally linked with them, were
the fearful 'boiling houses' in which high fever temperatures were artificially induced by a combination of doses of mercury with turkish
baths in occasionally successful attempts to suppress syphilis.
Another danger was that vice was almost invariably purveyed by
criminals, or those over whom criminals had control. London
naturally was the capital of crime: nowhere else were there such
obvious and tempting targets for the burglar, the confidence trickster
and the shoplifter. The streets were badly lit, the watch provided an
inadequate police, and the country roads radiating from the capital
were infested by highwaymen who were already being glamorized
(for instance the 'Golden Farmer') by enterprising journalists. The
latter made a killing out of ghosting spurious 'dying speeches', which

were sold to the crowds of cup-final proportions who watched outstanding hangings.

London life at the level of the masses was also qualitatively different from life in rural areas, market towns and even provincial
capitals, where men and women lived constantly among neighbours,
where privacy hardly existed, and some form of authority (master or
mistress, employer, clergy, parish officers) supervised most aspects of
daily life. Only in London did people live in anonymous masses,
with no one knowing or caring what they did or how they fared.
Uprooted immigrants, moving from one insanitary tenement to another at frequent intervals, encumbered by numbers of young children of whom few survived to adulthood, largely dependent on casual
labour for which the demand was usually far less than the supply
available, lived constantly on the edge of total destitution. Insecure
and largely pagan, untouched by any form of religion, the London
poor were a potential threat to property and order. But although the
word 'mob' was coined in the 1670s, serious outbreaks of violence
were not common during this period. There were only three major
riots. In 1668 the apprentices systematically attacked brothels; panic
and hysteria produced the Irish alarm in 1688, when rumours of the
approach of disbanded Irish soldiers led to attacks on London
catholics and foreign embassies; and in 1710 the impeachment of
Sacheverell led to violent attacks on another conspicuous minority
group, the dissenters and their meeting houses. But there was a constant under-current of minor disturbances, particularly during municipal and parliamentary elections—Southwark and Westminster
contained probably the most riotous electors in the country—and
the level of crime against both property and persons was always high.

By Anne's reign it was becoming apparent that money was gaining importance over birth or station in conferring power and influence. The blurring of lines dividing castes, the proliferation of
intermediate social groups, growing geographical mobility at least of
those in official positions and the professions from one region to
another, and their concentration in London, meant that persons
with pretensions or presumption could easily pass for gentlemen. But
the part played by money in corroding traditional values was fundamental and decisive. Some marxist historians claim that a market
economy came into existence during the middle years of the century, with inevitable superstructural changes in government, institutions and culture. But some go further, linking these suggested
qualitative changes to political revolution, the so-called English
Revolution of the 1640s and 1650s, and connecting them with puritanism as the appropriate ideology; in this way, developments that

took over a century to work and mature are all too often artificially concentrated and located in a short period. Admittedly, dramatic and novel developments did occur during the Interregnum, but it can only lead to distortion to suppose that they had a directly decisive effect on all subsequent English history.

The transition from subsistence to commercial agriculture, the opening of distant overseas markets and expansion of re-export trades that required long-term financing and more elaborate commercial organization, the functional separation of financial services from actual mercantile trading, can all be traced back to the closing years of the sixteenth century, but they were still developing trends at the time of the Restoration. There is obviously a connection between these long-term changes and the transformation of politics, but it is simplistic to assume that a model, bourgeois revolution had been accomplished in the 1640s and 1650s. Indeed, it is virtually impossible to demonstrate any direct connection between periods of economic depression and periods of particular political tension and crisis: for instance, the years of the Exclusion crisis (1679–81) do not seem to have coincided with abnormally adverse economic or social conditions. Hostility to royal absolutism was primarily political; even James II did not have the resources to try to develop mercantilist policies of the type operated by Colbert in France. Before the Revolution of 1688 the struggle between the court and the whigs extended into the trading community (for instance in elections to the East India Company board), but this was as a consequence of divisions within the world of politics; it cannot be said that the whigs had an economic policy that challenged that of the court.

Under the surface of politics, however, momentous changes were occurring, and a new ideology was emerging, whose key principles were contained or encapsulated in the words 'interest' and 'improvement'. Hobbes had asserted in *Leviathan* that in a state of nature and, he implied, when order broke down, all men would be actuated by the instinct of self-preservation. They would therefore accept rule by an all-powerful sovereign as the only way in which survival could be ensured. The reality turned out to be rather less stark, but nevertheless the traditional values of honour and loyalty, appropriate to castes determined by birth, implicit obedience to legitimate authority, acceptance of an overriding divine providential dispensation of human affairs, could no longer be relied on. Instead, by the end of this period 'interest' was the cement that bonded society. Men would act or obey—if it was made worth their while to do so. Governments had to attach men by making their private interests coincide with those of the public. At times, as under Danby in the 1670s, this took the form of crude bribery, but by Anne's reign a much more elaborate and sophisticated system of inducements had come into existence. Interest was now institutionalized through the management of the public revenues and especially the raising of massive loans.

Interest was also a key concept in the new moral system which became accepted after 1688 in most circles. The Restoration was followed by a spontaneous and widespread reaction against the hypocrisies and negative, prohibitive constraints of puritanism. This reaction took serious and intellectual, as well as frivolous and hedonistic, forms. There was a revulsion against dogmatic theology, and especially the doctrine of predestination, but this was combined with alarm at the growing paganism or religious indifference of the laity, and particularly the urban masses. By the 1690s the new church party of the latitudinarians, who praised reason as the 'candle of the Lord', encouraged scientific inquiry and behaved tolerantly towards those who differed from them, were in possession of key positions within the church. Always a minority among the anglican clergy, the latitudinarians nevertheless reflected in their sermons and emphasis on pastoral care the concerns of the new, mainly commercial and urban ways of life. They often used imagery and metaphors derived from commerce, they demonstrated that morality was *profitable* in this world as well as the next, and their reasons for enjoining men to charitable actions were certainly prudential.

The second key word of this period of emerging scientific inquiry and commercial, capitalistic development is 'improvement'. Men systematically examined a wide range of natural phenomena to discover how things or nature worked, with a view to considering whether they could be made to function better. In the first stage of an intellectual process that has helped as much as anything else to bring into existence our 'modern' world, the methods of scientific examination and analysis were applied to the study of society and government. John Graunt and Sir William Petty were the first to study society with the express purpose of seeing how it could be improved; with touching naivety they called this technique of applying scientific method to human affairs, 'True Politics'. Graunt and Petty developed the techniques of 'political arithmetic', using the statistical material available—the lists of births and deaths (categorized vaguely and very inaccurately) in the 'London Bills of Mortality', and rather more accurate material compiled for fiscal purposes. In a rudimentary and clumsy way they pioneered a potentially powerful intellectual method, that of 'political economy', a tradition which was to include Adam Smith, Malthus and Bentham, the most powerful and influential thinkers of the Britain of the Industrial Revolution.

Although intellectually influential, Petty's theories were not embodied in official policies. In France, by contrast, the mercantilist policies of Colbert were inspired by basically similar principles and provoked a coherent body of criticism. Fénélon's and Montesquieu's critiques of *étatisme*, of the arrogance and destructive selfishness of Louis xiv's absolutist policies, were only feebly (and insincerely) echoed in England by Bolingbroke and Swift. In England mercantilism never developed fully, but remained primarily a defensive mechanism against competitors in foreign trade. Ministers regulated, but did not attempt to direct or control trade and the economy by administrative as distinct from legislative means. Governmental intervention was frequently instigated by pressure groups who manipulated ministers and parliament alike in order to benefit sectional interests—for example in the prohibitions on the import of Irish cattle and Bengal textiles. The nearest that England came to a general debate on the role of the state in economic affairs was with the recoinage of 1696. The advocates of this reform of the currency, who accepted that it would have deflationary effects, were those who believed that the state should confine itself to creating the conditions in which an individual could improve his condition by his own efforts, or by the use of whatever wealth he possessed. Its opponents emphasized the need for the administration to encourage higher levels of consumption, but they did not advocate state control or direction of trade and industry. These critics could not show how higher consumption, and the increases in production that would be necessary, were to be obtained. They tended to assume that this would follow from the cheapening of credit, but both they and their twentieth-century apologists ignored the formidable technological limitations that made significant economic expansion difficult.

The one major change in the general structure of society during this period followed from the rise of the new monied interest, but important shifts did occur within each of the principal social classes. There is an immediately apparent contrast between the position, influence and fortunes of the aristocracy during this period, and in the eighty years that preceded the civil war which has been characterized as a time of general aristocratic decline. Some noble families declined (the Exclusionist peer, Eure, was virtually a pauper), some disappeared—the last of the Veres, the twentieth earl of Oxford died in 1703. But generally most of the nobility were wealthier than all but a handful of commoners, and the peerage was plentifully recruited from the ranks of the most substantial landowners, the most successful ministers and a few outstandingly able lawyers. After 1688 the ennoblement of Dutch and Huguenot servants of William caused the same kind of resentment that the Scots had provoked under James I, but a new category of peers was created by service in the wars against France; victorious generals and admirals entered the peerage in some numbers, but it was not until after 1714 that there was a substantial influx from the ranks of financiers and City magnates.

It was socially necessary for a peer to possess some land, but only a few peers wholly depended on agricultural income. Although systematic estate management techniques were being pioneered by magnates and were beginning to spread downwards, the largest incomes were derived from the development of London real estate, the profits of office, and investments after 1694 in government loans. However, for political reasons most noble families maintained large estates; these provided the territorial base that all but a few courtiers required, and were essential if the family influence was to last beyond the founder's lifetime. In most counties a small group of peers and their relations, together with the most substantial of the landowning gentry, monopolized the key positions, those that connected county life with the central government—the lord lieutenant, his deputies and the militia officers, the sheriff and the knights of the shire in parliament. Their way of life had to combine residence within the county or counties where they exercised local leadership with regular participation in political and social life in the capital. This enabled them to contract marriages for their children in the national or even international market, and to place sons and relations in the diplomatic, naval, military and court posts which they could claim in return for support of the administration. Some heads of families, usually not quite of the very first rank, personally served abroad as diplomats and increasingly as colonial governors, but prolonged absences overseas sometimes endangered their local interests—Pepys's patron Sandwich provides an example.

The income and patronage which magnates derived from office-holding was an important element in giving them both national and local influence. It is notable that the greatest political careers of the period were all of men who did not originally belong to the topmost social section, although all came from the substantial gentry, that is well up the social scale. Clarendon, a lawyer, came from a Wiltshire gentry family, and after his career was shipwrecked in 1667 it was his younger son, the later earl of Rochester, who carved out for himself a long and ultimately respected career. The two great Yorkshire rivals started in 1660 as Sir George Savile and Sir Thomas Osborne, both from good families but with restricted local influence. The first died as earl of Halifax, his line being extinguished soon afterwards, the latter ended as duke of Leeds and possessor of one of the largest estates and greatest fortunes in England. Thomas Clifford and John Churchill both came from minor west-country families; the former rose fastest of all between 1666 and 1672, when he became lord treasurer, but his fall the next year relegated his family to the obscurity of minor recusant nobility. John Churchill outshone all contemporaries, acquiring a European reputation such as no English subject had ever achieved, and amassing a fortune of unrivalled size. The two tory ministers of Anne's last years formed a contrasting social as well as politically incompatible pair. Harley came from a family that had achieved prominence in Herefordshire as parliamentarians and patrons of puritan ministers. He always retained a serious attitude to life, and patiently built up what he hoped would be a great and durable noble family. After marrying his son to the greatest heiress in England, Harley was dismayed when Anne refused to make his heir a duke. St John's paternal ancestors were disreputable minor royalist gentry, but on the female side he descended from the earls of Warwick. As a cosmopolitan he set himself to outshine his generation in spectacular but ephemeral ways. In a period containing much competition he gained a reputation as an outstanding wit and sexual athlete, in Paris as well as London, and treated his wife and relations with the same neglect that he showed his estate.

Success in politics carried many gentlemen into the ranks of the nobility, but with luck and ability the law was for a few the swiftest social escalator; Lord Chief Justice Saunders rose from the very bottom, having started life as a parochial orphan. Service as lord chancellor enabled Finch and Cowper to establish great and durable families. Somers and Jeffreys held the same office and the latter had the same aspiration, but political disaster in his case, and syphilis in the case of Somers, limited their achievement. Trade and industry were not yet recognized ways of achieving peerages, although several families with fortunes derived from mercantile trading were to get them in the years after Anne's death, and many such families found no difficulty in marrying their daughters (helped by big dowries) into the peerage.

Inevitably, some established noble families declined in fortune. The most spectacular failure (of a kind that would have been familiar to Elizabethans) was that of the second duke of Buckingham, son of James 1's favourite. He lived off his capital, dying bankrupt after squandering a vast fortune, frittering away the genuine and spontaneous popular support he could always evoke without effort, and wasting his considerable intellectual and artistic talents. Only the duke of Hamilton (killed in a duel in 1712) approached Buckingham in self-destructiveness, but in his case the family assets were saved by a capable female head, his mother Anne. Hamilton's killer, Mohun, who had twice been tried for murder, also dissipated his estate as well as his reputation. A few old families finally faded away; the last of the Pastons disappeared from Norfolk into penurious exile, but most established families now had the advantage of services at their disposal that had not been available to their ancestors.

The upper class made extensive use of professional servants – agents and bailiffs to administer rural and urban estates, lawyers to devise settlements and handle the purchase of properties, bankers to manage investments, surveyors to control mining operations. The availability of such skilled services greatly increased the capacity for survival of well endowed families: their fortunes and influence could endure a bad, mad or extravagant head. For instance, personal disabilities meant that the Cecils played an insignificant role during this period, but their great estates remained essentially intact. Whenever a family acquired an active head, the possession of large and secure estates enabled them quickly to become influential again; thus, after being dormant for generations, the Howards reassumed a leading role from 1681 in Norfolk, were given the lord lieutenancy in 1683, and led the county in 1688.

The return of the Howards to public life required a (temporary, as it transpired) conversion to protestantism. Most recusant nobility and gentry lived, from choice, quietly and inoffensively on their provincial estates, which were often in remote regions, and were reluctantly pressed into service as lords lieutenant and JPs by James II in 1686–8. The militants (many of them converts) and sympathizers with absolutist principles and policies who filled the court of Charles in 1670–73, and that of James in 1685–8, disappeared into exile at the jacobite court of St Germain and out of English life. At the other end of the religious spectrum, the dissenting way of life and behaviour could not easily be combined with participation in public duties or fashionable society (again with the exception of 1686–8). Apart from a few residual figures like the 'good lord' Wharton (died 1696), or an eccentric like William Penn, the Quaker and proprietor of Pennsylvania, few dissenters made any impact on national life. The dissenting churches suffered from a continuous process of social decapitation, losing in each generation those with the means to enter upper-class social life.

Although some of the most substantial gentry families had social aspirations to rise and enter the ranks of the aristocracy, the vast majority were content with the influence (regarded as theirs by right) which they possessed within their 'countries', a term that meant for some their counties, but for most their immediate neighbourhood, part of a shire. But although they saw themselves as the backbone of the nation, the provincial gentry felt increasingly that their position and influence were becoming insecure. Their differing

reactions to the social and economic factors that were responsible for
their unease tended to accentuate divisions within the ranks of the
gentry. They were far from constituting a homogeneous social class.
Gregory King's celebrated (and none too reliable) table broke down
the gentry into conventional, status divisions:

> 800 baronets (hereditary knights)—average income £880 per
> annum;
> 600 knights—average income £650 per annum;
> 3,000 esquires—average income £450 per annum;
> 12,000 gentlemen—average income £280 per annum.

But in practice the distinctions in status were becoming less important than differentials in income. Men with money and confidence
could, at least in London, circumvent social barriers. Social differences were blurred by the growth of the so-called pseudo-gentry,
that is families or individuals living in London, and after 1700 increasingly to be found in the main provincial capitals also, in the
style of gentry but without owning landed property, and often
without any very clear or sure sources of income. By traditional
standards a gentleman was one who was certified as armigerous—
entitled to bear a coat of arms—by the heralds who used to make
regular visitations of the counties. Their insistence on authentic
gentle birth, and an absolute separation for at least three generations
from the degrading pursuit of trade, industry or usury, was now
anachronistic: a gentleman was one who could pass himself off as
one.

Many of the English provincial gentry, particularly in the poorer
counties, were equivalents of the French *hoberaux*, the rural nobility
who wore their swords while ploughing to show that they were not
peasants. The 'parochial' or 'yeomanly' gentry, with incomes of
around £200 a year, unimproved estates and old houses, lacked the
means to buy military commissions, the education that would advance their sons in careers in the church or the law, or the dowries
that would enable their daughters to obtain good husbands. Often
they could not afford to mix socially with those who dispensed
patronage. The owners of small estates did not normally serve as JPS
(except in poorer and Welsh counties), but most were too grand to
serve in parish offices. They seldom left their region, not owning a
coach in which their womenfolk could travel, and only visited their
county town infrequently. But collectively they constituted a formidable group at county elections, one of the few occasions when they
assembled in large numbers, where they could give vehement and
often violent expression to their bitterness and frustrations. There
they could air the views and prejudices they derived from Dyer's

newsletters (a major tory influence) and their high-flying clerical neighbours.

Life for the gentry with incomes of £500 to £1,000 a year was much more varied. Such men expected to play a regular and independent role in county affairs and even national politics. Squires of this type filled the Cavalier Commons in 1661, but over the succeeding decades they were mostly to find an independent role beyond their means. Such men became pensioners of the court in order to offset the costs of residence in London during sessions, and they found the expenses of frequent elections—especially after the Triennial Act of 1694—increasingly difficult to meet. They had to form combinations or find a patron and, even if they had a strong interest in a local borough, they found it an uphill task to resist neighbouring magnates or intrusive men of money.

Electioneering was a common form of conspicuous expenditure and, from an economic point of view, second only to gambling as a cause of financial ruin. But aspiring gentry could not fall behind the local pace-setters. An old or cramped house would not be accepted as a rendezvous for the county. Charities had to be supported. A local figure had to occupy a position where favours could be obtained for individuals: their gratification demonstrated one's standing and influence. It was essential at least to be a JP, and to form one of the select group within the county who would be consulted on any matter of importance by the lord lieutenant, the bishop, the assize judge and MPs.

Maintaining a leading position became increasingly expensive (at least £1,000 a year by Anne's time), not because of inflation, but because of rising social norms and expectations. A widening gap developed between the squirearchy and a new social oligarchy. The former tended to be slow, or too poor, to adapt to changing circumstances, and many were too proud to accept subordinate rank under a magnate or party chief, although this reduced their participation in the distribution of patronage.

The anglican clergy generally and readily accepted a position of subordination to the aristocracy and gentry, but in contrast to the position after 1714 few even of the higher clergy came from noble or major gentry families—Compton (bishop of London), Crewe, the bishop, and Grenville, the dean, of Durham were exceptional. Although the parochial clergy, with a few envied and privileged exceptions, were generally poor, the clergy as a body were the most fervently and conspicuously loyal of all sections of the nation under Charles II. This loyalty was not only a result of the purges of dissidents in 1660–2; the anglican clergy sincerely believed that they

were the divinely ordained beneficiaries of a new, modern miracle—
the restoration of the virtually dismantled church. They now had the
duty of accomplishing God's work, they had a sacred trust to per-
form, and God would hold them personally accountable for their
stewardship.

In the first years after 1660 the morale of the anglican clergy was
extremely high. Both houses of parliament gave them unreserved
support. Led by a set of able and energetic bishops, the church,
purged of dissenters, began the mammoth task of physical, administrative, liturgical and educational reconstruction. The two universities were purged and then kept under strict control, at the price of
a fall in numbers of students and a dampening of intellectual life.
Inevitably, clerical confidence and euphoria did not last for long.
From as early as 1662 Charles showed he could not be relied on, and
by the 1670s parliament was also turning in favour of religious toleration. From personal experience in dealing with intransigent dissenting ministers and recalcitrant parishioners, the clergy were conscious
of their dependence on close and reliable support from lay authority.
To their dismay they became aware that such support was based on
considerations of political expediency, and might be withdrawn or
modified if circumstances changed—as they did in 1667–8, 1672 and
1678. The court contained many with catholic sympathies. The
country opposition tended to protect dissenters. But the church faced
an even wider danger, a moral crisis arising from the spread of indifference towards religion among all classes. Conscious that dissenters charged them with neglecting their duty to see that wickedness,
vice, blasphemy and atheism were suppressed, clergy of all ranks
tried with decreasing effect to instigate punitive action by magistrates and judges. However, a combination of inertia and incompetence, and a growing resentment against clerical pressures, led
many JPS besides those who were sympathetic to the dissenters to
neglect to enforce both penal and moral laws. Without their support
the ecclesiastical courts were only moderately effective, mainly
against minor offenders; there was no prerogative court like the old
High Commission abolished in 1641, and after 1688 a series of Indemnity Acts with retrospective application made the church courts
even more impotent.

The clergy, mostly underpaid, felt insecure. They were only too
well aware at the local level of dissenting hostility, and from 1678
they identified the whigs as enemies who would again destroy the
church. The parochial clergy as well as the bishops were almost
unanimous in opposing Exclusion and then, after the reversal of
alliances, James II's catholicizing policies of 1686–8. Such unity
among the clergy was in remarkable contrast to the divisions that

had existed before 1640, and is all the more surprising when one considers the disparities in standing and income that existed within the church. Most vicars and all curates were miserably poor, often earning little more than a labourer (although vicars at least had security of tenure). Some rectors and most of the higher dignitaries enjoyed relatively comfortable incomes. Most of the latter category held two or more livings *in commendam*, that is as absentees, paying a curate a low proportion of the stipend to do the actual pastoral work. Bishops were wealthy: Durham carried a stipend of over £3,000, and Lichfield at £730 and even St Davids at £450 were not to be disdained. There were known routes to high position; crown patronage led to the highest positions, university and private patrons controlled appointment to the better livings. Most clergy knew all too well that without connections and influence their prospects were dim; more begging letters were written by the clergy than by anyone else, and usually without response. Only by exceptional preaching skills could a few self-advertising clergy advance themselves through their own efforts.

After 1689 the unity of the church was shattered. About four hundred clergy refused to take the oaths to William and Mary, forming the non-juror church, and many of those who did stay in the established church were uneasy because of its apparent repudiation of the principles of divine right. It was a new world after 1689, a world of religious toleration in which the parish clergyman had to live in the same small community as dissenters who personally defied his authority, despised and often disparaged his ministrations and could no longer be suppressed by the law. The division between church and dissent was to endure as the main, and certainly the most visible, split in English society for over two centuries. Almost every town and village in England (although not yet in Wales) was divided into hostile sub-communities, and around these schisms there crystallized many other causes of division and tension—social, occupational and economic as well as political and personal. To make matters worse for the parish clergy, they suspected that their bishops were relatively unaware of this situation, and indifferent to the plight of those in daily competition with the dissenters. Whereas the latitudinarian bishops were friends of toleration, the lower clergy articulated their discontent in the slogan that the 'church is in danger', and consistently supported the hottest tories throughout the reigns of William and Anne.

For contemporaries the main social development was the rise of the monied interest. This was based on the increasing differentiation between those who were personally and directly engaged in trade, industrial production and retail selling, and those whose interests were primarily financial. Following the pattern of the early seventeenth century, this was at first usually a matter of career progression: older and successful merchants tended to turn to the financing of trade. But after 1688 a distinct class of professional financiers emerged to play an important role, and after 1695 a class of rentiers developed, living on interest payments, but not undertaking any economic activity themselves.

Those who were directly concerned with industrial production were, with a few exceptions, of comparatively restricted wealth and social importance. Apart from the shipyards that built vessels for the East Indies and West Indies trades, forges like the Crowley works at Winlaton-on-Tyne and a few breweries, the actual units of production were small. The bulk of textile manufactures (still easily the largest industry) were worked by the domestic system in the homes of the workers. Only the Foleys, originally Severn valley ironmasters, and some London and Southwark brewers, achieved fortunes and higher social status through manufacturing. Control over production in textiles was increasingly exercised by the middlemen who collected and marketed the finished products, put out the raw materials and often let the looms and other instruments of production to the workers. They supplied the credit which most producers lacked, and often handled and financed exports to overseas markets.

Middlemen, wholesalers (especially in London), merchants and ship-owners engaged in trade with northern Europe, France and the Low Countries (still by bulk and value the most important throughout the period) could make comparatively large profits and accumulate sizeable fortunes. The most successful merchants, particularly those engaged in the Spanish and Levant trades and members of the East India Company, often purchased property and estates in the country. But the trading and commercial interest lacked the capacity to rival the landed interest. Mercantile wealth, in the case of all but the most successful, consisted largely of business assets and working capital—stock in trade, raw materials, ships, debts, business property. These could not be easily or quickly realized. Furthermore, prosperity depended on the quality of personal management for there were few joint stock companies and no professional managers. A premature death or collapse of health, the succession of a minor, or an incompetent or profligate heir, could quickly ruin what were essentially family businesses or partnerships.

Collectively the City, through the court of aldermen and the East India and Levant Companies, frequently did exert considerable influence on the administration and in parliament (for action against the Dutch in 1664–5, for a ban on trade with France in 1678). But after 1689 the East India interest was divided into two rival companies, and it was the financial rather than the trading interest which had the ability to influence government.

The management of money was always more profitable than actual participation in trade, and after the establishment of the Bank of England it was also more secure. A new class of bankers (originating from goldsmiths, merchants, scriveners) first achieved prominence after the Second Dutch War, and the Stop of the Exchequer in 1672 was facilitated by the knowledge that the sight of the government defaulting on its obligations to a group of *nouveaux riches*, who had taken advantage of the crown's necessities, would not be unpopular. Like Fouquet's corrupt connections and French bankers during the War of the Spanish Succession, those who served the Stuarts before 1688 could make quick but always precarious profits, and at the cost of being the most hated group in the nation. They were literally at the king's mercy. By contrast those who invested in the Bank of England and other government loans ran only the risk that a Jacobite restoration would lead to a repudiation of all the debts of a usurping king. They enjoyed security, easily realizable assets, a satisfactory rate of interest and influence with the government. Financiers like Godfrey and Heathcote (governors of the Bank) were regularly consulted by sovereigns and ministers. Major policy decisions had to take into account their wishes and interests, for example over the deflationary recoinage of 1696. When Harley displaced the Godolphin administration in 1710, the survival of his new ministry initially depended on his ability to form a replacement set of financiers, to make the urgently needed financial advances and send remittances abroad, when Heathcote, Furnese and the Bank refused to do so.

It is not surprising that the 'monied interest', at whose head were the governors of the Bank, was hated by almost everyone, and particularly by the gentry and mere merchants who were being eclipsed. The men of money reduced other sections to dependence through their monopoly of credit—for long-term investment, normal trading transactions, in the form of mortgages and even loans to the improvident. They became conspicuously wealthy during the wars, at times of heavy and regular taxation. Many financiers were of foreign extraction. Almost all had climbed from obscure social origins. They were hated as parasites; they did not apparently create wealth, yet as they were becoming rich this must be at the expense of the nation generally. Moreover, their wealth was the product of financial transactions and currency manipulations that were totally unintelligible to the mass of the people.

By Gregory King's impressionistic calculations just over half the population lived in families that were below the subsistence line, in his phrase 'decreasing the wealth of the kingdom'. The bulk of the rural poor continued to consist of those without any rights or titles— unauthorized squatters on common land and reclaimed waste, land- less labourers dependent on seasonal demand for their labour, younger children of copyholders, small freeholders and tenant farmers for whom their families could make no provision, widows and orphans and, at the very base of the social scale, illegitimate children maintained by the parish, few of whom survived for long.

Despite extensive poverty, England (although not Scotland or Ireland) consolidated its position as the second European state (Holland being the first) to escape from recurrent crises of subsis- tence. Life by modern standards was precarious for all, but the whole community no longer lived—as all medieval Europe had done —on the edge of constant disaster. There were no general, and pro- bably not even local, famines of such magnitude as to justify the description of demographic catastrophes, that is when harvest failures decimated the population, sweeping away the old and the very young en masse, and so dislocating the population structure. The plague of 1665–6, which hit many provincial towns (Colchester was a very bad case) even harder than London, did not recur. There were serious harvest deficiencies in 1661–3, 1674–5, 1693 and 1709, reflected in soaring prices and serious disturbances in corn-growing areas against the export of foodstuffs. But in most years there were marginal, and from the 1700s fairly substantial, surpluses of basic foodstuffs.

As in twentieth-century third world countries, poverty of resources led to mass movements away from the rural areas of those for whom there was insufficient work, or things were going badly—younger children, labourers, evicted tenant farmers, failed tradesmen and artisans, irregular lovers, those who quarrelled with or deserted their families. Few had the resources to go to the colonies, although a proportion of the young emigrated as indentured servants. Some moved to the coal- and lead-mining districts, but the great magnet was London, even though (like modern Latin American capitals) it was not a centre of expanding industries, and could offer only casual and seasonal demands for unskilled labour. Newcomers found them- selves engaged in an unceasing fight for personal survival, and the difficulties of the very poor partly explain the relative freedom from mass disorders in the capital during this period.

Significantly, it was artisans, small masters and apprentices who were regarded with suspicion as likely to provoke disorders. Restoration ministers remembered the part that radical London had played in the 1640s. They feared that the resistance of the 'middling sort' of people to the laws against the dissenters indicated a continuing spirit of rebellion. Unrest at this social level was in reality due to a significant deterioration in their prospects. Lack of sufficient working capital and the difficulty (or prohibitive cost) of obtaining credit were making it hard for many small masters to survive. Most of those who completed their apprenticeships could not afford to set up on their own, but had reluctantly to work as journeymen under worsening terms. Some masters were taking on excessive numbers of apprentices, as a form of cheap and disciplined labour, who would eventually flood the labour market as new journeymen. Consequently labour in the textile industry adopted defensive stances —resisting any technical, labour-saving innovations, rioting to force the passage and enforcement of acts prohibiting the import of cheap Bengal manufactures, and periodically exploding with xenophobic hostility against foreign immigrants (the 'poor Palatine' refugees in 1709, Huguenots and the first Irish) who they loathed as cheap competitors in the labour market.

London always attracted special attention from ministers, and the JPs in and around the capital carried the heaviest burdens of work and responsibility. In rural areas the JPs were often purged for party political purposes, but so far as administration was concerned they were left very much to their own devices. Problems of what would now be called 'social control' were not acute. For example, the 1662 Act of Settlement restricted provision for the poor to the parish in which the pauper had been born; those applying to parochial officers elsewhere for relief had to be sent back to their native parish. On the face of it, this was a most drastic measure, and if enforced would have imposed harsh restrictions on population movements. But in reality it was not consistently enforced, and we now know that there was considerable mobility between parishes within a county or region, and the act could never have been enforced so far as the population of London was concerned. Nevertheless, there is evidence of rising tensions in the increase in the number of crimes (especially those against property) for which capital punishment was prescribed, and probably (although the evidence is not uniform) an increased proportion of those convicted were executed or transported.

Overall, by comparison with the periods that preceded and followed, this was not a time of social turmoil and dislocation. There were few enclosures. Industrial and commercial developments and mining were increasing the population of such areas as Tyneside, Birmingham and its surrounding villages, the Forest of Dean, but apart from London there was as yet no extraordinary urban expansion, no emergence of a second conurbation. Although party passions and religious differences divided every section of society, there was no challenge to the existing order from below. Intellectuals were not alienated, as they had been in early-Stuart England. The dissenters lost their former militancy through a long-term process of embourgeoisement, which included even the quakers. This was characteristic of the social trends of the period. English society was moving slowly, unevenly but inexorably towards a new structure, in which a new oligarchy would have predominant influence.

5 Foreign Policy, 1660–88

The collapse of the Commonwealth and the Restoration coincided with the emergence of a new European order after the treaty of the Pyrenees, which ended the Franco-Spanish war of 1635–59. The ascendancy of France was to be the dominant characteristic of late seventeenth-century Europe; with the peripheral exception of the Ottoman empire, it can be said that up to the 1680s France was the sole great power in Europe. Consequently nearly all the assumptions, principles and policies that had long been operative in the case of other states now had to be revised.

During the previous century and a half English rulers and their ministers, if they had an active foreign policy at all, could choose between a French or a Spanish alignment, and it was a practicable proposition to maintain neutrality in the long contest for supremacy between France and Spain. Ministers had often been divided into so-called French and Spanish parties, although English opinion generally was traditionally hostile towards Spain as the aggressive champion of the Counter-Reformation. There was far less ideological hostility towards France, where the Huguenots enjoyed toleration. France seemed to be the less dangerous of the great powers; there was no effective French fleet outside the Mediterranean, and the power of the crown was constantly contested and limited by the great nobility.

In the years after Louis xiv's assumption of power in 1661 the situation was totally transformed. He created the largest and most advanced army in Europe, and made full use of the most extensive and skilled diplomatic service in existence. Two further parts of his assertive policies fundamentally affected relations with England. During the 1660s Colbert rapidly constructed an entirely new, large and efficient fleet, well equipped with bases on the Atlantic coast—as revolutionary and formidable a challenge to English security as that posed by Tirpitz's new German navy in the twentieth century. This, moreover, was directly connected with concurrent policies of economic and mercantile development, backed by stringently enforced tariffs, which made France a new and unexpected competitor for English industrial, mercantile and colonial interests.

The expansion of French power under Louis XIV threatened English security and prosperity, and eventually it was to produce the first two in the long series of Anglo-French wars that ended only in 1815. But at first English reactions to the upsurge of French power were inconsistent, confused and uncertain. By later standards England's role should have been to try to check French power, to reduce Louis's capacity to establish what contemporaries called 'the New Universal Monarchy'. Indeed, the principle of the balance of power was formulated during this period, but neither Charles, James nor the majority of their ministers had the imagination and courage to accept the practical consequences of this principle. Down to 1688 English policy makers usually reacted to French moves. English intervention and influence in Europe had far less practical impact than French and Dutch intervention in domestic English politics, and the revolution of 1688 was itself a move, albeit a decisive one, in their struggle.

After 1688, under William's direction, English foreign policy assumed the basic forms which it was to retain for over two centuries. William and his English associates had tried from the mid-1670s to direct England into active participation in the alliances and war against France. Their failure had been due not only to French counter-intervention and the court's francophile sympathies, but because virtually the whole English political nation was insular, ignorant of European affairs and absorbed in domestic politics. The intrinsic difficulties of combining with other states whose interests were either separate from, or actually contradictory to, those of England, were exacerbated by the slowness with which ministers, parliament and public opinion absorbed the education in European realities which the Nine Years War provided. By taking on himself the direction of diplomacy and military operations, showing his distrust of nearly all his new subjects as incompetent, factious, corrupt or disloyal, William may have helped to retard this educative process. His success was posthumous—in the confidence, indeed arrogance, born of success, with which his successors, Marlborough and Godolphin, and even more the tory ministers of 1710–14, handled foreign affairs.

There was more continuity in foreign policy than in domestic affairs between the Commonwealth and the restored monarchy. This continuity was certainly not from choice, but largely the result of the economic and popular pressures that were brought to bear on Charles and his ministers. Republican foreign policy had been coloured by Cromwell's desire for a protestant policy, but the primary objective throughout was to ensure the survival of the regime, by depriving the exiled Stuarts of foreign assistance. To a lesser extent the monarchy was similarly concerned to render émigré groups harmless—in the 1660s republicans and fugitive regicides, after 1683 whigs implicated in the Rye House Plot. In the 1660s Spain gave rather ineffective support to republican plotters, as retribution for Charles's cynical but realistic repudiation of his obligations, and the help he was giving the rebel Portuguese. Charles had accepted a Spanish alliance in 1656 only as a second best, because Cromwell pre-empted him in concluding an alliance with France, which both men valued as the stronger power. By concluding this alliance Cromwell was operating a reverse balance of power policy, allying with the more dangerous power so as to neutralize it, and his success was remarkable considering the close personal links between the French and English royal families.

From his accession, Charles's own personal preference was for a close relationship with France, but he came under immediate and sustained pressure to concentrate on a policy of using the navy to renew and intensify pressure on the Dutch. The fleet had been the main instrument of power of the Commonwealth in foreign relations, the means by which it had extorted recognition from instinctively hostile sovereigns, and protected English commercial interests. Efficiently administered and vigorously directed by the council of state, the navy had penetrated the Mediterranean, the Tagus and the Baltic and even in 1659 exerted considerable influence in the latter. Less successfully, the navy had enabled Cromwell to formulate and attempt his 'western design' (1655) of conquering Spain's Caribbean possessions and trade. This provoked an inconclusive war that was terminated only by the Restoration, and exposed English merchant shipping to heavy losses as the condition of the navy deteriorated. But this failure was played down by the advocates of aggressive, mercantilist policies. The policy (associated with the Rump, rather than with Cromwell) of expanding foreign trade by such legislation as the Navigation Ordinance (1651), and using the navy to extort trade concessions and inflict damage on competitors, was the most influential legacy from the Interregnum. This line of argument, developed into the thesis that England should concentrate exclusively on a maritime and colonial strategy, and avoid continental diplomatic entanglements and military commitments, was to continue as a major principle well into the eighteenth century, consistently attracting 'country' support.

The navalist and mercantilist groups who involved England in the Second Dutch War were misled into thinking that the successes of 1652–4 would be easy to repeat. During that first war the Dutch fighting fleet, heavily out-gunned, had been shattered in battle. Blockades temporarily paralysed Dutch trade, and further heavy

damage was inflicted on the Dutch economy by the capture of more
than a thousand merchant ships and their cargoes. By late 1653 the
Dutch were losing both the will and the ability to continue the war.
Their credit was nearing exhaustion, political recriminations were
tearing the provinces apart, and the States General was ready to
settle on almost any terms. English mercantile interests had by then
formulated their war aims—to put the United Provinces in a state of
permanent dependence, so that all disputes between the two countries
could be resolved to England's advantage. But Cromwell was
not interested in economic advantages, only in preventing the
Stuarts receiving Dutch aid. Mercantilist critics bitterly attacked
him for losing the peace after others had won the war.

The peace of 1654 did not remove the basic causes of conflict that
had led to the war. These continued to fester. A new attempt at
settlement, by a treaty negotiated under Clarendon's direction in
1662, had little effect. The Dutch persisted with their proven tactic
of promising redress of English grievances (over the North Sea
fisheries, seizures of English ships in east Asia and west Africa), but
going no further than verbal concessions. However, Clarendon and
Charles knew that the navy (and particularly the dockyards) had
become run down during the last years of the Commonwealth, and
that there was insufficient money to restore its former strength and
efficiency in the near future. Existing resources were stretched in
protecting England's ally, Portugal, and the new possessions of
Bombay and Tangier, which came into English hands as a result of
Charles's marriage to Catherine of Braganza (April 1662). This marriage sharpened Spanish hostility, creating a danger that any attack
on the Dutch might precipitate a new war against Spain. This could
have serious economic as well as naval consequences, since attempts
to establish a close alliance with France achieved nothing. In 1662
Louis preferred to renew his treaty with the Dutch, and this reverse
left England isolated diplomatically.

The advocates of aggressive policies against the Dutch were unimpressed by, or largely unaware of, these symptoms of English
weakness. During 1660–64 pressures for renewed coercion of the
Dutch, including outright war if necessary, steadily mounted.
Merchant interests ensured the speedy re-enactment of the
Navigation Ordinance, in a strengthened statutory form in 1660.
Commodities could be exported from, or imported into, existing or
future colonies in Asia, Africa and America only in English or
colonial ships; to satisfy this regulation the ships had to have been
built in England, to be English owned, and threequarters of the crew
had to be English. Commodities from Europe must be shipped either
in English ships, or those belonging to the country of origin, so cutting

out the Dutch as middlemen, and this objective was also to be achieved by prohibiting the export of sugar, tobacco and dyeing woods from the colonies to any ports outside England and Ireland. The supplementary Statute of Frauds (1662) was even more explicitly anti-Dutch: it barred the import of wines, spices, tobacco and naval stores from the United Provinces (and Germany), and gave a narrow definition to the meaning of English ships, so as to prevent the Dutch using flags of convenience. Those who framed these acts had profited from experience since 1651, and the new provisions facilitated enforcement. The arrest and condemnation of Dutch ships for contravening the Navigation Act considerably increased tension.

Several distinct groups combined in urging, or undertaking, direct action. The Commons showed itself receptive to petitions and representations. Its address of April 1664 (drafted by Sir Thomas Clifford) denounced the Dutch as the major impediment to all chances of commercial expansion and national prosperity. MPs displayed a genuine and spontaneous hostility to the Dutch, causing Charles to write in June 1664: 'I never saw so great an appetite to a war as in both this town and country, especially in the parliament men.' Naval officers, including many who had served the Commonwealth, were eager for action and employment, and had influential patrons in the lord high admiral, James, and the lord general, Albemarle, whose importance and influence would be greatly magnified by a war. A group of courtiers and junior ministers, among whom William Coventry and the rising favourite Falmouth were prominent, saw Clarendon as an obstruction to effective administration as well as to their own careers. They expected to use Clarendon's dislike of any war, and all too obvious unfitness to conduct one, to procure his ruin. Several among these political adventurers, including James, were personally concerned with a group of London merchants—the Company of Royal Adventurers—who tried to win a share not only of west African trade, but also of the booming slave trade, from the most aggressive of Dutch merchant interests, the West India Company.

Hostilities between these two companies actually precipitated the war. Both instigated attacks by west African tribes on their competitor's trading posts and personnel. In January 1664 Holmes systematically plundered the Dutch posts, with a squadron sent from England. De Witt, pensionary of Holland and *de facto* head of the Dutch government, felt that this use of force constituted a challenge to which he must reply. He ordered de Ruyter to carry out a reprisal raid, which destroyed virtually all the English positions. De Witt knew that this move might provoke a general war, but he was convinced that failure to meet force with force would only encourage further English aggression. His judgement was confirmed by developments. The English were on the point of seizing New Amsterdam, and in December a Dutch convoy returning from Turkey was attacked off Gibraltar. De Witt's determined stand disproved the predictions which Sir George Downing, envoy at the Hague, had been making and which influenced the policy makers in London. Downing was far from being an advocate of war. He believed that the threat of force would extort concessions from the Dutch, that memories of the disasters of the first war, and fear of internal unrest inflamed by the Orangist party, would make de Witt seek peace at almost any price. In September 1664 Downing claimed that Dutch finances and credit were already severely strained, and that news of the generous grants of supply being made by parliament would lead the States General to adopt policies of appeasement. Downing's plan was to exert pressure in Europe and the narrow seas in order to force the Dutch to give way on all controverted questions and disputes in east Asia and west Africa.

Downing did not expect pressure to lead to a declared war, but he was confident that if one did break out, then a rapid and decisive victory could be achieved. England retained all the advantages that had been so skilfully exploited in 1652–3. Her geographical position stood 'like eagle's wings' between the Dutch ports and the oceanic trade routes. The prevailing westerly winds gave the English fleet the strategic (and often the tactical) initiative. English ports and anchorages were more advantageously sited than those on the exposed Dutch coast. Because of the shallows in the approaches to their ports, Dutch ships could never be so heavily gunned as their adversaries. Dutch merchant shipping, a veritable 'mountain of gold', represented a large and vulnerable target to English privateers.

The Second Dutch War started with English successes reminiscent of the first. In the weeks before the actual declaration of war (on 4 March 1665) several hundred prizes were taken, and in May the Dutch suffered their worst defeat in all three wars when their main fleet was routed off Lowestoft. But there was no effective exploitation of this victory, the number of prizes declined steadily, Dutch privateers began to operate against English shipping, and an attack on Dutch East Indiamen holed up in Bergen was repulsed. In 1666, when France entered the war as a reluctant enemy, faulty intelligence led to a division of the fleet with a squadron being detached to cover the expected arrival of the French fleet. The weakened main fleet met the Dutch in the Four Days' Fight (May) and suffered heavy losses, but in July it turned the tables by hammering the Dutch off the North Foreland, and later a huge concentration of enemy merchant ships was destroyed in the Vlie anchorage. The

Dutch had the reserves to survive such losses, but this major effort virtually exhausted English resources and produced moves for an end to the war. For financial and administrative reasons it was decided not to put the main fleet to sea in 1667, but the Dutch still had enough money for a massive effort. In an effort to deter the English from attempting another war of aggression, when they had recovered, de Witt overruled his admirals and insisted on the execution of the hazardous but brilliantly successful attack on Chatham, the burning of dockyard and ships (June), and a blockade of much of the English coast was established during the last weeks of hostilities.

What had started as a popular war ended catastrophically, and for a short time even the stability of the monarchy itself seemed to be in doubt. Albemarle (the former General Monk) had to be brought into prominence as a saviour of the nation. Responsibility for the failures really lay on the commanding admirals—particularly James, Sandwich and Allin—who followed an essentially piratical strategy. Instead of following up victories at sea by establishing close and prolonged blockades, the fleet was diverted into largely unproductive sweeps to capture prizes. Pursuit of private profit (and some of the prizes were later discovered to have been misappropriated) dominated the admirals' thinking. No clear strategical plan was developed. Naval administration deteriorated as the war progressed. Stocks of arms and stores were low at the start, and new replacement supplies had to be purchased at inflated prices. By the end of 1666 admiralty credit was exhausted, the seamen's morale had been destroyed by the use of promissory 'tickets' to pay their arrears— which they could not cash—and the dockyards lacked both the money and the materials to fit out a fleet.

The financial weaknesses of the government crippled the navy, and were aggravated by the coincidental disasters of the Plague and the Great Fire of London (September 1666). Practical experience totally disproved the arguments on which the mercantilist case for a war of profitable aggression had rested. Profits did not come. Losses of merchant ships taken by the Dutch seem more or less to have equalled the prizes captured. Merchants suffered more serious losses from lengthy dislocations of overseas and coastal trade. The Baltic was closed to English ships throughout the war. Because of the limited pool of seamen available it was impossible to make war and try to continue trade at anything like normal levels. Of course the Dutch were similarly affected, so the strength of their financial reserves and the superiority of their credit system became the decisive factors in determining the outcome of the war. The war had been launched with an unprecedentedly huge vote of supply, for £2,500,000, which it was thought would intimidate the Dutch, but this turned out to be a bluff. Money came in slowly, credit became increasingly expensive and finally failed altogether. War provided the acid test of the efficiency of seventeenth-century governments. Charles II's almost undirected administration failed the test.

The inadequacies of English diplomacy also contributed significantly to the failure. As the pressures for war mounted in 1664, belated moves were attempted to isolate the Dutch and procure allies against them. In view of the fact that no permanent representatives had been stationed in either country since 1660, it is not surprising that special missions sent in the autumn to Sweden and Denmark failed to obtain alliances with either. French offers to mediate in the disputes with the Dutch were disregarded, in the mistaken belief that French neutrality either had been, or could easily be, obtained. Louis's moves came as unpleasant surprises to the English council. At first he tried to keep both maritime powers dependent on him, holding out the prospect to England of a possible alliance but actually intending to mediate in favour of the Dutch, in order to obtain their acquiescence for his designs against the Spanish Netherlands. But early English victories in 1665 made Louis, like the German and Scandinavian states, fear that the United Provinces were about to fall under English domination. English propaganda, especially the grandiloquent claims to sovereignty of the narrow seas, was taken at its face value. Neutrals believed that England was getting into a position where it would establish a 'universal monarchy' at sea, and high-handed interference with neutral rights by privateers and prize-courts provoked resentment.

Louis also intervened to sabotage an ambitious attempt by Arlington to negotiate a series of alliances—with Munster, Sweden, Spain, Brandenburg and the Emperor. All except the first failed, and this was due to French, not Dutch, diplomatic intervention. Louis had ulterior motives for this, and for honouring his obligations to the Dutch by declaring war on England in January 1666. His policy was now concerned with a far more important issue than the war between the two maritime powers: the death of Philip IV in September 1665 opened up the whole question of the Spanish succession. Absorbed at first in their war, the Dutch and the English began to realize the implications for themselves of the 'devolutionary' claims that Louis put forward, for territories in the Spanish Netherlands. His invasion of Flanders in May 1667 hastened the conclusion of peace at Breda (21 July), and forced ministers in both countries to reconsider their policies. The peace itself settled nothing. Each power was confirmed in its conquests—New York for England, African ports and Surinam in the Caribbean for the Dutch. But the original causes of conflict were not resolved.

The interlude between the Second and Third Dutch Wars contained not one, but two, astonishing diplomatic revolutions. First, the English and the Dutch within a few months of ceasing hostilities against each other came together in January 1668 (with the later addition of Sweden) in the Triple Alliance, and this seemed to have achieved its apparent objective of checking France when Louis ended the War of Devolution in April 1668 (Treaty of Aachen). Subsequently in January 1670 the three allies agreed on aid to Spain, if France attacked again, and supply was requested from parliament in the 1671 session specifically to support the Triple Alliance. However, under the surface Charles was pursuing an entirely contradictory policy. Secret negotiations with France were aimed at ensuring French support in a new war which was being cold-bloodedly planned against the Dutch. In two secret treaties—Dover (May 1670) and the sham or 'simulated' treaty of December—an alliance was concluded between England and France, embodying the desire of their sovereigns to destroy the independence of the United Provinces.

From 1668 until his death there was to be a permanent discrepancy between Charles's avowed principles and policies, and those which he was really but secretly attempting. Even the leading ministers and diplomats found it difficult at any time and on any issue to known what were the king's real intentions, or to know what he was doing in secret, and their constant puzzlement and understandable mistrust were shared by foreign sovereigns, their ministers and their diplomatic representatives in London. Technically, there was nothing unconstitutional about Charles's conduct, since foreign affairs were exclusively a prerogative matter, and parliament had no right to be kept informed, still less to have its consent obtained; but it is sophistry to claim that Charles was primarily concerned with the national interest. His policy (and that of James later) was clearly dynastic; it was not the interests of England but those of the monarchy that were being promoted, and this was to be not only at the expense of other sovereigns, but also of his own subjects. In particular, Charles tried to use foreign alliances in order to achieve independence from parliament.

The Triple Alliance was extremely popular with parliament and public opinion, but for quite mistaken reasons. It was welcomed as the only way of limiting the growth of French power. The ease with which the French army took the most strongly fortified cities in the Spanish Netherlands in 1667, the appearance of a strong French fleet in the Channel, and customs impositions and fiscal discrimination against English goods and merchants were producing widespread hostility against France. But the Triple Alliance, largely the work of Arlington and Sir William Temple, was not an alliance against France, although the public saw it as such. Its immediate purpose had been to compel Spain to make concessions to France so that the war could be quickly ended. Only if Louis, from whom assurances had been received, refused to accept these concessions and continued military operations (as his exuberantly successful generals were urging) would the allies join with Spain and restore the frontiers of 1659. This was stipulated in a secret article (soon known to Louis), but it was the general acclaim that the treaty received, as a successful move to check French expansion, that made it appear to Louis as a possible obstacle to the realization of his next set of expansionist objectives. His solution was to engage Charles as an ally and instrument in the work of destroying the independence of the United Provinces.

Charles's motives for abandoning the Triple Alliance were far more devious. In the first place it was an assertion of personal authority. Freed from tutelage to Clarendon, Charles was determined to make the major policy decisions himself, and not to relapse into dependence on any individual minister. In a revealing letter to his sister, the duchess of Orléans, who acted as intermediary with Louis, Charles told her to drive out of Louis's head the idea 'that my ministers are anything but what I will have them, and that they have no partiality but to my interest and the good of England'. In other words all negotiations must be conducted with Charles himself or those whom he nominated, and these were not to include Buckingham, his would-be chief minister who was known to be eager for a French alliance but would have been easy to mislead and manipulate to serve French purposes. It was also a guarantee that Arlington, who had negotiated the Triple Alliance and was suspected by Louis as being pro-Spanish, would do as he was told and not obstruct an alliance with France. Most important of all, Charles ensured that the crucial negotiations must be conducted on a personal basis.

The preliminaries of the secret Treaty of Dover were settled in correspondence through 1669 and early 1670 by Charles and his sister. Only an inner group were aware of what was going on—James, Clifford, a catholic peer Arundell of Wardour, and (so as to involve him and head off future obstruction) Arlington. Not only were the normal diplomatic channels by-passed, but the other leading ministers were kept in ignorance. The principal provision of the treaty was a commitment to make war on the United Provinces jointly, with an auxiliary French fleet assisting the English, and an English army of 6,000 to serve with the French. English annexations were specified as Walcheren, Sluis and Kadzand, strategic areas that controlled the Scheldt estuary; in contrast French gains were not stated, and so were not limited. Another indication of England's status as junior partner can be found in the financial provisions. Charles originally pitched his demands very high, claiming £800,000 per annum as war subsidy (and another £200,000 for his conversion to catholicism); the treaty gave him £225,000 per annum for the war, and £150,000 on account of religion. This last sum was to be paid after ratification of the treaty, and not when Charles made his promised public declaration of his conversion to catholicism. As this shows, Louis was far from sharing Charles's assumed enthusiasm for the 'catholicity' clause. The former was concerned with preparing for war against the Dutch. Charles's declaration might prove to be a diversion since, as the treaty stated, it might provoke disorders in England necessitating the despatch of French aid: Louis undertook to send 6,000 soldiers if required.

Charles's motives for proposing to declare himself a catholic have puzzled historians; the probable explanation is that he was trying to improve his long-term bargaining position in relations with a much stronger partner. By secretly repudiating and reversing his public and popular foreign policy of the Triple Alliance, Charles was exposing himself, his heir and his ministers to the same kind of reaction and attacks that had assailed Strafford, Laud, Charles I and, more recently, Clarendon. Furthermore, this new adventure in foreign policy was inextricably connected with ambitious and risky domestic policies that were certain to excite general resentment. Charles needed the assurance of continuing, perhaps permanent, French support, but French foreign policy was notoriously calculating and amoral, operating on the machiavellian principle of *raison d'état*. Only by publicly committing Louis through an undertaking to give support not just for Charles personally or for the institution of the monarchy, but to maintain the catholic faith against a possible protestant rebellion, could Charles obtain any assurance that Louis would not stand aside (as he was to do in 1688) if rebellion threatened him with deposition and exile. It is not surprising that Louis showed no enthusiasm for this project of a public announcement of Charles's conversion, but preferred to concentrate on the preparation of the war.

Since three of the ministers in the so-called Cabal (Buckingham, Ashley and Lauderdale) knew nothing of the Dover Treaty, a bogus treaty had to be negotiated (December 1670) providing simply for the attack on the Dutch. Buckingham put himself forward as France's best friend in England, and had ambitions to command the army that would have to be raised, seeing this as a sure way of gaining political predominance under an absolutist system of government. Ashley, less secure in office, had to go along with royal policies, and his contacts with commercial interests were of some value because a *casus belli* had to be concocted. The real aim of the war was to free Charles from dependence on parliament and his subjects, but since obviously this could not be avowed, a semi-fraudulent commercial case was prepared by the committee of trade. The East India and Royal African Companies, and those who had settled in Surinam and been expropriated, were encouraged to put forward claims against the Dutch; but Clifford and Ashley were among the commissioners who handled the negotiations with the States General and made sure that no settlement was reached—although eventually in March 1672 the Dutch offered almost all that the English had demanded earlier. Downing replaced Temple at the Hague and lost no opportunity during his brief stay (December 1671–February 1672) to put pressure on de Witt. But when war was declared on 13 March 1672 the reasons given—disputes over the Indies, Surinam and the salute to the English flag symbolizing sovereignty over the narrow seas—made an unimpressive cover for naked aggression.

These commercial issues were pretexts. Once again the real reason for war was predatory greed—this time for power as well as wealth. In anticipation of an actual declaration of war, Dutch ships returning home with valuable cargoes were attacked, but almost symbolically the most ambitious attempt, an attack in the Channel on a lightly defended Smyrna convoy, failed miserably. After some preliminary cruising, the English and French fleets were surprised while revictualling off the Suffolk coast on 28 May, and in the action of Sole Bay the English were severely mauled and the admiral, Sandwich, killed. By comparison the French escaped serious damage, something that was attributed by the English officers to either cowardice or secret restraining orders. After refitting, the English fleet wasted the rest of the summer in unsuccessful hunts for enemy East Indiamen, so that at the end there was virtually nothing to show for an expensive campaign.

In the fighting on land the French won rapid and staggering victories. They overran the landward provinces of Gelderland and Overijssel, and captured Utrecht on 23 June. Even before this disaster a Dutch mission was sent to sue for peace, and it was already apparent to Charles and his ministers that Louis was now completely the master of the situation. Godolphin, who was accompanying Louis, reported that English interests were likely to be virtually ignored in the punitive peace that France would now impose. The English position was extremely weak. The fleet was unsuccessful. The war had been launched without financial reserves, and as early as the beginning of June doubts were being expressed as to how easily another campaign could be financed. Approaches were made to France for the promise of an increased subsidy, and the question raised as to whether parliament could be recalled in the autumn—so Louis was well aware of his ally's difficulties. Confident that the war was already won, he rejected the Dutch offers of concessions as insufficient. The terms he demanded showed how little account he took of England, and would have put both the United Provinces and the Spanish Netherlands permanently and completely at his mercy. France was to annex the Dutch Generality lands that lay between the two, receive an indemnity that would drain the republic of its money, establish a privileged position for the catholic minority under French protection, and dismantle all prohibitions and protective duties on French goods. Significantly and quite deliberately, Louis made no provision for the transfer to England of the strategically valuable areas around the Scheldt that had been promised at Dover; Charles was to be given only the remote port of Delfzijl in the north.

Two missions were hastily despatched to try to safeguard English pretensions; the first was headed by Halifax, but the second was headed by the two rivals to ministerial predominance, Arlington and Buckingham. Their mission was to persuade Louis not to make peace without incorporating the English claims—acknowledgement by the Dutch of English dominion over the narrow seas, an annual rent for fishing in the North Sea, an indemnity of £1,000,000, annexation of the Scheldt ports and Brille, and concessions in the Indies. Louis gave an impression of agreeing to these claims, but this soon became an academic question. This was because the missions failed in their second (and, as it proved, crucial) objective. This was to persuade William to save what he could for himself by accepting Charles's protection and turn himself into the dependant of England. This was a temptation of satanic proportions. The Dutch population was demoralized, the army inadequate to resist a determined French attack across the flooded polders. William himself at first thought, like the masses who gave the English diplomats a frenzied welcome as deliverers, that Charles would intervene to moderate the crushing French demands. He found that the offer to set him up as hereditary prince of the United Provinces was dependent on acceptance of the full French and English demands. William revealed the secret offers to the States General (which was resented as a breach of faith by Charles) and recommended their rejection; the resolution to do so (21 July) was the only reply that Charles and Louis received.

William subsequently concentrated on trying to separate the English from the French. His repeated offers to meet most of the English demands got no response because they were conditional on Charles making peace unilaterally, and this would mean the loss of

French subsidies. William then turned to political subversion, in order to force Charles to abandon the war and the French alliance. In the long term the Dutch could not afford to finance a naval war against England at the same time as trying to eject the French from their territory and constructing a general alliance against Louis. Military and diplomatic campaigning were always to be William's priority. In using unscrupulous methods William was also repaying the contempt and threats with which his approaches had been treated by Arlington and Charles. The first unofficial mission by Zas and Arton (January 1673), whose objective was to influence opinion, failed when both men were arrested as spies. In the parliamentary session that began in February 1673 the opposition concentrated exclusively in attacking the domestic policies that accompanied the war, but the war itself did not come into question; in return for royal acceptance of the Test Act and the king's withdrawal of the Declaration of Indulgence, parliament voted sufficient supply to finance another summer's campaign. However, in March there appeared a celebrated pamphlet, *England's Appeal from the Private Cabal at Whitehall to the Great Council of the Nation*, which was to produce direct criticism of the war itself in the autumn session, and to colour the attitude of a whole generation to foreign affairs. This pamphlet was the work of du Moulin, the earliest of a succession of able and devoted Huguenot servants of William. It presented the war and the French alliance as part of a dangerous conspiracy against the protestant religion and the liberties of Englishmen. Du Moulin depicted Louis as exploiting England in order to establish his 'universal monarchy', and Charles's ministers were portrayed as corrupt betrayers of their country's interests and independence.

Developments during the summer of 1673 confirmed and illustrated the arguments and charges of *England's Appeal*. The conference at Cologne failed to produce peace, because Louis maintained his harsh demands and the English emissaries had instructions not to make any separate agreement. There was now a serious danger that England would become involved in the imminent extension of the war to include Spain, and loss of all trade with Spain would be commercially disastrous. Three indecisive fleet actions were fought, and on each occasion the French were again accused of deliberately allowing the English to bear the brunt of action and losses. Failure to drive the enemy fleet from the Dutch coast meant that the army prepared for an invasion from the sea could not leave England. Its inaction provoked charges that it had never been intended for use abroad, but that its real purpose had been to stage a coup to make Charles absolute. In addition James's second marriage, to Mary of Modena, notoriously sponsored and arranged by French diplomacy,

underlined the dangers that du Moulin had described by symbolizing England's status as a French satellite and creating the prospect of
a catholic dynasty. The Commons refused to cooperate any further
in the war. Furious attacks on the French alliance forced a prorogation on 4 November and, when parliament reassembled in
January 1674, all Charles's attempts to argue that Dutch intransigence was responsible for obstructing the conclusion of peace had no
effect. By then a group of propagandists and MPs was working for
du Moulin, but the entire country opposition and independents in
both houses were demanding an early end to the war and the rup-
ture of the French alliance.

The Treaty of Westminster in February 1674 not only brought the
war to an inglorious end (the Dutch conceding only the salute to the
flag and a small indemnity), it also exploded the mercantilist thesis
on which all the Dutch wars had been based. There was no profit,
actual or potential, to offset the money expended on the wars. Heavy
taxation and higher customs, the pressing of ships and seamen, prohibitions on trade and the closure of the Baltic had all affected the
economy adversely. The treaty also represented a major diplomatic
triumph for William, but he was to have to pay a heavy price for this
success over the next decade. By appealing to public opinion,
generating universal distrust of the court and ministers, and encouraging parliamentary and pamphlet attacks on them, William counter-
mined France and destroyed the influence over English policy which
Louis had achieved. But he exacerbated, as well as exploited, weaknesses and negative characteristics in the English system of government. The suspicions and tensions that he and his agents created
were to persist. When William subsequently attempted to enlist
English resources on the side of the confederation fighting France, it
was the latter who imitated his techniques, and with almost equally
decisive effect.

By the autumn of 1677 the confederates had suffered a series of
defeats that imperilled the entire Spanish Netherlands, while a revolt
in Sicily and French victories over a combined Dutch and Spanish
fleet threatened to give Louis naval and commercial supremacy
in the Mediterranean. William desperately needed English aid in
order at least to try to restore a balance of power in Europe.
Characteristically, the favourable response which William's approaches received from Danby, Charles's chief minister from 1673 to
1679, was the result primarily of considerations in terms of domestic
politics, not foreign policy. Danby had not been involved as a principal in the policies of the Cabal, and in 1673–4 he had favoured
ending the Dutch war for financial reasons. Part of his ministerial

pose had from the start been an advertised aloofness from France, although he was privately aware of Charles's pro-French sympathies and continuing contacts with Louis. In 1677 Danby wished to make use of William's prestige, he saw advantages in raising an army, and he was looking ahead to a remoter future. Danby planned to get control of the reversionary interest, since both Charles and James were beginning to age. By sponsoring William's marriage (November) to Mary, James's elder daughter, Danby could hope to perpetuate his influence. Although a son was born to James's wife immediately after the marriage of Mary, displacing her in the line of succession, he soon sickened and died like several before him.

The royal marriage was accompanied by the conclusion of an alliance of mutual assistance (January 1678). At the same time missions were sent to Louis to urge him to accept peace on terms that were more favourable to the confederates than would be justified by the military situation. An expansion of the army was quickly carried out. A small force was sent to defend Ostend (February). But when parliament was asked to vote supply, the opposition engaged in systematic obstruction. Charles's sincerity in intending a war against France was openly questioned (and rightly, since he was secretly and simultaneously negotiating for a new French subsidy as the price of inaction). Charges were made that the expansion of the army to 40,000 men, which a war against France (as distinct from one against the Dutch) necessitated, was part of a royal and ministerial plot against the constitution, and that these forces would be used to set up absolutism at home, not to fight France. It is possible that this was precisely what Charles and Danby had in mind, at least as an option, but the opposition politicians who made these charges were themselves cooperating secretly with the French ambassador in return for subsidies. By intervening in the internal politics of England and the United Provinces, using domestic factions and utilizing the clumsy procedures of representative institutions, Louis scored a great diplomatic triumph at the Nijmegen conference. He concluded peace with the States General over William's head (31 July), and as this was a separate peace with the Dutch republicans leaving the confederates to fend for themselves, the effect was to disintegrate the confederation and discredit William.

However, Louis had to realize that there was now a permanent danger that William would, directly or indirectly, gain influence over Charles and assume the direction of English foreign policy. In December 1678, prompted by the French ambassador, some of the opposition leaders revealed secret correspondence implicating Danby in negotiations for a French subsidy, at a time that he was publicly calling for war against Louis, and was raising an army for that purpose. Louis could not trust Charles's frequently repeated professions of friendship since he knew that a king of England could be compelled by his ministers, or parliamentary pressure or poverty, to adopt policies that he disliked. Louis therefore set himself to exploit those negative characteristics of English politics that William had used in 1672–3. France subsidized the opposition in 1678. English ministers and diplomats were purchased with pensions. When the political crisis over the Exclusion bill intensified and divided the entire nation into hostile parties, French policies of subversion were far more likely to succeed than were the constructive attempts by William to settle the differences between court and parliament, so that England could again play a positive role in European affairs. William attempted the impossible, but for him (as again in 1688) a solution to the internal crisis was not an end in itself, but a necessary preliminary to making England a credible and effective member of the new alliance that he was painfully reconstructing in order to check France.

During 1679–80 Charles acquiesced when his ministers pursued a cosmetic foreign policy of putting together a new anti-French alliance, but they had no chance of success while whig leaders pressed for Exclusion. Foreign states would not associate with a kingdom that seemed to be on the brink of another suicidally destructive civil war; only the desperately weak Spaniards concluded a treaty of mutual assistance (June 1680). Nor did Charles meet with any response when he appealed in 1679 to Louis for subsidies to enable him to subsist without parliament. French interests were being served by the continuing confrontation between king and parliament. Louis cared nothing for the interests of the monarchy in England (as he was to prove again in 1688); political divisions and confusion prevented England from playing an active role in Europe. Only when it seemed likely that Charles and his ministers would come to the conclusion that William alone could rescue the court from its domestic enemies did Louis intervene. The secret agreement of April 1681 permanently neutralized England. In return for subsidies Charles agreed not to call parliament again, and this ensured that he could not have an active or independent foreign policy.

This agreement rendered futile the visit of William to England in July, during which he severely damaged his reputation and influence. William's associates, Temple, Sidney and Sunderland, had repeatedly advised him to intervene as the only man who could restore national unity. The basis of the settlement he was expected to impose was the exclusion of James, since William made it clear that he rejected the alternative of limitations on the prerogative, and believed that James's accession would precipitate a civil war. But

William had no control over the whigs, nor even so far as we know
any contacts with their leaders, and by 1681 Charles had committed
himself irrevocably against Exclusion. Although William did not
know the details of how Charles had sold himself to Louis, his
reception in 1681, and the indifference which the English court
showed as Louis made spectacular new gains—Strasbourg and
Luxemburg among them—made England useless. In November
1683 Spain, goaded by piecemeal acts of aggression, declared war on
France. William failed to get any support for action to aid her from
either the States General or England, who reneged on the treaty of
1680. All William's work to build a new alliance to check Louis was
undone.

English foreign policy from April 1681 until the Revolution of
1688 can best be described as shadow-boxing. Louis was content
with English inactivity. He did not now need a naval ally, since his
fleet was as strong as the English and Dutch combined. Charles,
playing out time, had long forgotten and abandoned his attempts (in
1668–70) to persuade Louis to limit his navy. Tangier was abandoned to save money (1683). James continued this inactivity in
foreign affairs; the only perceptible difference from Charles is that he
saw positive advantages in English neutrality, especially as the possibility of a new European war increased. In 1687–8 quite serious
differences arose between the English and Dutch East India
Companies, over Bantam in Java, that could easily have produced a
new Dutch war, but James made no attempt to use these differences
as a *casus belli*, as had been done in 1665 and 1672. Whether Louis
would allow James to remain neutral in the general war that was
likely to break out in the very near future was, however, something
that William could not leave to him. He had to prevent a repetition
of the catastrophic situation of 1672, when the Dutch faced overwhelming naval as well as military power. William had no alternative but to pre-empt a possible alliance between James and Louis,
but his far more ambitious objective in invading England in 1688
was to add English resources to those available in the new alliance
being formed against France.

6 The Fall of
the Commonwealth and
the Restoration

The impression of strength and durability given by the Protectorate when Richard peacefully succeeded his father, Oliver Cromwell, on 3 September 1658, proved deceptive. Although the royalists were, and continued to be, powerless to destroy the republic, Oliver had never gained the willing consent of the nation. It is an historical truism to conclude that Cromwell's government depended on military power, but it is less often realized that at no time in his career did he find it an easy task to command an army that was always partly politicized, and in which subaltern officers and rankers were conscious of their potential power. Indeed, Oliver's ability to control the officer corps, and to maintain discipline over the ranks, had been the precondition for the survival of the Protectorate, and Richard faced an almost impossible task in having to take over as commander-in-chief as well as Protector. He made an intelligent attempt to widen the basis of public support for his regime, by a process of civilianization calculated to appeal to the gentry (including even former royalists) who served as JPs and making parliament a more active partner. But he fell from power in April 1659 as a direct result of losing control over the army.

Those who supplanted Richard—the Rump, Generals Fleetwood and Lambert—were equally unsuccessful in solving this problem. The largely politicized army played the dominant role throughout the period from Oliver's death to the return of the king: any decision or policy that went against its interests or ignored its reactions could not succeed. Monk's temporary greatness, his extraordinary achievement in effecting the Restoration, depended absolutely on his unique ability to lead and control his officers and men. A far lesser man than Oliver, lacking a sense of mission and allowing himself to fade into relative (if lucrative) unimportance in the years after 1660, nevertheless Monk alone equalled Oliver Cromwell in his mastery of the complex, difficult but politically decisive techniques of military management and army politics. Monk also had the common sense to realize that he should not try to set himself up as lord protector, as he was urged by many of his officers, and also by Bordeaux, the French ambassador. The collapse of all authority which plunged England into a state of virtual anarchy by December 1659, the fragmentation and demoralization of republican and sectarian groups, the steady contraction of their already narrow bases of support, widespread and virulent antimilitary feeling which was reflected in refusals to pay taxes, all left Monk with no alternative but to recall the exiled monarch.

This last phase of the Commonwealth was a period of intense but predominantly sterile political ferment. A revival of polemical pamphleteering and impassioned rhetorical debate produced negative, regurgitated or unrealistic propositions. It is striking how almost all the proposals were literally reactionary: parliamentary republicans wanted to go back to 1653, when the Rump Parliament had been forcibly dispersed by Cromwell; military activists worked for a return to 1647–8, years of the Putney and Whitehall debates in the council of the army and of constitutions formulated by politically conscious soldiers. The presbyterian oligarchs hoped to revive the Isle of Wight Treaty of 1648, and by imposing severe restrictions on a restored monarchy to perpetuate the influence of the parliamentarian section of the old political nation. Each of these groups claimed to represent and promote the liberties of the nation, and true religion, but in the months after Oliver's death they successively revealed themselves as primarily concerned to impose their own narrow concepts and sectional interests on the rest of the nation. Justified in their own language and thought as divinely appointed to rule, sectaries, officers, rumpers, presbyterian clergy and magnates, were seen and resented as impostors by the broader masses as well as by the old, displaced section of the political nation that had supported the monarchy.

The prospect of continuing anarchical disorders and arbitrary, purposeless changes enhanced the attractions of the old monarchical order, which alone could appeal to the whole nation. Thanks to Charles's own political shrewdness, and the consistent constitutionalism of his chief advisers, Hyde and Ormonde, the return of the monarchy promised civil, in place of sword or military, government, general union and virtually universal indemnity, legal not arbitrary justice, lower taxes, peace with Spain and renewed commercial prosperity, and finally no commitment to a partisan religious settlement. Yet although all but entrenched minority groups desired a restoration, such was the exclusive and dominant power of even an insubordinate and divided army that no one could see how it was to be brought about. Eventually the army itself became the unwitting agent of restoration, once Monk out-manoeuvred his rivals and made the decision. Like his old master, Oliver, Monk went further than he originally intended or expected, and once he knew what had to be done he succeeded in concealing his intentions.

Contemporaries often described the Restoration as a divinely ordained miracle. The sudden and unexpected deliverance from usurpation and tyranny was interpreted as a restoration of the natural and divine order, the correction of temporarily triumphant aberrations. In the twentieth century, with a belief in progress, most historians see revolutions as the dynamic factor in historical development, as the primary agents of change. By contrast, restorations tend to be seen as intrinsically futile attempts to put the clock back. But in the seventeenth century stability not change was assumed to be the normal state, and it was generally thought that the changes which undesirably but undoubtedly did occur formed a cyclical pattern, with events and situations repeating themselves, so that it was entirely practicable to return to the positions which existed before 1642, to undo or rectify all the destructive changes which had taken place since then.

This widespread belief that the experiences and developments of the Interregnum could be ignored, the hope that the former order could be restored in a perfect form that would confer union and prosperity on a divided and near-demoralized nation, meant that expectations were pitched impossibly high in 1660. Disillusionment was inevitable, but it was to be significantly increased by the mistakes and partisan character of the Restoration settlement.

Despite an almost ridiculous lack of experience—he had held no important civil or military office—Richard made an initially favourable impression as protector. He was inferior in personality and ability to his brother, Henry, who commanded the forces in Ireland but was feared by many in the army as another dictator. Richard's undisputed succession was greeted with genuine relief; addresses from the army, religious congregations, counties and corporations pledged loyal support. After Richard's ignominious fall these addresses were to be derided, but in 1658 they reflected general hopes for internal peace and stability. Furthermore, Richard was not personally associated with compromising acts and policies—the execution of Charles 1, the expulsion of the Rump, the special tribunals or the rule of the major-generals. His frank and open character, his sincerity and modesty attracted approval.

Richard displayed flexibility and firmness in successfully resolving what could have become a dangerous crisis with the army. Meetings of officers had been occurring during the last weeks of

Oliver's life, but they increased in size and frequency during October and began to develop disquieting political characteristics. These meetings were attended by as many as three hundred officers from units stationed throughout the British Isles. In behaviour they followed the pattern established at Putney, Windsor and Whitehall in 1647–8, which derived from the prayer meetings of the sects. Within such meetings considerations of rank were often suspended, and any individual could speak freely, frequently in quasi-religious and emotive language calculated to produce a highly charged atmosphere and a sense of unity and collective purpose, which could be exploited by a militant minority to mould and manipulate their colleagues, to isolate and intimidate sceptics, and to stampede a meeting into extreme courses of action.

The army meetings in the next year, 1659, were largely dominated by relatively junior officers and rankers, but in 1658 Fleetwood, the leading general (whose susceptibility to pressure was not yet apparent), and the other so-called grandees were able to contain the militants. Fleetwood had both personal and political obligations to the Protectorate. His military career had been promoted by Oliver, and he became Richard's brother-in-law in 1652 by marrying Ireton's widow, Bridget Cromwell. Fleetwood was a reliable officer, who had never been associated with army radicals or dissident politicians, but like Oliver he had made himself conspicuous as a champion of the religious sectaries. Events were to show that religious radicalism was largely a spent force by 1659, and Fleetwood had a weakness in that he had never had to deal on his own with politically inspired army disaffection. Personally, he was irresolute, having an unmilitary but at the time not uncommon tendency to break into tears at times of tension, and reproach himself for unworthiness. The grandees recognized soldiers' grievances, especially on arrears of over a year's pay, but they discouraged radical demands for a purge of officers denounced as Oliver's creatures, and for the dismissal of some of Richard's civilian ministers as enemies of the army; at this stage few of the majors and captains were prepared to go along with the subaltern and ranker activists. The grandees accepted Richard's firm response, that he would try to satisfy direct army grievances but not demands that would confer independence on the army. Fleetwood was promoted to lieutenant-general, but Richard remained commander-in-chief, and would not abandon the power of nominating officers, or agree that no officer would ever be removed except after court-martial, that is by fellow officers. On the other hand, Richard promised to consult the generals over appointments, some arrears were paid, and by taking his stand on the constitution (the Humble Petition and Advice) which provided him with a regular income for the maintenance of the army, he demonstrated the point that the economic interests of the soldiers would be best served by supporting him.

The army remained quiescent until the following March, but it was still a potential threat. The most highly politicized units were those stationed in and around London, and the commanders of detached and more effectively disciplined armies urged that action should be taken to bring them under control. Henry Cromwell wrote from Ireland advising Fleetwood to prevent his regiments interfering in politics, but did not suggest how this was to be done. Monk from Edinburgh was more specific in advocating to Richard a purge, through the device of retrenchment, but neither Richard nor Fleetwood had the authority to attempt such drastic action, and none of the senior officers genuinely loyal to Richard—Goffe, Ingoldsby, Montagu—had enough influence to act as effective rivals to the militants. Nor were Richard's civilian ministers of any assistance; they left him to cope with the army on his own, but the further extent of their inadequacy was to be fully realized only in the mismanagement of the parliamentary session that began on 27 January 1659.

The elections were held on the old system of representation, abandoning the redistribution from small boroughs to the counties which had been operated in 1654 and 1656—another indication of the shallow-rooted nature of the Commonwealth's constitutional experiments. There was considerable competition for seats, with many contested elections, but Richard and the ministers do not seem to have engaged in systematic electioneering, and on the eve of the session they were uncertain of the likely composition of the Commons. In the event, the numerical strength of parties was not to prove the decisive factor; debates were to show that there was a majority ready to follow an official lead, few crypto-royalists were returned, and the determined and vocal republican minority was defeated in every important division.

The basic reason for the failure of the session was the same as that for Oliver's difficulties with all his parliaments: insufficient or unskilful attention was given to detailed management. No clear lead was given to MPs, concerted tactics were not worked out, so that a handful of stubborn and determined republicans won a tactical ascendancy. Endless obstruction and filibustering, the use of every procedural device and legalistic trick, enabled them to render the session sterile: not a single bill was passed, not a penny voted. At the start, by introducing a bill for the recognition of the protector and the constitution, the court gave the republicans an opportunity to attack the loosely drafted Humble Petition and Advice, concentrating against its quasi-monarchical aspects. The Other House, the second chamber composed of nominees of the protector, mainly salaried judges, councillors and colonels, was attacked as a puppet body. The republicans also called for the expulsion of the MPS from Scotland and Ireland, or at least their suspension until the legality of the union had been debated.

Superficially, the results were inconclusive. All votes against the official interpretation of the constitution were defeated, but no bill of recognition passed, and the doubts expressed in debates made an impression outside the Commons. The main outcome of the session was a destructive widening and publicization of divisions. In debates ranging over past events, the republicans condemned Oliver's rule as a period of tyranny and economic depression, while praising the years of the Rump as a time of governmental solvency, national prosperity and godly rule. This provoked their opponents into denunciations of the Rump as having been a self-perpetuating, self-interested and corrupt band of usurpers who had grabbed power by violating the rights of parliament in Pride's Purge (1648). Later in 1660 this fundamental split between the republican rumpers, and the MPS secluded by Pride, was to emerge even more sharply and signal the end of the Commonwealth itself; but the other division which developed in the spring of 1659 was to be immediately fatal to the protectorate.

Republican obstruction of parliamentary business coincided with an ominous revival of political agitation within the army. Early in February, officers meeting at Fleetwood's residence, Wallingford House, proposed to petition parliament over soldiers' grievances, but desisted when warned by Richard. However, radical officers continued to canvass, pamphlets were circulated calling on soldiers to act against tyranny, and a connection was established with the republican opposition in parliament. Former officers made themselves conspicuous in the Commons, especially Lambert who had been second in command to Oliver until dismissed in 1657 for refusing to accept the new constitution, and Packer who had been the chief victim of the last purge of the army. John Lambert was a brilliant field commander and the most glamorous of public men, but he had always been as much a politician as a soldier since he helped Ireton draft the Heads of the Proposals in 1647. Although many contemporaries distrusted him as being too ambitious, he had established his republican reputation by heading the opposition to Oliver becoming king in 1656. In 1657 he had been dismissed for resisting the imposition of a loyalty oath. He did not have to take an active part in initiating the agitation that led to Richard's fall, but he was likely to be the chief beneficiary of political change. The emergence of Lambert and Packer as leaders of opposition posed a direct challenge not only to Richard, but also to Fleetwood and the grandees.

Lack of unity destroyed the Protectorate: each component section of the administration reacted separately, and in a different manner, to the radical challenge. This challenge began when a general council of the army was allowed to meet on 2 April, composed largely of politicized officers and men, many of whom had been in London and away from their units for months. The representation which this council produced, an abrasive document demanding a purge of 'wicked' ministers as well as payment of arrears, was drafted by a newly formed group of middle officers and rankers, who deliberately excluded all grandees from their proceedings. Richard answered in vague but conciliatory terms, but permitted a further meeting, on 13 April, which demanded that a serving officer should replace him as commander-in-chief.

Richard and the parliamentary majority failed to coordinate their attempts to check the gathering momentum of political activity in the army. Another general council had been arranged for 20 April; two days before this, a group of independent MPs took the initiative, since no lead was forthcoming from the ministers and court managers, by moving that general councils should not meet without permission, and that all serving officers must undertake not to disturb parliament. Revealing their mounting fears, at the same time they tried to reassure ordinary soldiers by promising (yet again) to pay arrears and pass an indemnity act; but the main resolutions, combined with talk of retrenchment, enabled the radical propagandists to persuade officers and men that extensive purges, with disbandment of whole units, were being planned. On the same day, the 18th, without consulting his ministers, Richard prohibited the planned general meeting, and ordered absentee officers to return to their regiments.

These moves merely provoked intense radical activity, so that on 20 April some MPs proposed that parliament should withdraw into the City for protection, and moves were made to put the militia into a state of readiness. The crisis was decided on the next day. Again without receiving any official lead or directive, MPs voted by 163–87 to vest command of the forces in Richard, the Commons and the Other House, that is under civil authority. This defiant stand made no real impression, since republicans and radicals knew that Thurloe (and probably other ministers) were promising to obtain the dissolution of parliament in an effort to retain office. On the other hand, the attitude of parliament probably encouraged Richard to gamble in an attempt to assert his command. He ordered a rendezvous at

Whitehall, and once sufficient men had assembled under reliable officers he intended to use them to arrest radical agitators, and probably Fleetwood and his associates as well.

The dissidents knew that Richard would not be supported; they had canvassed colonels and reckoned that most would not go to Whitehall, and that those who did would not be followed by their subalterns and men. Only a few hundred turned up at Whitehall; instead the bulk of the regiments assembled at a rival rendezvous at St James. Visibly powerless and humiliated, Richard capitulated, agreeing to dissolve parliament, and in return the grandees agreed to continue him in office as nominal protector. Parliament was dissolved on 22 April, but the grandees quickly found that they could not honour their promise. Fleetwood and his associates were isolated and in danger of falling with Richard, since junior officers were establishing a rival political centre and were being encouraged by republican leaders, especially Hesilrige and Vane. They disapproved of senior officers who owed their appointment to Oliver, whereas Lambert, Packer and others were politically acceptable to the radicals because they had been dismissed by Oliver.

Consequently Fleetwood and the serving grandees were compelled to collaborate with Lambert, and had to accept the republican demand for the restoration of the Rump as the only legitimate representative body entitled to govern. A declaration was made on 6 May, and the next day about fifty MPs reassembled at Westminster. On 19 May a council of state was formed of twenty-one MPs and ten others—including only three officers, an under-representation that was to be a source of future trouble. Richard was never formally deposed or arrested, but allowed to fade away; the Protectorate was treated as having been from the first a mere usurpation, since on its own interpretation the Rump could be dissolved only with its own consent, so that everything done since 1653 was invalid.

By 1659 the Rump's claims to be the authentic representative of the nation were unconvincing, and the republicans justified its exclusive right to govern by legalistic arguments that persuaded only those who stood to gain from them. On 9 May MPs secluded from the Commons in 1648 tried to resume their seats, but were repulsed on the argument that Pride's Purge had been sanctioned by a quorate House of Commons. The army was firmly put in its subordinate place; the Rump refused to give Fleetwood independent powers as commander-in-chief, and insisted that all commissions had to be validated by itself. A projected indemnity act was drafted in such a way as to leave officers and soldiers insecure. The Rump undertook a nationwide purge of JPs, and officials who had served the

Cromwells too faithfully were dismissed.

In general the Rump was trapped in the same dilemma as in 1649–53. Its small size (at a maximum about 110, in practice about sixty working MPs) put an intolerable burden on the activists, and emphasized its unrepresentative character. A date was set by which it would vote its own dissolution—7 May 1660—but discussions on the form which a permanent constitution was to take were intermittent, and proved to be inconclusive. The problem was insoluble. To its self-righteous and doctrinaire republican members the Rump was the embodiment of the good old cause, an incomparable assembly of the godly and well-intentioned. But unfortunately free elections (like those to Richard's parliament, even though ex-royalists had been excluded) were likely to return only a minority of godly men, and a majority of the lukewarm and uncommitted. The younger generation did not share the principles and dogmas of the ageing parliamentary veterans of the Rump, who despairingly feared that their good work would be undone by a new parliament. Although an unrestricted single-chamber parliament could not be trusted, there was no agreement on the kind of checks and controls that should be provided—rigid qualifications to be imposed on candidates standing for election and returning officers, a senate or nominated upper house (favoured by most army officers, but suspiciously resembling the Cromwellian Other House) or, as the junior officers and men advocated, a rigid written constitution resembling those proposed by the levellers in 1647–9. But the lack of urgency with which the issue was discussed raised doubts (as in 1653) whether the Rump did intend to relinquish power in the foreseeable future.

Urgent practical problems could not be evaded or postponed. The Rump found it almost impossible to raise enough money, either by taxes or loans, to meet the costs of government. Consequently the state of the fleet deteriorated and shipping losses to Spanish privateers mounted, and so far from reducing the arrears for which Richard had been criticized, current army pay could not be met. An efficient and satisfied army was all the more necessary because during the summer evidence accumulated of serious preparations being made for a general royalist insurrection, and the peace concluded between France and Spain would increase the chances of foreign intervention on Charles's behalf. The royalist threat, culminating in Booth's rising on 31 July in Cheshire, postponed an outright conflict between the Rump and the army; considering the precariousness of the political situation, it was wildly unrealistic for the doctrinaire republicans (except Vane who began to associate with the military radicals) to refuse to make a real attempt to conciliate the army on whose support their own survival depended.

The key issue concerned army commissions. A purge of officers closely identified with the Protectorate, about 160 in all, created only a limited reaction since many of them had been repudiated by their men in April. Difficulties arose over their replacements. Lambert, Fleetwood and the other senior officers pushed their own protégés, the civilian committee men sponsored officers who had been dismissed by Oliver for plotting and disaffection, particularly those associated with the anabaptists and other minor sects. Both groups also blatantly sought to advance friends and relatives. At one stage a serious clash threatened to develop with the Scottish army. Underlining his approval, and that of his army, for the restoration of the Rump, Monk asked that his regiments in Scotland should be exempted from extensive purges. His letter was badly received, and Monk found it expedient to acquiesce in the changes that were ordered, while taking steps to minimize the influence of officers foisted on him.

During the summer of 1659 dissatisfaction at all levels in the English army found expression in pamphlets, agitation and remonstrances which heightened political consciousness within the ranks, and infuriated the Rump republicans. Unwisely, they failed to see the resemblance with the unrest that had preceded Richard's fall, or to draw the logical conclusion that the army must be carefully handled and reassured. Instead they provokingly contrasted its restiveness under their government, which they claimed to be the embodiment and protector of liberties, with its supine acceptance of the tyrant Oliver Cromwell. This blind and insulting attitude, and continued neglect of soldiers' grievances, made all ranks ready to respond to assertive leadership. This was not forthcoming from the senior general, Fleetwood, but Lambert was dynamic, ambitious and popular. Ultimately, he may well have been aiming at becoming protector, but in 1659 his immediate aims were first to gain an ascendancy within the army, and then to make the army the senior partner in government. A superficially glamorous figure, quick to act but without foreseeing the consequences of decisive action, and contemptuous of civilians, Lambert was an early example of the kind of military politician who has appeared so often in Africa, the Arab world and Latin America in the twentieth century.

Lambert's prestige was enhanced by his quick suppression of Booth's rebellion, at Winnington Bridge on 18 August. Three aspects of this rebellion deserve attention. It was intended to be a countrywide insurrection, but such were the weaknesses and divisions among the royalists that serious progress was made only in Lancashire and Cheshire. Its temporary success there was entirely due to leadership and support from the 'presbyterians'—former parliamentarians who had been alienated since Pride's Purge and the execution of Charles I—whereas in other regions the old cavaliers failed to honour their promises to royalist agents. Secondly, Booth did not proclaim the king, or declare in favour of the conditional restoration of the monarchy, but his call for a free parliament was generally understood to imply this. Finally, the rising was badly mistimed; had it been delayed for only a few weeks it would have coincided with an open breach between the army and the Rump.

This breach was opened by the Derby petition, which was organized in mid-September by a group of middle-ranking officers. At first Lambert was not involved, but he responded to the activists' appeals when the Rump refused to reward him for his defeat of Booth by promoting him to major-general. The petition raised general issues by demanding a political settlement acceptable to the army, including a second chamber of parliament that republicans were unlikely to accept. While demanding security in military command for Lambert and Fleetwood, the officers called for a widespread purge of all magistrates and corporations that had not actively supported the government during Booth's rising, which would have established the principle that the army had a right to intervene in purely political matters. The Rump was even more alarmed by the resurgence of political agitation which followed, with circular letters being sent to all units soliciting support. Some republicans favoured immediate action; their leader, Hesilrige, recklessly moved on 22 September that Lambert should be sent to the Tower, but after reading the petition the majority acted more cautiously. A resolution condemning the petition was defeated by thirty-one votes to twenty-five, but the organizers were rebuked for their proceedings, and ordered not to repeat them.

As officers reassembled in London, political agitation was resumed. On 5 October a new petition was presented to the Rump, vindicating the Derby petition and calling for the punishment of all who (like Hesilrige) misrepresented it. In effect this was a demand for recognition by the Rump of the army and its council of officers as an equal partner in government. But even now most Rump members hesitated before rejecting such demands. The Rump took action only when it was learnt that activists were undermining the loyalty of regiments commanded by reliable officers. On 11 October a bill was passed through all its stages invalidating all measures and grants passed during the Protectorate, unless specifically approved retrospectively by the Rump, and making it treason to levy taxes without parliamentary consent. The first provision went directly against army demands, the second was intended to discourage any forcible dissolution of the Rump by showing that bankruptcy would face a military government. These votes were published, and this appeal to the nation against the army was an acknowledgement that a breach was imminent. On 12 October the Rump asserted direct control, dismissing the nine politically most prominent officers headed by Lambert, and suppressed the office of commander-in-chief, demoting Fleetwood to one of seven commissioners for the army (Monk and Hesilrige being others). Simultaneously, practical steps were taken to rally officers and soldiers for the defence of parliament, so that there was at least a show of resistance on 13 October when Lambert's regiments blockaded Westminster, refusing admission to the Speaker and MPs. But by the evening it became apparent that the loyal soldiers were not prepared to fight. The council of state found itself powerless.

After the drama of this coup there followed (as in April) a curious political hiatus, which revealed how little thought had been given to longer-term consequences. The Rump was dispersed, but the impotent council of state sat until 25 October, and a quorum of its army commissioners continued to sit even after that date. The council of the army, Lambert's body of supporters with Fleetwood tagging on, set up a committee to work out a permanent constitution, but it was not until the 26th that a joint civil-military executive committee of safety began to function. Lambert, Fleetwood and the other officers had put themselves into an untenable position, with everyone attributing their action to ambition. In April there had been something, even if it was only the Rump, to put in the place of Richard, but now there was nothing. The committee of safety set itself the modest aim of getting forty members of the Rump to meet, on condition that they recognized the army's action and its demands, but they failed to obtain the requisite pledges. The only prominent civilians to collaborate with the army were Vane and Salwey. Elections were unthinkable for the hostile attitude of the City of London indicated the feelings of the mass of the population towards an army which was necessarily living at free quarter, and whose discipline and morale were steadily deteriorating as arrears of pay continued to accumulate. A bankrupt state, with unpayable debts of over £2,000,000 and faced by general refusals to pay taxes or advance money, could offer no prospect of relief.

To complete their problems, Lambert and the committee of safety encountered a direct challenge from several detached commands—the garrisons at Portsmouth and Hull, the fleet, and especially the armies of occupation in Ireland and Scotland. Eventually Monk and the army in Scotland were to play the decisive role. There had been doubts in April as to whether he would acquiesce in Richard's removal, but Monk had subsequently approved the recall of the Rump in carefully phrased terms that were intended to warn the army against infringing parliamentary rights, and the Rump against neglecting army interests. Both groups had ignored him until they needed his support or approval, and virtually all the grandees and politicians underestimated his influence and power. Many historians, like most of his contemporaries at first, have paid too little attention to George Monk (or Monck), describing him as almost an accidental agent of change. Undoubtedly Monk, a professional soldier from early life in the Dutch service and then in Ireland, was a rough and boorish man (with an even less presentable wife) but he had a reserve and caution that were to prove prime assets in the crisis of 1659–60. Politically, he was not actively committed. He had been loyal to Oliver, who had given him his commands, but earlier he had spent two years in the Tower as a royalist prisoner of war. He was in Scotland in 1650–52 and continuously after 1654, out of the mainstream of events, but two pieces of his military experience were to prove relevant. He had always succeeded, both in Ireland and Scotland, in maintaining the morale of his troops even in atrociously adverse conditions, and he had effectively suppressed disaffection over pay that radical officers had tried to exploit.

The remoteness and isolation of the regiments in Scotland proved to be an advantage. Monk and his colonels were not absentee officers, politicking in London, but knew their subordinates and were known to them: unlike those of Lambert, his well-officered units were not to disintegrate under pressure. More generally, Monk had alternative options which gave him decisive advantages over each of the groups which tried to oppose him. In dealing with Lambert and Fleetwood, Monk took a stand on the illegality of their forcible dispersion of parliament, and demanded the recall of the Rump. Later, when the Rump tried to undermine his authority, Monk was strengthened by the large number of addresses from the provinces presented to him, which showed how little support the Rump really possessed. In dealing with the Rump Monk held the ace of trumps; when he chose to do so, he could overwhelm the republicans by sponsoring the return to the Commons of the secluded members (a clear majority) who had been kept out by arbitrary force since Pride's Purge in 1648.

Monk's prime asset throughout 1659–60 was his effective control over his army. All activities were closely supervised. He would not permit signatures to be collected for the Derby petition or later representations, but gave a lead to his officers by drafting a declaration which condemned the coup and demanded the recall of the Rump

(20 October). This declaration alarmed Lambert, who not only despatched a reproachful letter justifying the English army's actions, but also arranged for officers to go to Scotland to spread propaganda and undermine Monk's authority. These agents were arrested, or carefully watched, but Monk opened negotiations by sending a delegation to London. It is doubtful whether he expected to succeed in anything more than gaining time, since the negotiators' instructions insisted on the recall of the Rump, with security for it to continue sitting until 6 May, and on the need for parliamentary approval before any taxes were levied. Monk also stipulated recognition of the purge of unreliable officers which he had carried out in Scotland on his own initiative, with approval of the replacement appointments, and a demand that no decision by the council of the army in London should be valid without the concurrence of the officers in Scotland and Ireland. The only concession offered was an indemnity to cover the period since 1 October. However the commissioners failed to insist on these stiff conditions, signing an agreement on 15 November that was defective on two vital points: the Rump was not to be recalled, but instead a delegate council of the army was to determine a new constitution, and a joint commission of seven officers from each of the English and Scottish armies was to investigate all recent dismissals, so giving them a right to question Monk's recent purge of dissidents.

The same confidence and determination that had led Monk to make such stiff demands now led him to repudiate the agreement on 24 November, the day after Lambert arrived at Newcastle to command the forces assembling there for an advance into Scotland. At this stage more than at any other, everything depended on Monk's ability to keep the loyalty of his army. His commissioners had signed the agreement only because they were told that the Scottish army was disintegrating, and at the time not only individual officers and men but some squadrons of cavalry and outlying garrisons were defecting to Lambert. But throughout the whole crisis Monk succeeded in keeping his main army united and disciplined. This was a great achievement, on which all his successes were based. Monk quoted Coligny, the Huguenot leader in the French wars of religion, as saying that 'it was a horrible thing to command an army of volunteers', but he knew how to handle a partly politicized army. He convened a series of councils, carefully arranging business and proceedings so that after full and free discussion favourable votes were taken. Soldiers were catechized into a knowledge of their duties. A weekly gazette and propaganda pamphlets were published, ministers' sermons were censored. Potentially mutinous units were disbanded.

The most important of all techniques of military management were those relating to the choice and employment of officers. Monk acted with great subtlety. While declaring for the Rump he reinstated officers whom the Rump had forced him to remove or demote—their loyalty would be to Monk personally. Officers foisted on him by the Rump were either removed, sent to remote commands or left behind in Scotland when the army invaded England. This thorough preparation paid off. Remonstrances and emissaries from Lambert's army, from London and from sectarian congregations had little effect, whereas in contrast Lambert's army quickly became demoralized and unwilling to fight, and the forces in the south of England broke up. Lack of pay, the absence of mutual confidence between officers (many of whom were speculating in debentures issued to soldiers in lieu of pay) and men, resentment at the blatantly ambitious power-play of the senior officers, awareness of mounting hatred of the army, all infected Lambert's ranks with defeatism.

In mid-December Monk's and Lambert's armies were only thirty miles apart, but the collapse in the south undermined all Lambert's plans. On 3 December officers loyal to the Rump seized control of the Portsmouth garrison; on the 20th the forces sent against them defected. The fleet declared for the Rump and blockaded the Thames. The council of officers met for the last time on 23 December, appropriately ratifying an elaborate and futile project for a permanent constitution. On the next day the Speaker's authority was recognized, and the Rump reassembled on 26 December. This restoration would not have been possible but for Monk's stand, but the opponents of the Rump had collapsed from their own weaknesses and were now no longer a danger. Monk was still in Scotland and in no position to exert direct influence on decisions in London. The Speaker's letter informing him of the restoration of the Rump contained no invitation to come to London, but despite this and the apparent end to the crisis, Monk's army crossed the Tweed on 1 January. He realized that the republican politicians would be no more likely to accept his advice than they had that of Lambert and Fleetwood, and he had well founded suspicions that they had no real intention of dissolving parliament by May.

The Rump's conduct between 26 December and Monk's arrival in London on 3 February did not enhance its reputation. Those who presented petitions of which it disapproved were imprisoned. An attempt by secluded members to take their seats was repulsed, and writs were ordered for elections to fill their places—although nothing was done. A declaration on 23 January stated that there was no intention of perpetuating the Rump's life, but its vagueness showed that there was no agreement on what form a future constitution should take. A massive purge of the army removed nearly half the officers, but in appointing replacements there was rampant jobbery on behalf of relatives and associates of MPs. Popular lack of trust in the Rump was reflected in continued refusals to pay taxes, which left the soldiers' pay even further in arrears.

Monk arrived in London uncommitted to any specific policies. On his way he had been presented with many addresses calling for a free parliament or for the readmission of the secluded members, but he had not been able to indicate his feelings since he was under close scrutiny by two leading Rump MPs who were particularly suspicious of any contacts with secluded members or the City of London. Monk had been warned by his chaplain, Gumble, who had come up on a political reconnaissance, that the Rump was fundamentally hostile to him as an independent military politician, as a popular hero, and because of his past collaboration with the Protectorate. This meant that Monk had to continue to give first priority to the maintenance of discipline within his army. He insisted that other forces should be removed from around London before his own men arrived, fearing that the latter would be infected by the others' indiscipline and restiveness. But his own men must continue to receive regular pay (hitherto financed by Scottish revenues) if their loyalty was to endure, and he could not afford to antagonize either the Rump or the City, although they were now on the worst of terms.

Monk's speech to the Rump on 6 February was a skilfully balanced performance. He described the addresses which he had received, and reported his non-committal replies. While indicating his own (probably feigned) acquiescence in their continued exclusion of the secluded members, he gave a warning against any imposition of new, discriminatory oaths and emphasized the desperate anxiety of the 'sober part' of the nation for a permanent settlement. But despite his diplomatic words the speech was very badly received by the Rump. It was interpreted as a bid for popularity, as reflecting on the sectarian militants who were pledging support for the Rump, and as implying negligence or injustice in their conduct of government. By reacting sharply and maliciously the Rump precipitated its own fall. It ordered the arrest of those who had presented addresses to Monk. On 9 February it contrived a machiavellian move to embroil the general with his potential allies in the City. Using the pretext of a move to get the Common Council to declare that it would withhold taxes until there was a full and free parliament, the Rump ordered Monk to reduce the City to a defenceless state by removing the temporary defences erected the previous December, and to arrest eleven prominent citizens. When reporting that he had carried out these orders, and that the Common Council would now be submissive, Monk asked the Rump to abandon further action. Instead, it ordered him to demolish the city gates, suspended the Common Council, and began to consider how to rig future city elections. This harsh and intransigent attitude infuriated not only the City but Monk's officers who openly declared that they could now understand why Lambert had dispersed the Rump. This showed that they would support Monk, but there was no need for him to use crude force against the Rump. After consulting his senior subordinates Monk ordered his army to take up quarters in the City; this was done on 11 February. Then Monk and fifteen officers sent a sharp protest to the Rump, complaining against its consideration of new restrictive oaths on office-holders, demanding the issuing of writs to fill vacant seats by election, and reminding members that a dissolution must come by 6 May. In the City Monk caused the lord mayor to summon the Common Council (although it had been suppressed by the Rump), and publicized his actions.

The Rump responded by demoting Monk. It appointed a new commission to control the army, with Monk as a junior member. It was now, during a lull, that Monk played his trump card. He had already established contacts with many of the secluded members, and convoked meetings with them on 14, 17 and 18 February, so that it was an easy task to organize the return under military protection of over ninety secluded members to the Commons on 21 February. This move was generally welcomed. Some secluded members had tried to force re-entry the previous May, when the Rump was restored, and again when it was brought back in December. A third repulse, on 6 January, led to a well-publicized protest, and many addresses had asked Monk to readmit them. Moreover, although Monk got a council of his officers to issue a letter to provincial units explaining that this action was necessary to ensure that money was voted to pay the army, and did not entail any alteration of the constitution, it was soon generally understood that the re-entry of the secluded members marked the end of the Commonwealth.

The readmitted members swamped the republicans. They began by establishing a new council of state and appointed Monk commander-in-chief. For the next few weeks Monk still had to concentrate on keeping control over the army, suppressing an agitation in March for a declaration against any rule by a single person, and reassuring officers and men about arrears. But the real issue was not whether the monarchy should be restored, but the form that such a restoration should take. At first royalist agents knew nothing about Monk's intention—only as late as 17 March did Sir John Grenville make the first contact—but speculated uneasily that he might set

himself up as protector, or reinstate Richard Cromwell. Then, when
reports showed that Monk favoured a restoration, they feared that
he would insist on stringent limitations on the king.

It was not so much Monk's own political associations, but those
of his leading advisers, that gave this impression. Many of
them—Morrice, Knight and Annesley, the new president of the
council of state—were closely linked with the aristocratic group of
presbyterian parliamentarians headed by Manchester and
Northumberland. Furthermore, not only were these presbyterian
leaders politically experienced and socially influential, but they
alone at this time had an apparently coherent policy and an organized following. Booth's rising had shown that the presbyterians
were more united and effective than the old cavaliers. Monk put
command of the militia, and the commission of the peace, into their
hands. Presbyterians controlled most of the corporations, and their
ministers possessed more influence and prestige than the clergy of
other denominations. Elections to Oliver's and Richard's parliaments had consistently returned presbyterian majorities, and the
qualifications that restricted candidates for the forthcoming elections
to men who had not supported Charles I promised a Convention
parliament similarly composed.

The presbyterian party was known to wish to impose as the price
of restoration a revised version of the Isle of Wight Treaty negotiated
with Charles I in 1648. This would give parliament control over the
militia for fifteen years, and permanently over appointments to the
great offices of state and major legal posts. The royal veto would be
suspended. Bishops would be re-established, but their authority was
to be diluted by the institution of diocesan synods, and the church
would be even weaker financially since confiscated church lands
were not to be restored. Neither Charles nor Edward Hyde, his chief
minister in exile, could accept the predominance of parliament
which such a treaty would perpetuate, but there were formidable
impediments to the imposition of such conditions. Constitutionally, a
treaty would have to be incorporated in a statute, but since the
Convention would technically be an irregular assembly (since it was
elected on writs issued by the council of state, not the king), its status
as a legal parliament and all its acts would have to be validated
retrospectively by the next parliament, and there could be no certainty that this would be done. Indeed, once Charles returned, any
attempt to force through such a treaty would have probably precipitated a premature dissolution, perhaps before an act of indemnity had passed, and this could have led to a violent royalist
reaction.

During the session of the Convention the presbyterians lacked the strength, skill and stamina to impose conditions. Their aristocratic chiefs were an isolated, rather inactive and divided group. Some were concerned only with the acquisition of office. Few gave any lead, either in the elections or during the session. Presbyterians in the council of state failed to persuade Monk of the necessity for conditions, but by pretending to Charles that Monk was in favour (when the king knew that he was not) they revealed the weakness of their position. Unexpectedly, the presbyterians failed entirely to dominate the elections, in which over a hundred former or crypto-royalists were returned. Those who favoured restrictions on the monarchy failed to gain the necessary influence during the session, which began on 25 April, so that an assiduous and intelligently directed minority was able to block presbyterian policies on most major issues. The other formerly active groups did not matter at all: no Cromwellian interest survived, and only eighteen members who had sat in the Rump in 1659 were elected, of whom five were unseated.

The complete transformation in the king's position owed everything immediately to Monk, and more generally to the reaction in public opinion in favour of the monarchy, and little or nothing to the royal ministers abroad or cavalier agents in Britain. After Booth's defeat both groups watched the rapid succession of events with bewilderment, and the advice which Charles received was frequently rendered obsolete by unexpected changes. The only consistent line was to try to identify the man or party with the greatest power in Britain and to win him or them for the king. For a time it was calculated that Lambert could be gained, then it was hoped that Lambert and Monk would fight each other to the death, with varying opinions on which was likely to be victorious, or faith was put on Lawson and the fleet, a presbyterian rising in London, and even Henry Cromwell in Ireland was thought to be a possible agent of restoration.

Equally over-optimistically, but much more dangerously, approaches were made for aid from foreign states. In 1659, after experiencing the futility of relying on Spanish promises, Marshall Turenne was asked to provide 3,000 men as a private venture, but by 1660 reliance on official help from France was the policy advocated by the main dissident faction among the royalist exiles. This was the Louvre group centred on the queen-mother, who was an inveterate enemy of Hyde. Led by Jermyn it consisted of those who combined a sympathy for catholicism with incipient tendencies towards absolutism.

Hyde's main service in the months before the Convention met was to remain inactive. All who offered their services to the king were appropriately answered, but by avoiding premature commitment to any immediate course of action, or to any particular form of settlement, Hyde preserved the widest scope for manoeuvre on Charles's part. This was the basis of the astonishing ease with which the actual restoration was effected, an almost faultless political performance by Charles and Hyde, both in general, in declarations of constitutional principle, and in detailed political negotiations. The keynote was struck by the Declaration of Breda (4 April), with a general appeal for unity. Apart from a tiny minority of regicides and fanatical sectarians, all sections of the nation were reassured by the promises of indulgence to all tender consciences (provided that they kept the peace), and of a general indemnity for all past offences. The army was promised early payment of arrears, and on such detailed matters as the land settlement parliament was given the responsibility of presenting proposals.

The actual process of restoration took just over two months. On 16 March the Long Parliament at last dissolved itself. In the middle of the elections for the Convention there was a brief scare when Lambert escaped from the Tower (9 April) and appointed a rendezvous for republicans and soldiers at Edgehill, but comparatively few responded, and those who assembled would not fight when confronted by Monk's troops (22 April). The Convention met on 25 April. On 1 May both houses formally read Charles's Declaration of Breda, which had been drafted on 4 April, and proceeded to draw up an answer and to elect deputations to present it to the king (7 May). On 8 May Charles was proclaimed in London. He met the parliamentary delegations at the Hague on 14 May, disembarked at Dover on the 25th and entered London four days later, his thirtieth birthday.

An underlying theme, that the restoration was one of parliament as much as of the monarchy, was reiterated in royal messages to the Convention. In letters accompanying the Declaration of Breda, Charles asserted the interdependence of crown and parliament, adding that not only was parliament a necessary part of the constitution, but that it was equally essential for it to respect the authority of the crown. The usurping governments of the recent past were stigmatized as having been based on 'private and particular ends and ambition', whereas the Convention now had the opportunity to repair the ravages which had been inflicted on the constitution, liberties and properties of the nation. No attempt was made to pressurize the Convention; parliamentary forms and privileges were meticulously respected—in sharp contrast with the arbitrary and partisan interference with parliamentary freedom over the past twenty years. Indeed Charles and Hyde acquiesced in frequently peremptory behaviour by the Convention House of Commons, which sometimes took executive action almost in the manner of the Long Parliament. It got an order in council withdrawn until the matter of cloth exports had been examined by the Commons, it stipulated that leases of ecclesiastical lands should not be made until a bill had been debated, and orders were sent to London and provincial towns to hasten payment of poll money so that army disbanding could be accelerated. The Lords were warned against delays, and their attempt to name poll money commissioners was vetoed. The most striking example was the Commons' disregard for Charles's stated preference for a prorogation in September; instead the House insisted that there should be an adjournment, which meant that unfinished measures could be resumed. By comparison the Cavalier Parliament was to behave in a much more deferential manner.

Although parliament was restored as an essential part of the constitution, Charles and Hyde regarded it as a subordinate part. The subjects were entitled to liberties, that is specific rights appropriate to their birth and station in society, not to liberty in the abstract, or the right to participate in government; the latter belonged only to those chosen by the king as privy councillors, officers, judges and justices, to those summoned to the Lords or returned to the Commons, or elected to municipal offices. The return of the old order meant that once again there was a place for everything, and now everything should be in its proper, legal place. As Bridgeman said at the trial of the regicides in October, the people had as great a privilege as the king in their lives, liberties and properties, but 'it is not the sharing of government that is for the liberty and benefit of the people; but it is how they may have their lives and liberties and estates safely secured under government'.

The old order was the natural order. Its restoration, so far from being unrealistic or futile, provided the easiest and logical solution to all contemporary problems. Hyde told the Convention that Charles hoped it would join with him in restoring 'the whole nation to its primitive temper and integrity, to its old good manners, its old good humour and its old good nature'. Using an astrological metaphor he asserted that all the motions of the past twenty years had been unnatural, proceeding from the influence of a malignant star that had now expired, so that 'the good genius of this kingdom is become superior . . . and our own good old stars govern us again'. One important corollary should be noticed. If the recent past was an unnatural period then it should be consigned to oblivion; nothing was to be learnt from it, little could be gained by studying its events, and all past animosities and divisions must be forgotten. A general act of indemnity and pardon was an essential precondition of the process of restoring the old order. As in the old Jewish practice, the regicides, who alone were excepted unconditionally for punishment, played a ritual role as scapegoats. The thirteen who were executed (ten in October 1660, three in 1662) carried the burden of the nation's sins.

It was very much to the credit of Charles and Hyde that a wider proscription, or a general cavalier revenge, were avoided. Hyde took great care to discourage royalists from provocatively demanding, or after 1660 attempting, revenge for their past sufferings on their former enemies. Pardons were freely issued to anxious or vulnerable individuals; only Vane (executed in 1662) was singled out for harsh treatment, Charles regarding him as too dangerous to live. Personal vendettas were discouraged. The decision as to who should be excepted from the general pardon was left to the Convention, where it was former parliamentarians led by Prynne who endeavoured to extend the number. The debates which decided on the exceptions show that the whole process was intrinsically unsavoury and time-consuming—as it was to be again in the Convention of 1689. A basic resolution on 8 June, that in addition to the regicides only twenty persons should be excepted (although not executed) led to prolonged discussions. Members followed their particular prejudices, nominated personal enemies and engaged in distasteful bargaining. Later it was proposed to except whole categories of offenders—men associated with the Rump or Oliver's administration, those who petitioned against Charles I in 1648, those who drafted the Instrument of Government, officials and judges in the high courts of justice set up as special tribunals to try royalist plotters, and the major-generals. The debates revealed a widespread spirit of malicious vindictiveness, understandable after two decades of strife, but which threatened to inject a new strain of virulence into politics should the Restoration settlement fail to produce general and lasting satisfaction.

The bill of pardon, indemnity and oblivion passed the Commons on 11 July, after a reminder from Charles of the need for its early enactment. But the Lords showed even less sense of urgency. Amendments were introduced in favour of individual peers, and belated attempts were made to extend the number to be excepted. Further interventions by Charles were needed before the bill finally passed; it received the royal assent on 29 August. In theory it restored national unity, granting a pardon to all individuals and bodies corporate for actions committed under orders from all forms of authority during the civil wars and the usurpation. Apart from those concerned in the king's trial and execution (fifty-one in all), twenty-nine others were to be punished or disqualified from holding any office. There can be little doubt that the accelerated decline and early disappearance of the defeated republican and Cromwellian parties were ensured by this avoidance of a harsh and general proscription. Although most regicides died bravely, believing that they were sealing with their blood the good old cause, no cult ever developed around their martyrdom, and later generations forgot them.

The second major issue that had been left to parliament, that of settling the proprietorship of land sold or confiscated during the Civil War and Interregnum, surprisingly faded into relative unimportance, and was finally disposed of without the need for legislation. Before the Restoration the land question had seemed likely to provide an intractable problem, since Charles had committed himself to the return of confiscated property, while Monk in response to pressure publicly insisted in 1660 that new proprietors must either be confirmed or compensated. Land changes fell into two categories. Most royalist landowners had had to sell land in order to pay composition fines imposed by the victorious parliamentarians, and subsequent differential taxation; legally these were voluntary sales, not confiscations. It would have been administratively and juridically impossible to reverse these changes, especially in the absence of any register of lands. Dr Thirsk has shown why there was no great demand for this to be attempted; a high proportion of alienated land had been recovered through purchase by its former royalist owners before 1660, although this did not prevent the less able or the unfortunate who failed to accomplish recovery from complaining bitterly that their interests were being betrayed. Some land had been confiscated by the Interregnum authorities. Crown estates, including those of the queen-mother, were simply resumed. Church property presented more difficult problems. Some peers and MPs who disliked laudian episcopacy wished to confirm those who had purchased ecclesiastical lands, or at least to legislate stipulating favourable conditions or compensation for them, and there was general sympathy for tenants who had bought their leases, as distinct from speculative purchasers. In the face of considerable legal complexities, parliament left the matter to a royal commission, set up on 7 October. Such reference of a complicated and time-consuming task to a commission was probably inevitable, but the absence of any statutory restraints enabled the church in general, and certain bishops and cathedral chapters in particular, to drive very hard bargains and to exact heavy renewal fines for leases—conduct that was very profitable financially, but which was to contribute substantially to the revival of anticlerical sentiment.

Some prominent cavaliers had lost their estates after being convicted by Interregnum courts or declared guilty of treason by ordinance. These confiscations were neither ratified nor invalidated by the

act for the confirmation of judicial proceedings; consequently some
peers resorted to private bills to restore their estates, despite a discouraging attitude by Charles. Some but not all of these bills passed,
depending on how much political influence was possessed by their
beneficiaries, thus adding to the resentment felt and expressed by
rank-and-file cavaliers who complained that they were ignored and
neglected.

Charles and Hyde were able to prevent a serious crisis developing
over the most controversial issue, of how to regularize the confused
religious situation and then to provide for a permanent settlement.
The religious issue provoked a sharp split within the Convention. In
the Declaration of Breda Charles had promised a liberty to tender
consciences, provided they did not disturb the peace, and his consent
to any act of parliament which might permanently establish such a
liberty. But whereas Charles could safely leave the questions of indemnity and land to parliament, all his actions during 1660 show that
he did not wish to have his ecclesiastical prerogatives permanently
restricted by a parliament in which presbyterian influences were
strong. At this time he shared Hyde's determination to secure the full
re-establishment of the doctrine and government of the Church of
England under bishops, and to make only minimal concessions to
the presbyterians, and none to the sects.
    Charles, Hyde and their ecclesiastical advisers (a small group of
divines headed by Sheldon, Morley and Barwick, who had been
active royalist agents) were in a tight position, with restricted room
for manoeuvre. If they delayed moving towards restoring the old
order, there was a danger that the presbyterians would entrench
themselves and that temporary concessions would solidify into a permanent settlement. On the other hand, to respond openly to anglican calls for action to restore the old order of a church governed by
iure divino bishops would enrage the majority in the Convention, and
there was no possibility of dissolving the Convention until the Act of
Indemnity had been passed, money voted and the army disbanded.
    Operating under these constraints, Charles and Hyde achieved a
clear-cut tactical victory. They conceded ground only on matters of
temporary significance, particularly on the question of settling ministers in their livings. Many parishes were occupied by men who had
been put in by the Long Parliament, or had been invited by congregations, or had simply intruded themselves. These ministers were
now vulnerable to legal action by ejected anglican clergy or by the
lay patrons of the livings. Many intruders were blatant heretics,
lacked formal ordination, or were closely associated with Cromwell
or the Rump; but however desirable their removal, anarchy would

result if hundreds of individuals were left to take action, legal or physical. On 9 May a bill was introduced, and on 1 June a proclamation was issued, both for maintaining existing ministers. In practice the latter was not universally observed, and in taking action many anglican zealots made no distinction between the discredited and friendless anabaptists and fanatics, and the presbyterian ministers whose interests would be protected by the Convention. The issue was raised in a general form when the marquis of Hertford, on regaining the chancellorship of Oxford University on 6 June, took steps for a general purge of university and college posts. Ejected or threatened presbyterians petitioned the Commons, who revived the bill to maintain ministers, and the court managers could do no more than delay this measure, which received the royal assent on 13 September.

While this bill occupied the attention of the Convention, Hyde with the assistance of Sheldon and Morley was quietly preparing for the transformation of the church, using the royal powers of ecclesiastical patronage to appoint convinced episcopalians to vacant livings in the gift of the crown, reconstituting cathedral chapters, and selecting suitable candidates for nomination as bishops. The Convention inadvertently helped him by a decision to transfer discussion of matters of doctrine and liturgy to a 'synod' of clergy. This put an end to a bill which had been introduced for the settlement of a strictly protestant church, with specific provisions against the type of innovations which Laud had tried to enforce. Bishops would have had elected clergy associated with them in the exercise of their functions, the Book of Common Prayer would be modified, clergy excused from using ceremonies to which they objected, and the Elizabethan Act of Uniformity would be suspended until a synod had met. But it took time to convene a fully prepared synod, and when presbyterians and anglican clergy did meet, on 22 October, it was in an informal meeting.

The resulting Worcester House declaration of 25 October gave the appearance of offering the presbyterians extensive concessions, but only as an interim measure until a synod could meet. Presbyters were to be associated with bishops, old puritan demands were met on confirmation and excommunication, and objectionable ceremonies were made optional. The sincerity of this declaration is very dubious. On 28 October the first batch of new bishops was consecrated, and their strictly anglican, almost laudian, character was to prove a much more accurate reflection of the court's intentions.

This only became indisputably clear late in November. Parliament reassembled on 6 November, but it was not until the 24th that the presbyterian majority belatedly voted to introduce a bill to convert the Worcester House declaration into a statute, so making it the basis of the permanent religious settlement. Since an early dissolution had already been announced, it was doubtful whether enough time remained for the bill to pass. But it was preferable for the court to organize vigorous resistance to the measure than to allow the bill to lapse with the dissolution. The court managers actually achieved a decisive victory. On 28 November the Commons rejected the bill, on its second reading, by 183 votes to 157.

This victory was the final result of hard, continuous attention to detail on the part of the king's managers throughout the life of the Convention. In the early stages, although on the defensive, they had delayed and impeded the large but unorganized, undirected and incoherent presbyterian majority; only in August, when many supporters left London for the country, did court pressure on the presbyterians weaken. An ascendancy in day-to-day proceedings, the knowledge that the court had a majority in the Lords, steady reinforcement by waverers and defectors from the ranks of their opponents, private encouragement from Charles and Hyde, produced a confidence and aggression that the presbyterians could not match. The latter could no longer count on Monk as an active politician.They were deserted by former leaders like Annesley who accepted offices, and no generally acceptable replacements could be found. Furthermore this important court achievement in securing mastery over the Convention was reinforced by the confident knowledge that the movement of opinion, and the extension of royal authority, were certain to produce a majority favourable to the court and the church in the next parliament.

By the end of 1660, the king had consolidated his position to the point where he was almost totally secure. The army was being rapidly disbanded. The bishops and orthodox clergy were gradually extending their influence. Former royalists increasingly commanded the militia, and filled the commission of the peace. Evidence of plotting by former republican officers and some sectaries created alarm in the last weeks of the year, but there was no real danger of a serious rebellion. The primary reasons for this were psycho-political. The Restoration, a miracle of divine intervention according to its adherents and beneficiaries, shattered the rationale as well as the morale of those who had vainly tried to prevent it. Oliver Cromwell, Fleetwood, Hesilrige, Vane and Milton, despite their differences had all shared the conviction that, by a series of military victories and political revolutions, God had put them in power in order to further a divine plan. Their successes had been due to Him, not to their own abilities or advantages. The Restoration could only mean that God had turned away from them. The overthrow of the Protectorate and

Commonwealth, the fall of the saints and the collapse of the good old cause, could be explained only as a form of divine judgement. In these circumstances Christian duty indicated acceptance of God's will in a quietist, passive rather than militant attitude. Apart from the millenarians, for whom catastrophe was a preliminary to the latter days and the second coming of Christ, and who logically but ineffectively staged a minor rising in London under Venner (January 1661), the sectaries sank into resigned political inactivity.

The one institutional royal weakness, already apparent by the end of 1660 and destined to become increasingly serious in its effects, lay in the chronic shortage of money which followed from the errors and miscalculations of the financial settlement. However, a moral weakness was also to undermine the achievements of the Restoration and frustrate all hopes of union, harmony and stability. Few participants behaved in a disinterested fashion, many were literally demoralized as well as disappointed by the frenzied scramble for offices, grants and pensions. Since there were never enough to satisfy all aspirants, recriminations were inevitable. Particularly bitter resentment was expressed at the successes achieved by such adroit opportunists as Anthony Ashley Cooper, and personal favourites. The blatant use of patronage for material profit by Clarendon's entourage, the intolerable arrogance of the undeservedly successful, conspicuous expenditure and luxurious immorality at court after years of poverty in exile or retirement, the readiness of almost everyone in Whitehall to sell himself or herself, excited corrosive resentment among those excluded from the feast. Partly because of its ease and unexpectedness, the success of the Restoration was corrupting: most of the major gains went to those who had contributed little towards it.

7 Clarendon's Ministry, 1660–67

Despite rumours of plots during the last months of 1660, and the minor London insurrection by Venner's fanatics in January 1661, Charles's position was essentially strong. The plotters were almost universally discredited and unpopular because of their past behaviour as republican activists in the politicized army of 1659–60, and no longer had any influence in the small army which Charles retained (and remodelled) as the basis of order. Episcopalian clergy were now in possession of the key positions in the church. Old cavaliers, together with gentry of the younger generation from both royalist and parliamentarian family backgrounds, were being appointed to commanding positions in the militia and the commission of the peace. Whereas at court disappointed aspirants for offices and pensions already formed a potentially disturbing faction, there was as yet no sign of division in the provinces within the ranks of the cavaliers. This unity, and the opportunity for service and influence which the Restoration gave to the younger generation of gentry who had been largely excluded by the Commonwealth regimes, ensured the return of an overwhelmingly loyal House of Commons in the elections of January and February 1661. The so-called 'presbyterians' were reduced to what could now be regarded as a residual minority of older men, whom the younger generation was not likely to respect or follow.

Charles had taken care that the Convention should not make either the political or the religious settlement. The character of the settlement imposed by the Cavalier Parliament was negative, preventive and partisan. The objective was not so much to undo the legislation of the Long Parliament—all ordinances passed since 1642 without royal assent were automatically invalidated—but to prevent any repetition. In this the Cavalier Parliament was conclusively successful. It cannot be emphasized too strongly that the mid-seventeenth century 'English Revolution' was not decisive in its effects. The last verdict on all the issues that had been fought over during the civil wars was that of the Cavalier Parliament. Its initial legislation was consciously backward looking, but at the same time entirely new issues were emerging, conditions were changing, and a new generation with a different mentality and outlook began to turn away from old, sterile or exhausted topics to entirely new questions. This is seen particularly in the sphere of religion, where the educated laity was losing most of its interest in theology and controversy, and sometimes in religion itself. From the mid-1660s the main contest came to centre on the desirability of toleration, and most of the arguments deployed were political, social or even economic—the actual religious aspects and considerations were almost secondary. The bishops who had at last vanquished presbyterians and sectaries found to their alarm that their realm was being invaded by widespread religious indifferentism, immorality in all sections of society, profaneness and atheism.

It was the same in politics. Parliament used submissive language. By passing the Militia Acts (1661, 1662) and the Act to Preserve the Person of the King (1661), it explicitly disavowed any intention of challenging royal supremacy within the constitution. But Charles found that (unlike any of his predecessors) he could not live without annual parliamentary sessions and, although Clarendon was slow to appreciate this, the art of directing and managing parliament now became the most vital ministerial skill, on which depended the success of any policy. Similarly, fears by independent peers and MPs that the crown might become permanently independent of parliament, the law and the cooperation of the nation, took new forms. The prerogative methods and institutions used by Charles I—ship money, Star Chamber, High Commission, the Council of the North, forced loans—were not revived in 1660–61, or even seriously considered, except by a few clerics. Absolutism or arbitrary government now meant government on the French model, as it was being developed and operated by Louis XIV in the years after his assumption of personal power in 1661. This fear of absolutism, perceptible as early as 1663, later became increasingly connected with alarm at the advance of catholicism and was to form the main constituent in the development of systematic opposition.

Charles's personal qualities and defects, the differences between his principles and practices and his father's, established new political patterns. Charles's failings are well known—his laziness and neglect of routine government business, his susceptibility to persuasion (especially by women), his opportunism and shabby readiness to abandon servants who were unfortunate or became unpopular, his toleration of shameless importunity and personal impudence. All these characteristics stemmed from the cynically low estimate of human nature which he had formed during the years of exile, and which was confirmed by the general scramble for office and reward which accompanied the Restoration. From the beginning no one could be certain about Charles's statements and intentions, and as a result all ministers invariably lived in a state of anxiety. This behaviour was deliberate. The key to Charles's character, and the principal explanation for his success in surviving as king with the royal prerogatives intact (which comes as near as we can to describing his 'objectives') lay in his skill at the art of dissimulation. Charles was adept at concealing his passions and purposes, at deceiving or misleading all those with whom he had dealings—on the assumption that everyone approaching him invariably had ulterior purposes in mind.

Charles's success in dissimulating his feelings and intentions has led to very different historical verdicts on his personality and achievement. Less often noticed were the immediate effects of the uncertainty he generated. He deceived the presbyterians in 1660, but his acquiescence in the subsequent recovery of the church by the bishops could not be taken as guaranteeing unswerving support. From 1662 there were serious doubts about the sincerity of his anglicanism. Another important (and deliberate) ambiguity resulted from his conscious adoption of mixed, and often bitterly divided ministries. At first Clarendon was balanced by Monk, then by Bennet. Another disadvantage for ministers was that they could never rely on their being the most influential advisers. Unofficial intermediaries like Daniel O'Neill, Sir John Baber and Sir Richard Bellings often acted for the king, and offered advice without the knowledge of the ministers.

Brisk efficiency as well as loyalty marked the first session of the new parliament, May 1661–May 1662. A particularly effective Speaker, Sir Edward Turner, controlled proceedings. Committees were packed with reliable men. All MPS were ordered to take the sacrament (only five made difficulties); this was in contrast to the failure of the 'presbyterians' in the Convention to enforce the disqualification of royalists. Those who now wished to oppose the direction of the Restoration settlement were exposed as an impotent minority when the Commons resolved by 228 votes to 103 that the Covenant should be publicly burnt.

Based on the premise that the Civil War had been caused by the factious and seditious practices of Pym and his demagogic associates, the legislation passed by the Cavalier Parliament was expressly intended to prevent any repetition of the agitational techniques that had been used in 1640–42. The Act to Preserve the Person and Government of the King made it treason to imprison or restrain the sovereign, and extended to writing, printing, preaching and speaking those penalties already attached to acting against royal authority. Anyone asserting that Charles was a papist, or trying to introduce popery, was to be disqualified from holding office. This established a principle that the court tried to enact in a more positive and general form in 1665 and 1675, by proposing oaths on officers not to endeavour any alteration of the existing forms of government in either church or state. The Act against Tumultuous Petitioning (1661) employed the same principle in making a distinction between petitions for simple redress of personal grievances, and those that implied alterations in any matters established by law; the latter required some form of official sanction from JPs or a grand jury, and no petition was to be presented by more than twenty persons.

Another act of 1661 restored bishops to the House of Lords, and removed the disqualification on clergy from holding lay offices. The ecclesiastical courts were restored. An act of 1662 gave justices acting on information from churchwardens the power to remove paupers, or those who might become charges on the poor rates, from their place of settlement to their birthplace. The reason was to prevent wealthier parishes becoming overburdened, but the effects were to put a substantial part of the population at the mercy of parish officers as well as of the remoter justices.

The Militia Act (1661) was based on an explicit repudiation of the claim that Charles I had rejected, and that had produced the breach with the Long Parliament in 1642. It declared that

> The sole supreme government, command and disposition of the militia and of all the forces by sea and land, and of all forts . . . is, and by the laws of England ever was, the undoubted right of his majesty . . . and that both or either of the houses of parliament cannot, nor ought to pretend to the same.

There appears to have been some hesitation and opposition to such an unreserved and total abandonment of any share in the control of the forces, but the Act was confirmed in 1662 although in later years it was regretted as opening the way to military government under the crown.

The other major controversial act concerned a matter that was to prove to be a major issue in Restoration politics, control over the municipal corporations. The bill, 'for well ordering of corporations', which was given a first reading on 19 June 1661, and received the royal assent in December, was at times strongly contested; its committal on 20 June was carried by 185 to 136, but it finally passed by an easy majority of 182 to 77. Particularly significant was the way in which the Commons re-examined their attitude and made amend-

ments when the full implications were understood. An act was made
necessary by legal uncertainties in many corporations. The Act of
Indemnity (1660) covered charters only in very general terms, and
the privy council had received many petitions for the renewal of
charters, confirmation of privileges, or for reinstatement from individuals ejected by republican governments. Many corporations
were divided into factions that perpetuated the tensions and conflicts
of the recent past, and it was judged unsafe for men identified with
the Commonwealth to remain in office. But there was a danger that
in the process of providing for security and loyal influence, the crown
might be able to obtain permanent and decisive advantages.
Initially, ministers proposed using prerogative methods: they stipulated that in issuing new charters the king was to have the nomination of recorders and town clerks, and voting in parliamentary
elections was to be restricted to members of the municipal common
councils. This would have contracted the urban electorate by over
ninety-five per cent, and no Commons, however loyal, would have
acquiesced in such a fundamental change promulgated without its
own consent.

In debates on the bill a corresponding attempt was made to obtain advantages for existing MPs and their local associates. It was
proposed that the commissioners who were to purge the corporations
should be nominated by the sitting MPs, and that they should be
eligible to serve themselves. Later this proposal was dropped, but the
Commons rejected amendments by the Lords that would have
forced all corporations to renew their charters, without any guarantee
that the king would confirm their existing rights. In the outcome, the
Corporation Act established a working partnership between king
and gentry. Charles nominated the commissioners, but he chose men
who were acceptable to the Commons and local cavalier interests,
not agents of centralization. Institutional rights were safeguarded;
charters were not to be questioned for anything done before May
1661, so that general renewals were not demanded. However, the
powers of the commissioners to purge and replace individuals were
almost unlimited. In addition to tendering the oaths of allegiance
and supremacy to all office-holders, who after 1663 were also to have
to take the anglican sacrament, they were empowered to dismiss
officers even if they took these oaths, and they could nominate as
replacements anyone who was or had been an inhabitant. These
provisions were designed to ensure that office-holding would be
reserved for the well affected and, although the commissioners'
powers expired in March 1663, by then many MPs had used the
process to entrench their personal interest in corporations.

The general effect of these acts may be described as the restoration of the old 'political nation', that is the recovery of full and exclusive control over administration in the localities by the traditional ruling class, the gentry, together with their parochial and urban associates and dependants. But the other half of the Restoration settlement, the partisan religious legislation in the so-called Clarendon Code, re-introduced an element of division and bitterness into politics at all levels, splitting the gentry in the localities, and perpetuating for a decade the old rifts which had been effaced during 1660, between families who had fought for the king and those who had adhered to the Long Parliament.

The Restoration church settlement was largely the achievement, both for good and for ill, of probably the ablest and certainly the most resolute of all contemporary statesmen, Gilbert Sheldon, who left an indelible impression on the life of the nation. First as bishop of London, then from 1663 archbishop of Canterbury, he reconstructed the virtually ruined Church of England, placed it under full epis-copal government, and equipped it with a liturgy and prayer book that remained in use until the mid-twentieth century. He created an alliance with the gentry that was to operate as a major factor in English politics and social life for over two centuries. In achieving all this he also widened and institutionalized what was to continue as the fundamental division in English society for two centuries, that between church and dissent. It is this negative achievement that has received most attention from historians, who have rightly blamed Sheldon for initiating the last prolonged phase of religious perse-cution, but this moral condemnation has led many of them to ignore or misrepresent the other aspects of his career.

Sheldon has generally been seen as a laudian, the product of a world that was dying if not dead, his policy as both hateful and futile. Certainly Sheldon shared Laud's principles and objectives a well-ordered church embracing the entire nation, using a uniform liturgy and inseparably connected with royal government. However, Sheldon had not been a fervent laudian, or an advocate of arminian innovations in the period before the civil war; though never an in-tellectual (he was warden of All Souls), he was accepted readily as a member of the liberal Great Tew circle associated with Falkland. The experiences that formed his post-Restoration attitudes and policies had been acquired later, during his time as Charles I's chief (and, for a while, only) confidential adviser in 1646–7 and again during the Isle of Wight treaty negotiations. Although his advice then, about which we know virtually nothing, proved to be disas-trous in its consequences, Sheldon formulated what at that time must have seemed the quixotic objective of nothing less than a total restoration of the ruined Church of England, and he had the faith to work for this throughout the Commonwealth. Sheldon was largely successful in precisely those areas where Laud had failed disastrously. Nothing could be in sharper contrast than the way in which Sheldon converted the formerly hostile and anticlerical gentry into allies and active champions of anglican interests. The parochial clergy who before 1640 had included a significant proportion of refractory puritan activists were transformed by purges, discipline and education into a fervently loyal and reliable clerical body. The universities were remodelled so as to produce a new generation of young clergy sympathetic and obedient to the establishment. Above all, Sheldon systematically enlisted the support of parliament. Whereas Laud had been detested as a main prop of royal absolutism, Sheldon identified the church with the common law, putting the authority of statutes above the exercise of the royal prerogative.

A partisan religious settlement could hardly have been avoided. Toleration was associated with Cromwell and the Commonwealth, and religious dissent was equated with political faction. Animosities and vindictiveness among the orthodox clergy diminished the chances of instituting either toleration or comprehension, that is the grant of concessions to permit presbyterian clergy to remain within the established church. Clergy who had been cruelly maltreated and humiliated by the Long Parliament and its county committees, the 'triers', and sometimes their own parishioners, were disinclined to extend charity to old enemies or seek a general reconciliation. The militancy of formerly victimized clergy led to the summary ejection during 1660 of nearly 700 intruders, men who could show no legal title to the livings which they occupied at the expense of surviving legal incumbents or lay patrons. Those who were nominated as bishops in the autumn of 1660—a group of exceptionally determined and able men including Morley, Cosin and Henchman—made effective use of this spirit. Sheldon and his colleagues established an identity of principles and interests between the higher and the parochial clergy that was to survive intact all the very considerable (and in 1660 unexpected) strains and crises of the years up to 1688—the sudden changes of royal policy, James's conversion to catholicism, the alliance between the dissenters and the whigs, the open challenge from catholicism in 1685–8. Unlike Laud, both Sheldon and his successor Sancroft could depend on the unity and loyalty of all clergy, apart from a few isolated eccentrics, and only after the Revolution of 1688 did a rift reappear between the hierarchy and the lower clergy.

Sheldon's alliance with the gentry was little less impressive in its results, rewarding him for all the skill and industry which he devoted to it. Sheldon personally paid great attention to winning over peers and MPS; his dinners at Lambeth palace were a feature of parliamentary sessions, and he advised his bishops to establish and conserve close personal relations with the leading laity in their dioceses. In 1660 when the Convention passed an act to settle existing ministers in their livings, and again in 1662 when it was suggested that royal dispensations should enable leading and selected presbyterians to continue in theirs, Sheldon aggressively upheld the rights of the patrons of livings to exercise their legal powers, and such patrons included many gentry as well as university colleges and cathedral chapters. When the Corporation Act was being debated he warned against half-measures and called for action against those office-holders who retained links with dissenting congregations, thus identifying the issue of occasional conformity—which was to be a major cause of political controversy for over fifty years. In 1664, by a bold personal initiative taken entirely on his own authority, Sheldon concluded a verbal agreement with Clarendon by which in future the clergy were to be subject to parliamentary taxation, instead of imposing taxes on themselves in Convocation. This move is usually criticized because as a result Convocation ceased to meet as often and regularly as in the past. But it ended the possibility of serious conflict with the Commons in the event of Convocation voting money at a time when (as in 1640) the Commons were denying the king supply in order to force through certain measures. The side-effects were also important in strengthening the alliance with the gentry. From this time the clergy voted in parliamentary elections, and soon emerged as a formidable and united block supporting loyal candidates.

The basis of the alliance with the gentry was the assumption that religious uniformity was a necessary prerequisite for political unity, stability and peace. The avoidance of faction and schism was explicitly stated as the reason for the Act of Uniformity, which received the royal assent on 19 May 1662. This statute followed the breakdown of the Savoy Conference (April–August 1661) between the bishops and some leading presbyterian clergy to agree on formulae which would allow presbyterian clergy, or more accurately those clergy with scruples, to conform to the church. The actual obstacles which impeded unity can be traced back, as subjects of open and almost continuous contention, at least as far back as the Hampton Court Conference of 1604. With great tactical shrewdness (and overall lack of wider perspective) Sheldon insisted that the onus was on the presbyterian representatives to suggest possible changes, but by simply objecting and finally rejecting all proposals, he created the impression that the bishops had never intended to negotiate or to even consider concessions. In practice it was the underlying implications of what was being demanded that convinced the bishops (as in 1604) of the futility and danger of the proceedings. These changes, framed by Richard Baxter, would have given the clergy the option to omit certain objectionable ceremonies, and to use a directory in place of the Book of Common Prayer. It would have meant a variation in religious practice from parish to parish, and the effective authority of the bishop and archdeacon would have been substantially reduced.

This was exactly the opposite of what the Act of Uniformity provided. Conformity in outward observances, not doctrine, was the objective. Variety, spontaneity and independent judgement on the part of the clergy were feared, because the laity might be led astray. All clergy were ordered to use the Common Prayer, and no other form of service, and to declare their 'unfeigned assent and consent to all and every thing contained and prescribed' within it. They must have received ordination by a bishop, take oaths pledging non-resistance to royal authority, disclaim the Covenant, and subscribe all Thirty-Nine Articles. Those who failed to meet these stringent requirements were ejected on 24 August 1662 from their livings or university positions, and disqualified from teaching in public schools. Nearly a thousand clergy, the celebrated 'Bartholomew men', left the church as a result; this major and dramatic secession marks the symbolic birth of English religious non-conformity. So far from introducing national uniformity and religious unity, the Act permanently divided the nation. But it should be remembered that for both Sheldon and Baxter the religious settlement was not a matter of political expedience, but of theological right and wrong; compromises which incorporated any recognition of erroneous principles or practices simply could not be accepted.

However, on the part of parliament the Act of Uniformity was primarily a political matter: religious dissidents were politically dangerous and must be forced to obey the laws. To allow individual clergy or laymen to follow the dictates of their own consciences would undermine authority. Consequently acts were passed in 1664 and 1670 to suppress all conventicles, that is unauthorized religious meetings, with differential penalties for all attending, officiating at, or providing premises for, such meetings. An act of 1665 excluded all ministers who had been ejected from livings from residing within a five-mile radius, or in any corporation or parliamentary constituency. In addition, the Licensing Act of 1662 was directed as much at preventing the publication and dissemination of dissenting literature as at suppressing material judged politically seditious.

These acts, known as the Clarendon Code, were enforced as long as dissent and sedition were equated. In the early years Sheldon greatly increased their effectiveness by brilliant organization. In 1660 he had prepared the way for the episcopal take-over of the church by unobtrusive and skilful use of royal patronage, and by carefully reconstituting the cathedral chapters. In 1661 he remodelled Convocation, eliminating actual or potential dissidents. He was ready in August 1662 to replace the ministers who refused to conform—over a hundred in London alone—so that the crisis which many had expected, of empty pulpits and pastorless parishes, was avoided and the quality of the clergy whom he put in was remarkably high. During the Plague Sheldon was (with Monk) one of the few prominent men who stayed in the capital, and he tried without great success to order the City clergy to stay at their posts. Before the passage of the Five Mile Act in 1665, which Sheldon himself helped to draft, he had already prepared lists of dissenting clergy with their current addresses in prohibited areas, for despatch to the JPs to ensure immediate and systematic enforcement.

Sheldon displayed the same ability and energy in the herculean administrative task of physical and organizational reconstruction. Cathedrals, parish churches and parsonages had frequently been neglected, plundered or vandalized during the Interregnum. Church furnishings and service books were missing. Glebe lands and charitable funds had often been misappropriated. Few clergy had been ordained during two decades by the surviving bishops, and many of those reinstated in 1660 were old and ailing. The church needed rejuvenation. The refusal of ministers to conform in 1662 faced Sheldon with over a thousand vacancies that had to be filled, but this was done, with great care being taken to maintain high standards. In addition schools and universities had to be regulated.

The immensity of these administrative tasks, on top of the active political involvement which absorbed much episcopal time and attention, especially in attendance in the Lords, precluded any far-reaching attempt at reforms. Furthermore, the keynote of the restoration of the church was simply the insistence that the church was recovering only what belonged to it by law, that is properties, institutions and jurisdictions which were defined and delimited. To have considered changes—for instance reforms of the ecclesiastical courts or redistribution of clerical incomes—would have obscured the principle that the church was entitled to certain fixed rights, and should be put in possession of them. Certainly there was a lack of creative imagination, a legalistic narrowness and considerable inflexibility (all personal characteristics of Sheldon himself), and many clergy made themselves excessively unpopular by insisting on their full profits when negotiating with tenants and renewing leases. But the church derived great strength and resolution from the knowledge that its rights and privileges were based on the law, and this fact became even more important when Charles showed how little he was to be relied upon.

In the Declaration of Breda Charles had left the forms of a religious settlement to parliament, but he actively supported Clarendon's successful postponement of permanent legislation until the Convention had been replaced by a more anglican parliament. The king continued to acquiesce in his minister's policy during the first months of the Cavalier Parliament, but as the uniformity act neared completion he began to show disquieting signs of initiating an independent and divergent policy. In June 1662 Monk introduced the king to a delegation of presbyterian ministers asking for relief; Clarendon was insufficiently sure of his own influence to advise that they should be rebuffed, but would have conceded a three-month suspension of the Act. It was left to the bishops, acting with the king's legal advisers, to force abandonment of the proposals for concessions. But on 27 August, just after the Act came into force, Charles floated the idea of granting dispensations to individual ministers, provided that they petitioned for them. This would have made them into direct dependants of the crown, but as well as guaranteeing their good political behaviour it would also, as Sheldon pointed out in a vehement protest, grant them immunity from effective authority and so undermine the position of the bishops. Taking an intransigent stand on the letter of the law, he forced a withdrawal of the proposal.

The third move was much more dangerous to the church, both in itself and in its wider implications. Early in June Sir Henry Bennet suggested that Charles should let the Act come into operation and then subsequently announce his intention to give relief. Ominously, he coupled this with advice that it would be wise to give concessions only from a position of strength, and advocated the 'temporary' raising of military units to preserve order. Ostensibly this was to be just for the period when dissenters might challenge the Act of Uniformity, but obviously the subsequent introduction of toleration could be used to justify the retention of the military. Even more provocative was the transparent plan to enable catholics, as well as dissenters, to take advantage of the suspension of the penal laws by the royal prerogative. Consequently, the announcement of the Declaration of Indulgence, on 26 December 1662, produced a political explosion. Again Sheldon headed opposition, working closely with parliamentary critics of the prerogative powers on which the Declaration was based, whereas at first Clarendon appears to have at least acquiesced in the new policy. In the face of concerted protests Charles quickly gave way, and Sheldon achieved another victory when he forced the abandonment of a bill for indulgence for dissenters (but not catholics), which was introduced in the Lords by two junior ministers, Ashley and Robartes, in February 1663.

Although the attempt to grant toleration by prerogative methods collapsed so quickly in the face of anglican intransigence, this first Declaration of Indulgence demonstrated the availability of an alternative politico-religious strategy for the king and his ministers to follow. This connected toleration with the use of the suspending power—and so enhancement of the prerogative—and promised benefits for the catholics and dissenters, who could be used as replacements for the anglicans as instruments or allies for the king. Although it failed so abysmally and quickly in 1662–3, this line of policy was to be revived in 1672–3, and again in 1687–8. This first attempt also brought forward Sheldon and his fellow bishops as champions of the supremacy of statutes and, even more important, as defenders of protestantism against the advance of popery. As in Laud's day, the attempt to enforce religious conformity soon created tensions, and inevitably made the bishops unpopular in certain circles. However Sheldon's sustained, successful and public opposition to the grant of any concessions for the catholics prevented bishops who were engaged in repressing dissenters from being effectively accused of crypto-popery, as Laud had been. By resisting royal policy, Sheldon obtained for the bishops a reputation for protestant integrity that was to survive whig smears, and his example inspired the seven bishops in their defiance of James in 1688.

Episcopal determination.was in sharp contrast with Clarendon's lack of resolution. The bishops derived confidence from the knowledge that they were the men in possession. Having achieved full authority over the church, Sheldon and his colleagues rode out the storm which overwhelmed Clarendon. A less complete restoration of the church, or the loss of unity and cohesion that concessions to the presbyterians would have inevitably produced, must have left the church exposed to changes reflecting the principles or policies of expediency of the Cabal ministers. In practice, in 1668 Sheldon routed the attempt, inspired by Buckingham, to pass bills of comprehension and indulgence, and he was still strong enough in 1673 to block a further bill of toleration. With its morale unimpaired, the church endured the unsympathetic Cabal ministry, and in alliance with a majority in the Commons forced the abandonment of all its policies. Under Danby, and again in 1681–6 when Rochester was chief minister, the anglican interest formed by Sheldon, and continued by Sancroft and Compton, formed the basis of the two most successful of Charles's administrations, and his disciples provided the main body of popular toryism down to 1714.

The character and composition of the dissenting sects were largely determined by the way in which the old Elizabethan and the new laws passed after 1660 were actually enforced. This varied considerably from place to place, mainly reflecting the different attitudes of the county and corporation magistrates, and from time to time. The repressive laws were enforced with rigour, on a nationwide scale, only in times of acute insecurity (1664–6, 1670, 1681–5), while at other times (1667–70, 1672–4, 1679–81) the dissenters benefited from official or tacit toleration. Consequently, the size of the dissenting community was constantly fluctuating: during periods when there was no risk in doing so the congregations at their religious meetings were swelled by large numbers of people, who clearly preferred the dissenting services and preaching to the anglican, but in times of severe enforcement of the laws they fell away in droves to conform to the established church. Only a hard core was left of ministers who had been ejected from the church in 1660–62 but generally defied the laws by conducting illegal religious meetings (conventicles), despite the heavy penalties for doing so, and laymen who provided the places for conventicles or persisted in attending them. But this hard core was far from being homogeneous, and the character of all the sects changed during the period of intermittent repression.

The presbyterians were well served and, in the absence of lay leadership after 1660, mainly directed by a large number of well-educated and devoted ministers who had gone into the wilderness in 1660–62 rather than conform, but were divided among themselves about their fundamental objectives. Many of their laity and clergy (Baxter, for example) occasionally attended anglican services and aimed at comprehension, that is a new religious settlement containing sufficient concessions for them to be able to re-enter a modified anglican church, but a zealous minority rejected any form of reunion, remaining as intransigent in their hostility to any version of episcopacy and the anglican liturgy as the majority of Scottish presbyterians. The English presbyterians were socially superior to the other dissenting sects, but although many of the aristocracy and gentry who had lived through the 1640s and 1650s as adults maintained existing contact with them (particularly by keeping ejected ministers as household chaplains) and remained generally sympathetic, few of the male members of such families regularly attended conventicles or boycotted anglican services, and contacts weakened further in the next generation. When toleration was finally established on a statutory basis in 1689, and the last attempt at comprehension failed in 1689–90, the presbyterians emerged with solid and respectable urban congregations, overwhelmingly middle class in composition and concerned to preserve their own faith and values rather than to expand and proselytize.

The independents or congregationalists were for a time after 1660 treated as being politically very dangerous because of their past associations with Cromwell and because their congregations contained a number of discharged officers and soldiers who had been political activists in 1658–60 and were suspected of being engaged in plotting against Charles II. The independents believed in the virtual autonomy of each congregation; this enabled them to operate more effectively during periods of repression than the presbyterians, who could not maintain national and regional synods, or enforce the strict theological uniformity which they had practiced during the Interregnum. The independents were not interested in comprehension, but were united in wanting toleration, as were the baptists, who were also associated in the minds of the Restoration authorities with political extremism and condemned by the clergy as heretics. There was a distinct social difference between independents and baptists: the latter's members were largely drawn from the poorer peasantry and urban working class, whereas the independents tended to be artisans, tradesmen and tenant farmers. The baptist clergy had less authority within their congregations than the other dissenting clergy; the democratic practices of self-government and the absence of any form of deference to clerical authority kept radical ideas alive among the baptists during a period when they found little effective expression in political movements. It should be remembered also that the Restoration generation of baptists produced the greatest popular classic in English literature, John Bunyan's *Pilgrim's Progress*.

The other conspicuously radical sect, the quakers or Society of Friends, provoked even deeper suspicion. Their total refusal to compromise with the world's vanities and demands—symbolized by such practices as their rejection of oath-taking, their use of the familiar second-person singular in addressing everyone, demonstrating that all were brothers and sisters, and their refusal to take off their caps to superiors—led to their being suspected as subversives who wanted to dissolve all forms of authority. At first their direct action tactics—disturbing church services, threatening all sinners from Charles down with God's wrath—aroused popular antagonism or exasperation, but subsequently their extraordinary steadfastness under the most savage and sustained repression dispelled some of their general unpopularity. But their ability to survive harsh repression, their flexible but very successful organization to help those who were suffering, their continued and active attempts to proselytize at a time when other sects were concentrating on bare survival, confirmed the official attitude of hostility to them. However, they had in William Penn an unusually well placed protector, who in 1686 obtained for them James II's favour. With toleration there began the extraordinary transformation of the quakers from the most radical of the dissenting sects into a largely self-sufficient community, with the business prosperity of individual members largely based on implicit trust in their personal integrity and reputation for fair-dealing.

Although the anglican clergy and magistrates claimed that they were only enforcing laws made for the purpose of uniting the nation in the protestant religion and preventing rebellion, and were not indulging in the kind of bigoted persecution associated with popery, their zealous activity up to 1687 did tend to alienate all but the most committed anglicans. Action against the dissenters often involved using discreditable and damaging methods. Informers had to be used to sniff out conventicles, the Restoration statutes giving them as reward a proportion of the fines imposed, and such men were usually the scum of society. Although often unattractively self-righteous, most dissenters who were harassed by magistrates and clergy were respectable tradesmen or farmers, and when they were jailed for long periods, or their stock was distrained, heavy losses were incurred by their partners or employees. As in Laud's day, it was claimed that religious repression was causing economic depression, and commercial expansion and general prosperity were promised as the results of toleration in the royal Declarations of Indulgence of 1672, 1687 and 1688. Furthermore, there was one grievance that conformist laymen shared with the dissenters—tithe. Nobody liked paying it, and its burden became disproportionately heavy in years of depression caused by bad harvests, so that many small landowners had goods distrained, sharing the experience of the dissenters whose refusals to pay were based on principle.

The failure of the attempt after the Restoration to coerce the dissenters into conformity and submission to the established church is revealing of the weaknesses and (in every sense of the word) amateurishness of English local government. In France a centralized administration, operating through the *intendants* and using the army in the infamous *dragonnades*, quickly eliminated the much larger Huguenot minority. In England the dissenters constituted, according to Compton's census of 1676, rather less than five per cent of the population, and this may be accepted as an approximate estimate of the hard core. Although so few, they survived more because of the deficiencies of local administration than because of the action of those among the political nation who claimed to be sympathetic to them and advocates of toleration. Shaftesbury and James both tried to exploit them, and when toleration was granted by the statute of 1689 it was a grudging, almost a minimum, concession. Nevertheless, the end of repression eased the lives of the dissenters, but the failure of comprehension finalized their separation from the mainstream of English intellectual and political life. The separatist, introverted, characteristics that had been acquired during the period of persecution were to remain as characteristics of what was later, after the rise of methodism, to be called the old dissent.

Clarendon's explanations, in the *Continuation* of his history, for his post-Restoration failure are unintentionally revealing. By blaming Charles's indolence, the enmity of his mistress Barbara Castlemaine, William Coventry and Henry Bennet, that is by concentrating on personalities and by sneering at those like Coventry and George Downing who were trying to tackle the main problems of government by introducing new methods, Clarendon showed how little he understood the reasons for his increasing ineffectiveness and unpopularity in the years before his fall in 1667. He failed conspicuously in all three principal areas of government and politics. From the start he was most vulnerable at court, not just because he was detested by the favourites and mistresses, but more fundamentally because he failed to understand Charles. By negatively deploring his failings and resenting his younger friends, instead of trying to influence and guide the king, Clarendon provoked personal animosity against a censorious minister, and expended the debt of obligation that Charles owed him for services during the years of exile.

Similarly, Clarendon never fully appreciated the need to manage parliament, and especially the Commons. He deprecated, and for a time prevented, any distribution of offices and pensions to build a court interest, although this inaction tempted pretenders to royal favour. A backbench adventurer, Sir Richard Temple, offered in 1663 to undertake for the king, and obtain the supply and legislation that he required. The erratic catholic earl of Bristol launched an impeachment, calculating that Clarendon would be abandoned as a sacrifice to appease parliamentary discontent. Both attempts were ineptly prepared and failed, but Charles saw that management was essential. Overriding Clarendon's objections, he forced him to admit Bennet into the role of principal parliamentary manager, although the latter almost immediately began to develop a line of policy at variance with that of the senior ministers. Although forty-five years old Bennet posed as the leader of the younger generation of courtiers, and paraded his loyal services to the crown by wearing a black patch on the bridge of his nose, where he had been slashed by a roundhead in a skirmish. His services as royalist agent in Madrid after 1658 had given him diplomatic experience and reputation, but also gave rise to (justified) reports that he had become a catholic, or at least a sympathizer.

Clarendon's failure to dominate government, that is the decision making processes and chief executive duties, was his fatal weakness. He did not believe that there should be a chief minister, and certainly he did not try consistently to behave as one himself. Clarendon held to the view that only the king should command, and that the activities of the great officers of state should be coordinated through the agency of the privy council. But it soon became obvious that Charles had no intention of playing the same kind of controlling role as Louis xiv and the privy council was too large and heterogeneous to function effectively and expeditiously. Clarendon also handicapped himself by becoming lord chancellor. This office involved a burden of routine administration that broke his health, and only part of which (clerical and judicial patronage) possessed direct political importance. He failed to see that the key position was now the treasury. Not only did he not assume this office himself, when it became obvious that Charles would not take an active part in governing and that the privy council would not function in the way that Clarendon hoped it would, but he retained Southampton as lord treasurer although both politically and administratively he proved to be a virtual passenger. Southampton failed to assert himself on general issues. He actually surrendered control of treasury patronage to the king, which meant in practice that other ministers were free to scramble competitively for it. Within his own sphere Southampton made no sustained attempt either to rectify the initial miscalculations which meant that the crown had an inadequate revenue, or to restrain extravagant expediture. Like Clarendon he suffered from bad health, and handed over actual control of administration to a competent subordinate, Sir Philip Warwick, who lacked the ambition and standing to attempt to rectify ministerial and administrative defects, still less to give direction to government as a whole.

These failures to provide firm leadership were all the more damaging because of the mixed composition of the ministry. At first Charles had no choice in the matter. He had obligations to Monk, and had to admit his retinue—Morrice as secretary of state, Ashley as chancellor of the exchequer, Manchester and Anglesey. This suited Clarendon, since there was a danger that otherwise these so-called presbyterian ministers might unite with the dissident court faction associated with the queen-mother, but after 1662 Monk faded into relative unimportance. Thereafter Clarendon's position was constantly endangered. He failed to check the meteoric rise of Charles's favourite, Falmouth, who was on the verge of becoming chief minister when he was killed at sea in 1665. Clarendon had also to accept Bennet as secretary of state (1662), although he knew that the latter was working to undermine him. Bennet attracted younger aspirants for office, both those who simply saw Clarendon as an obstacle to their own advancement and those, of whom William Coventry and George Downing were the ablest and most articulate, who were frustrated by Clarendon's complacency, inertia and obstruction of all administrative and fiscal changes.

A short-lived return to the institutions and methods of 1640 followed the Restoration, in both the household and the offices of state. Appointments were made to some places for life. Clarendon deplored and prevented as far as he could any innovation, any variation from traditional practices; for instance, he opposed the appointment of commissioners in addition to a lord high admiral. But two factors made restoration of the old order untenable. Desperate shortage of money forced Charles, in what can be seen as a symbolic act, to make drastic reductions in the household in 1662, and subsequent insolvency made fiscal experimentation unavoidable. Secondly, in pre-industrial societies war, and especially naval war with its complex and expensive logistical problems, posed the most difficult set of tasks that relatively rudimentary governmental machines had to undertake. So the fact could not be concealed that the relative failure of the Dutch war of 1665–7 was due directly to the incompetence of royal government, in sharp and humiliating contrast to the success that the Rump government had achieved in 1652–4. It followed that although Clarendon was not responsible for instigating the war, he carried the responsibility for its dismal outcome.

However, Clarendon's weaknesses had already been exposed in the difficult parliamentary session of 1663, that is before the Dutch war began. The session opened with the Commons endeavouring to prevent any future repetition of the Declaration of Indulgence. Asserting its right as representative of the nation, the house claimed that by passing statutes such as the Act of Uniformity it had deprived the royal Declaration of Breda (1660) of all validity, so that the king was no longer bound by his pre-Restoration promises, but was now bound by a statute which had received his assent. In the face of this uncompromising attitude Charles adopted a soft approach, asking MPs to trust him, explaining how he loved parliaments and had always favoured the church, and almost begging for money. Voluntarily he submitted a state of the revenue to the house, but it was slow to respond. Consequently, in June Charles intervened again, this time more harshly, rebuking MPs for their lack of warmth, and warning that he would find it difficult to preserve peace within the kingdom unless he was granted supply. Even then a sizeable minority (111 to 159) still opposed supply, and the money voted was in the obsolete form of subsidies, the pre-1642 form of direct taxation.

Other difficulties demonstrated the inadequacy of court leadership and management. An attempt to repeal the 1641 Triennial Act

came to nothing. A bill against the sale of offices was moved by
independents so as to embarrass the court. The need for Charles to
intervene personally was in itself a sign of ministerial incompetence,
so it is not surprising that he insisted on Clarendon enlarging the
group that was consulted occasionally on parliamentary affairs, to
include Bennet, Coventry and Clifford. Bitterly resentful at having
to share influence with young and energetic men who blatantly
aimed at supplanting him, Clarendon obstinately deplored efforts to
procure the election of royal servants at by-elections, condemned the
use of financial inducements, and opposed the idea of Charles personally canvassing MPS as being demeaning and prejudicial to royal
authority. Only Bristol's folly in launching an ill-timed and
maliciously inspired attempt at an impeachment in July saved
Clarendon from the consequences of mismanagement.

By contrast the next session of March to May 1664 was well organized. It saw the accomplishment of a drastic emasculation of the
Triennial Act, the passage of an act to improve collection of the
hearth tax that had failed in 1663, and the severe act against conventicles. The most far-reaching development showed that it was
the new managers who were now in control: Clifford introduced the
motion that was designed to lead to war, which declared that the
Dutch represented the greatest obstruction to trade. Raising money
for the war absorbed virtually the whole of the 1664–5 session, but
the votes of supply passed during the short Oxford session of October
1665 included fiscal innovations that marked a further decline in
Clarendon's authority and influence. Downing proposed appropriat-
ing a new grant of £1,250,000 as security for repayment of a loan.
Lord Treasurer Southampton and Clarendon, who had not been
consulted, opposed this proposition but were forced to give way by
Charles himself. Ministers were publicly divided on a series of proposals, including a bill which passed the Commons against the import of Irish cattle, a bill to impose a test oath on all office holders
which failed to pass, and over attacks against Sandwich, one of the
admirals, for embezzling prize cargoes.

With accumulating strains from heavy taxation on an economy
depressed by dislocation of trade, caused by losses of ships and
foreign markets, and aggravated by the plague, resentment against
continued demands for supply could not be avoided. The session of
1666–7 reflected the growth of discontent. Clarendon virtually lost
control. The session degenerated into confusion as factions within the
court competed with each other, and an increasingly coherent opposition began to form. Impeachment was revived, although after considerable discussion no case was actually presented to the lords
(against viscount Mordaunt, not an important political figure). The

contentious act prohibiting Irish cattle imports was passed, to the fury of Clarendon's ally Ormonde, the lord lieutenant. A provocative proposal for a general excise had to be dropped. An unofficial suggestion for the hated hearth tax to be bought up by a once and for all lump sum, which could have earned the court some popularity, was not proceeded with. Tensions were created by clashes between the Lords and Commons over the patent issued to the Canary Company.

Acute dissatisfaction with the incompetence and alleged corruption of the administration also led the Commons to make a demand that represented an undisguised innovation with far-reaching implications. This was for the appointment of commissioners to inspect the public accounts, and report back to the Commons. In the 1690s such a commission was to become the device by means of which Robert Harley effected parliamentary control over the executive, and even in 1667 its potential power to restrict and control the conduct of government was already understood. There were also more immediate reasons why Charles resisted. The appointment of commissioners was objectionable because it was 'tacked' to a supply bill, that is it formed an inseparable part of the vote of taxes. The opposition clearly intended to use the commission to collect material for an onslaught on the ministers, and to justify restricting further supply. Clarendon was aware of the danger to himself, and on constitutional grounds would have dissolved parliament rather than give way. Charles would have vetoed the bill, but in a roundabout way he managed to postpone the threatened invasion of his prerogative. The Lords was used to block the appointment of commissioners, but instead the house asked Charles to appoint them himself. But when he did so in March 1667, naming men who were not MPS, most of the commissioners were doubtful about their authority to act without a statute, and when consulted the judges were also unsure and failed to remove their misgivings. As a result this commission never acted, and in December Charles had to accept one appointed by parliament.

Charles's retention of Clarendon meant association with a minister who had lost the capacity for constructive action. Clarendon talked of dissolving parliament, but this was impractical because financial necessities would require calling a new one, and a bill introduced in January to limit not only MPS, but also electors, to those who had received the anglican sacrament, had made no progress. On Southampton's death in May 1667, Clarendon opposed putting the treasury into commission, although he had no qualified candidate for this key post. His objections were disregarded, as were his subsequent proposals for a treasury commission in a traditional form,

composed of great officers who were already overburdened, and
lacked the necessary expertise to rescue royal finances from their near
bankrupt state. The new commission was appointed without reference to Clarendon. Albemarle (formerly Monk) was put in as a
figurehead, and Ashley as chancellor of the exchequer was belatedly
added, but the three members who mattered (William Coventry,
Clifford and Duncombe) were not only junior royal servants who
had been critical of Clarendon's administration in general, but were
determined to break with Southampton's obsolete methods.
Immediately they initiated long overdue changes, and politically
their appointment and administrative innovations left Clarendon
hopelessly and visibly isolated.

The humiliation of the successful Dutch attack on Chatham (May
1667) and Clarendon's clumsy reaction to this disaster, finally
necessitated a change of ministry. The naval failures of 1666 had
conclusively proved that war could not easily be made to produce
immediate profits. They had produced a disastrously wrong policy
decision. On the assumption that an early peace could be concluded,
and in order to free seamen to man merchant ships, and so get trade
moving again, the main fleet was to be laid up in 1667. Only detached squadrons were sent out to protect trade, but for coast defence
purposes new military units were raised. The result was politically
provocative, but militarily ineffective. The squadrons failed to protect trade, the soldiers could not prevent the Dutch entering the
Medway. Suspicions developed that these army units were in fact
designed to form a standing army which would enable the ministers
to govern without parliament. Commissions issued to their officers
were identical with those given to regular officers. Pay for the men
was provided by ordering that money raised through assessments for
the support of the militia should be illegally diverted for the new
units, and free quartering of soldiers on householders was also used,
although it too was illegal.

Inept handling of parliament strengthened these fears that
Clarendon and his son-in-law James were pressing Charles to introduce military government. Parliament had been prorogued until
October, but it was recalled on 25 July, because an early conclusion
of peace was now in doubt. Nothing had been prepared. The king
did not make a speech to guide peers and members, as was customary. Not surprisingly opposition MPs seized the opportunity to
attack the court for raising the army, and after virulent speeches a
unanimous vote passed for its disbandment. Knowing that petitions
were ready for presentation to the Commons, to inflame it still more
against the court, Charles prorogued on 29 July. Nothing had been
gained. MPs were furious at being summoned to London, and then

sent home again after four days. Rumours circulated about Charles's intentions—dissolution, military government, illegal taxes—and his conduct was interpreted as being designed to protect his minister. All this guaranteed an unmanageable session when parliament was called—unless a sacrifice could be offered.

Clarendon provided the obvious scapegoat. He had become almost universally detested. He had no powerful friends, apart from James and Ormonde. The new treasury commissioners were already discarding many of the old governmental methods without reference to him. Crucially, Charles was becoming totally dissatisfied. There had never been any personal warmth in the relationship, but Charles had relied on Clarendon's experience. Mismanagement of the war and royal finances, the gap of incomprehension between Clarendon and subordinate ministers who were trying to rectify administrative weaknesses, the certainty that parliament would exploit the crown's desperate financial position, made Clarendon a liability. Even the bishops were dissociating themselves; they had advised against a dissolution, fearing that elections would produce an unfavourable Commons. There was also a great deal of politically irrelevant pressure on Charles to remove Clarendon, especially from mistresses and courtiers who played on personal differences between the two men, but the decisive influences were those of Buckingham and Coventry. The former promised a favourable parliamentary session, including grants of supply; the latter argued that Clarendon's removal was a pre-requisite for the essential reorganization of administration. Like a butterfly in a collector's album, Buckingham has been fixed for ever in Dryden's mordant lines:

A man so various, that he seem'd to be
Not one, but all Mankind's Epitome.
Stiff in Opinions, always in the wrong;
Was everything by starts, and nothing long:
But in the course of one revolving Moon,
Was Chymyst, Fidler, States-Man and Buffoon:
Then all for Women, Painting, Rhyming, Drinking:
Besides ten thousand freaks that dy'd in thinking. . . .
Rayling and praising were his usual Themes;
And both (to show his Judgement) in Extremes.

Yet some of the aura of mystery and greatness that had been attached to his tragic father, James I's favourite, remained with the second duke. When he exerted himself he could arouse popular feeling, and radicals and the advocates of religious toleration in the late 1660s were prepared to build a political interest for him. Having been brought up with Charles, as a foster-brother, and sharing the same cynical and dilettante tastes, Buckingham also possessed influence at court. But all his assets wasted away—his wealth dissolved, his health broke and he found himself overtaken first by his Cabal colleagues and then by Shaftesbury as organizer of opposition.

Clarendon's dismissal on 30 August marked the end of the Restoration era. The entirely separate and distinct impeachment which was launched in October, first on the lesser count of misdemeanours, but from the 26th on charges of treason, marked the beginning of a new era, with new issues and new political alignments.

The impeachment served the interests only of those who now aspired to secure themselves in office and influence. The attacks were led by Buckingham and his followers, young and ambitious men like Edward Seymour and Richard Temple, who aimed to destroy Clarendon so that he could never recover, and if necessary would put him to death. As a side effect these vicious attacks would also shatter the old cavalier interest beyond repair, making entirely new policies possible. Significantly many of those who had pressed for Clarendon's removal (conspicuously Coventry) abstained from joining in the impeachment, and unexpectedly virtually all the old 'presbyterian' opposition and a section of the old cavalier interest rallied to his defence.

Technically, the prosecution case was weak. There was no hard evidence on which to substantiate charges of treason. This was apparent despite the ferocity of the attacks made by Seymour and Vaughan. Buckingham was therefore obliged to involve Charles in overcoming obstruction and resistance in the Commons, and this opposition could be expected to be even stronger in the Lords. Yet even with Charles identifying himself with the prosecution, the Commons rejected by 172 to 103 the first article, alleging that Clarendon had committed treason by advocating the dissolution of parliament and rule by an army. A second major check came when the Lords refused to commit him to the Tower on general charges, although this had been done in Strafford's case in 1640. The weight of opposition in both Houses meant that a bill of attainder declaring him guilty without having to prove it (on the model of 1641) was unlikely to succeed, but an equally ruthless method was considered—the establishment of a special court of twenty-four peers presided over by a new lord steward. Knowing that this court would be packed with his enemies, Clarendon fled to France on 27 November.

Superficially Charles was liberated by the removal of an incompetent and unpopular minister whom he had grown to detest, whereas he was on terms of easy familiarity with several of the new ministers. He was now free to explore the possibility of entirely new policies: Clarendon's removal coincided with the first moves for an understanding with Louis xiv. But the power of the crown was not really increased. James, who opposed the impeachment of his father-in-law, commented that by encouraging the Commons to destroy a fallen minister, Charles weakened the position of all later ministers. Knowing that they could not depend on royal protection against parliamentary attacks, all future ministers were obliged to put their own interests first, and to give a higher priority to self-protection than to stubborn advocacy or execution of royal policies.

Partly in order to protect themselves, Clarendon's successors invented the processes of systematic parliamentary management, but there was a more comprehensive and permanent way of securing themselves—by superseding parliament altogether. The Cabal ministers soon found it difficult to maintain control over the Commons which they had used to help destroy Clarendon. Consequently, they began to think of putting themselves into the same state of inviolable ministerial security that Louis xiv's servants possessed. In France ministers were responsible to an active and autocratic sovereign, but Charles did not apparently have either the determination or the application to business that would enable him to master his ministers. The absolutism at which the Cabal ministers aimed would in reality have meant ministerial rather than royal absolutism.

8 The Cabal

Despite the discontent and alarms caused by the disasters of the Second Dutch War, the position of the monarchy was secure in 1667 and Clarendon's fall had no immediately appreciable effects. Buckingham's failure to manage parliament in 1668, and specifically to obtain concessions for the dissenters, meant that there was no reversal or major modification of the main principles of the Restoration Settlement. But under the surface Charles now had freedom to develop a secret line of policy that was to produce the Dover treaty of alliance with France (May 1670), and in 1672 the Third Dutch War and the Declaration of Indulgence.

Charles's secret policy may accurately be described as absolutist. The objective was to make the king independent of his subjects, and in particular to free him from having to rely on the cooperation of parliament. Such a policy was influenced, perhaps directly inspired, by developments in contemporary Europe, above all in France, but English-style absolutism would have differed in important respects from European models. In France, and also in Sweden, Denmark and Brandenburg–Prussia, absolutist policies aimed at increasing the power of the monarchy primarily for purposes of foreign war, and territorial conquest or defence. The first priority was the creation and maintenance of a large, professional standing army, officered by disciplined aristocrats. All governmental policies were aimed at creating and concentrating power. Wealth and prosperity were to be exploited to increase the power of the monarch, both within his kingdom and in relation to other states. Merchants and entrepreneurs in France were allotted an entirely subordinate position, which reflected the comparatively undeveloped and undiversified state of the French economy. Colbert had to foster and protect, often actually establish, industries and trades, and many of his enterprises depended for survival on subsidies. Continuously subject to ministerial supervision and directives, merchants and industrialists seldom took important initiatives or significantly influenced ministerial decisions. Only after Colbert's death, from the 1690s, did they begin to behave more independently, and even then they lacked the institutional means to force changes in the policies of which they were critical. They were socially and politically uninfluential by comparison with the aristocracy, whose reduction to obedience, and a varyingly effective imposition of service to the crown, formed the essential basis of absolutism in late seventeenth-century France, Sweden, Brandenburg–Prussia, and later also in Russia.

In England, society was already far more complex in structure. A significant investment in trade, industry, mining and urban real estate came from the aristocracy and gentry; merchants and financiers had for a century been large-scale purchasers of land. This far more varied and subdivided social structure, together with the unique institution of parliament and an economy in which exports and foreign trade were traditionally important, meant that absolutism necessarily took different forms in England. The first and crucial step towards achieving it must be to make the king independent of parliament, especially in financial matters, and the only practicable way of achieving financial independence seemed to lie in expanding overseas commerce, which would directly benefit the crown through greatly increased customs revenue yields, and indirectly through larger yields from other taxes on consumption. This wealth derived from trade also had the advantage of being more easily and quickly realizable—in the forms of tax payments, advances and loans—than wealth from agriculture. The emphasis on trade expansion gave first priority to the strengthening and maintenance of the navy; after 1660 an army was needed for security against internal disaffection, but its role was defensive and comparatively minor. The dynamic and offensive element in late-Stuart absolutism, symbolized by the inflated claim to the sovereignty of the seas, can be found in the attempts to seize a larger share of European trade, and to secure more of the increasingly valuable trade in colonial products from America, west Africa and east Asia.

Charles I's ship-money fleet represented the first systematic attempt to challenge Dutch commercial dominance. Maladministration made it ineffective even before the collapse of royal authority in 1640–42. After the Civil Wars, the Rump began to exert pressure on the Dutch, passing the Navigation Ordinance in 1651, but the advantages gained in the hard-fought first Dutch war were largely thrown away by Cromwell in the peace treaty of 1654, and heavy losses were suffered during his ill-conceived Spanish war. Like the Rump, the Convention Parliament showed itself responsive to the interests and representations of mercantile groups. This was not in any way because of continuity of membership or similarity of political outlook—they could hardly have been more dissimilar—but because commercial interests had become accustomed

to petitioning parliament for legislative action to remedy grievances and rectify defects in the existing laws. Regular sessions after
1660, and the flexibility of the committee system of the Commons,
ensured a continuation of this extremely significant process. In practical terms it meant that parliament was to prove a successful representative body, reducing the effectiveness of royal and ministerial attempts to exploit mercantile needs and to claim credit for
advancing their interests.

In 1660 the Convention re-enacted the Navigation Act in a
strengthened form, by requiring 'enumerated' goods (sugar, tobacco,
cotton, dyestuffs) to be exported from the plantations to England in
English ships, and undertook a thorough review of the book of rates.
This established the basis of customs policy for over a century, by
systematically increasing the duties on imported manufactures, while
lowering those on raw materials and on exports of English manufactured goods. Neither of these measures seems to have been inspired
by ministers, and Clarendon strongly disapproved of the intense
pressure which both houses of parliament began to exert for an
aggressive anti-Dutch policy, culminating in the resolution of 21 April
1664, which virtually called for war. But the failure of the war,
combined with the massive cost incurred, very largely eliminated
spontaneous, uncritical popular enthusiasm for wars of commercial
aggression directed against the Dutch. Increasing evidence of unexpected French naval and commercial expansion, and the realization that it would take decades of expanded trade to recoup the
money spent on a naval war, exposed as simplistic the previously
accepted argument that by destroying Dutch naval power the main
obstacle to expansion of trade and wealth would be removed.
Nevertheless for their own, ulterior reasons Charles and Clifford
were set on a planned, unprovoked third Dutch war. This was to be
represented as another struggle for commercial supremacy, but the
real objectives were political. The initiative came entirely from
Charles and his ministers. Parliament had demanded action in 1664,
but in 1672 war was prepared and launched while parliament was
deliberately kept prorogued and, had it proved as successful as
Charles hoped, he would have been freed from the necessity of re-
calling the Cavalier Parliament. Victory was intended to give him
decisively greater power over his subjects at home, as well as over
the Dutch.

The French alliance that led to the Third Dutch War was the
result of Charles's own personal and secret policy decisions, and not
the work of the so-called Cabal ministry. This familiar title is misleading because it implies a cohesion and unity of purpose that never

existed among the ministers of 1667–73. Each minister worked for himself, if necessary at the expense of his colleagues, and ministerial combinations, reputations and influence were constantly changing. The feud between Arlington and Buckingham bitterly divided the administration. Clarendon's successors were no more effective in managing parliament than he had been. Buckingham's attempt to relieve the dissenters so as to gain an alliance with a block of opposition members, by introducing proposals for toleration and comprehension in the session of 1668, failed abysmally. Instead, the Commons passed a new and severe bill against conventicles; this was held up in the Lords, and again in the 1669 session, but the campaign to force it through (successful in 1670) gave cohesion and a sense of purpose to a combination of 'country' members and former Clarendonians, working in close cooperation with Sheldon, that were absent among the court's supporters. Buckingham also achieved indifferent success in obtaining money—in 1668 only an additional £300,000, while in 1669 parliament had to be prorogued before supply had been voted. An interminable and bitter dispute between the two houses over the Lords' claim to jurisdiction in a law case, *Skinner* v. *the East India Company*, seriously impeded business in both sessions. Yet, despite these failures and his erratic and often scandalous behaviour, Buckingham kept office and the king's apparent favour, whereas Charles discarded the ablest of his junior ministers, Sir William Coventry, who was one of the initiators of a serious attempt to strengthen the basis of monarchical authority. Charles hated Coventry personally, and allowed this hatred to sway his judgement in March 1669 when, after a farcical quarrel with Buckingham, Coventry was dismissed from the privy council and the treasury commission. At the latter he, Clifford, Duncombe and Ashley, with Sir George Downing as secretary, had begun systematically to reform procedures and methods of administration, the necessary preliminary to making Charles solvent.

This promising, but long-term, development needs to be taken into account when judging the wisdom of Charles's decision to ally with France, and to receive subsidies in return for the commitment to join in an offensive war against the Dutch, when he was still encumbered by the debts of the Second Dutch War. In the short term, improvements in the supervision of branches of the revenue and the enforcement of control over expenditure by spending departments were unlikely to produce spectacular results, but they were evidence of sustained attention to business and largely disinterested service—qualities that had previously been rarely combined. The decision in 1670 to institute direct collection of the hearth money—to be followed in 1671 by direct collection of the customs—demonstrated an intention and the capacity to put royal finances on a proper basis. Significantly, parliament was favourably impressed. Usually MPs feared that royal solvency would imperil the life of parliament, and in a facile way they had attributed royal insolvency to the corruption of Charles's officers; in the 1669 session, acting on evidence from the commission for public accounts, the Commons had spent a great deal of its time in furious attacks on Carteret, the former treasurer of the navy. But in 1670–71 it voted the most generous extraordinary supply of the whole reign. A subsidy was granted for the navy, additional duties on wine for eight years, additional excise for six years, a law duty for nine, and further duties on imported goods were proposed.

From Charles's point of view there were two major disadvantages in accepting this generosity as the start of a partnership with a loyal and anglican majority, of the kind that Danby was to construct in the years after 1673. Although not explicitly conditional, these grants would not have been forthcoming if the court had resisted or rejected measures initiated by this majority, especially the Conventicle Act of 1670. There were signs that the dominant group of unofficial members in the Commons were assuming leadership and undertaking legislative initiatives, in default of effective leadership by the ministers, and this would have seriously restricted the king's freedom to decide the main direction of policy. The customs duties which were drafted, but not passed, in 1670–71 would have prohibited the import of some French commodities, and put virtually prohibitive duties on silks and linens. Admittedly compensatory increases on sugar and tobacco would have prevented the total yield to the revenue being reduced, but the whole line of policy was entirely at variance with the king's secret alliance with France. Prohibition and discriminatory duties were a response to pressure from merchants for retaliation against Colbert's tariffs of 1664 and 1667, which had made it difficult to sell English textiles in France. Charles and the ambassador in Paris had made half-hearted representations to Louis, and negotiations had opened for a commercial treaty, but once Louis secured the English alliance at Dover he lost all interest, and a full commercial agreement was never concluded. Charles also showed no interest, a fact that disproves the myth created by Stuart apologists that he was genuinely concerned with maritime and commercial matters. Royal and ministerial inaction led to these proposals from the Commons, which were likely to be popular because they were directed against France.

Retaliatory action against French goods, which could start a trade war, was dangerous from Charles's point of view because it would strengthen support within the country for the Triple Alliance, and make it much more difficult for him to reverse his alliances. The Triple Alliance originated in the defensive alliance of January 1668 with the Dutch, which Sweden later joined. Its real purpose had been to end the War of Devolution between France and Spain by forcing the latter to accept a settlement; only if France refused to limit its demands and engaged in an all-out war would the signatories intervene to defend the Spanish Netherlands. But most people in England and Holland wrongly interpreted the Triple Alliance as anti-French, and when Louis ended the war by the Treaty of Aachen (April 1668) it was incorrectly credited with having checked his plans of conquest. Public and parliamentary opinion was strongly anti-French, and this was exploited by spokesmen for the court (who were not in the secret of Charles's diplomacy) during the 1670–71 session, when demands for supply were justified as necessary to make the Triple Alliance effective. But in reality the ships for which money was voted were intended by Charles to reinforce the fleet for a new war of aggression against the Dutch.

It would be an understatement to say that Charles was playing a dangerous as well as discreditable game. His motives for doing so are still far from agreed, but it is clear that James and the celebrated Cabal of (in order of importance as well as initials) Clifford, Arlington, Buckingham and Ashley, with Lauderdale, merely followed Charles's lead. The secret Treaty of Dover was his achievement, and only he knew everything about the details and ramifications of the agreement with Louis. The preliminary but crucial stage of the negotiations was conducted by correspondence between Charles and his surviving sister, Henrietta, wife of Louis's brother, the duc d'Orléans. Their regular correspondence had touched on important diplomatic matters earlier, notably in 1664–6 when Charles tried unsuccessfully to prevent the French helping the Dutch, but the personal letters assumed the role of negotiations from the late autumn of 1668. A cipher was exchanged in December. Then on 25 January 1669, according to James, the king revealed his intentions to him, Arlington, Clifford and Arundell, a catholic peer. He outlined a plan to combine a proposed alliance with France with a future public declaration of his conversion to catholicism, thus originating the two main principles that were to be embodied in the secret Treaty of Dover in May 1670.

This French alliance was from the first designed to produce and win a new war against the Dutch, in which the overwhelming power of France on land, and the combined fleets of France and England, together with the systematic diplomatic isolation of the Dutch, were confidently expected to result in a quick and decisive victory. The prospect of numerous prizes, a war indemnity of up to £1,000,000, and Louis's undertaking to pay £225,000 annually during the war, and another £150,000 at the time when Charles declared himself a catholic, provided the prospect of an actually profitable war. Royal prestige, damaged by the Chatham disaster, would be repaired and James had a new opportunity for naval glory and power. In the long term the agreed annexation of Walcheren and Kadzand would enable England to put pressure on the Dutch whenever this was necessary, and certainly to force them to observe punitive peace terms, provisions that would give English commerce permanent competitive advantages. These territories controlled access to Antwerp. This could be used either as a valuable diplomatic counter in negotiations with Spain, or with France when the Spanish succession issue came to be decided, or it could be exploited to open the hitherto closed port to English ships. This meant that although Charles dropped his earlier insistence on Louis limiting the strength of his fleet and concluding a commercial treaty, it could be claimed that English trade would benefit—and royal revenues would be appreciably increased.

The 'catholicity' clause of Treaty of Dover has puzzled historians, who are not even agreed that at this time Charles sincerely intended to embrace catholicism. Was this undertaking, to declare himself an open catholic, with Louis promising subsidies and armed assistance with a force of 6,000 men if the declaration provoked rebellion, really intended? It has been suggested that it was a device to extract more money from Louis, or to give Charles control over the timing of the war, or to bind Arlington and Clifford to James and Charles. But by this clause Charles exposed himself to French blackmail, and although Henrietta was enraptured it seems doubtful whether Louis was greatly attracted by the prospect of Charles's conversion. Originally the conversion was to precede the declaration of war against the Dutch, although the timing was left to Charles's discretion, but this was later reversed. This change provides a clue to Charles's motives. Personal reasons did play a part; this act would unite in one faith all Charles I's surviving children. More generally a public declaration of catholicism would follow the successful outcome of the war, and would both symbolize and contribute to the independence from his subjects which Charles hoped to achieve. In addition Charles could expect (literally) eternal credit for ensuring that catholicism would never be eradicated as a major force from English life.

Most important of all there was a major element of shrewd political calculation. The open declaration of conversion, and the establishment of catholicism as a public faith under French protection, would make it impossible for Louis arbitrarily to abandon the alliance with England at some future date, in order to suit some shift in his constantly flexible European diplomacy. The alliance in 1670 was only a temporary expedient for Louis, to enable him to crush the Dutch, but if Charles and James were to base their whole attempt to establish royal absolutism on the support of France, they needed some assurance that such support was secure and permanent. In Charles's own experience French attitudes towards him had always been arbitrary and governed by the cold, dispassionate principle of 'reason of state'. Despite Charles's close personal relationship to the French royal family, as eldest son of a daughter of France, Mazarin allied with the regicide protector, and even after Cromwell's death he had contemptuously rejected Charles's approaches for help in 1659. Louis preferred another republican government when he renewed the alliance with the Dutch in 1662, repulsing Charles's rival overtures. French behaviour in later years strengthens this interpretation of the calculations underlying the catholicity clause: Louis was to subsidize the opposition in 1678 against the crown, at the end of that year he stage-managed the fall of Danby which plunged England into the Exclusion Crisis, and in 1680–81 he hesitated before finally giving minimum aid to rescue the monarchy from the whigs. In 1688 while publicly giving the false impression that they were allied, Louis left James to face William's invasion unaided. In 1689–90 he supplied him with insufficient aid to recover his lost kingdoms, but with just sufficient to divert William and allied resources from the war in Europe.

In 1670 Charles knew that he was allying with a much stronger sovereign, who could afford to abandon the alliance with England once the predatory war against the Dutch had been won. If Charles was to embark on a policy of making himself independent from his subjects he needed the assurance of long-term French support. Only by Charles publicly declaring himself a catholic could he tie Louis. The promise of money and, if necessary, an army would be a binding commitment—considerations of prestige, as well as the rivalry with the Emperor for the role of champion of the interests of the catholic church, would make it difficult for Louis to retract, and so precipitate the collapse of the catholic cause throughout the British Isles. At the price of proclaiming himself dependent on French aid, Charles would have done everything possible to achieve immunity from the exercise at his, and his catholic heirs', expense of the prevalent French political principle, the machiavellian maxims of reason of state, the subordination of all other considerations to the pursuit of national self-interest.

The other principal participants in the Dover Treaty, James and Clifford, were simple men of faith and action. By his part James completed the recovery of his influence from the nadir into which it

had been plunged by his defence of Clarendon. In particular it
secured his right to the succession, which had emerged as an issue
during the preceding spring session, when Buckingham and Ashley
had pushed the Roos divorce bill (the first to permit remarriage) as a
dress rehearsal, or try-out, for Charles to discard the queen and contract a new and protestant marriage. Clifford has usually been depicted as the least important minister of the Cabal. Up to 1670 he
was the work-horse, employed on a variety of duties. He had served
at sea and as a diplomat in Scandinavia during the Dutch war. First
as comptroller, and then as treasurer, of the king's household, he
acted as dispenser of patronage at court and as manager and spokesman in the Commons. From 1667 he served on the new treasury
commission, emerging after Coventry's dismissal in March 1669 as
the effective leader, and the only commissioner in the Commons.
Although unfamiliar with France and the French language, his entire trustworthiness led Charles to use him for the last stages of the
negotiations preceding the conclusion of the Dover Treaty. Up to
this point Clifford was still regarded as Arlington's protégé, but his
energy and determination in implementing the secret policy elevated
him—first in royal favour, and then in office—above his former
patron. Clifford had no reservations or hesitations about the Dover
policies. He was moving towards personal conversion to catholicism.
An implacable enemy of the Dutch, he willingly sabotaged negotiations to strengthen the Triple Alliance to which Charles was still
publicly pledged. Ready to move quickly and take risks, he advocated and took responsibility for bold courses—the Stop of the
Exchequer and the Declaration of Indulgence were largely his
work—so that it was logical for Charles to appoint him in November
1672 to the most important office, as lord treasurer. But if his rise
was faster than that of his rivals, he failed in all his policies, and his
fall was abrupt and complete. His treasurership lasted only to June
1673, and he died a broken man in October.

By comparison Arlington's caution ensured his survival, political
and personal, and survival represented his objective throughout a
long ministerial career. Arlington had not joined actively in the attacks on Clarendon, rightly fearing that Buckingham had marked
him down as the next victim. Negotiation of the Triple Alliance had
strengthened his position, but Arlington was always acutely aware of
the complexities of the European diplomatic situation (unlike
Clifford), and of the risk of becoming identified as the enemy of
France. He had therefore reinsured himself in the autumn of 1668 by
suggesting a French alliance. This ensured that despite his timidity,
especially over religion (he became a catholic years later on his
death-bed), he was included in the secret of Charles's intentions, and

in the conclusion of the Dover Treaty. Since Buckingham was excluded this put Arlington in a position of security as a member of the confidential inner ring. Of necessity Arlington would always go along with Charles, and this meant that when the Dover policy eventually failed Arlington acquiesced in its abandonment.

In addition to minor ministers like Lord Keeper Bridgeman, three leading ministers, Ashley, Buckingham and Lauderdale, were not in the secret of the Dover Treaty. For their benefit, Louis, the French ambassador and Charles's other ministers went through the elaborate farce of the simulated treaty. This treaty, concluded in December 1670, was also secret, but omitted the clause about Charles declaring himself a catholic. The money already promised for that purpose was now lumped together with the money for the war, whose date was left to Louis to determine. Buckingham, who went to France to push the negotiations along, was convinced that this treaty of alliance would enlist French support for his becoming chief minister, displacing Arlington whom he knew Louis distrusted. Buckingham posed as France's best friend in English politics in order to strengthen his claim to the command of the English army which was to be sent to join the land offensive against the Dutch, but which would subsequently become even more important as the physical basis of English absolutism. He and Ashley also hoped to gain sectional credit by describing the war as the means of expanding trade and shipping, as a new mercantile offensive. However, Ashley's part in the king's new policies was insubstantial. He acquiesced but did not lead, or even get asked for advice. In the treasury commission Ashley was totally eclipsed by Clifford, and he would have lost the chancellorship of the exchequer (a relatively minor post) had he not followed his colleagues. Lauderdale was even less influential so far as English affairs were concerned, and suffered a setback when his premature proposals for a union of England and Scotland failed.

The agreement that the war should begin in the spring of 1672 left ample time for both logistical and political preparation. Two major policy moves deserve detailed attention, both advocated and executed by Clifford; the Stop of the Exchequer and the Declaration of Indulgence.

The Stop on 2 January 1672 was necessary in order to free revenue for immediate expenditure on the fleet. The new treasury commission of 1667 had regularized methods which were used in anticipating taxes, by ordering payments to be made 'in course', that is in a fixed order to those who had advanced money. This had unforeseen consequences. An increasing proportion of actual revenue had to be allocated for these payments, because a ring of bankers found it more profitable to buy orders for payment (often at large discounts), rather than lend money directly to the crown, and other smaller investors preferred to deposit their money with these bankers rather than lend to Charles. The result was a crippling shortage of ready money, and in purely financial terms the crown was in a weak position to bargain for loans with the dominant group who had money to lend. Politically, the bankers were very vulnerable. The Commons interpreted the bankers' operations as continuing manipulation of the king's necessities, by the only group who had done conspicuously well out of the disastrous Second Dutch War. Virulent attacks on bankers made in November 1669, October and November 1670, and January 1671 promised a relatively favourable reaction to the Stop, which Clifford had in mind from November 1667, and expressed the frustrated hostility of country gentlemen to a new plutocracy. MPs deplored the concentration of wealth in a few hands, they connected the prosperity of London bankers with the depressed state of the provinces and of agriculture. They were blamed for the shortage of coin and low rents—'as interest goes up, land goes down'—and the men who took advantage of Charles were also accused of exploiting landowners by their mortgages which too often encouraged extravagance. Bankers always make good scapegoats, but the most ominous speeches were those that compared Backwell and the London bankers with the corrupt ring of *financiers* associated with Fouquet in France, which Colbert destroyed in the years after 1662. Clifford, who significantly used the past tense in 1671 in saying that the bankers 'have been necessary evils', was indeed following Colbert's example when, by the Stop, he repudiated the orders for payment, ruining bankers who were not clients or part of the patronage system which he was constructing. His flexibility in meeting some of the payments, so as to ensure that depositors could be repaid by some favoured bankers, paid handsome political dividends. In the short term the Stop was not greatly or widely resented, but it did mean that if the war did not prove decisive in a single campaign, then parliament would have to be recalled and asked for extraordinary supply—loans on any scale could not be obtained otherwise.

The Declaration of Indulgence, on 15 March 1672, formed another part of the immediate preparations for war: by granting religious toleration Charles would secure internal peace and union. Inevitably the Declaration raised wider issues, and to appreciate these it should be seen as part of a wholly alternative political strategy that was available to Charles and James throughout their reigns. The so-called Clarendon Code had identified the restored monarchy with the established Church of England and with the legislative and judicial attempt to impose religious uniformity by coercive means. The assumption that religious dissent was inherently connected with political faction and the principles of rebellion had been generally accepted in the 1660s, when memories of the recent past and continued republican plotting made all dissenters objects of suspicion. Fear of the dissenters revived in 1670, when those in London made an ill-judged but systematic effort to resist the enforcement of the Conventicle Act, but generally in years of peace and prosperity the old animosities towards the dissenters were slowly subsiding.

Charles had never shared them. His declaration from Breda in 1660 had contained a conditional promise of liberty to tender consciences, provided that they did not disturb the peace. Charles then tried to give relief to dissenters by his declaration of December 1662, and he backed a bill in the Lords in 1663. In 1668 he acquiesced in Buckingham's attempt to pass comprehension and toleration bills, and appointed some bishops who were sympathetic to these unsuccessful moves. None of his chief ministers in 1672 were identified with the established church, but all agreed on the benefits to be derived from the institution of religious toleration by prerogative means. Moreover, although after the enforced withdrawal of the 1672 declaration Charles never reverted to a policy of toleration, it was to be revived in a much more thorough and systematic manner by James in 1686-8.

The Declaration began by reversing the anglican argument on the necessity for coercion: the 'sad experience of twelve years' showed that forcible courses did not work. Dissenters were to be allowed certain rights, but under direct royal authority and on sufferance. The penal laws were suspended. Public worship was allowed to all protestant dissenters who requested and took out licences; about 1,500 were issued. This was accompanied by a warning that any abuse of liberty, specifically by seditious preaching, would lead to withdrawal of all privileges. A serious attempt was made to balance these concessions to the dissenters by giving guarantees (much fuller than James's in 1687 and 1688) to reassure the anglican clergy. There was to be no change in the doctrine, discipline and government of the church, its revenues were confirmed (there had been rumours that all dean and chapter lands would be sold for the benefit of the crown), and only conformists were to be capable of holding livings. But these guarantees could not conceal the wish of the king and his ministers to disassociate themselves from an exclusive and permanent connection with the church, a connection which they now evaluated as a liability rather than an asset.

Charles hoped to free himself from dependence on parliament, as well as the church, by issuing the Declaration. The majority in parliament had not only rejected toleration in 1668, but passed the severe Conventicle Act (1670), which Archbishop Sheldon encouraged JPS to enforce systematically. A strong revival of parliamentary and popular anti-catholic sentiment also threatened to restrict the king's freedom of action. Accepting the risk of antagonizing the anglicans, the ministers now expected to convert the dissenters into dependants and instruments of the crown who, in return for toleration, were to uphold the prerogative methods by which it was instituted. There could also be electoral advantages from winning their support, and this possibility opened up the option of dissolving the Cavalier Parliament and calling a new one, which was to be seriously considered in 1673. But the policy rested on two fallacies. First, ministers overestimated both the numerical strength and the dynamism of the dissenters. Allowing them free exercise of their religion did not significantly weaken the established church, and they used their freedom cautiously—there was no revival of the old, burning missionary zeal to make converts and expand their strength. Politically, too they were largely passive—welcoming and accepting toleration but expressing a preference for it to be granted by statutory, not prerogative, means. Secondly, the Declaration was not taken at its face value: it was widely interpreted as intended primarily to benefit the catholics. Unlike the protestant dissenters, the catholics were permitted only private worship, but the difference was illusory and nobody was deceived. Private worship was all that catholics wanted, since their organization was based on chapels in private houses, and they knew that public worship would merely inflame popular anti-catholic prejudices. In fact opinion reacted violently against any concessions to catholics, and if parliament had to be recalled the Declaration would be vulnerable, both as an allegedly illegal exercise of pretended prerogative powers and as a cover for the advance of catholicism.

The Declaration preceded war on the Dutch by two days. The summer's campaign at sea failed to bring decisive success, but an autumn parliamentary session was avoided by the unscrupulous device of keeping the fleet out of its bases, so that the seamen did not have to be paid off. The remodelling of the ministry, with Clifford becoming lord treasurer and Shaftesbury lord chancellor, indicated a determination to persevere with the war and its accompanying policy of toleration, but new parliamentary supplies were needed if a fleet was to be fitted out for 1673.

The session of February–March 1673 marked the end of this attempt to establish absolutism, and it saw Charles suffer the heaviest political reverses of his entire reign. Two points stand out. First, the opposition that defeated Charles and Clifford and dismantled their policies, was largely spontaneous: it owed little to formal organization or leadership. Secondly, although this opposition made use of arguments against the ministry derived from the Dutch propaganda pamphlets that were circulating at this time, the parliamentary attacks were directed not against the war as such, but against the policies that accompanied it, and their effects were to persist long after the war had been ended.

At the beginning of the session Charles boldly asserted his determination to stand by the Declaration, and defended the war as just and necessary. Shaftesbury (the former Ashley, who was promoted to an earldom) capped this with a vicious onslaught against the Dutch, culminating in the slogan *delenda est Carthago*, which Cato had constantly used to urge the total destruction of Rome's rival. Parliament was unimpressed. Shaftesbury's vehemence was interpreted as personally necessary to clear himself from suspicions that he had been in contact with Dutch secret agents. The Commons were incensed against him for having issued writs for by-elections without the Speaker's authorization. This gave an opportunity to a new 'country' opposition, composed of backbenchers with both royalist and parliamentarian backgrounds, to force Charles to retreat and repudiate his chancellor. But on the main issue of the Declaration this opposition cannot be described as spoiling for a fight; the crucial debate on 10 February started hesitantly with MPs reluctant to speak, and when a lead was indicated it was by young or relatively obscure men. However, the result was conclusive, the house voting by 168 to 116 'that penal statutes, in matters ecclesiastical, cannot be suspended but by act of parliament'. Charles tried to avoid a surrender when he replied (24 February) to an address containing this forthright statement. He disclaimed any right of suspending laws concerned with properties or liberties, disavowed any intention of altering the doctrine or discipline of the church, and offered to assent to any bill containing provisions for indulgence. The Commons immediately saw that no renunciation of the suspending power in ecclesiastical matters was being made, and maintained pressure to pin Charles down, insisting in tactful phrases that he had been misinformed if he believed that he possessed such a power. If admitted, it 'might tend to the interrupting of the free course of the laws, and altering the legislative power, which hath always been acknowledged to reside in your Majesty and your two houses of parliament'.

It became clear that unless Charles gave way the Commons would hold back the urgently needed supply of money, a bill for which had passed through its preliminary stages. Ministers now seriously considered dissolving parliament and holding new elections, but in addition to the uncertain composition of a new Commons, there would have been insufficient time for elections and for the new parliament to vote supply in time to raise loans for spending on the fleet. After the Stop, and without such security, loans would not be forthcoming. A minor tactical manoeuvre, playing the Lords off against the Commons, proved futile. Significantly, the final decision was virtually the work of the French ambassador, who made it clear that in the event of a dissolution money would not be provided by Louis, whereas it would be if Charles dropped the Declaration and concentrated on prosecuting the war—which of course would serve French interests directly. As a result Charles withdrew the Declaration on 8 March, using the formula that had been suggested in the Commons' address, 'that what hath been done in that particular shall not for the future be drawn into consequence or example'.

A similar surrender had to be made over the even more vital test bill. Debates on this issue in parliament reflected the intensity of anti-papist feelings in the country, creating an atmosphere of fears and suspicion that was to persist for decades. Although there was no certain knowledge of Charles's real plans or secret treaty commitments, suspicions were general that the war was a cover for the advance of absolutism and catholicism. Catholics were suspected of having been infiltrated into high offices, with Clifford as the prime suspect, and into commissions in the army which had been expanded the previous year, ostensibly to fight the Dutch but in reality, it was believed, to dispense with parliament and the militia, and set up an arbitrary government comparable with Cromwell's.

The test originated in a debate on 28 February, when an address was voted calling for action against priests, and for oaths to be put to all officers and men in the army. The bill, read for the first time on 5 March, attempted to secure the permanent and complete exclusion of all catholics from public offices. In addition to the existing oaths of allegiance and supremacy, all office-holders must in future take the sacrament according to the rites of the Church of England, accompanied by a declaration repudiating the central catholic doctrine of transubstantiation, which was designed to close all loopholes. This bill and the enforced abandonment of the Declaration destroyed Charles's attempt to make himself absolute. James and Clifford resigned their offices as lord admiral and lord treasurer, but this tacit admission of their change of faith actually had the effect of increasing fears of catholicism and distrust of the court. Nothing less than an entire change of policy could reassure parliamentary and public opinion, but Charles was determined to continue the war, hoping that by landing the army on the Zeeland coast a decision could be reached.

By accepting the Test Act Charles suffered a major reduction in prestige and patronage powers. The act restricted the crown's choice of persons who could be employed, and James was to resent this restriction as totally unacceptable; in November 1685 he concentrated on trying to secure its repeal, and he was then to use his prerogative powers in order to circumvent it.

The Cabal was to remain actively infamous in reputation as long as the danger of absolutism continued to exist. Its policies fatally associated assertions and exercise of the royal prerogative with the advance of popery and alliance with France, and by doing so imparted an atmosphere of tension and crisis to politics that was to subside only after the Revolution of 1688. Experience of the Cabal forewarned the nation against the basically similar, if more sophisticated and elaborate, policies of James in 1686–8.

However, royal authority could be strengthened in practical ways by an alternative and fundamentally different political strategy, of depending on a conditional alliance with the Church of England and the country gentry. First, under Danby in the years after 1673, and later under more favourable circumstances and with greater success by Rochester after 1681, Charles permitted an experiment with this line of policy.

9 Danby as Lord Treasurer, 1673–8

The concessions which Charles was forced to make early in 1673 did not at first improve his position. Parliament granted money in return for the withdrawal of the Declaration of Indulgence and the acceptance of the Test Act, but the summer's naval campaign on which the money was largely spent proved indecisive. James's and Clifford's enforced retirement, instead of diminishing tension, actually confirmed suspicions and increased fears of popery. Ministers defended their individual interests rather than those of the crown, quarrelling publicly among themselves. In two short and acrimonious sessions (October–November 1673 and January–February 1674) a handful of court spokesmen tried to contain a rampant opposition which attacked ministers, introduced bills to reduce royal powers, and refused supply. Wild rumours and seditious libels, fed by Dutch propaganda, created tension and uncertainty throughout the nation.

The first step towards an improvement came when Charles, having decided not to dissolve parliament (which was now over twelve years old), replaced Clifford as lord treasurer by a comparatively obscure junior minister, Sir Thomas Osborne, in July 1673. At first only a stop-gap, Osborne (who was in 1674 to become earl of Danby) proved unexpectedly successful in a number of complementary ways and soon made himself indispensable. Improved financial administration enabled Charles to subsist. By formulating a coherent and attractive policy, and developing and using new techniques of political management, he rallied and marshalled parliamentary support for the court. So long as he was successful Charles supported and accepted Danby as his chief minister, but apart from a mutual lack of personal regard the relationship between the two men was always flawed by the divergence of their views on two crucial issues. The real and permanent basis of Danby's successful management of parliament was not, as most contemporaries believed, the use of corruption and influence, but his advocacy of specifically anglican principles and policies, and a foreign policy that repudiated the French orientation that had characterized the Cabal. But neither of these new departures in policy were really approved by Charles, and both were actively opposed by James and many of Danby's ministerial colleagues.

Danby was fully aware of royal reservations about his policies, and of his own inadequacies as a courtier. He tried to make himself secure, seeking if possible to put his tenure of office on a permanent footing. He produced three major policy initiatives—a non-resistance test in 1675, the marriage of Mary to William of Orange in 1677 and, following an alliance with the Dutch, an apparently active anti-French foreign policy in 1678. The relation between king and minister was the reverse of that during the Cabal; then Charles had made the decisions, and his ministers implemented them, but now it was the minister who led. But it was a major and ineradicable source of weakness that at no time did Danby enjoy full or sincere royal approval and support.

Danby's insecurity was further increased by his total dependence on the existing and increasingly unrepresentative parliament for his political survival. All his policies and managerial techniques were designed to maximize support in a 'standing' parliament elected long ago, in 1661. Opposition leaders knew as well as Danby that if Charles could be forced or persuaded to dissolve, the subsequent general elections could not be managed or controlled by the court, and swings in local electoral interests, combined with changes in public opinion produced by opposition propaganda, would inevitably result in a transformation. For over five years the opposition failed to force a dissolution, but the mounting frustration that resulted was itself dangerous. The longer Danby survived and the Cavalier Parliament continued, the greater was the probability that its eventual dissolution would sweep away the minister, and destroy all his methods of political control.

During the summer of 1673, Clifford's resignation left the administration drifting, while a hard-fought but inconclusive naval campaign continued. Danby, who was critically ill for weeks after his appointment, did not yet possess sufficient authority to influence Charles to end the war or to develop a distinctive policy. He faced open hostility from Arlington, who had wanted the treasury put in commission, not under a lord treasurer, and worked for the removal of a man whom he regarded as the protégé of his rival Buckingham. Moreover, the latter did not give Danby consistent support. In addition, another rival court group, headed by the idol of the old cavaliers and former lord lieutenant of Ireland, Ormonde, contained in Sir William Coventry a candidate better qualified than Danby for the administration and reform of royal finances. On another front Danby soon discovered that one of his subordinates, the chancellor of the exchequer Duncombe, was intriguing against him. Considering all these dangers, it was entirely appropriate for Shaftesbury, when swearing Danby in, to point out that the attributes that had brought him to high office differed from those that would keep him there.

Danby began by trying to reduce royal expenditure, but immediate results were modest, and he owed his emergence as chief minister largely to the mistakes and mutual enmity of his superiors. The short autumn session of parliament was disastrous for the court. On its first meeting (20 October 1673) Lord Chancellor Shaftesbury delayed ordering an immediate, formal prorogation, a delay that had damaging consequences, and which Charles and some ministers believed was deliberate and malicious. It enabled opposition members to pass an address through the Commons calling on Charles to prevent the consummation of James's second marriage (already solemnized by proxy) with Mary of Modena, and demanding that he should marry a protestant. Like James I at the time of the similarly unpopular Spanish marriage negotiations, Charles resented such representations as an invasion of his prerogative, but this extraordinarily ill-timed and provocative marriage (negotiated with French assistance) and the violent Commons' reaction against it, represent the first steps on the road to Exclusion and the Revolution of 1688. It opened up the prospect of a catholic dynasty, since there could now be little doubt of James's conversion. But a royal rebuke did not prevent a second address which used highly coloured language and arguments that were to be heard continuously for two decades: men's minds were being filled with jealousies and discontents, fears of the growth of popery were being confirmed and the king was being brought into alliances (with France) prejudicial to the protestant religion itself.

The session, lasting only a week, produced total deadlock. In the spring the Commons had attacked the Cabal's domestic policies but financed the war; now they refused supply for what was denounced as a catholic war, one into which England had been dragged by France. Some speeches were echoes of Dutch propaganda, especially du Moulin's celebrated pamphlet, *England's Appeal*. The failure of the war was used to refute the mercantilist thesis of aggressive commercial war. Particularly violent attacks were directed against the army. Complaints of soldiers' misbehaviour, forcible billeting on householders, and the alleged exercise of martial law, led to the army being voted a grievance. Fears were openly expressed that the newly raised regiments would be retained when peace came, and the expanded army used to establish arbitrary government. When the opposition proposed to start a systematic offensive against the ministers, beginning with Lauderdale, Charles checked them by a sudden prorogation.

The Commons showed themselves equally intransigent in the next session (7 January–24 February 1674), but Danby initiated a coherent court policy designed to rally moderate opinion. The opposition resisted appeals for money, and introduced bills to protect liberties and the protestant religion against encroachment and subversion. Acting on Danby's advice, Charles responded flexibly. He allowed a committee to examine the (heavily expurgated) articles of the French alliance, assuring MPs that no other treaty existed! Cosmetic actions such as banishing catholics from court, and punishing soldiers' crimes severely, were quoted to show that Charles should be trusted, and more seriously some regiments were disbanded. In private Danby was urging the conclusion of an early peace, but Charles was still claiming publicly and privately that Dutch arrogance prevented this.

Using Lord Keeper Finch, a staunch anglican and constitutionalist who had replaced Shaftesbury in November, Danby carefully and cleverly disassociated himself from the policies of the Cabal. In his opening speech to parliament Finch emphasized that a new start was to be made. Peers and MPs were flattered into seeing themselves as the agents of a new act of restoration; it was their role to revive the state, to resolve the crisis happily with a new and blessed revolution, disappointing those dangerous men 'who wait for the languishing and declination of the present government'. Both houses voted thanks (the Commons by a comfortable margin of 191 to 139). MPs also noticed a deliberate and glaring omission in the speech. It had contained nothing to vindicate the past conduct of those ministers who had served in the Cabal.

This was tantamount to announcing that Arlington and Buckingham were expendable, whereas in the previous session the prospect of attacks on ministers had led to a snap prorogation. Now both men knew that they must organize their own defence without assistance from either Charles or Danby, and consequently both followed an unprecedented course of action to avoid sharing Clarendon's fate. On 13 January, the day after the Commons voted for the removal of all obnoxious and dangerous councillors, a letter was received from Buckingham offering to explain his conduct in person. The voluntary appearance of a minister and a peer before the lower house, remarkable and unprecedented in itself, and Buckingham's stated readiness to accept the Commons as the arbiter of ministers' fate, showed that he believed that the balance of political power had shifted. Buckingham also tried to establish his credentials as a potential leader of opposition. Rather unconvincingly he put all the blame for the breaking of the Triple Alliance on Arlington, and accused him of talking of setting up 'government by an army'. Buckingham also attempted to demonstrate that he had acted and worked closely with Shaftesbury, knowing that the latter after his dismissal as lord chancellor the previous November was establishing connections with the opposition in both houses.

Buckingham's two appearances were ill-prepared and clumsily executed. He had not consulted Charles who was resentful, and he did not dissuade the Commons from voting for his removal from all offices. Buckingham's humiliation was increased by the failure of the over-ambitious attempt launched by his followers to have Arlington impeached. They were correct in thinking that only an impeachment, or the threat of one, would induce Charles to remove Arlington, but the operation required substantiation of detailed articles. After asking Charles's permission to appear in person before the Commons, Arlington put up a much more skilful defence. He explained that the council as a whole had agreed to all major policies, such as the Declaration of Indulgence, and refrained from simply blaming Buckingham and Shaftesbury, while cleverly hinting that the former had been particularly insistent on close links with France. Arlington's partisans defeated an address for his removal, but this was a private victory which if anything weakened Danby, since it ensured that Arlington retained Charles's favour, and remained a rival minister.

Danby's immediate concern was to end the Dutch war at the earliest possible date, and he used the Commons' refusal of supply to persuade the king to abandon his preference for continuing the French alliance and the war for at least another campaign. On Danby's advice, Charles reversed his previous stand by communicating to parliament peace proposals from the States General and asking for guidance. Some members argued that having no responsibility for a destructive and unnecessary war, they should leave Charles to end it as best as he could, while others tried to make mischief by raising the question of relations with, and commitments to, France. But on 27 January the Commons voted for a speedy peace; the Lords concurred on 2 February. In fact peace was quickly made, but its announcement to parliament on 11 February did not disarm the opposition. Charles accompanied his announcement of peace by a request for money to enable the army to be disbanded, to a strength smaller than that of 1663. The Commons had asked for such a reduction, but they were not prepared to pay for it, and

committed themselves to the intransigent principle 'that the continuing of any standing forces other than the militia is a great grievance
and vexatious to the people'.

As this vote showed the opposition now controlled parliamentary
business. It pressed forward with a series of bills—to improve the
efficacy of *habeas corpus*; to change judges' tenure (to the formula
quamdiu se bene gesserit) so as to render them independent of royal and
ministerial pressure; to regulate parliamentary elections, requiring
candidates to be inhabitants or property owners in the constituency;
to ensure better attendance by members at Westminster; to ease
sheriffs' monetary burdens; to disqualify papists from sitting in either
house; and to prevent the illegal exaction of money without parliamentary consent, with a clause to ensure that customs should
expire when Charles died. These proposals added up to what was
virtually an opposition programme, designed to appeal to uncommitted as well as partisan opinion by attempting to make parliament
more independent, and raising for the first time the controversial
issue of 'limitations', of an attempt to safeguard liberties under a
papist successor.

By proroguing parliament on 24 February 1674 Danby killed all
these bills, but it was now essential for him to formulate his own
distinctive ministerial policy. He had to rally the dispirited followers
of the court—anglicans in the provinces, as well as the peers and
MPs who had lost the initiative in the two last sessions. Equally
essential was his need to diminish the influence of his rivals at court,
and to find a way of persuading Charles to give him consistent
support.

By the time parliament reassembled, on 13 April 1675, Danby had
emerged as the chief minister. He now proclaimed himself the
authentic champion of the traditional principles of church and
monarchy, reviving the Clarendonian alliance with the bishops and
clergy, and appealing to old cavaliers and the moderate gentry.

Danby's astuteness and determination to establish himself for a
lengthy tenure of office could already be seen in the resourceful way
he used the peace negotiations in February 1674 to establish a lasting
connection with William of Orange. This immediately reduced the
influence of Arlington, who was replaced as secretary of state in
September by a subordinate bureaucrat, Williamson, who was useful
in developing the systematic use of patronage to build up influence
in parliament, but was not likely to become a major politician in his
own right. Competent in handling routine diplomatic business,
Williamson was also a useful link-man with the anglican clergy, and
the recommendations that emerged from a meeting which he

arranged with the bishops were to be the main planks in Danby's new policy. They called for the enforcement of the laws against both papists and dissenters, and especially for the withdrawal of the licences issued under the Declaration of Indulgence. This was done in January 1675. In addition, by good housekeeping and the bold step of temporarily suspending payment of all salaries and pensions, Danby began to gain some control over expenditure, and forced many courtiers into supplicant attitudes. Most of the extraordinary revenues voted in 1670–71 still had some years to run, so that Danby did not have to ask parliament for further supply.

Danby's object in calling the session that began in April 1675 was to make an ambitious and determined attempt to disarm, or in effect eliminate, parliamentary opposition, and so secure himself and all future ministers from the vicious attacks that had threatened or destroyed all major royal servants since the Restoration. The principle that all MPs should be subjected to a loyalty test had been suggested by the bishops in February, and was embodied in a bill introduced in the Lords on 15 April. This bill represented an elaborated version of the proposal that Clarendon had tried to rush through the thinly attended Oxford session of 1665. It stipulated that all MPs and officers must undertake not to attempt any alteration of the government as established in either church or state. This provision would have prevented any attempt at fundamental change or reforms, and would have imposed an entirely new restriction on all legislative initiatives; it was no coincidence that among Danby's closest associates was Edward Seymour, an outstandingly authoritarian and assertive Speaker, whose role would have been to disallow motions, and take steps to punish contravenors of the test.

The proposed bill also imposed on all MPs and officers the oath against the lawfulness of resistance to royal authority which clergy already had to take. This included the words 'or against those that are commissioned' by the king. Suspicions were voiced that this was intended to justify a standing army, and there was a real basis for these fears. One of the expected by-products of enforcing the laws against recusants and dissenters was a regular supply of money from fines, that Danby hoped would eventually be sufficient to pay salaries to sheriffs, justices and militia officers. The aim was avowedly the professionalization of local government, a major step in the direction of royal absolutism.

The test bill was strenuously opposed in the Lords for an almost unprecedented seventeen days, but an organized bloc of court peers, with the bishops as its nucleus, carried all the main clauses, although on one amendment the majority fell to one. By rejecting an amendment to add 'by force or fraud' to the description of the actions that would be illegal, which would legitimize constitutional attempts to make changes in existing laws, Danby confirmed suspicions that he wished to silence all effective opposition. The bill brought Shaftesbury into the open as the recognized spokesman, and soon the acknowledged leader, of the opposition. At the end of 1674 he had discussions with country opposition members, and later publicized his position in a widely circulated letter to the earl of Carlisle (3 February 1675). In this he vindicated the legitimacy of his attitudes, declaring himself ready to serve the king—but only if parliament was dissolved, and Charles undertook to have frequent parliaments in the future. Since this would mean frequent elections the entire character of politics would be transformed, greatly weakening the power of the king and of ministers who regarded themselves as primarily responsible to him. By emphasizing that he would not be bought by a mere offer of office, Shaftesbury not only asserted the purity of his motives, but skilfully made it exceedingly difficult for any other opponent of the court to accept office independently of himself, and he specifically named his main rivals for leadership of the opposition, Halifax and Sir William Coventry, as potential defectors. Finally, the letter contained one notable and deliberate omission: Shaftesbury did not denounce James, in an effort to separate him from Danby's interest.

The country opposition made detailed preparations for the session. Bills were introduced to improve *habeas corpus*, against non-parliamentary taxation, to exclude papists from parliament and to eliminate placemen. The last proposal was rejected after fiercely contested debates, the others lapsed with the prorogation. The main opposition set-piece, a formal impeachment of Danby, ended in ignominious failure. The articles were cleverly drafted to appeal to a wide range of interests; charges that he was extravagantly enriching himself, and a rapacious family, were designed to infuriate simple country gentlemen, and were substantiated by an interpretation of recent administrative changes at the exchequer as primarily a cover for massive fraud and embezzlement. Commercial interests were expected to feel aggrieved by alleged manipulation of exchequer payments. But as in so many seventeenth-century impeachments the articles could not be substantiated to the satisfaction of moderate members. Danby had received advance notice of the threat and organized an effective defence. He received support from James, who abandoned a flirtation with the opposition which had been based on his dislike of the renewed prosecutions of catholics. When the second article failed in the Commons, by 181 to 105, the opposition would have dropped the remainder. But Danby's lieutenants insisted on examining the other articles so as to discredit all the charges, and prevent their being revived in a future session.

Despite this major setback the opposition fought fiercely and achieved two propaganda successes. Alarm at the continuing increase in French power, and fear that despite Danby's public attitudes the court was still secretly sympathetic to France, found expression in violent denunciations of the recruitment of soldiers for the French service. Danby was also vulnerable because of his association with Lauderdale, the one survivor of the Cabal who retained the full confidence of Charles, because of his unique ability to control Scotland. In the opposition view Lauderdale had already achieved there what Danby was trying to do in England—the establishment of a government based on a strong standing army. Consequently, debates on Lauderdale generated bitter criticism, but voting addresses for his removal could never amount to more than a demonstration, ignored by Charles.

Nevertheless, Shaftesbury and the opposition achieved a major triumph by blocking the crucial bill for a non-resistance test. They prolonged and aggravated a conflict between the two houses over the jurisdiction of the Lords in relation to the privileges of the Commons, as posed by the case of *Shirley* v. *Fagg*. Shaftesbury championed the Lords' case, and some of his associates deliberately antagonized the Commons, provoking members into taking arbitrary action preventing a compromise settlement that would have given time and opportunity for a resumption of debates on the test. Danby coolly championed the Commons, calculating that he could in any case rely on an automatic majority in the upper house, while by favouring the lower he hoped to earn gratitude sufficient to get the test passed. His strategy was ruined in the end by the arrogance of his ally, Speaker Seymour, who by arresting lawyers for daring to plead before the Lords made a settlement impossible.

The case of *Shirley* v. *Fagg* eventually produced a complete deadlock, and necessitated a prorogation and abandonment of the test bill. Never again was Danby to come so close to achieving his objective of rendering all opposition impotent. But he could not abandon his overall political strategy of gaining control over parliament, because his own tenure of office largely depended on it. He knew that Charles was constantly tempted by an alternative line of royal policy in which parliament had no place. Indeed, shortly before parliament met again (on 13 October 1675) Charles concluded a secret agreement with Louis, by which he agreed to dissolve if parliament refused to vote supply, or showed itself hostile to France; in return he was to get an annual subsidy of £100,000. Such a dissolution would at the least mean a drastic reduction in Danby's influence and ministerial importance, the French faction at court would become predominant, and Danby's power-base in the Cavalier Parliament would disappear.

The weeks before parliament met were filled with ministerial preparations on a large scale, which amounted to the first really systematic attempt to organize a working majority. There had been talk of undertakers in the past, and Clifford and Danby had tried to influence members in 1669–70, but there had never been anything as elaborate as this campaign. The secretaries of state despatched circular letters urging all those whom they reckoned as court supporters to attend from the beginning. Lists were compiled of those who should be approached because they had a particular influence with, or over, named members, and those officially connected with ministers were also canvassed. But the estimated total of royal servants and dependants is less impressive when subjected to analysis. Most had been appointed to their positions before Danby became minister, and were not necessarily loyal to him. A few held life-offices and so could not be dismissed. Several were noted as having been absent from the last session, and there was a shortage of government servants willing and able to speak in debates and in this way to reduce the almost insupportable burden borne by the two secretaries. As a longer-term investment Danby also began to construct a bloc of pensioners. Responsibility for paying compensation to those who had formerly been concerned in farming the excise was transferred to the minister so that he would have a hold on them, and payments from secret service funds were now increasingly used to strengthen the court interest in parliament.

Contrary to the contemporary myth created by such propagandists as Marvell, the results were far from spectacular. There were only about thirty actual pensioners in the Commons. Danby's principal agent, Wiseman, reported that in addition to a hundred dependants he could undertake for another seventy-nine, and had hopes of a further ninety, if they were approached with tact and care. This would have amounted to a considerable majority, and even Danby's own lower estimate of 230 would have been enough, but in the event the highest court vote during the session was only 171; the opposition went one better, getting 172 on a crucial division.

As a result the session again ended in stalemate. Charles opened by asking for supply to repay debts and anticipations, and for building ships. He tried to meet criticism by promising to be a 'better husband' in expenditure, adding that he had not been as extravagant as some would have the world believe. He got a grudging and critical response. Some MPs argued that no extraordinary supply was needed, and there was no question of money being voted to discharge anticipations. When a grant was made (of £300,000) the

opposition tied it to an appropriation of the customs to the maintenance of the navy, which would restrict Danby's ability to alter the
pattern of expenditure. In addition his elaborate preparations
proved to be counter-productive. Opposition members attended in
strength from the start of the session, and leaders used the preparations to excite moderate members against the court. They were denounced as an insidious and indirect way of achieving the same
general objective as the abortive test of the previous session—the
subordination of parliament and the silencing of all criticism of the
executive. The Commons ordered a committee to examine 'what
members have had guineas, promises, rewards or letters to corrupt
their votes'. This reaction against ministerial intervention led to
another attempt to pass a series of laws for the preservation of allegedly
endangered liberties, but these had little chance of passing, and the
main opposition hope was to force the dissolution of the 'standing'
parliament.

The opposition did not know of Charles's contract with Louis to
dissolve, if the session proved unsatisfactory, but they had hopes of
detaching James from the court interest by promises of toleration,
including some relief for catholics. These manoeuvres enabled the
opposition to press home attacks in the Lords, where an address
calling for a dissolution was defeated (20 November) by only fifty
votes to forty-eight. This narrow vote forced Danby to prorogue; he
could not afford a weakening of his position in the upper house, since
the still unresolved case of *Shirley* v. *Fagg* was being revived in
the Commons, and if Danby again championed the cause of the
Commons he would antagonize some of his followers among the
peers. But the prorogation, announced on 22 November, took everyone by surprise because it was for the unprecedentedly long period
of fifteen months. This decision enabled Danby to retrieve his set-
backs. The length of the prorogation was successfully used to convince Louis that a subsidy should still be paid, although originally a
dissolution had been stipulated. Secondly, such a long period
without a parliament to act as the forum and focus for opposition
would certainly reduce political excitement, and Danby planned to
impose curbs on expressions of opinion during this period.

Despite his attempts to build up a bloc of reliable peers and members, Danby could not afford to ignore public opinion and the
attempts being made to influence it against him. He was under particularly damaging attack at this time. Inspired and possibly written
by Shaftesbury, a *Letter from a Person of Quality to his Friend in the
Country* appeared early in November, making a devastatingly effective appeal to popular prejudices. Based on the crude but often persuasive conspiracy theory of politics, and harnessing anticlerical feel-

ing, the argument started with the hard fact of Danby's unsuccessful test, which it claimed with justification had been intended to confer a monopoly of office and influence on old cavaliers and rigid anglicans. The pamphlet then elaborated the thesis of a design by the bishops and their political champions to establish absolutism, so trying to convert Danby's close association with Sheldon and the bench of bishops into a sinister conspiracy against liberties which allegedly went back to the time of Laud, whose name still excited execration. The continuity of this asserted conspiracy, with Danby as its current agent, also enabled the author to connect him with policies undertaken by Clarendon and Clifford, at a time when he had had no influence on major policy decisions, and to associate Danby with the raising of the army in 1672, which in reality he had disbanded as quickly as possible in 1673–4. But although the pamphlet exaggerated Danby's role as the advocate of absolutist policies, it was correct in arguing that he wished to transform the character of politics and make government more authoritarian. Another telling argument was conveyed by depicting the court as a party, that is as a section organized primarily for the purpose of benefiting its members, literally at the expense of the nation, which would have to pay twice, in money and by the loss of liberties.

The publication of the *Letter* coincided with the parliamentary session, making Danby's task more difficult. Once it was over Danby attempted to clamp down on the coffee houses which had become centres for political discussion, and the dissemination of pamphlets of all kinds. He was only very partially successful, having to abandon an attempt to suppress their licences. Nor was he able to banish opposition leaders from London to their provincial homes: Shaftesbury refused to go voluntarily, and Danby's colleagues refused to act on his suggestion that Shaftesbury should be sent to the Tower. In this proposed severity there is an indication of the frustration Danby felt at having his policies blocked. He faced a dilemma common to all authoritarian governments. Close censorship gave unlicensed pamphlets a scarcity value, leading the public to pass on and accept the wildest rumours and most scandalous libels. During the long prorogation a disturbing incident showed Danby that he could not relax control. Jenks, a City radical, used the June 1676 elections for sheriffs to make a violent and greatly applauded speech on national political issues. He claimed that a popish plot was being actively prepared to procure James's immediate succession, and called on the City authorities to petition the king to call a new parliament, on the grounds that the Cavalier Parliament had been automatically dissolved by a prorogation of more than twelve months. It was disquieting that the lord mayor had not intervened to silence

Jenks, who was in fact anticipating arguments that were to be developed by Oates and the whigs during the Popish Plot. Consequently Danby reacted with severity. Jenks was interrogated by the council and held in the Tower without trial, and strenuous (but unsuccessful) efforts were used to make him implicate Shaftesbury and Buckingham in his demonstration.

At court Danby used the long prorogation to strengthen his influence. He broke up an alliance between James and Arlington. Those who had proved unreliable were purged, including Halifax and Holles. Control over secret service money was confided to a member of his family, Charles Bertie. Canvassing and listing of MPs also continued, and extensive changes were made in the commission of the peace for all counties. Opposition pamphlets were answered, and their leaders were counter-attacked with arguments that were basically similar to those employed on their behalf: there was a conspiracy afoot, but it was by the opportunist Shaftesbury and his opposition colleagues; it went back to 'Forty-one' and had the same aims as the conspiracy that had set the kingdom ablaze with civil war, being intended to gratify the ambitions of a few restless and wicked men who were working to deceive and mislead men of good will.

As early as June 1676 a committee of the council began to prepare for the next session, which began in February 1677. At first the developments of this session seemed to indicate that Danby's position as chief minister was becoming impregnable. Shaftesbury and Buckingham committed a major error by claiming that the fifteen months prorogation had automatically dissolved parliament and that therefore all further proceedings would be invalid. Few peers agreed. The majority, egged on by Danby, treated this proposition as a scandalous reflection on parliament, and committed the two leaders (together with Wharton and Salisbury) to the Tower, thus decapitating the opposition. The Commons gave even less support to Shaftesbury's argument; although all peers would be summoned to a new parliament, many MPs suspected that they had little chance of re-election. The court managers carried all before them. The additional excise was renewed, £600,000 voted for ships, and an attempt to appropriate tunnage and poundage was defeated. But as if to confirm opposition suspicions, parliament was adjourned once the money had been voted, and in May, when the session was resumed, Charles made parliament doubt whether he really did intend to check the advance of French power, by his insistence that money must be voted before he committed himself to an active foreign policy. He rebuffed an address demanding that he inform the

Commons of his alliances as a condition for supply, treating it as a violation of his prerogative.

By responding brusquely to the Commons, adjourning parliament, and so ensuring that England would be a spectator while further French advances were made during the summer of 1677, Charles was putting Danby in a critically false position. The latter's ability to manage parliament depended on his being generally trusted to follow policies of distinctive anglicanism and independence from France. But he could never prevent Charles from considering or following policies that were quite separate from, or even directly contradictory to, his own line. An adjournment of parliament to December, and the failure to conclude any alliance with the Dutch, publicly associated Danby with the duplicity of which Charles was now suspected. In fact, in the parallel area of secret politics Danby was in even greater difficulties. James was unfriendly. Buckingham's influence was reviving immediately after he was released from the Tower. Danby could not prevent Charles renewing negotiations for a further French subsidy, and was so conscious of the precariousness of his influence that in July he allowed himself to be drawn into these negotiations, if only over the mechanics of the amount of money, and how and when it was to be paid, and not over the political content of the agreement.

The failure to do anything to check France made it imperative for Danby to rehabilitate his reputation, and although he was primarily an unscrupulous political operator concerned to secure himself, he was increasingly and genuinely alarmed by the dangerous consequences of Louis's advances. The conquest of the whole Spanish Netherlands was now possible. William's credit in Holland, and with his allies, was shaken by a series of defeats. His Dutch republican opponents were eager for peace, and ready to play off France against their own *stadtholder*. Similarly the pro-French elements at Whitehall would become stronger if Louis could dictate peace. One course of action offered a solution to all these problems; by concluding a closer connection with William, by bringing him into English affairs through a marriage with James's daughter Mary, Danby could hope to consolidate his own position, keep Charles to an anti-French line which the national interest demanded, and even in the very long term perhaps perpetuate his own administration, by winning the favour of the most probable heir after Charles's death (since James was generally expected to pre-decease his brother).

The marriage solemnized on 4 November 1677 put Danby in a position to construct what in the next century was called a reversionary interest. Danby could hope to combine continued favour with the reigning monarch with the promise of its future continuation. But in practice shorter-term considerations were paramount. In concert with William, Danby first attempted to gain a diplomatic triumph, by persuading Louis to concede more generous terms than the European situation warranted. When this failed Danby was ready to risk all-out war against France. He calculated that anti-French feelings were sufficiently strong to persuade parliament to vote supply, and from his ministerial angle there were now advantages in making Charles depend on parliament. This would make Danby absolutely indispensable as the one minister capable of managing both houses. War would break clandestine royal negotiations with Louis, and convince the latter that Charles could not be trusted and therefore was not worth purchasing by subsidies. War would also increase the amount of patronage at Danby's disposal, and enhance further the importance of his unrivalled ability to maintain royal solvency.

For a time a clear policy emerged. On 31 December an alliance was signed with the Dutch, setting out the terms for peace which Charles undertook to obtain—if necessary by the use of force. A general alliance followed in March 1678. Parliament was told that treaties had been concluded, and in asking for supply to raise an army of 30–40,000 men and a fleet, Charles indicated that he would accept appropriation of the money voted for their maintenance. The army was levied very quickly, and an advance force was sent to save Ostend in February.

The sequel is one of the most confused periods of this or any other reign, with Commons and king reproaching each other for neglecting the interests of the nation in the face of the French threat. Charles was pursuing two entirely contradictory policies simultaneously, one public, one secret. On 17 May he negotiated a secret agreement with Louis, promising disbandment of the army, prorogation of parliament and neutrality in return for a subsidy. What Charles did not know was that Louis was already subsidizing his most bitter opponents in the Commons, encouraging them to obstruct all royal policies, and especially supply. Some of these French pensioners encouraged the opposition to pitch demands at an unrealizably high level, proposing that no peace should be made except on the basis of the 1659 Pyrenees Treaty, forcing Louis to abandon all his acquisitions. A poll tax was voted, but this was accompanied by a three-year prohibition on the import of French commodities, which would reduce revenue from customs.

Leaders of the country opposition spread suspicions and distrust. They made charges that the army was being raised only on the pretext of foreign war, but was really intended to serve as the basis of arbitrary government at home. Consequently when at the end of

May Louis and the States General were apparently on the point of
concluding a truce, and an early peace came into prospect, the
Commons voted £619,000 for disbanding. To complicate matters
Louis then refused to evacuate some of his conquests, until lost
possessions were restored to his Swedish ally. Danby clumsily
attempted to exploit the danger that the war would be prolonged
by demanding an increase of £300,000 a year in the ordinary revenue,
that is for the rest of the reign. The Commons refused even to consider this, but voted extraordinary grants specifically for disbanding.

Yet most of the army was still in being in October, even though
France and the Dutch signed the Treaty of Nijmegen on 31 July. It
is impossible to penetrate Danby's real intentions at this time, but it
does appear that he seriously contemplated using the army to maintain his own and the king's authority, perhaps in conjuction with a
dissolution of parliament, and a period of ruling without calling
another. Otherwise it is difficult to understand why he did not
disband as quickly as possible (as in 1673–4) in order to save money.
James, as before in 1673 and later in 1679, was advocating a very
strong line—dissolution, the arrest of opposition leaders and a permanent increase in army strength. In the next year Danby made
similar suggestions from the Tower, but by then the crisis had come.
In 1678 Charles was unwilling to commit himself so irrevocably, or
to identify himself too closely with a minister whose policies were
beginning to go wrong.

This examination of Danby's difficulties shows how deceptive appearances could be. For opposition MPs and pamphleteers (like
Marvell) Danby was the infinitely powerful and devious puppet-
master, controlling the weak Charles, and manipulating packs of
corrupt officers, peers and members. The opposition after years of
frustration feared that his hold on power was impregnable, and that
one of his attempts to establish royal and ministerial absolutism must
inevitably succeed. In reality the impression of full power and per-
manence was illusory. Apart from the failures to establish himself by
the test in 1675, or by war in 1678, Danby at no time enjoyed
security of ministerial tenure. He could never rely on Charles. Many
of his parliamentary dependants were equally unreliable. He could
monitor and contain, but never eliminate, French influence and intrigues at court. Most important of all Danby, unlike Walpole and
Newcastle in the next century, presided over and sought to exploit a
system of politics that was not in equilibrium. Charles and Danby
feared parliament; the country opposition believed that king and
minister were working to undermine the constitution. Danby absolutely depended on the employment in a standing parliament of
managerial techniques that would make it very difficult for courtiers

to gain re-election, if general elections ever took place. The opposition believed that these techniques were not being used for the merely routine business of maintaining a working majority, but were part of a design to destroy parliamentary independence. They feared either that a captive parliament would be used as the instrument by which absolutism would be established, or that French assistance would make Charles sufficiently independent to enable him to dispense with parliament for all time. Politics were already in a chronic state of tension and generalized suspicions, even before the 'revelations' of the Popish Plot in the autumn of 1678 excited the most violent passions and hysteria throughout the nation.

10 The Exclusion Crisis

The Popish Plot precipitated the Exclusion Crisis of 1679–81 which threatened at times to erupt into a major revolution. Remembering the pattern of events after 1640 many men pessimistically predicted a similar series of disasters—civil war, social upheaval and, as a likely consequence of any appeal to force, the imposition of arbitrary government in the form of either an absolute monarchy (as in France after the Frondes), or another military dictatorship resembling the harsh rule of the Rump, and of Cromwell and his major-generals. In the event there was no violence, despite the seriousness of the crisis. At first sight this is surprising, considering that political excitement rose at times to the point of general hysteria, and that passionate partisanship eventually engulfed a high percentage of the whole population, producing a division into two bitterly hostile factions.

The main explanation for the absence of violence is that the whole character of politics was transformed at the onset of the crisis. Active participation had been confined for years to a small segment of the nation, the officials and dependants of the court and members of the increasingly unrepresentative parliament. The dissolution of the 'standing' Cavalier Parliament in January 1679 destroyed the obstacle that had dammed up politics, and in place of stagnation a torrent of changes and developments swept away Danby's policies and systems of management. In this altered situation the new parliament, and especially the Commons, became the focus of all politics as whig energies were concentrated for over two years on attempts to enact the bill excluding James from the succession, which gave its name to the crisis.

This concentration made the first whigs an essentially parliamentary movement. Their most successful appeal to the people took the form of organizing mass petitions demanding that Charles should let parliament meet; their propaganda constantly emphasized the rights of parliament, and their party organization reached its highest stage of development in the 1681 parliamentary elections. As whig leader, Shaftesbury subordinated everything to Exclusion, spending all the resources and energies of the whigs on the unsuccessful campaign to pass it into law. But by convincing his followers that success was ultimately certain he kept them disciplined and under his control as a parliamentary movement for most of the period of crisis, and it was only in the desperate last stages that some whigs turned to consider using extra-parliamentary methods—a *coup d'état*, assassination of Charles and James or a general insurrection.

This concentration on enacting a single measure also meant that the Exclusion parliaments proved to be legislatively barren. The crisis produced not statutes but parties. Shaftesbury created the first whigs, the earliest recognizable party. By doing so he divided the nation and called into existence as a counterweight the first tories. Both whigs and tories are unmistakably parties, units far more coherent, disciplined, organized and united than mere aggregates of groups and interests based on family or territorial connections. But if parties came into existence, this did not mean recognition of a party system. The rage of party was such that neither whigs nor tories would acknowledge that the behaviour and principles of their opponents were legal and constitutional. Each party claimed that it exclusively represented the well-affected majority of the nation, and denounced the other as a self-seeking and subversive faction. The whigs believed that their policy of Exclusion was opposed only by a parasitical court and its creatures, who were subservient to James and secretly sympathetic to catholicism. The tories despised the whigs as comprising a mass of the rabble, led by a clique of conspirators who cynically exploited alleged grievances and the protestant religion in order to gratify their lust for power.

By maintaining the newly raised army throughout the summer of 1678, despite the end of the European war, and by using for its maintenance money that parliament had voted for disbanding, Danby was taking a dangerous risk. Certain parliamentary resentment at such an illegal diversion of funds could easily develop into more generalized fears that this army was intended to be used to establish arbitrary government. Unknown to Danby and Charles its continued existence also disturbed Louis. He had destroyed the confederation of European powers by inducing the States General to make a separate peace at Nijmegen, regardless of their allies' interests and despite William's opposition. In order to perpetuate and deepen William's isolation Louis now set out to nullify the Anglo-Dutch alliance. Charles was ready to promise that it would be a dead letter, in return for a subsidy, but Louis did not trust Danby. The latter had been responsible for the marriage between William and Mary, he had threatened war against France and, so long as the army existed, he was a potential obstacle to the development of new French expansionist policies. Barrillon, the French ambassador in London, was therefore given instructions to undermine the lord treasurer by exploiting the close relationship which he had formed with a section of the country opposition, who were now reinforced by the former ambassador in Paris, Ralph Montagu.

This prepared attack would probably have destroyed Danby on its own, but his difficulties were greatly increased by the 'discovery' in the autumn of the Popish Plot. The excitement which the alleged revelations generated, the sensational events which followed in quick and unpredictable succession, supplied a popular dimension to politics. Parliament, judges and juries now came under popular pressure. The country opposition which had for years been accusing the court of neglecting to enforce the laws against the catholics now tried to claim a monopoly of anti-papist zeal, and aimed to take over investigation of the revelations.

Despite Charles's own suspicions, it is very unlikely that the original discoveries were the work of the opposition. August, then as now a politically dead season, was a poor choice for attracting publicity. The informers were obscure or disreputable—Israel Tonge, a crazy visionary, Titus Oates, a disgraced clergyman who had lived on Jesuit charity while feigning conversion, threadbare adventurers with bogus military titles like Bedloe and (later) Dangerfield, dissatisfied or discarded servants of catholic notables (Bolron, Dugdale). Their stories of Jesuit plots to murder Charles, set fire to London (again), raise a catholic army and incite a foreign invasion, lacked novelty. Under questioning before the council, later in law courts presided over by indulgent judges, their evidence was frequently exposed as badly constructed and riddled with improbabilities and contradictions. Yet this band of shabby perjurers set the nation ablaze with fear and apprehension, and precipitated a prolonged crisis.

The underlying reasons for their influence and persuasiveness have to be related to the deep-rooted protestant tradition in English history. John Foxe's thesis in *Actes and Monuments* that England had a national destiny to fulfil in advancing the interests of true religion was still one of the most powerful influences colouring English attitudes. Even though successive kings and ministers neglected to act the role of militant champions of European protestantism, England remained vulnerable as a prime target for papist malice and aggression. Catholicism was identified in the public mind with foreign influences, and specifically with the great European power which possessed or threatened to possess a dominant position—Spain in the first half of the century, Louis xiv in the years after 1661—to the point where not only English interests but national independence itself were threatened. Both these powers successively intervened in English domestic politics, building up an interest at court, and protected native catholics. Consequently, in the defensive struggle which contemporaries believed they were fighting against the growth of foreign-supported catholicism, the protestant religion was equated with national integrity and independence.

The strength and persistence of this hatred and fear of catholicism give an indication of a deep-seated sense of insecurity and generalized apprehension about the future. The catholics numbered less than two per cent of the total population and (apart from London) their main pockets of strength were in remote and backward rural areas, and most catholic laymen were known by their neighbours to be politically inactive and innocuous. The danger was believed to derive from hidden or secret catholics, 'protestants in masquerade', many of them in high office and strategic places, whose number defied estimation but was usually grotesquely overstated. Furthermore, catholic laymen were thought to be dominated by the politically active and fanatical clerical firebrands, especially the Jesuits, who were plotting to seize and utilize the machinery of the state to achieve elimination of heresy. Allegations that they would coerce, depose or even assassinate sovereigns, break faith and repudiate agreements once they had served their purpose, engage in merciless persecution as a means of procuring conversions, were demonstrated by citing the familiar events of Mary's reign. Following the collapse of the Commonwealth and the eclipse of republicanism, the catholic church alone offered a clear, coherent and comprehensive challenge to every aspect of the established order. Its highly disciplined organization had defied a century's intermittent attempts to suppress it. Catholics were united by common loyalty to the pope, and possessed the motive and dedication to attempt the overthrow of the existing order (moral, social and intellectual as well as political and ecclesiastical), replacing it with an alternative that was based on totally different principles and practices.

Developments after 1673 seemed to give immediate substance to these fears. James's absence from anglican worship and his resignation of all English offices left little doubt that if Charles died first he would be succeeded by a catholic. James's second wife made their household a centre of catholic activity, rather as Henrietta Maria had done. As earlier in the century, the court generally was highly suspect, despite Danby's pursuit of a distinctively anglican policy. Unfortunately for him the charges that he was secretly favouring popery, made with particular venom by the poet and opposition MP Andrew Marvell in his *Account of the Growth of Popery and Arbitrary Government*, began to acquire some plausibility just before the outbreak of the Popish Plot. His new political alliance with James largely effaced the favourable impression Danby had hoped to make by the marriage of Mary to William. The retention of the expanded army deepened suspicions, and the discovery that many of the officers were papists recently returned from the French service contributed to the belief that there was an actual design to establish both popery and absolute government.

The first revelations accused catholic conspirators of preparing to murder Charles, massacre protestants and introduce an army from abroad. Charles was sceptical after he caught Oates in lies when he appeared before the council on 29 September, and treated the plot as no more than a threat against his life, playing down the wider implications. He also intended to reserve the investigation to routine administrative methods—the council and the judges—but made a damaging mistake by failing to ensure that this was done. Danby was obliged to probe the evidence thoroughly. He needed to discover whether the informers had been primed by any prominent opponent (or aspiring colleague). He expected to keep the witnesses under control, since they had at first addressed themselves to the ministers, and probably calculated that the dangerous situation which their evidence would reveal could be used to justify retention of the newly raised army regiments. By energetic investigation he would demonstrate his own protestant zeal.

In addition to denouncing priests who had befriended him, Oates named Edward Coleman as a principal conspirator. Coleman had acted as secretary first to James and then to the duchess, serving them as confidential agent, and was well known as a catholic lobbyist at Westminster. When he was arrested a cache of his correspondence was seized, dating back to 1675. Some of it was highly incriminating, showing that a trusted member of James's entourage had been discussing with foreign catholic notables (including Louis's Jesuit confessor) detailed schemes to dissolve parliament, establish toleration and advance catholic interests. Nothing could have been more damaging in implicating James, whom Oates had unimaginatively cleared of any complicity in the plot. When all the letters were deciphered they were to provide the basis of the case for Exclusion.

A second sensational development had even more explosive, although short-term, effects. Oates swore his information on 28 September before a prominent magistrate, Sir Edmund Berry Godfrey, who was known to be sympathetic to dissenters. This may make it appear surprising that Godfrey at once gave Coleman a warning about Oates's allegations, but Coleman had established contacts with London magistrates, on James's behalf, as part of a campaign to stop prosecutions of both recusants and dissenters. The real surprise is that Coleman then destroyed only his most recent letters, but kept incriminating correspondence from three years back. What happened next is an impenetrable mystery. Godfrey disappeared. On 17 October his body was found. Contemporaries mourned him as the first victim of the papists. Hysterical fears of an impending massacre of all protestants gripped London, and anti-papist excitement quickly enveloped all sections of the population, provincial as well as metropolitan. Godfrey's murder and Coleman's letters apparently provided irrefutable proof of the plot, and the common danger necessitated emergency measures.

It is not surprising that defendants fared badly in the series of trials that began in November. Thirteen were condemned either for treason (complicity in the plot to assassinate Charles) or for Godfrey's murder, and another three were executed for officiating as priests. Judges freely admitted hearsay evidence, often introduced cases with prejudicial statements about the plot in general, displayed bias in summing up the evidence and disparaged defence witnesses. Not until July 1679, when Sir George Wakeman (formerly physician to the queen) and three Benedictines were acquitted, were Oates and the other prosecution witnesses subjected to any severe question-ing, and in that case their evidence was shot to pieces. However, they had by then left an indelible impression on the public mind; it was from the quickly published and widely circulated accounts of the trials that the people obtained most of their information about the plot and its ramifications.

In the autumn session of 1678 both Lords and Commons quickly exploited popular excitement to justify taking what was effectively executive action. Oates and other informers were heard at the bar of the Commons, and the lord chief justice was asked to arrest the catholic peers whom he named. The two houses appointed com-mittees empowered to send for men and papers, to inquire into the plot, and to suggest remedies. Specific actions were demanded: the lord mayor was virtually instructed to increase security precautions, and the Commons sent the council a list of suspects who were to be named in a proclamation. Interrogatory committees of peers and MPS subjected Coleman to intensive and repeated questioning. He could have saved his life by implicating James, with incalculable effects, but he gave nothing away. Nevertheless his letters inevitably brought James's position into question. The Commons passed an additional test bill to exclude catholics (including peers) from parlia-ment. In the Lords Shaftesbury raised, but did not press, a sugges-tion that James might be thought to be obstructing investigation of the plot. On 4 November his opposition lieutenants in the Commons formally proposed that James should be barred from the king's presence and councils. On direct instructions from Charles this was strenuously resisted by court members, and on 6 November the latter counter-attacked by demanding investigation of another aspect of Coleman's activities—his distribution of French money to (mainly opposition) MPS.

On 9 November Charles took a major initiative. It was he who first explicitly raised the whole general issue of the succession, and put forward at this early stage the policy of 'limitations', which was to be offered as the royal alternative to Exclusion throughout the crisis. Charles promised assent to

> such reasonable bills as should be presented, to make them safe in the reign of any successor, so as they tend not to impeach the right of succession, nor the descent of the crown in the true line.

Significantly limitations imposed on royal powers must not apply either in Charles's own lifetime, or in the reign of any future protestant sovereign. Charles proceeded to give a firm lead to the court. Secretary Williamson, sent to the Tower by the Commons for signing army commissions to catholics, was promptly freed. A militia bill which would have put it temporarily out of royal control was vetoed. Danby after some hesitation earlier now committed himself to James, rallying support to insert a proviso exempting him from the new test bill; this passed in the Commons by 158 to 156 (21 November). These were severe checks to the opposition, and nothing would be further from the truth than to assume that the Plot revelations automatically gave it the ascendancy. If it was to regain the initiative it was necessary to widen the attack on the court, to fix in the public mind the danger of absolutism as well as that from popery.

A group of opposition members had it in their power to destroy Danby from 11 November, when the Commons upheld the election of Ralph Montagu for Northampton, so giving him the protection of privilege. After being dismissed as ambassador in Paris he had retained correspondence incriminating Danby in negotiations for a French subsidy, at a time when he had been asking parliament for money and raising an army for a war against France. Danby suspected that an attack was impending, but it was delayed by opposition fears that it would be unsafe to launch a deadly attack until the army had been disbanded, and so was no longer available for a ministerial coup. Eventually Danby got in his attack first. On 19 December orders were given to seize Montagu's papers on the grounds that he had been negotiating without authorization with the papal nuncio in Paris. At this point Montagu revealed his secret

papers, which had already been read by some of his principal opposition colleagues. These were produced and read in the house. Using
carefully prepared tactics, and taking full advantage of the spontaneous reaction of those uninstructed members for whom these
papers confirmed all their worst suspicions of ministerial duplicity, the
opposition pressed lethally effective charges against Danby, and at
the end of the debate the Commons voted by 179 to 116 that there
was sufficient matter for an impeachment.

This was effectively the end of Danby—and of the Cavalier
Parliament. The opposition ascendancy was now such that the
Commons disregarded papers produced by Charles Bertie, Danby's
confidential agent, implicating opposition leaders in French intrigues. On 21 December recommittal of the draft articles of impeachment was rejected by 179 to 135, the word 'traitorous' retained by
179 to 141, and the absurd allegation that Danby was 'popishly
affected' was voted by 143 to 119. The Commons at least was now
out of Danby's control, even though the Lords declined to commit
him into custody. Indeed there was now a real danger that the whole
court would be dragged down by the disintegration of Danby's
power and influence. To gain time for radically new moves and
manoeuvres, Charles prorogued parliament on 30 December, dissolved
it on 24 January, and called a new one to meet on 6 March 1679.

Dissolution of the Cavalier Parliament had for long been
Shaftesbury's immediate objective. Now it took place under
optimum conditions for the opposition. The revelations of Danby's
duplicity did not actually corroborate any evidence given about the
plot—but corroboration had not been demanded in ordinary plot
trials either. For most contemporaries it was enough to show that
there was a popish plot, and now a parallel design to establish absolutism. Spontaneous excitement caused by the Plot was still high
during the early months of 1679, but there was as yet no general
polarization into hostile parties, and the elections were certainly not
fought over the issue of Exclusion. Indeed these first months of 1679
were a time of flux: Danby's fall left a political vacuum, and the
dissolution of the standing Cavalier Parliament broke up the old
political patterns.

Two factors determined the new pattern that was to persist
throughout the crisis. First, Charles emerged as a politician in his own
right, quite unrecognizable compared with the usually indolent but
intermittently active figure of past years. This meant that Danby
had no successor as chief minister, and the startling moves of the
spring were made on Charles's own initiative. He created a
European sensation by sending James abroad just before parliament
met; despite an accompanying and widely publicized statement by

Charles that he had never been married to anyone but the queen, James (and virtually everyone else) wrongly interpreted this exile as the preliminary to his being abandoned in favour of Monmouth. Charles gained peace of mind from exiling James, who had been pressing him to adopt the most provocative repressive measures, such as arresting opposition leaders, garrisoning the Tower to overawe London and dissolving parliament. This advice was more suited to fighting a civil war than avoiding one, but then James was convinced that a rebellion was inevitable if Charles resisted Exclusion.

It is perhaps surprising, and it was certainly a gross mistake on his part, that Shaftesbury did not correctly evaluate Charles's new style, his new-found determination. Quite rightly Shaftesbury did not trust Charles, but quite wrongly he persisted in seeing him as weak and irresolute. He was not impressed by Charles's second sensational move, the dissolution of the privy council and its replacement (announced on 21 April) by a council of an entirely new type. Smaller in size (thirty members), it was to include independent and even opposition politicians, with the theoretical aim of resolving differences and problems before they hardened into open political rifts. James was staggered by Shaftesbury's appointment as lord president of this new council, and by the inclusion of others who he regarded as his inveterate enemies—Halifax and Essex, an honest but easily led opposition peer who became first treasury commissioner. Sunderland, not an obvious choice, was appointed secretary of state.

This surprise move demonstrates Charles's skill as a tactician, and also the limits of what tactics could achieve. He opened up dazzling opportunities to a complete new set of aspiring politicians who had been blocked by Danby's dominance—Halifax, Sunderland, Laurence Hyde, Godolphin, Essex and several of Shaftesbury's lieutenants. Shaftesbury himself was enticingly tempted with what he could easily convert into the position of chief minister for his remaining years, and had he (and Essex) been no more than insatiably ambitious opportunists this move would have won them for the Court and disrupted the opposition. In any case many of the opposition rank and file feared that their leaders were about to defect and renege on their principles.

In reality, Shaftesbury resisted temptation. The second new factor which determined the character of the Exclusion Crisis was of course his decision to commit himself and the opposition irrevocably to the policy of Exclusion. This commitment was increasingly to produce political polarization, it made Shaftesbury's leadership of the opposition virtually impregnable, and the necessity for its passage gave his followers cohesion and determination. The whig strategy of insisting on Exclusion could not be deflected by such clever tactical

moves as the new privy council, but from the first it rested on a
fallacious estimate by Shaftesbury of Charles's character and intentions. It depended on the assumption that, as so often in the recent
past, Charles would give way before sustained pressure, whatever he
said or promised to the contrary. There was therefore from the start
a fatal flaw in the arguments which Shaftesbury used to justify the
concentration on passing Exclusion, which he now imposed on his
followers, in parliament and in the country.

Shaftesbury made Exclusion the central opposition policy in the
course of the 1679 session, but it was not an issue during the
February elections. The main factor which produced such sweeping
changes in representation (over 320 places changed hands) was the
length of time that had elapsed since the last elections: of the members who were displaced 170 had been elected in 1661, and another
fifty-five at by-elections during the 1660s. Representation remained
unchanged in only thirty-four double and seven single member constituencies. Many members had neglected to look after their local
interest, or had quarrelled with their patrons or former associates.
After so many years without opportunities, there was intense competition for seats, with new families and a new generation of candidates thrusting themselves forward. Consequently, attempts made
to arrange for an agreed distribution of seats by means of informal
county meetings of gentry, so as to avoid contests and expense, did
not often succeed. A few attempts at guidance by lords lieutenant
were resented by electors and independent candidates, and the
attempts of returning officers to favour associates of Danby were
fiercely denounced. Dependants of the court, and especially those who
had been named in pamphlets as pensioners, found themselves at a
serious disadvantage. Popular electorates were influenced against
them, Danby could offer them no assistance (he found great difficulty in obtaining seats for his own family), and the court had fewer
than thirty places at its disposal. There was little time in any case for
systematic direction or intervention from the centre, by either the
court or Shaftesbury and his associates. These elections of the spring
of 1679 were largely decided by the interplay of local forces, with the
revulsion against Danby and his methods of parliamentary management as a background factor. The issues which were to dominate
proceedings in the next three parliaments hardly surfaced at all.

The sweeping changes produced by the elections led to widely
discrepant estimates of the composition and likely character of the
new parliament. Some observers estimated court strength as low as
thirty, but Charles was initially reassured by the return of men of
substance, who he thought would have a moderating influence.
Shaftesbury probably knew more about the world of politics than

anyone: in a systematic analysis he divided those members who had sat in the Cavalier Parliament and were re-elected into 153 opponents and ninety-eight supporters of the court. Those who had not sat in the last parliament divided into sixty potential courtiers, 149 likely opponents, with thirty-six doubtful. But these estimates, like the impressionistic ones that were current, derived from past attitudes towards Danby and his policies. With Danby's removal from the office of lord treasurer (13 March) and the emergence of Exclusion in May as the central issue, entirely new alignments were bound to develop.

The first weeks of the new parliament were very confused. Danby provoked an explosive reaction by arranging as compensation for his loss of office a promotion in the peerage, and a pension of £5,000 a year, as well as a pardon. An incensed Commons renewed impeachment proceedings. On the first day of the session, 6 March, Charles acting under Danby's advice rejected the Commons' choice of Speaker, Edward Seymour, and tried to install a nominee of his own, so antagonizing the new house at the very outset. Eventually a compromise candidate, Gregory, was accepted but opposition spokesmen used the bitter dispute to inflame feelings against the court. They set out systematically to educate the new members. Oates and other witnesses were heard at the bar of the house, extracts from the *Journals* about the plot were reproduced, and the key committee of secrecy (twelve of its fifteen members were prominent opponents of the court) timed its reports so as to influence proceedings.

The opposition leaders in the Commons did not slavishly follow Shaftesbury's lead, and some of the new and necessarily inexperienced members achieved a rather premature influence when, at the end of April, several of the former recognized spokesmen for the country opposition were compromised by being named to the new privy council. Too much time was given to attacks against Danby, but an actual impeachment presented such formidable legal and organizational problems that it could not be mounted quickly; Danby could be expected to put up a stubborn defence, and the pardon he had received from the king might be used by his friends in the lords, who included almost all the bishops, to bar any impeachment. It would have been wiser to begin with an impeachment of one of the five catholic peers accused of complicity in the Plot, and this could also have been used to deter Charles from attempting an early prorogation or dissolution, which could be represented as an attempt to stifle punishment of high-placed plotters. But the attacks made on Danby enabled the opposition to develop the theme that liberties as well as religion were being endangered by a design to establish absolutism by the popish plotters.

From this position it was easy to move, on 27 April, to the crucial
vote that James, being a papist, had given the greatest encouragement to the plot. This vote compelled Charles to make a stand. On
30 April he repeated his readiness to ensure that the powers of a
papist successor should be limited. The latter was to give up all
ecclesiastical patronage, and appointments to the great offices of
state and the judicial bench were to be made by parliament, as well
as those of JPs, lords lieutenant and deputies. This offer did not
deflect Shaftesbury and his supporters from pressing on with
Exclusion, but it was essential from Charles's point of view that,
when Exclusion was proposed, both parliament and the nation
should be aware that an alternative existed.

The case against limitations was twofold. First there was doubt as
to whether Charles could be trusted when he made this apparently
straightforward offer of guarantees. Montagu's revelations had
shown that Charles as well as Danby had deliberately deceived parliament in 1678 over the intended war against France, and by this
time nobody could have any real faith in what Charles said or promised. Limitations could prove to be a trap. Their enactment would
involve a mass of time-consuming, detailed legislation. The court
could engage in effective obstruction, especially in the Lords, in
what were relatively short sessions, and nothing could be easier than
to kill the necessary bills by a prorogation. By contrast the Exclusion
bill was short and simple. Its passage would involve few technical
difficulties, and it had the great merit of being immediately intelligible to all.

Secondly, it was doubtful whether limitations, even if enacted in a
statute, would be constitutionally binding on a catholic successor. It
was argued that (as after Henry VII's accession) all such legislation
would be invalidated by the fact of James becoming king.
Furthermore, a sovereign could free himself from restrictions by
using his dispensing power or, as in 1662 and 1672, the suspending
power. Limitations in the whig view would delude the people with
security, when in fact none existed. The case for Exclusion was first
openly developed on 11 May, as the only way of providing security
for religion and liberties, but the weightier speeches in the debate
were made against the proposal and were delivered by former opposition spokesmen (Capel, Cavendish and Powle) who were now
members of the new council. But at the end of the debate the court
yielded the question for fear of exposing their numerical weakness.
When a division was challenged, on the second reading on 21 May,
the court was heavily defeated by 207 to 128, although the number
of abstentions (almost exactly one third of the house) came as a
surprise.

The arguments in favour of Exclusion were simple and intelligible to all, including the politically unsophisticated masses. It was alleged that James's conversion to catholicism had so antagonized a fiercely protestant nation that he knew he could never rely on voluntary cooperation in government by his subjects. This would leave him with no alternative but to rule as an absolute king. The principles of catholicism were identified by the whigs with absolutism, those of protestantism with the law and the constitution. James would have to make constant use of his prerogative powers and rely on an army; only from the court, catholic Ireland and France could he be assured of support, an unholy trinity indeed. Furthermore, James was known to have a high interpretation of the royal prerogative, and to be impatient of legal restraints.

The Exclusion bill was deceptively simple. It disabled James by name, with the succession going to the next in line—James's protestant daughter, Mary—and it also perpetuated James's banishment and rendered treasonable any attempt to uphold his right. But this was only the first, if decisive step. Once James had been excluded, and all his active supporters proscribed by making treasonable any upholding of his rights, it would be possible to amend the provision about the succession—it was this possibility that kept Charles's illegitimate son Monmouth in hopes—as well as to impose significant restrictions on the prerogative. Limitations were rejected as a substitute for Exclusion, but they would have been welcomed as an additional set of measures applying to all future rulers. Acceptance of Exclusion by Charles would have amounted to an act of surrender, leaving him with reduced powers as a 'Doge of Venice', and rendering the monarchy permanently dependent on parliament.

Charles made his opposition clear in council and proceeded to prorogue parliament (27 May), and then dissolve (12 July). This not only killed Exclusion, but gave its opponents the opportunity to challenge Shaftesbury's supporters in fresh elections. In this they relied heavily on lords lieutenant to give a lead to the loyal gentry, and the clergy made themselves conspicuous in supporting anti-Exclusionist candidates. The results were unimpressive. In many constituencies, notably London, loyal candidates could not risk a poll, and the exclusionists won particularly clear victories in some county elections. Thirty-two of those who had voted for Exclusion (15.4 per cent) did not retain their seats; of the members who had voted against the bill the number was forty-nine (38.3 per cent). It is more difficult to be precise about the affiliations and opinions of those newly elected, but at least sixty-two can be identified as whigs in the next session, but only twenty-nine as tories.

There is some evidence of more electoral organization on the whig side, but the main development was the unprecedentedly large output of electoral propaganda in the form of pamphlets and newspapers which depicted those who voted against Exclusion as betrayers of the liberties and religion of the nation—some (especially former pensioners of Danby) as conscious traitors, others as the dupes of the court. But widespread and effective political organization developed not so much during the generally rather one-sided parliamentary elections of August and September 1679, as in the subsequent campaign of mass agitation, through petitions calling for parliament to be allowed to meet.

At the time of the elections many whigs feared that a long parliamentary session was not to be expected, but Charles's tactic of successively proroguing parliament (seven times, for a period of just over a year, from 7 October 1679 until it met on 21 October 1680) took them by surprise. This prerogative power of prorogation and dissolution, which Charles I had fatally surrendered in 1641, was the ace in the royal pack. Shaftesbury could never counter its use, but he did succeed in preserving the unity and morale of the whigs during the months without parliament, and he actually extended popular support for Exclusion. The mass petitions organized during the winter were not expected to achieve their ostensible objective of forcing Charles to concede an early session of parliament, but were rather a device to maintain pressure on the crown and court by ensuring that political activity and interest continued at an abnormally high level. Petitions educated public opinion in the case for Exclusion, their unfavourable reception by Charles perpetuated suspicion of the court. Petitioning necessitated mass organization and publicization of the whig case. Canvassers were employed in large numbers, deputations were carefully selected to present the subscribed petitions to Charles, and whig journalists took care to report successes and play down the occasional failures.

On his side Charles also took action. Recognizing the influence of the opposition press, prosecutions for seditious libel were ordered and a series of trials during the summer of 1680 (Care, Curtis, Smith and Harris) temporarily silenced most of the whig journalists, although pamphlets continued to appear. Charles went out of his way to snub whig petitioners, but he imitated their technique by encouraging the organization of direct answers or repudiations in the form of 'abhorrences', addresses denouncing petitions as unconstitutional attempts to put the king under improper pressure. Some of these abhorrences received popular support, although most originated from official bodies such as loyal corporations, but the challenge which they posed to Shaftesbury's claim to represent the nation added to the animosity between the two factions, into which an increasingly large part of the nation was now being sharply divided. Another development added to whig fears and anger. A sham 'Meal-tub Plot' was discovered in the autumn of 1679; this was an attempt by catholic militants to plant incriminating papers on whig activists, suggesting that they were contemplating treasonable resistance to the crown.

The whigs were also alarmed by the other main developments during the prorogation—the revival of James's influence, and the purging of the administration. Charles fell seriously ill in August 1679, and although he quickly recovered, the leading ministers (Sunderland, Halifax and Essex) had already recalled James from exile, fearing that Charles's death would plunge the country into civil war. James agreed to withdraw again only on conditions: his place of exile was changed to Edinburgh, where the Scottish admin-istration was put in his hands, and a balance was created by sending Monmouth abroad to Holland, although the latter was not deprived of his offices. But when Monmouth returned without leave in Nov-ember, using as a pretext the fact that he had been named in the sham Meal-tub Plot, he was stripped of all his offices, and left de-pendent for reinstatement on the promises made to him by Shaftesbury and the whigs. It is from this time that Monmouth, who came increasingly under the influence of a political adventurer, Sir Thomas Armstrong, began to aspire to the succession, or at least to becoming regent if and when Exclusion passed.

Shaftesbury was dismissed as lord president in October, and four whigs resigned from the council in January. Essex remained, al-though increasingly uneasy at the king's attitudes. Generally, the political nation was becoming divided into irrevocably hostile fac-tions. Shaftesbury made extensive use of Monmouth's popularity, sending him on a spectacularly successful tour of the west country during the summer of 1680, but he did not commit himself to accept-ing Monmouth's tenuous claims to the throne, since there was a strong school of opinion among the whigs opposed to giving them any consideration. Unity would be essential if Exclusion was to be forced through. In June 1680 Shaftesbury and the whig leaders de-monstrated their determination to stick to Exclusion, and impressed public opinion with their confidence, when they attempted to have James presented by the Westminster grand jury for trial as a recu-sant, and the duchess of Portsmouth (Charles's chief mistress) as a prostitute. An act of such flagrant defiance was intended to show that compromise was impossible, and when the judges suppressed the charge they were in turn denounced.

The whigs dominated the Commons in the second Exclusion Parliament that finally began on 21 October 1680. Before it began

Charles was offered money and the right to name his successor in return for agreeing to Exclusion, but of course he refused. His warning that only limitations on a catholic successor were acceptable, and his concoction of a largely bogus anti-French foreign policy, did not deter the whigs from pushing a new Exclusion bill quickly through the commons, with the tories offering only token resistance. The bill was presented to the Lords on 15 November but, in an unusual move which showed the strength of their opposition to the proposal, a majority of sixty-three to thirty threw it out on the first reading.

This sharp repulse brought Shaftesbury and the whigs face to face with their inescapable difficulty. Only Charles could ensure the passage of Exclusion through the Lords. The basic whig assumption had been that eventually he would agree, provided that he was put under such intense pressure that he could plead that he had no alternative. Sunderland also had come to believe that Charles really wanted to be forced to agree, hence his and Godolphin's votes for the bill, and their advice to William to add his weight to those arguing for Exclusion as the only way of avoiding civil war. Now the ignominious defeat of the bill exposed these arguments as based on illusions. It was Charles's openly hostile attitude, rather than Halifax's eloquence or even the unanimous stand of the bishops, that had been responsible. After this defeat Exclusion could be achieved only by showing the king that all government would become impracticable unless he gave way, in other words by systematic obstruction and the mounting of such intense pressure as to amount to direct coercion.

During the rest of what was now a broken-backed session, the whigs used their ascendancy in the Commons to address for the removal of Halifax, and voted for impeachments of several ministers, judges and provincial tories. As a gesture to reward their support, the principal Elizabethan act against dissenters was repealed, although by a court trick it was not presented for the royal assent. Stafford, the least important of the papist peers who had been in the Tower for two years, was impeached, convicted and executed. But Exclusion could not be reintroduced during the session, so that although they voted menacing resolutions against anyone advising the king to dissolve or prorogue, the whigs welcomed the end of the second Exclusion Parliament. On 7 January 1681 they responded to yet another message from Charles warning the house that he would not agree to Exclusion, and reminding them of the alternative of limitations, with the argument that there could be no security without Exclusion and that 'to rely upon any other means or remedies without such a bill, is not only insufficient but dangerous'. They warned that no supply would be voted until Exclusion had passed, and on 10 January, having notice of an imminent prorogation, they passed a series of intransigent resolutions to show that they accepted the king's challenge, and were ready for a final, all-out offensive in new elections.

The elections of February 1681 were the most highly organized of the three. The striking new development was the presentation to whig candidates, on their being elected, of sets of instructions from their constituents (in reality centrally organized by the whig leaders), which insisted on Exclusion and rejected limitations. A spate of pamphlets told the electors that all was now at stake. They were particularly asked to ignore local considerations and connections; only those who had proved their staunch attachment to religion and liberties (that is had supported Exclusion) deserved re-election. Echoing recent resolutions by the Commons, pamphleteers identified the court and the tories with the pro-French interest, and alleged that these subverters of the constitution were hoping to gain election by massive bribery.

There were a number of fierce contests, with both parties mobilizing their aristocratic members to make appearances at polls and circulate recommendatory letters. The tory challenge made insufficient impact significantly to reduce whig predominance in the new Commons; the net whig loss was only six places, and overall the tories gained fewer than twenty. The whigs held on to constituencies of each type—especially counties and large boroughs with wide franchises, where the tories were rarely able to offer a serious challenge, and corporations where royal orders to enforce the Corporation Act and exclude dissenters and doubtful conformists had been ignored. However, it was a first sign of whig weakness that some of their former members did not seek re-election.

Charles ordered the parliament, summoned for 21 March, to meet at Oxford. This would rule out a possible whig tactic of withdrawing from Westminster into the City, and it would deprive the whigs of the moral (and possible physical) support of the London radicals. Naturally, the whigs denounced this switch as an attempt at intimidation, and some London radicals accompanied their representatives to Oxford as a bodyguard against an alleged plan to stage a military coup; but by doing so they were playing into the king's hands. Charles's opening speech was addressed as much to the nation as to the assembled parliament. He carefully established his own reasonableness, by promising to consider favourably any expedient that safeguarded both the interests of religion and the rights of the monarchy. Asserting his own distaste for arbitrary government, Charles warned that he would not allow others to ignore the laws. He was setting up whig intransigence and extremism as the real danger to liberties and order. In order to prepare the nation for the early dissolution which he had already planned, Charles cited the unreasonable resolutions of 7 and 10 January, the wilful whig rejection of all royal approaches and their refusal to consider any alternative to Exclusion.

The whigs ignored this warning. They hoped to prevent an early dissolution by launching an impeachment of Fitzharris. He was a government agent who had been caught while preparing to plant treasonable papers on leading whigs, and had then been disavowed by those who instructed him. He was now ready to turn his evidence to the advantage of the whigs and incriminate associates of James; this could be given the maximum publicity by an impeachment, and it was calculated that Charles would be deterred from dissolving by the fear of being accused of suppressing vital evidence. A long debate on 26 March ended in a resolution for a new Exclusion bill. But although the tories did not challenge a division, the alternative of limitations was now spelled out in detail. Littleton proposed a regency to secure government in protestant hands under a catholic, with James permanently exiled although retaining the mere title of king. The whigs answered with their standard argument that only Exclusion could bring security, and it was while they were in the middle of debating the first reading of a new bill that Charles surprised them by the snap dissolution of 28 March, putting an end to Exclusion, and effectively to the first whigs also.

Charles had not had to allow the Oxford Parliament to sit, and he used whig intransigence during the brief session as part of an elaborate political and propaganda manoeuvre to discredit his opponents. Royal finances were being prudently administered by Hyde, so that Charles was unmoved by the whig threat to withhold all supply. He had renewed serious negotiations with Louis from the beginning of the year, and found that the latter was now prepared to pay a subsidy which would help Charles to govern without parliament, and by doing so would guarantee against William gaining increased influence in England through a regency scheme. By a verbal agreement concluded finally on 1 April, and known only to Charles and Hyde, Louis promised to pay two million livres in the first year, with one and a half million in each of the following years. In return Charles promised not to honour a mutual assistance treaty concluded with Spain in 1680, and in effect undertook not to allow parliament to meet.

The dissolution of the Oxford Parliament finally shattered Shaftesbury's thesis that Charles could be persuaded or coerced into conceding Exclusion. Whig claims that another parliament would have to be summoned could not conceal the bankruptcy of Shaftesbury's political strategy; although Charles did promise to make further use of parliaments in his declaration of April 1681, he had no intention of doing so. Shaftesbury was now in a major dilemma. Unlike Pym, he could not use violence or the threat of violence because Charles possessed an adequate army, militia who were carefully modelled and led by reliable officers (especially in London, where the lieutenancy was closely supervised), and enough money to maintain both forces.

Psychologically, Shaftesbury could not easily contemplate using any form of open force. By 1681 fear of another civil war had become as potent a feeling among the people as hostility to popery. He had had no alternative but to rely on legislative methods, but it should not be forgotten that the first whigs never controlled parliament, only the Commons. Only if Charles had given way would the opposition of the Lords have been overcome. Anti-papist feeling, support for the union of all protestants, anticlericalism, hostility to pensioners and courtiers, and fears of French influence, had all been exacerbated and exploited by whig propaganda, and mobilized to make the whig domination over the Commons impregnable. But once Charles felt that he could safely dispense with parliament, whig strength quickly collapsed.

Constitutionally, there was nothing Shaftesbury could do to counter skilled use of the prerogative powers of dissolution and prorogation. On the other hand, Charles and his tory allies were able convincingly to adopt and imitate whig techniques: the king appealed to the nation in his opening speech to the Oxford Parliament and in the April Declaration, tory journalists developed a crude but highly effective propaganda campaign depicting the whigs as would-be authors of another civil war, tory addresses and even instructions to members were organized in 1681, and in the large cities (London, Bristol, Norwich) tory electioneering machines contested whig dominance. Although unsuccessful as a whole in the 1681 elections, the very existence and the activities of the first tories refuted whig claims exclusively to represent the nation.

However, in the last resort the defeat of the whigs was Charles's achievement. Throughout the crisis his judgement was almost faultless. In 1679 he rejected advice from Danby and James that he should refuse to make any concessions and suppress the opposition, a course of action that would have infallibly caused a new civil war. Instead, he tricked Shaftesbury by giving him the false hope of being eventually converted to Exclusion. Written off by Louis in 1679 and by William in 1680, Charles rejected the temptation which was extended to him by Shaftesbury (and in 1680 by Sunderland and the duchess of Portsmouth also) of winning relief from whig pressure by giving way on Exclusion. Politically this would have meant impotence, not a characteristic associated with Charles in any form, but Charles waited until it was safe to use his prerogative powers. Only when the time was ripe did he put an end to the quite unprecedented dependence on parliament that had existed since 1660. Moreover, the alliance with the tories meant that governing without a parliament in the years after 1681 was not seen by most people as a stage on the way to absolutism. Not only did Charles emerge from the Exclusion Crisis as incontestably the strongest seventeenth-century monarch, but he did so as a constitutional ruler.

11 The Tory Reaction, 1681–6

Whig historical tradition has attached the title of the 'Stuart revenge' to the years after 1681. Persistent whigs, and dissenters generally, did suffer severe repression, but this does not justify calling it a period of tyranny or absolutism. During these years Charles and his tory and anglican allies achieved a belated realization of the cavalier principles and aims of 1661. The dominant tories, as constitutionalists, genuinely believed that the subversive beliefs and actions of their whig opponents necessitated the use against them of the full extent of the available legal powers, but under Charles there was only one major infringement of the law: no parliament was called in 1684, as stipulated by the triennial act of 1641. Charles made no attempt to enlarge the permanent powers of the monarchy. He had a static conception of royal rights, he was satisfied with the secure and comfortable position which he had achieved by defeating the first whigs, and in a sense can be described as playing out time. In contrast, James committed himself to dynamic policies to extend prerogative powers, free the crown from the restrictions imposed by the Test Acts, while his catholicism impelled him to secure effective toleration for his co-religionists.

As a result James came up against the limits of tory loyalty. In theory, tories were devoted to the anglican principles of non-resistance and absolute obedience, but in the parliamentary debates of November 1685 James received a warning that, in practice, the loyalty that they offered was conditional. Ignoring these warnings, James's use of prerogative methods during 1686 further offended tory constitutionalism, reviving old fears that there was a necessary connection between catholicism and absolutism. Tory reactions faced James with a crucial decision. Either he must accept effective limits on his authority, or he could look for new allies, and adopt new policies and methods, in order to attain his full objectives.

By their political skill Charles and his ministers made the personal government of 1681–5 incomparably more effective, secure and generally acceptable than that of Charles I in 1629–40. Its strength depended primarily on the establishment of financial solvency, which was largely the work of Rochester, the first treasury commissioner. Substantial cuts were made in expenditure during the Exclusion Crisis, particularly by suspending or delaying payment of pensions and salaries, and retrenchment was continued after the crisis subsided. Rochester freed the treasury from political interference by the privy council, so that effective control could be achieved over departmental expenditure, and a significant reduction in the floating debt led to savings in interest payments. European peace and the expiry of the prohibition on French commodities (March 1681) produced an expansion in trade; administrative reorganization in the customs and excise ensured that royal finances benefited to the full. Even more crucial was Rochester's influence over Charles himself. Previous ministers had not been able to prevent royal expenditure rising to waste any surpluses that appeared, but Rochester succeeded in restraining Charles.

Secondly, Charles freed himself from any prospect of having to finance an expensive foreign policy. The verbal agreement concluded with the French ambassador in April 1681 brought modest subsidies (not all of which were actually paid) in return for Charles's undertaking not to honour his treaties with Spain and the Dutch, if war developed over French encroachments into the Spanish Netherlands. This can be seen as an ignoble sell-out of national interests but, by skilful diplomatic manoeuvring and calculated deceit, Charles and Rochester avoided being exposed for what they were, the puppets of Louis. With greater ease they also evaded William's attempts, abetted by Halifax, to commit them to the anti-French camp. This would have necessitated calling a parliament, with all its attendant risks and uncertainties. Only Halifax among ministers was in favour. An inactive foreign policy was enforced by the pledge which Louis extorted in 1681 not to allow any meeting of parliament, but by giving this undertaking Charles was only confirming a decision which he had already made for reasons of domestic politics.

The absence of parliament after two decades in which every year except two (1672 and 1676) had seen a session, no prospect of one meeting in the foreseeable future, transformed the character of politics once again and significantly altered the relationship between Charles and his tory allies. During the Exclusion Crisis and its immediate aftermath the tories served as active and aggressive auxiliaries against the whigs, adopting many originally whig political techniques—popular addresses, electoral organization, press propaganda with a mass appeal, urban political clubs. But once the whigs had lost control over London (September 1682) such activism became unnecessary and undesirable, since it maintained an atmosphere of political excitement. For contemporaries, party politics and divisions were abnormal and dangerous; the tories, therefore, were now encouraged to assume a more passive role, primarily supportive of legally constituted authority. In some large cities, such as Norwich and Bristol, where tory enthusiasts had played a decisive part in the struggle for control, there was some reluctance to relapse into relative inactivity, but generally most tories lived up to their principles of loyalty.

One tory maxim proclaimed that 'steady loyalty is the only foundation of true felicity'. Subjects should obey and trust their divinely instituted superiors, lay and ecclesiastical. With no elections in prospect the king, ministers and tories did not need to affect popularity. In his 1681 Declaration, Charles appealed to the nation against Shaftesbury and the whig parliaments, but by 1683 at the time of the Rye House Plot he sternly required unconditional loyalty from all. In demanding voluntary and willing subjection to authority, Charles emphasized the argument that the alternative was another civil war. Tory propaganda, vigorously directed by L'Estrange, expanded the theme that the whigs were concerned only to exploit popular grievances in order to advance their own subversive purposes, not to relieve the people who were being cynically used. Whig leaders were depicted as atheists who championed true protestantism, beggars and gamblers who upheld property rights, patriots eager to sell themselves. Tories tended not to see, or admit, that the people or sections of the nation could have legitimate causes for discontent, requiring expression and redress but Charles's ministers possessed one exceptionally strong advantage. The very low level of taxation, the absence of illegal exactions, and the relatively high levels of foreign trade and domestic production refuted whig claims that England was suffering under a new tyranny similar to the personal government of Charles I. There were no extraordinary taxes on which opposition could focus, and indeed the lightness of taxation during the prosperity of Charles's last years was to form the background of the later tory myth of how government should be conducted when, after 1688, the nation became burdened by war taxation and debt.

Tory strength derived from those who were satisfied with the status quo; it was concentrated particularly in the provincial gentry, the virtually united anglican clergy, together with their connections and dependants. They all assumed—too readily, believing their own propaganda—a permanent identity of interests with the crown, but after 1681 their loyalty was secured by the total monopoly of local offices in the militia and corporations and as JPs which they were given. All identifiable whigs were ejected from the customs, excise and admiralty employment. Enforcement of the Corporation Act, and actions of *quo warranto* against municipal charters gave tories domination over corporate towns. Tory sheriffs empanelled tory juries. Tory grand juries were the sole mouthpiece to represent local views and grievances. Significantly, if at first sight paradoxically, it was only at court that the tories were less than predominant. Rochester had to contend with the rehabilitated Sunderland (from 1682) for James's as well as Charles's favour, and he could never eliminate Halifax's influence. During 1684 he had to repulse a full-scale attack by Halifax on his conduct of treasury affairs, and by the end of the year he virtually admitted defeat by accepting honourable exile as lord lieutenant in Ireland. Halifax's advocacy of a parliament made him a potential threat to the other ministers. Elections and the need to manage proceedings might give him an advantage by enabling him to put into practice his principles of trimming, that is of constructing a counter-weight to the tories, composed of independent politicians and gentry, William's connections and repentant whigs.

Halifax's approaches to former whigs, especially his attempts in 1682 and 1684 to get Monmouth restored to favour, were unforgivable in tory eyes. Whatever the tories stood for, their most important characteristic and the cement that held them together was their hatred for the whigs. This operated at all levels. In tory eyes the whigs constituted a detestable and dangerous faction, ready to plunge the nation into rebellion and disorder. Anglican clergy feared that whig calls for protestant unity disguised an intention of destroying the established church, and they saw that whigs and dissenters worked together. Officers and courtiers knew that many whigs, like Montagu and Winnington, a former solicitor general, had not entirely abandoned their hopes of getting into office. More generally, throughout English society and not just in the sphere of politics, deep and lasting divisions had been created during the Exclusion Crisis in every county and nearly every borough. Personal detestation separated whigs from tories. Neither could credit their enemies with good faith or good intentions. Consequently a persistent attachment to whig principles, attempts to continue any form of political activity after the dissolution of the Oxford Parliament, were interpreted as a direct challenge to the local and central authority of the king's government.

The aim of the first attempt at repression was to eliminate Shaftesbury, and to prosecute those whigs who could be clearly exposed in court as dangerous subversives. Shaftesbury, arrested in July 1681, was vulnerable because many of the Irish perjurers whom he had imported to 'prove' the existence of an Irish popish plot in 1680–81 defected to the court, and were soon happy to fabricate evidence against their former paymaster. The other selected victims were Howard of Escrick (the most disreputable whig peer and a former Dutch secret agent), Rouse who as whig under-sheriff in London had managed evidence for the whigs, and finally College, a popular organizer in London, who had made himself conspicuous by leading a company of whig militants to Oxford, ostensibly to protect whig leaders during the parliamentary session. Only the last was convicted and executed. Shaftesbury owed his life to the sheriffs of London and Middlesex, who uniquely were elected, not nominated by the king. They knew that if a grand jury presented a true bill, that is that there was a case to answer, Shaftesbury would be tried by a packed court—by twenty-four selected enemies from among his peers, sitting as the court of the lord high steward. By empanelling a packed whig grand jury the whig sheriffs not only saved Shaftesbury and Rouse, but halted the crown's judicial offensive. Unusually, but quite legitimately, the grand jury subjected the prosecution witnesses to a searching examination which discredited their evidence, and then proceeded by an ignoramus verdict to dismiss the prosecution case. The whig leaders were temporarily safe, until a new set of witnesses could be obtained and organized. College had earlier been similarly cleared by a London grand jury, but in August his case was switched to Oxford, where a conviction was easily obtained. This minor success, the publication by the king of the draft of a whig association found among Shaftesbury's papers and even the appearance of Dryden's two great political satires, *Absalom and Achitophel* and *The Medal*, could not detract from a striking if essentially defensive whig victory.

Although the whig leaders were saved, and a wider proscription possibly averted, the dissenters were now exposed to the most severe, sustained and effective persecution of the whole period. In the 1670s the clergy had often found it increasingly difficult to persuade magistrates to enforce the existing laws, but after 1681 there were few JPs sympathetic to dissenters. Tory clergy and gentry hated the dissenters for consistently supporting the whigs, and saw in dissenting principles and practices the living spirit of law-breaking and potential rebellion. Frightened of another rebellion, most JPs were eager to act, and willingly followed directives from Whitehall to enforce the penal laws systematically against protestant dissenters. Conventicles were suppressed. The Five Mile and Corporation Acts were used to destroy dissenting organizations in the boroughs. The Elizabethan acts enforced intermittently in the past against the catholics were now employed against dissenters, producing some revenue to the crown but more profit for corrupt local officials and informers. Attempts by dissenters to organize defence and distress funds, to harass informers, and to use delaying legal tactics had the effect of confirming the belief that it was politically necessary to compel them to observe the law. The total number of dissenting conventicles, and the strength of many congregations, were substantially reduced as occasional dissenters and the more faint-hearted found it unsafe to retain any connection, but a hard-core of dedicated adherents remained, few dissenting clergy were silenced, and the quakers staunchly defied the harshest treatment.

After the Oxford dissolution the whigs retained only one governmental platform, the City of London, but even there they suffered a decisive defeat. In 1681 they won the elections for sheriffs, but lost those for lord mayor. The crucial struggle centred on the 1682 elections. Moore, the tory lord mayor, actively encouraged by Charles and the ministers, nominated Dudley North for one of the two sheriffs' places. The whigs denied his right to do so, but their attempt (by the out-going sheriffs) to hold a poll for both places was declared invalid, and as constituting a riot. A second tory was declared elected, and a partisan scrutiny of the livery lists of those entitled to vote produced a majority for another tory lord mayor. Aided by sharp electoral practice, these successes were also a reward for years of careful attention to City affairs by the government. Even though it had not been able to prevent whig control throughout the Exclusion Crisis, a Tory party had been constructed and fostered, which now beat the whigs at their own game of civic politics, before the *quo warranto* action procured the forfeiture of London's charter.

Tory sheriffs meant tory juries. Shaftesbury thought it prudent to withdraw at once, first into hiding and then to Amsterdam (December), where he died in January 1683. He at least remained totally intransigent—as an old and sick man he had nothing to lose—advising Monmouth to stage an insurrection in August 1682, during a tour of the north west, where he received a tumultuous popular welcome. Monmouth ignored this advice. He, Russell (heir to the earl of Bedford and Shaftesbury's lieutenant) and Essex, the chief aristocratic whig leaders, were slow to come round to the idea of organizing resistance. For a time they hoped that a European war would compel Charles to call a parliament in order to ask for supply. Monmouth made personal approaches to the court, but in May 1683 he tried to secure a general settlement. He asked for a parliament in order to pass an act of indemnity and pardon that would finally end political tensions and heal party divisions; in return he promised that no moves would be made against James. There was no reason for ministers to accept this proposal. Elections would reanimate local divisions and passions. Despite purges and *quo warranto* actions there would be a risk of a large block of former exclusionist whigs being elected, whom the aristocratic leaders might not be able to control. Monmouth's promises might not be honoured, and yet another abrupt dissolution would raise the political temperature.

It is not surprising that, when they realized that no parliament would be allowed, some of the whig leaders discussed the possibility of staging a coup. Monmouth's visit to the north west in 1682 had shown that it was still possible to raise popular support for the whig cause. Despite their electoral defeats the whigs still had the remains of a political machine in London, where an independent group of radicals was also discussing plans for a rebellion, together with the idea of assassinating Charles and James. But although much of the evidence is contradictory, it is doubtful whether these discussions went any further than talk. The strength of the army, especially in the area around London, the intrinsic difficulties of arming and organizing the large number of men that would be needed, the lack of trust between the aristocratic and radical leaders and difficulties of communication between groups posed formidable difficulties which remained unresolved. Lax security allowed knowledge of the discussions and plans to spread, so that when men on the fringes turned informer (June 1683), ample detailed evidence confirmed all the assumptions about whig rebelliousness that tory propaganda had already established.

There are close parallels between this Rye House Plot which centred on a plan to assassinate Charles and James on their return from Newmarket, and the way it was treated, and the earlier Popish Plot. Much of the evidence by the informers was false and fabricated, sometimes grotesquely exaggerated, but it was accepted because it fitted into current preconceptions about the conspiratorial and traitorous nature of the whig faction. Believing that their duty was to crush the king's enemies, judges intimidated juries, guided or interrupted witnesses, harassed defendants and created prejudice by repeated references to the plot as a proven fact. Hearsay and accomplices' evidence, particularly that by the whig adventurer, lord Howard of Escrick, was admitted. Defendants were not given sufficient time to prepare their defence or to summon witnesses. Consequently, the crop of whig martyrs produced in 1683, and venerated for over a century, was almost as large as that of catholic and Irish saints in 1678–81. Russell and several plotters implicated in the murder plans (including Rouse who had been cleared in 1681) were convicted and executed in July. Algernon Sydney, the other most notable victim, was convicted in December—partly on the basis of notes for his book on government. Charles and James both displayed a venomous animosity against him, comparable to that against Vane in 1662, and they were also determined to destroy Sir Thomas Armstrong, whom they blamed for leading Monmouth into opposition and encouraging his pretensions to the crown. Having fled abroad, Armstrong was kidnapped at Leiden, and shipped to London, then peremptorily executed as an outlaw, without being allowed to stand trial. Other whig refugees, including Lord Grey, remained in Holland.

While prominent and personally obnoxious whigs were prosecuted for treason, the provincial whig gentry were intimidated and humiliated by their local tory rivals. Their houses were searched for arms (few were found), grand juries presented the leading whigs in several counties as disaffected and bound them over to be of good behaviour, and offers to submit and reconcile themselves to their local enemies were usually rejected. But in political terms such treatment hardly constituted severe repression. Ministers (if not local enemies) were satisfied when whigs lapsed into inactivity, refrained from organizing or assisting resistance to the surrender or forfeiture of municipal charters, and abstained from putting themselves forward as candidates in the 1685 elections. Few former whig gentry showed any eagerness to support Monmouth in his rebellion in that year; the rank and file whigs who rallied to him in the west country were those who had really suffered in the unremitting, and often savagely conducted, campaign against the dissenters and their sympathizers in a region where they were particularly strong.

Charles's principles and practice in selecting and employing ministers differed significantly from those adopted by James. Charles carefully preserved a balance, never allowing his brother to become predominant; Halifax was kept as a counterweight, even though none of his policies were accepted. Despite his invaluable services as financial administrator, Rochester was similarly limited by the readmission of Sunderland to court, and his associates (like Seymour) were kept out of key offices. James rejected this policy of balancing one minister against another. He believed that like all other subjects his ministers should display unconditional obedience to his decisions; the king could appoint whom he pleased and entirely on his own terms. So on his accession in February 1685 he unexpectedly retained Halifax, as president of the council, although he detested him personally and distrusted his opinions as quasi-republican, because he needed him to influence the forthcoming parliament. On the other hand he demoted the earl of Bath, although he was head of a conspicuously loyal family and the most important provincial magnate in terms of electoral influence. Ministers were expected to share this royal disregard for personal considerations, to serve with any colleague whom James appointed (including catholics from early 1686), and not to press their own personal interests.

When Charles died (6 February 1685) there was still some fear that disorders would be provoked by the accession of an openly catholic king, but England remained as quiet as on the day after Cromwell's death. James began by giving reassurances to those whose support he needed. He explained to Louis that it was necessary to call a parliament in order to get revenues voted. He promised the Church of England, in a statement to the privy council later repeated to parliament, that remembering its loyalty in the 'worst of times' he would always take care to defend and support it. James added for the benefit of the tories that he would preserve the existing government in state as well as church, and respect property rights. But from the start there were signs of a new royal style—more formality in official behaviour, and bluntness and directness in royal statements. James insisted on worshipping publicly, attending mass in full state. He ordered the continued collection of customs and excise in anticipation of its grant by parliament, although this was technically illegal. Former exclusionists who approached him, offering to submit, were told that they must prove the sincerity of their penitence by withdrawing from any part in the elections for a new parliament.

These elections were supervised, rather than directed, by the ministers. Remembering the Exclusionist triumphs of 1679 and 1681, there were entirely unjustified fears at court that many whigs might be returned, to the point that it would be difficult to get an adequate financial settlement for the king. In practice no whig organization functioned during the elections, except in one or two counties. On the court side Sunderland despatched circular letters to lords lieutenant and provincial notables, asking them to help elect 'good members'. Later he sent recommendations of named individuals for specific seats, but these numbered fewer than twenty. In general, although by the *quo warranto* actions against the corporations, and the subsequent issuing of new charters (fifty-one between 1681 and Charles's death, and another forty-seven immediately after James's accession) the crown had created the conditions for the electoral victories of 1685, the executants and principal beneficiaries were the provincial tories, and above all tory gentry. The new charters named the new officers in the towns, who had formerly been elected, and most of them were nominees or dependants of the local tory gentry. In places where the parliamentary franchise was vested in the corporation this change in itself ensured success, and elsewhere it put the tories at an advantage because the returning officers favoured them.

Furthermore, the new officers and magistrates by enforcing the penal laws broke up most of the previously dominant dissenting interests in many of the smaller towns, especially in the west country. The results were conclusive; out of 195 MPs returned by boroughs that had been issued with new charters only nine can be described as whigs, and most of the tories elected were local gentry, not townsmen—or courtiers.

Lords lieutenant did not 'care for' elections in the sense of dictating the choice of candidates; this was done by carefully establishing a consensus within a county, consulting the country gentry (but not the townsmen) at each stage. County meetings were convoked, at which the disposal of seats for the county and most of the boroughs was usually agreed, sometimes after prolonged bargaining, once at least only after a ballot by those present. All participants were then expected to use their common interest in favour of the agreed candidates; this was important since part of the strategy was to set up so strong an interest beforehand that it would be obviously futile for dissidents or independents to stand. There was a widespread desire to avoid polls and contested elections, which would be divisive, generate excitement, give opportunities for political declarations and also cost money. Returning officers could also be relied on to aid these agreed candidates. In several places independents were refused a poll, or (as in the Surrey election) the time and place of the poll were arbitrarily and privately changed. Furthermore, such malpractices had no damaging repercussions; although petitions to the Commons presented by defeated or frustrated candidates reached an unprecedented total of sixty-six, they were ignored, being simply buried in committee by the tory majority. Only one case went to a division, when a prominent whig (Freke) was unseated by 224 to 60 votes.

The new House of Commons was overwhelmingly tory. Fewer than forty old whigs were returned, and half that number of new men with even vague whig connections. Constituencies that had been in the iron grip of the whigs during the Exclusion elections now succumbed to tories without a contest. Only in Buckinghamshire, where Thomas Wharton overpowered a protégé of Jeffreys, and in the small Dorset boroughs where they failed, is there any evidence of a coherent whig organization. The sweeping changes in representation gave the court an additional advantage. The high proportion of inexperienced MPs (there were twenty-seven counties and 112 boroughs where both MPs were new) gave the court managers their opportunity to establish an ascendancy and control of proceedings that was in sharp contrast to the opposition domination in 1679–81.

However, the Commons started with a gaffe. An address was

agreed in grand committee calling on the king to prosecute all non-conformists, which by implication would have included catholics. When James's surprised reaction was explained, the Commons immediately responded by amendments making it clear that the address was directed against protestant dissenters only. The Commons did not question James's unauthorized collection of revenues, and accepted his warning in the first royal speech that they must not try to ration him financially in an attempt to ensure frequent parliaments. They gave him an adequate but not lavish financial settlement by renewing Charles's life revenues, without apparently making any systematic evaluation of either their past, or the potential, yield. Additional revenues, in the form of indirect taxes, were also voted in order to discharge Charles's debts and anticipations, and to replenish naval and ordnance stores. From the first day of the session (19 May) members were aware of the danger posed by Argyll's expedition against Scotland, and when Monmouth landed in Dorset parliament promptly voted further supply to meet the emergency.

The crisis provoked by Monmouth's rebellion, which historians tend to underestimate because of the speed with which it was suppressed, bound king and parliament to each other. A bill of attainder, introduced on 15 June, was rushed through without opposition; this declared him a traitor and as a result he was later executed without trial. When Seymour, usually persuasive and influential, made a blistering attack on the recent use of the new charters to return members whom he regarded as creatures of the court (and of his west-country rival, Bath), and proposed that they should be suspended from sitting until an inquiry had been made, the house failed to respond. Such suspensions would have hampered the conduct of business at a time when in their eyes members faced a mortal danger—not so much a military victory by Monmouth and the radical whigs, but rather the incalculable dangers of another prolonged civil war.

Monmouth's rebellion provides a vivid revelation of the strength and character of grass-roots whig support in the west country. Had the rebellion spread to other areas where the whigs had been strong—the north west, East Anglia, above all London—regional variations would have been apparent, but the common features of popular, radical whiggery are clear. Those who responded to Monmouth were men who for the most part had a social and political status that placed them in the boundary zone, just within or just outside the political nation. Many were freeholders or urban voters, or with favourable returning officers could pass as such, eligible for parochial offices, serving as rankers in the militia. Most still retained a connection with the land, combining small-scale farming with textile work, mining, artisan crafts or retailing. Nearly all lived just above, or precariously on, another boundary, that of self-sufficiency. Yet if these west-country provincials were individually insignificant and uninfluential by national standards, they had a tradition of independence. Their fathers had, under Blake's inspired leadership, defied and defeated the royalist gentry during the civil war. They had themselves overwhelmed court candidates during the Exclusion elections. Somerset and Dorset boroughs had offered relatively stubborn resistance to the combined attack by the crown and the local gentry, although by 1685 tories controlled municipal governments and succeeded in the parliamentary elections. Furthermore, despite harsh persecution and sustained pressure, the spirit and influence of religious dissent had not been stamped out.

A catalyst was needed to convert stubborn, but essentially defensive west-country whiggery into an active and aggressive movement. Monmouth supplied this, even though he landed at Lyme in Dorset (11 June) with only eighty-two men and a quantity of arms. In an age when such diversions were few he had created an ineradicable impression by his spectacular 'western progress' in 1680. Politically incompetent, militarily hesitant, Monmouth possessed charisma. Affable, handsome, athletic, a glamorous yet popular figure he (like Boulanger in France in the 1880s) had all the qualifications to raise a great mass movement, and lead it to total disaster. Nevertheless, for all his ineptitude during a rebellion that lasted less than a month, Monmouth was indispensable to provide a focus for feelings that were otherwise diffuse, and by his presence he imparted a confidence to his followers that he himself did not feel.

Monmouth's first declaration (published on landing) was skilfully drafted to attract immediate support. Its general thesis followed familiar whig lines: government was originally instituted for the benefit of the nation, and in England a set of restrictions ensured 'that the rights reserved unto the people tended to render the king honourable and great, and the prerogatives settled on the prince were in order to the subjects' protection and safety'. But unfortunately there had been a conspiracy to destroy the protestant religion and the rights of the nation which, after a whig view of the recent past had been given, culminated in James's usurpation. The remedies proposed, like the history, were whiggish and very much in the spirit of 1681—annual parliaments, no standing army, repeal of all laws against the dissenters including the Corporation Act, restoration of charters, elective sheriffs, free juries and independent judges. Monmouth left his own title to the crown to a parliament, and the only inflammatory note was the claim that James had poisoned his brother Charles and should be tried for this crime. The second declaration of 20 June, in which Monmouth precipitately assumed the crown for himself, was a panic measure and reflected the failure of former whigs among the gentry to give him support. Most had no choice, since James carried out preventive arrests of suspects. More serious still for Monmouth was the failure of the London radicals to make any move to support him, and the absence of diversionary risings elsewhere.

Nevertheless, it is significant that Monmouth's bold appearance did actually produce a rebellion, in contrast to the endless and inconclusive planning by royalists in the 1650s, the futile plotting by republicans in the early 1660s and the posturing by jacobites after 1688. There was sufficient social and political cohesion for him to form an army of over 4,000 men in a matter of days. Adequately officered—except for Grey's cavalry—it offered Monmouth a slim chance of success, but his failure to gamble everything on seizing Bristol forced the rebels on to the defensive. Morale slumped, desertions occurred, and the final catastrophe at Sedgemoor (6 July) became inevitable. Monmouth was forced to the desperate gamble of a night attack by his untrained troops on the royal army; a premature alarm led to a massacre. The savage judicial repression which followed made Jeffreys infamous, and it should be contrasted with the leniency with which Argyll's followers were treated after his abject defeat, whereas customarily repression of dissidents in Scotland was much more severe. The explanation is that Argyll's had been a feudal rebellion by clansmen who had an obligation to support their chief. Despite the presence with Argyll of ideologue radicals, his aim had not been to overthrow the entire political order. Monmouth on the other hand, like the Covenanters who had waged a ferocious guerrilla war through the 1670s, mobilized popular forces of discontent that were seen by conservatives as constituting an explicit and uncompromising challenge to the principles on which order and monarchical authority were based. Security could be restored only if they were ruthlessly eliminated.

During Monmouth's rebellion the tories as a whole rallied enthusiastically to James, cooperating in parliament and raising volunteers. They interpreted the defeat of Monmouth as finally securing the crown and the nation from whig rebellion. A series of trials weakened the old whig leadership further: Hampden and Cornish were tried for complicity in the Rye House Plot, new witnesses now becoming available, while three Exclusionist peers Delamere, Brandon and Stamford were charged with assisting Monmouth. In October tories were pleased when James dismissed Halifax, whom they never trusted. They did not realize that this dismissal was the first sign of a change of direction by James, and on his side James failed to anticipate the hostile reaction that his new policies would provoke from his tory allies.

When parliament reassembled in November James began by announcing that he intended to keep the army at its considerably enlarged emergency strength of 14,000, since the campaign in the west had exposed the ineffectiveness of the militia. He added, even more provocatively, that this army contained catholic officers who had not taken the test, and that he was determined to continue their commissions. In general James concluded by confidently asking for further supply, to pay for the army, and warned both houses that there were wicked men ready to stir up opposition. In fact it was these proposals themselves that revived opposition, which had the same characteristics as the old country opposition in the Cavalier Parliament, and whose members disclaimed any resemblance to the whigs.

James's disparagement of the militia betrayed an insulting intention of dispensing with the cooperation of the tory gentry. The opposition, led by men like Clarges who had consistently resisted Exclusion, widened the issues by suggesting that expansion of the standing army was a first step towards the introduction of absolutism: 'to trust to mercenary force alone, is to give up all our liberties at once.' Voting supply for the army was tantamount to accepting the principle of standing forces, and it was said that as a consequence parliament might never meet again. One suggested amendment anticipated post-1688 practice by proposing that supply should be voted for one year only, which would have forced James to accompany a standing army with annual sessions of parliament. James's admission that many officers were catholics raised the political temperature even further, reviving the old fears that a necessary connection existed between popery and absolutism. This gave real importance to the defeat of the court by one vote (183 to 182) on a procedural matter, whether to give priority to supply, or to consideration of James's statement about catholic army officers. The Commons approved an address warning the king that their incapacity to serve could be removed only by an act of parliament, but although a bill was promised to indemnify these officers from penalties already incurred, James was asked to ensure that such illegal commissions should not be granted in future. The Commons did progress with votes for supply, without formally linking them to the army issue, but for James their attitude was one of insubordination.

He was even more outraged by the conduct of the Lords. An openly aggressive group of peers was more explicit in denouncing as illegal the appointment of catholic officers, and out-manoeuvred an unready court (ineptly led by Lord Chancellor Jeffreys) by asking for the judges to be consulted over the legality of the commissions. They also took the initiative in approaching MPs to coordinate tactics, so that James was faced with the prospect of a dominant opposition controlling proceedings in both houses—something the whigs had never achieved during the Exclusion Crisis. Even though the court had won a series of divisions in committee on supply, so that a substantial addition to the revenue would be lost, James was disconcerted by the way opposition had developed despite his specific warnings, and determined not to allow it time to expand its influence still further. On 20 November he prorogued parliament until February, and immediately dismissed from their offices all MPs who had voted against the court. This parliament was never to sit again, and the breach between James and the tories could not be prevented from widening. Reflecting back on the debates, the tories were more than ever determined to uphold the tests imposed on office-holders as the principal defence against catholicism, and they began to see James as being misled by his ministers and pushed into extreme courses by the catholic militants, 'the cursed bigots, the Jesuitical party'.

James did not abandon hope of persuading the tories to concede his demands. Early in 1686 he initiated the process known as 'closeting', canvassing peers and MPs to agree to repeal the tests and the penal laws that discriminated against the catholics. In his own eyes these demands were not extreme. He wanted anglicans and tories to accept catholics as equals in both civil and religious rights, to insert his co-religionists in the ranks of the political nation. But by starting in the most politically sensitive of all areas—the army—James created suspicions which all his later moves served to confirm. Attempts to give benefits to the catholics were interpreted as aimed at undermining the anglican church, and by attempting to realize his objectives by prerogative methods, especially the use of the dispensing power, James gave the impression to those who suspected him that he was deliberately subverting the law and the constitution.

James began by issuing a large batch of dispensations on 23 November, enabling catholics to hold office without taking the tests. Protections were sent to give catholics immunity from the penal laws and to refund fines, but apart from the quakers who benefited in May 1686 there was as yet no question of relief for the protestant dissenters. It was expected that only a few openly political churchmen, led by Compton the bishop of London who had been dismissed from the Council in December, would object. James assumed that the majority of the clergy would remain true to their frequently expressed doctrines of non-resistance and passive obedience to royal orders and authority, and would continue to uphold the prerogative powers of the crown. Two churchmen who did so, Cartwright and Parker, were promoted to the sees of Chester and Oxford; both were well known as energetic opponents of the dissenters. In time it became clear that James had made a serious miscalculation. Congenitally unable, or unwilling, to understand the point of view of anyone who disagreed with him, he grossly underestimated the strength and persistence of genuine antagonism to catholicism among anglican gentry and clergy. Their reluctance to accept catholics as equals he attributed to self-interest; anglican clergy feared the loss of privileges, and lacked confidence that they could defend convincingly their erroneous doctrines in fair competition. Tories defended the test for equally selfish reasons, in order to preserve for themselves a monopoly of offices.

During 1686 the failure of closeting, and a continuing hostility towards catholics, forced James to realize that he would have to exert pressure on tories and anglicans if he was to attain his objectives. In March he ordered 'Directions concerning Preaching' to be issued. These prohibited polemical sermons, and were resented as handicapping anglicans in defending their faith against catholic controversialists who were now able to publish freely. To enforce the Directions James revived the royal prerogative court (abolished in 1641) under the title of the Ecclesiastical Commission (July). It made an example of Compton, suspending him in September from his episcopal functions for disobeying a royal order to discipline archdeacon Sharp for reflecting in a sermon on catholic doctrines. Under James's protection an open catholic church organization now emerged as an apparently formidable challenge to the established church, with public worship in an expanding chain of chapels, schools, charities and religious houses, able to mount an active campaign of preaching, publishing and proselytizing. Catholic political influence was also rapidly increasing. After the case of *Godden* v. *Hales*, in which the judges upheld the king's power to issue dispensations (June), appointments of catholics to offices were made on an extensive scale, with recommendations being made by a 'catholic cabinet' among the ministers, assisted by Sunderland.

The validity of tory and anglican political principles was being undermined by experience under James's catholicizing policies. The hostile tory reaction disappointed James, but in no way deterred him. He expected his chief minister Rochester to agree to become a catholic but when, after long hesitation, he declined to do so James dismissed him. Other office-holders who refused to give James the pledges he demanded, and over 250 JPs, were also discharged. Such wide purges narrowed the basis of James's administration, leaving him dependent on a collection of inexperienced catholics, careerists and opportunists, but there is no evidence to suggest that the actual quality of government was adversely affected. The weakness of James's position lay in the fact that he could not achieve anything permanent by using prerogative methods. Already many tories were beginning to look forward to James's death, when Mary's accession and a new parliament would enable them to undo all James's work. Security for the catholics in their new privileges could be achieved only by statutory repeal of the penal laws and tests, and if this was to be achieved, and subsequent repeal blocked, it was necessary to extend toleration and equality of civil rights to dissenters as well. This would create an interest sufficiently strong to defeat any future tory reaction. Consequently the refusals by most tories to assist him forced James to the previously unthinkable step of allying with his old and mortal enemies, the whigs, and to resume the role he had once attempted, of acting as champion of toleration for all.

12 James II and the Revolution of 1688

In justifying the Revolution of 1688 the Convention Parliament claimed, in the Bill of Rights (1689), that James II had endeavoured 'to subvert and extirpate the protestant religion, and the laws and liberties of this kingdom'. This was an overstated, propaganda statement. It is true that it was James, rather than his successful enemies, who acted as a revolutionary in the sequence of events that led to his overthrow, but he was a revolutionary in the methods and techniques that he employed, not in the objectives that he was trying to attain. These objectives were far less extreme than his suspicious subjects believed, going no further than establishing a basis for royal absolutism. Religious toleration was intended to free the crown from its existing dependence on the established Church of England, and create a permanent counterweight in a legally secure catholic church. The repeal of the Test Acts of 1673 and 1678 would restore to the king unrestricted freedom in appointing to offices. Expansion and improvement of the standing army would rule out rebellion, and amendment of the *habeas corpus* laws would make it possible to keep political offenders and suspects in custody indefinitely.

Had these proposals been carried into effect, James's position and powers would have been more extensive and secure than those of Charles I and II, but they would have still been much weaker than those of Louis XIV. The intolerably provocative element in James's policies consisted of his abandonment of the traditional allies of the monarchy, and his use of political techniques of agitation and electoral organization that had formerly been used by Shaftesbury and the first whigs, in the attempt to exclude James from the crown. When he found that the tory gentry and anglican clergy resisted his attempts throughout 1686 to persuade them to collaborate with him, he discarded them, dissolving the loyal parliament of 1685, and looked for new, subservient instruments and allies to supplement the numerically inadequate catholics. By doing so he made the anglican clergy realize that there was an incompatibility between their often-

proclaimed principles of unconditional passive obedience to authority, and the total inadmissibility of resistance to the king, and
the need to preserve the church. James also converted the tories,
who had from the first been auxiliaries of the court, into a 'country'
opposition party that never subsequently lost its suspicions of governmental abuse of power. At the same time most whigs were reserved
in their attitude to James, although a minority collaborated with
him. Deceived by a king whose right to succeed they had preserved
during the Exclusion Crisis, the tories joined with their old whig
enemies in carrying out the Revolution. Although many tories had
reservations about dethroning James in favour of William and Mary,
they were as committed as the whigs to the subsequent legislation
aimed at preventing any future king ever using the same methods in
the future—the suspending of, and dispensing with, statutes by prerogative power, the maintenance of a standing army without parliamentary consent, and the systematic electoral campaign aimed at
packing a subservient parliament.

The achievement of limits on the powers of the crown, rather than
their abolition, together with the participation of the conservative
tory gentry and anglican clergy, have made many historians doubt
whether the events of 1688–9 did really constitute an authentic revolution. However, they finally and conclusively put an end to the
possibility of royal absolutism being established in the British Isles, of
the kind that was dominant in most European states in the late
seventeenth century. Furthermore, James's policies, especially his extremely elaborate and systematic attempt to pack parliament by
manipulating the general elections planned for October 1688, affected a very high proportion of the politically conscious who possessed
the franchise. Most members of the political nation were individually canvassed by James's representatives, and put under direct
pressure in 1687–8. Individuals had to declare themselves openly, for
or against royal demands. Consequently the Revolution of 1688 was
not a matter of 'high politics' or abstract principle. James's policies
affected a wide spectrum of opinion, and the opposition that they
provoked was something far more than an upper-class conspiracy or
'aristocratic revolution'. The Revolution of 1688 was no mere palace
coup.

It was not from choice that James turned to the use of radical
methods that ended by alienating his subjects from him. The failure
of his attempts to persuade the tories to collaborate with him in
repealing the penal laws and the tests, the unexpected resistance of
the anglican clergy to his efforts to give the catholics an equally
privileged position with their own, forced James to a crucial

re-appraisal. He could abandon these policies, or discard his old allies. James was never deterred or influenced by opposition. He chose to intensify and systematize his efforts to achieve those objectives on which he had set his heart. In January 1687 he dismissed Lord Treasurer Rochester who, after some hesitation, had refused to abandon tory and anglican principles. This was followed by extensive purges of tories from local offices. In April James issued the first Declaration of Indulgence, extending religious toleration to dissenters as well as to catholics. Parliament, after being repeatedly prorogued, was dissolved on 2 July. Later that month the first mass purge of municipal office-holders was undertaken (in London), from which was to develop a persistent and large-scale campaign of regulating the corporations, as a preliminary to managing parliamentary elections.

In order to understand these policies of James II, and the hostile reactions that they provoked, it is necessary to examine the assumptions and expectations on which they were based. Underlying James's establishment of universal toleration were two fallacious beliefs. First, he expected that in conditions of peaceful coexistence and free competition catholicism would make significant advances, mainly at the expense of the Church of England. Secondly, James and his advisers thought that, actually or at least potentially, the catholics and the dissenters combined were equal in strength to the established church. Toleration was expected to undermine anglican authority and self-confidence; deprived of the coercive penal laws the clergy would lose their hold over parochial congregations. On the other hand the total cessation of religious persecution would foster social harmony and economic prosperity. The Declaration of Indulgence emphasized these advantages, and James's propagandists took over the whig argument that toleration had been a primary reason for Dutch economic success. Moreover, thanks to James's army, public toleration of diverse faiths posed no threat to peace and public order. James's political plans would be greatly assisted. Toleration would extinguish the religious friction and enmities, national and local, which careerist tories and whig demagogues had encouraged and exploited; they would lose their power bases in anglican intransigence or dissenting grievances. James hoped to convert dissenting gratitude into political support for the parliamentary candidates whom he sponsored, and who would be pre-engaged to repeal the penal laws by a statute.

In practice toleration failed to produce all these expected advantages. It is true that James in England (like Calvert, another catholic, in America) was the effective founder of practical religious liberty: it was not politically selective, like Cromwell's, and extended much more widely than the toleration established by the Convention in 1689. But the catholics reaped few advantages; their missionary campaign in 1686–8 was remarkably ineffective, producing relatively few converts, and these mostly of indifferent quality. Paradoxically, the main conversion achieved was that of the anglican clergy to the principle of conceding limited toleration to the protestant dissenters. But the visible activity of the catholics, especially the mass of pamphlets and books that they distributed, greatly alarmed public opinion. Anti-papist sentiments, temporarily discredited among the better educated after the exposure of Oates and his perjuries, regained currency, and the old whig rallying cry of the need for protestant unity in the face of the papist menace revived strongly and persuasively. Such arguments did not wreck James's attempt to translate dissenting gratitude into electoral support, but they did hamper the efforts made by such associates and agents as William Penn, Lobb and Howe to organize pledges of support for the king.

In his private conversations with the French ambassador, James described his ultimate objective as the 'establishment' of catholicism in England. By this he meant that the rights and freedoms he was conferring on the catholic church were to be perpetual and irreversible, not that he intended to make catholicism the national or state church in place of the anglican, still less to compel all his subjects to become catholics. James had to operate under two restraints. First, catholic organization and resources in England (and those of the crown also) were inadequate to attempt or even contemplate the kind of spectacular and forcible mass conversions that a ruthless, centralized and militarized administration, working with a confident and aggressive church leadership, had just achieved in France after the revocation of the Edict of Nantes (October 1685). Secondly, until June 1688 James had protestant heirs—his daughters Mary and Anne, then William. He extended toleration to dissenters, and started the campaign to pack parliament, so that an alliance of catholics and dissenters would be created sufficiently strong to prevent these heirs reversing his policies by reimposing the tests and penal laws.

Yet by his provocative attempts to put pressure on the anglican clergy James ensured a strong protestant reaction against all his policies, and generated widespread distrust of his sincerity and intentions. In 1686–7 he did not initiate direct action against the anglican church and its clergy, but enough was done to make them feel threatened. An ecclesiastical prerogative court was revived, despite the provisions of the statute of 1641 that had abolished the old High Commission. This new court, the Ecclesiastical Commission, was used in 1686 to suspend the most political and protestant-minded of the bishops from his functions (Compton of London). The other case created equal alarm and indignation, making the Commission appear to be the potential instrument of catholicization. The case of Magdalen College arose from a stubbornly but clumsily enforced attempt to impose a catholic president on the wealthiest of Oxford colleges. The fellows were deprived for resisting, and the college was turned into a catholic preserve; this constituted an infringement of property rights, as well as undermining a central anglican strength, its monopoly over higher education. This move antagonized a large number of influential patrons and alumni, who were powerless to check the process in the Commission, but made open demonstrations of their indignation. Further alarm about James's intentions was created when he issued dispensations to enable anglican clergy who turned catholic to retain their livings. Only a few did so, but suspicions were intensified when James kept key positions in the church unfilled, particularly the archbishopric of York from April 1686. Rumours spread that this see was to be given to a catholic, with the Jesuit Petre (a bogeyman because of his close association with James) as favourite, or that it would serve as a reward for conversion to any existing anglican bishop.

Until the second Declaration of Indulgence, in April 1688, the clergy as a whole were not directly affected by royal policies, except insofar as they had to learn to live and officiate in conditions of toleration. Anglican fears stemmed from the inadequacy of the guarantees contained in the 1687 Declaration, which promised security to the clergy in their possessions and the free exercise of their religion, but as individuals, and deliberately and conspicuously failed to give any such securities to legal entities within the church—cathedral chapters, universities, colleges, schools and charitable foundations—or to the church itself as an institution. This omission was repeated in the second Declaration (27 April 1688), which was accompanied by an ill-considered attempt to pressurize every individual clergyman, a move that had the effect of uniting virtually the whole church behind the defiant stand made on this occasion by its episcopal leaders. The bishops were ordered to instruct all their clergy to read the Declaration from the pulpit on two successive Sundays. If they did so this would give the appearance of acquiescence in James's policies, but if they refused, or bishops or their officials declined to transmit the order, then widespread prosecutions could follow. It was rumoured that the Ecclesiastical Commission would be used (and its subservience to royal orders could be taken for granted) to suspend offenders. This would deprive the church of independent leaders at a critical time, leaving it under the control of the minority of higher clergy who were ready to do what James wanted. Suspension would also mean the elimination of all clerics who might obstruct royal candidates in the forthcoming parliamentary elections, and several bishops who might oppose his policies in the House of Lords.

James was not in fact counting on suspensions, since he did not expect widespread refusals, still less open defiance from the bishops. He was taken completely by surprise when on 18 May the seven bishops, led by Sancroft, the archbishop of Canterbury, and including James's own protégé, Turner, bishop of Ely, petitioned him, asking that they should be excused from distributing and reading the Declaration. James's assumptions about the unquestioning obedience and loyalty he could expect from the clergy were shattered by the bishops' statement that the suspending power on which the Declaration rested was illegal, and he wrongly believed that the bishops were responsible for the printed (and garbled) version of the petition which appeared in London that same night. The Declaration was due to be read on the 20th, which gave James insufficient time to repair the damage. Very few London clergy read the Declaration, and it was to be expected that the provincial clergy would generally follow their example. The bishops could not be allowed immunity from prosecution, because they had challenged the legality of the suspending power. Nevertheless, James's ministers were divided, with some (including Sunderland, the most astute) appreciating the danger. If the bishops were convicted of seditious libel for publishing their petition, and suspended or deprived, this would decapitate the Church of England, and inflame the nation by an apparent intention to ruin protestantism. On the other hand if the bishops were acquitted, James's prestige would be severely damaged.

The trial provided a focal point on which all those opposed to his policies could concentrate, and a stage on which the issues could be dramatized to his disadvantage. He was out-manoeuvred at every stage. The bishops refused to give recognizances to appear at their trial, and so had to be committed to the Tower. Their imprisonment, although brief, heightened alarm and enlisted sympathy. At the trial, defence counsel repeatedly and categorically declared the suspending power, the basis of the Declaration, to be totally illegal. The judges permitted them to say things that could not have been possible outside the court-room, and their speeches were soon to appear in print in avidly read accounts of the trial. Crowds surrounded Westminster Hall, while peers and other prominent sympathizers sat in the public gallery to ensure that the trial was fairly conducted and discourage intimidation of the jury. But the attitude of the judges was the most revealing feature. They knew that any display of favour to the bishops would result in instant dismissal. On the other hand to press for conviction—the usual role for judges in political trials (as had been the case during the Popish Plot and Rye House Plot trials)—would mean upholding the legality of the very doubtful suspending power, as well as depriving the anglican church of its fathers in God. Any future parliament, provided that it was free and not subservient, in other words if James's attempts at packing had failed, would certainly impeach those who upheld the king's exercise of unconstitutional powers—just as Charles 1's judges had been impeached in 1640. One judge (Powell) passed a vote of no-confidence in his master by openly siding with the defendants. Lord Chief Justice Wright and Holloway tried to take refuge in a technical point, of whether the petition had been published, and then left to the jury the question of whether the petition was libellous—a course of action that was irregular since it was for the judges to decide on this point of law; the Seven Bishops Case was not followed in eighteenth-century press cases until the law was amended by Fox's Libel Act (1792). Only the catholic Alibone, who sat on the bench in virtue of a dispensation, tried to protect James's interests. This lack of judicial resolution encouraged the jury to acquit, and James's unconcealed and petulant resentment completed the débâcle. By bringing a prosecution he convicted himself of having designs against the church. Its failure left relations between the anglican clergy and the leaders of the political nation (both whigs and tories) far closer than they had been at any time since 1660.

James's second major objective was to achieve repeal of the tests, so enabling catholics and dissenters to hold administrative, military and local offices. Equality of civil rights was intended to break the existing anglican monopoly which, James believed, was deterring many men from conversion to catholicism. In his view the Test Acts of 1673 and 1678 constituted major encroachments on the prerogative and an intolerable restriction of the royal powers of patronage. James wished to give the catholics a share of offices that would be permanent and outlive himself. Furthermore, he believed that only they were wholly and unreservedly loyal to the crown. Consequently in 1687-8 he purged all office-holders who showed, by their insistence on the retention of the tests, that they would serve the crown only on their own conditions. Dispensations enabled catholics to take their places, but James planned to repeal the tests by statute so as to make their appointments legally unassailable. He was gradually working towards the creation of a distinct catholic interest strongly and permanently entrenched in the administration.

According to a later plan drafted in exile at St Germain, one among the five treasury commissioners and one of the two secretaries of state were always to be catholic. Catholics were to be predominant in appointments at court, as personal attendants on the king and queen, and even more significantly they were to control the army. The secretary of war was to be a catholic, and also *ex officio* member of the seven-man cabinet council. He was to have far more power than the existing secretary *for* war, and the projected office was clearly modelled on the new French system, in which Le Tellier and Louvois had held such a position and had used it to become the principal ministers of Louis XIV. Characteristically, James made a bad choice of catholic minister for this crucial appointment. The earl of Dover lacked dynamism or even administrative aptitude, and allegedly made use of his office primarily to enrich himself by selling commissions. However, some progress was made in increasing the proportion of catholic officers and men in the army, although far less than James wished—or the alarmed public believed. For him, a predominantly catholic army was the prerequisite for a monarchy that would at last cease to be dependent on the cooperation of the subjects, and after the birth of the prince of Wales in 1688, for the perpetuation of all his policies. The remodelling of the army in Ireland was completed by the beginning of 1688, but although progress in England was far slower, James was sufficiently confident of success to allow the county militia to fall into decay.

In attempting to pack a parliament that would repeal the tests and penal laws, James initiated the most intensive process of canvassing and questioning that has ever been attempted in English history, bringing pressure to bear directly on virtually every individual within, or on the fringes of, the political nation. By doing so he brought home to each person the vital importance of the issues involved: these were not a matter of 'high politics', or something that concerned only the gentry, but involved even those eligible only for humble parochial offices. As the trial of the seven bishops dramatized the issues, so James's purges and regulations, and the systematic campaign to pack parliament generalized them as widely as Shaftesbury had done during the Exclusion Crisis.

The base for James's organizational activity in 1687–8 can be found in the earlier addresses that had pledged support for the crown from local bodies—JPs, grand juries, corporations, livery companies, loyal associations and clergy. Originating in tory counter-addresses to whig petitions during the Exclusion Crisis, they were subsequently orchestrated—to welcome Charles's Declaration after the dissolution of the Oxford Parliament, to deplore Shaftesbury's Association project in 1681–2 and the Rye House Plot in 1683, and to promise loyalty on James's accession. The addresses that welcomed the first Declaration of Indulgence, which were largely organized by William Penn the quaker, foreshadowed a change of political alliances; most of them came from dissenting congregations. Up to October 1687, out of more than 200 addresses, only six came from the anglican clergy, and only twenty-seven from the corporations that returned members to parliament. Tory opposition blocked many attempts to organize addresses, JPs and lords lieutenant were often apathetic or actually discouraging. These failures indicated to James those areas where investigations and purges were needed. The earliest changes were made in London, where the lieutenancy was remodelled in August 1687, and over a thousand members of livery companies were dismissed. Nationally, eleven changes of lords lieutenant were made. The new men (who included catholics) were instructed on 25 October to institute a general canvass of all JPs, deputy lieutenants, and those judged capable and fit to serve in these offices. Meetings were convened between November 1687 and March 1688 at which three questions were put to several thousand men, including principal catholics and dissenters. First, if they were elected to the next parliament, would they pre-engage themselves to repeal of the tests and penal laws? If not intending to stand, would they pledge themselves to vote for candidates who had given such an undertaking? Finally, would they promise to live in peace and charity with those of different religious persuasions, that is would they accept toleration?

James made it clear that those who gave unsatisfactory answers would lose their offices, and that favourable replies would lead to consideration as replacements for those purged. The returns which have survived for about half the counties show that just over half those who were questioned gave definite answers; twenty-six per cent agreed, twenty-seven per cent refused, to consent to repeal of the tests and penal laws. The remainder gave ambiguous answers or, especially in Wales where Beaufort the lord lieutenant was not effective, evaded giving any answer. The returns were used to transform the commission of the peace and the lieutenancy. Sweeping purges of refusers led to the installation of numerous catholics and dissenters, and from among those giving favourable replies a number were selected to stand as parliamentary candidates.

The second aspect of James's preparations to pack a collaborationist parliament was the even more intensive and thorough regulation of the corporations. Under the supervision of a commission set up in November 1687, itinerant agents systematically and repeatedly inspected every corporate town in England and Wales, questioned the office-holders, listed men suitable to serve as replace-

ments for the unreliable, and reported on the structure and character of local politics and interests to an office in London run by
Robert Brent, a catholic lawyer and confidential agent to James,
who was also responsible for receiving and processing the answers to
the three questions put by the lords lieutenant. Between November
1687 and March 1688 Brent's agents concentrated on purging the
corporations and putting in new men. In April agents were sent into
the provinces to start constructing electoral interests, and further
purges were effected in June on the basis of their reports. At the
same time salaried officials in the provinces were canvassed and
pressurized—the excise in March, the customs in May. During July,
August and September a further stage saw the issuing of thirty-one
new charters to corporations, and finally in September the agents
were sent into the field again to complete preparations, knowing
that orders in council had been made (on 24 August) for the issuing
of parliamentary writs on 18 September. Sunderland, as coordinator
of the king's electoral activities and repeating in a much more systematic form the work he had done in 1685, sent out instructions to
individual, named, candidates and to lords lieutenant.

The threat of invasion by William forced James to order the writs
to be recalled on 28 September, so that all these intensive electoral
preparations were never put to the test. Nevertheless their effect was
considerable. They represented the most elaborate and formidable
attempt ever made to bring into existence a parliament that would
do what the sovereign wanted. Had James succeeded in the
elections, he would have been able to make the crown absolute by
statutory means. The king and his ministers could have achieved
practical and permanent independence by obtaining a larger
revenue—which would have made it possible to transform local
officials into a salaried class, modifications of *habeas corpus*, and
statutory backing for martial law. James had already achieved an
absolute authority in Scotland, where a far weaker parliament had
been dominated and manipulated. If, as Brent's agents claimed, a
working majority could be returned of members pre-engaged to obey
James, then national and individual liberties would lie at the mercy
of a sovereign who was distrusted because of his religion, and was
known to take a high view of his prerogative rights. Moreover, after
the birth of a healthy son, on 10 June 1688, James at last had the
prospect of ensuring that his policies would be continued after his
own death.

James's campaign should also be translated into terms of personal,
day-to-day politics. It involved an intrusion by the central government into the affairs of the localities on an unprecedented scale.
Every individual with influence and political experience was

personally pressurized, and a high proportion of office holders was displaced. Tories who prided themselves on loyalty to the crown found
themselves supplanted by a heterogeneous collection of catholics,
dissenters and former whigs. Often these changes involved social
change also, with petty or parochial gentry and urban tradesmen
taking places traditionally occupied by the more substantial gentry.
It was noticeable that very few country tories agreed to collaborate,
whereas the whigs were divided. Some were so eager to supplant
their hated local tory rivals, who had been put in by royal intervention in 1681–3, that they were now willing to use the king's offers to
recover their places. Adventurers and careerists thought only of personal advantage, the most conspicuous being William Williams, the
former whig Speaker, who prosecuted the seven bishops and became
solicitor-general. Even the radicals were split. Many had been in
exile since 1683 or 1685, and produced a stream of virulent pamphlets attacking James, but most of his regulators and electoral agents
were men who had formerly served or supported Shaftesbury.

Similarly, while very few prominent anglicans collaborated with
James, the dissenters were deeply divided. In 1686–7 Penn took a
leading part in advocating acceptance of James's offers as sincere
and beneficial, and he was despatched on an unsuccessful mission to
persuade William and Mary to consent to repeal of the penal laws
and tests. But by the summer of 1688 he had developed reservations,
especially about the tests and the attempt to pack parliament.
Clearly this was unsatisfactory for James. He found that dissenters
accepted the benefits of toleration, but the presbyterians in particular were unwilling to show their gratitude by publicly supporting
repeal of the tests. All dissenters faced a dilemma. Could they trust
James's sincerity, when the recent Revocation of the Edict of Nantes
by Louis xiv confirmed the belief that catholicism and toleration
were fundamentally incompatible? On the other hand, could they
really expect toleration, or even connivance, from the bishops and
anglican clergy at whose hands they had suffered so severely in
1681–6? Many dissenters were also pessimistic about William's intentions, fearing that he was determined to preserve the anglican
establishment strictly.

Divisions proliferated among the dissenters. Presbyterian clergy
were the most cautious and, by the time of the trial of the bishops,
had chosen to associate themselves with the anglicans in a modified
form of protestant alliance; comprehension, that is their reincorpo-
ration within the anglican church as a result of concessions to satisfy
their scruples, again became a possibility. Congregationalist and
baptist clergy, and still more the quakers, generally collaborated
with James. Dissenting laymen, striving for revenge and an ascen-

dancy in a new round of political in-fighting with predominantly anglican rivals within the corporations, allied with James and provided the bulk of his collaborators. However, James's alliance with the dissenters was dangerously vulnerable in one important aspect: their support for him would evaporate if an overpowering cry for protestant unity could be organized, and this was to be achieved by William's propagandists.

James's need to solicit support from any section of his subjects was confined to these electoral preparations. Otherwise, thanks to a competent administration and an efficient army, with garrisons in all large provincial towns and around (though not in) London, he could dispense with the cooperation of his subjects. Refusals to collaborate, or even successful disobedience as in the case of the bishops, could not stop or reverse James's policies. Only intervention from outside could accomplish this, and it was both necessary and logical for a significant section of his opponents to look to William as the only possible person to defeat royal plans.

William has been depicted as scheming to seize possession of the English crown in order to satisfy a life's ambition, but in reality he never regarded influence in, or control over, England as an end in itself, but rather as the necessary means of strengthening the forces available to him, in his self-imposed task of checking and defeating French aggression. At the time of his marriage in 1677, William had wanted early English entry into the European war; this had not been forthcoming. Later he believed, wrongly, that Charles would ultimately have to make major concessions to his domestic opponents, and William preferred Exclusion to the alternative of limitations, because the latter would weaken the monarchy to the point where an effective foreign policy might become impossible. Consequently, he connived at a memorandum from the States General in 1680 advocating Exclusion, and during a visit to England in July 1681 he tried to reconcile Charles with the whigs, although he had had no direct contacts with the whig leaders and had not realized how intransigent they were. This visit proved to be a disaster. Charles and James never lost the distrust of William which they then acquired. On his side, William retained a most unfavourable impression of the irresponsibility and selfishness of all English politicians, but particularly of the whigs, concluding that the latter were intent on exploiting him for personal and party advantage. England remained a French-subsidized neutral, reneging on its European obligations, and so allowing Louis to achieve further advances in 1681–3.

After 1685, Mary was heiress presumptive, but she received no allowance or recognition from James. Nevertheless, a reversionary interest of politicians looking forward to the next reign began to form. William's correspondence with England widened in its range. He maintained a close watch on developments, as James discarded tory support, declared for toleration and began to try to pack parliament. Using various diplomatic pretexts, William despatched special missions for reconnaissance purposes, Dijkvelt in February and Zuylestein in August 1687. Without committing himself to any course of action, William used the pensionary of Holland, Fagel, to indicate his disapproval of James's policies: Fagel's letter condemning attempts to repeal the penal laws and tests was given maximum publicity.

In September 1687 William took the first step towards putting James under pressure. An extensive and clandestine network of informants and agents was organized by his most trusted servants, Bentinck, Dijkvelt, Sidney and Johnstone. Bentinck, who became earl of Portland in 1689, had served William faithfully since boyhood days and was to continue as his chief confidant until displaced by Keppel in the last years of William's life. Sidney was disliked and despised by many of his contemporaries as an arrogant, drunken adventurer, and in the 1690s his limitations became apparent during his term as secretary, but William trusted him implicitly. He was 'the great wheel on whom the Revolution turned', doing much of the clandestine work in England in partnership with Johnstone, who came from a notable covenanting family. Dijkvelt was mainly employed in preparative work in Europe. This network kept William informed of James's plans and intentions as well as his decisions. It was used to sound out, and later to influence, prominent individuals, and to distribute vast quantities of printed propaganda with a popular appeal. But by April 1688, a surprisingly late date, William realized that he would have to intervene in England himself, and with an army, if James's policies were to be prevented from coming to fruition. Even then the timing of such intervention was uncertain, as William was involved in dangerous developments in Europe.

During the summer of 1688 a new European war was threatened by the disputed election to the key German electorate of Cologne. This created formidable problems for William. Spain was bound to become involved, and as the French would certainly infringe the sovereignty of the Spanish Netherlands and of Liège, where there was another disputed election, Dutch security could soon be imperilled. If this happened, William would have neither time nor resources to intervene in England. On the other hand Louis would do all in his power to draw James in on the French side. Already his ability to make use of James had been demonstrated when, under persuasion from the French ambassador, orders had been issued for the return of all English, Scottish and Irish subjects serving in six long-established regiments maintained by the States General, a move intended to embarrass William and weaken the Dutch forces. But Louis delayed his military offensive into the Rhineland until the end of September, so giving William a winter to spare. Louis could not move his forces to invade the Low Countries until the next spring, or send significant aid to James during what William planned to be a very short campaign.

William's freedom to act coincided with the climax of alarm and tension within England. The protracted campaign to pack parliament was about to be put to the test in the October general elections. The birth of the prince of Wales on 10 June was bound to have important effects. His mother, the queen, would become regent if James died, and she quickly emerged as a new political factor. Her influence would benefit the group of actively francophile ministers, who were pressing James for resolute action, and it was in order to gain her continuing favour that Sunderland became a convert to catholicism before the end of June. Catholicizing policies were certain to be intensified, and the long-term political prospects were now transformed. A catholic dynasty would mean the perpetuation of all James's policies, and the chances of an early protestant reaction under Mary receded. On the other hand the prosecution and acquittal of the bishops had reawakened anti-papist sentiment to a pitch not much less than in the hysterical panic of 1678. This was the line heavily stressed by William's popular propaganda, and it led to almost universal acceptance of a crude and fantastic invention—the charge that the infant prince was not the queen's child, but had been smuggled into Whitehall in the celebrated warming-pan. This fable suited both versions of what had allegedly happened: either the queen's pregnancy had never been genuine, or she had had a baby but it had died.

Another reason for William to take early action was the information that James was not only expanding his army, but intended to remodel it during the winter. This would involve increasing the proportion of catholic officers, which had been less than twelve per cent in 1687. Most serving officers came from the tory and anglican land-owning class; they were, paradoxically, the only section of James's subjects that had not been pressurized by canvassing and questioning. While they served in what was now James's main power base, nearly all their relations and associates in other branches of the administration had been interrogated and discarded. James intended to change this, to purge and catholicize the English army as he had recently the Irish army. This process also involved filling the ranks with Irish catholics; officers in the key Portsmouth garrison who objected were court-martialled and dismissed. In the short run these moves operated to William's advantage. They facilitated the subversive work of his partisans among the officers, especially the Rose Tavern group, and they led directly to the large-scale defections that were to undermine the morale of James's army in November. But they made early intervention imperative. William could not afford a full-scale military campaign against the numerically formidable English army; all his plans depended on the fulfilment of the assurances he received that this army was so disaffected that it would not offer serious resistance.

In addition to denouncing James's catholicizing policies, William's propagandists charged the king with being a French puppet. In reality this was not true; indeed, Louis used the crisis to try to reduce James to the kind of dependence which the latter had set himself to avoid. French plans would be served by diverting William to England, while Louis destroyed the League of Augsburg by a military and diplomatic offensive in Germany. He would then be free to rescue James from William. But in 1688 French dispositions made it impossible for any significant pressure to be exerted on William to deter him from invading. Despite this, the French envoy at the Hague formally warned the States General against any intervention in England, so confirming in the minds of both the Dutch and English publics the picture of James as the puppet of Louis, and the notion that the two catholic kings were linked in an alliance of religion.

This move damaged James immensely at a time when he was left isolated to defend himself against a threat which he was slow to recognize. Until September James concentrated almost entirely on his parliamentary preparations. When he appreciated the danger of William intervening, his first (uncharacteristic) move was to offer concessions. He insincerely suggested to the Dutch that they should cooperate to check French expansion. This was laughed at. The domestic concessions were more serious, as they amounted to an abandonment of his principal policies in such ways that it would have been difficult to renew them. The Ecclesiastical Commission was abolished, and its victims the Magdalen College fellows reinstated. Orders were given to restore the forfeited charters, including London's. Men put into municipal offices by the regulators were to be ejected, and an investigation of the conduct of the regulators and electoral agents was promised. Tories were offered their former places in the lieutenancy and commission of the peace. The writs for parliamentary elections were withdrawn, which was logical as the whole campaign of packing was now in ruins.

These concessions were totally ineffective. They were obviously made under pressure, and most men rightly suspected that they would be withdrawn if James overcame William. It was part of the anti-papist myth that no catholic could ever be trusted to keep faith with heretics, and by abandoning his policies and allies in a second political reversal as complete as that of 1687, James lost all credibility, and gained nothing. He sacrificed his ex-whig collaborators. Sunderland was dismissed (27 October), but this was far too late to have any effect. Tories generally turned down reinstatement; the clergy refused to give open pledges of support and condemnation of rebellion. It was impossible for James suddenly to free himself from the resentments and suspicions he had generated by his arbitrary policies. By trying to pack parliament he had antagonized all tories and most of the gentry-based electoral interests; now that the campaign had been called off, and Brent's agents discarded, a freely elected parliament must mean one strongly antagonistic to James and the court. This was the assumption both of William and of those who rallied to him when they called (as Monk had done in 1660) for a free parliament. There could be no doubt that such a free parliament would try to ensure against any future repetition of royal policies, as the bishops knew when, in reply to an appeal by James, they declared that parliament should decide whether the king had a dispensing and suspending power; they also demanded that catholics should be barred from state offices, and their ecclesiastical organization prohibited.

Trusting in the strength of the army and not wishing to have to rely on his subjects, James had allowed the militia to fall into decay, except in London. This meant that when James concentrated his troops into a field army to oppose William's advance on London the provinces were left uncovered. William's partisans were able to seize the main provincial centres—Chester, York, Nottingham, Hull, Northampton and Norwich—during the last ten days of November.

Nevertheless the existence of the English standing army complicated William's plans. By invading in early winter he faced unavoidable risks, and he was depleting the defences of the United Provinces at the outset of a European war. It is not an exaggeration to say that everything depended on the assurances that he had received from the English serving officers who were protestants (as distinct from the Scots, Irish and catholics) that they would defect at the most opportune moment, and that their action would disintegrate the army. Their performance of these promises, the precipitate collapse of military morale and cohesion, removed the danger of a prolonged land war in England. Many of these officers had tory associations, and their support helped to broaden the basis of William's appeal, enabling him to escape attempts by the radical whigs to tie him to themselves and what would have been an exclusively whig set of policies.

William landed in Torbay on 5 November, entering Exeter four days later. The story that initial lack of support almost led him to re-embark has no foundation; whig and tory gentry began to join in large numbers from the 12th. Defections from James's army began on the 16th. When the king arrived at the Salisbury rendezvous on the 19th he found an army that was rapidly becoming demoralized, and its uncertainty infected him. William was out of reach of a sudden offensive—he left Exeter on the 21st—but, by leaving the army on 24 November to return to London, James was, without realizing it, changing the character of the crisis from a military into a political contest, and he was even less well equipped for this. On 17 November, just before joining his army, James rejected a petition from a group of peers and bishops, calling for the convocation of a free parliament, but now on 30 November he reversed this decision. By proclamation James announced that a parliament would meet on 15 January, promised a general pardon that would enable William's adherents to stand as candidates, and also undertook to safeguard the Church of England. He ended by announcing that commissioners would be sent to negotiate with William.

This proclamation was the signal for the start of a period of intense political manoeuvring. English politicians were in their element, but neither James nor William welcomed the proposals that were advanced. James was becoming convinced that his life, and the even more precious lives of his wife and son, were endangered, and that security could be found only by taking refuge in France. He sent his wife and son away on 8 December, and left himself two days later. William's objection to the negotiations arose from a realization that his position was as yet insufficiently strong. He did not wish to have to accept arbitration between himself and James by the bishops, whom he mistrusted, and a group of tory peers who had stayed in London. His supporters, especially those who had taken the very considerable risk of joining in William's invasion force, or had risen in the provinces, were furious at the possibility of such men negotiating a compromise.

James's precipitate flight and his last actions, which were intended to produce an anarchical lack of order, changed the situation and suited both William and his leading adherents. Before he fled, James ordered the cancelling of parliamentary writs that had not been issued, had the Great Seal (needed to authenticate major state decisions) thrown into the Thames, and disbanded the army—without disarming the soldiers, many of them Irish. By deliberately creating a governmental vacuum, James forced even the most loyal politicians into taking action to preserve public order. Spontaneous but momentarily dangerous anti-catholic riots broke out in London, which threatened to turn into general mob attacks on property. In face of this danger an assembly of peers and bishops met at Guildhall on 11 December, and established a kind of provisional government for London. Similarly, in the provinces, when disbanding led to rumours that ravaging and murdering bands of soldiers were approaching, the 'Irish alarms', the gentry mustered the semi-defunct militia, taking over control from a virtually paralysed commission of the peace and lieutenancy.

Unfortunately for William, James failed to reach France at the first attempt. Intercepted by Kentish fishermen and beaten up, he returned to London on 16 December, when William was still some distance away. Now the latter had to use pressure to induce James to leave again, on the 18th agreeing to Rochester as his asylum in the correct expectation that from there he would soon escape to France. During these few days tories and anglican clergy vainly tried to dissuade James from doing so, but although he left secretly on the 22nd this second escape was too obviously to William's advantage, and was to be represented by jacobite propaganda as the culmination of William's conspiracy to usurp the throne. On the other hand, the anarchy that James had deliberately created horrified and frightened the entire propertied class, and his destruction of the Great Seal and withdrawal of the writs made William the indispensable agent in restoring order and government.

William convoked an assembly over Christmas to advise him. The peers, and a lower house composed of surviving members of Charles II's parliaments (but not those who had sat only in 1685, the implication being that that had not been a free parliament), together with aldermen and common councilmen of London, asked him to take on the administration, and to issue circular letters for elections to return members to a convention parliament, which was to meet on 22 January. It was a remarkable sign of the speed with which normal life was restored that these elections took place in peaceful conditions, without abnormal acrimony, and on traditional lines. It was as if there had been no revolution, no Irish alarms, no campaign to organize elections; in the counties the gentry had already reasserted their old dominant position by early January.

Besides the urgent question of settling immediately the form that government was to take, the Convention had to deal with fundamental constitutional problems that its predecessors had failed to solve,

both the Long Parliament in 1640–42 and the Convention of 1660.
In 1689 the essential basis was laid for a durable settlement, and the
government established under William and Mary was accepted by
the vast majority of the nation. Its strength was tested by a prolonged and unprecedentedly difficult and expensive war against
France. However, in the short term the Convention quickly divided
into factional parties, whose constant quarrels poisoned politics and
greatly added to William's difficulties.

The Revolution Settlement was pragmatic in character. The
Convention was indistinguishable in its composition and proceedings
from other parliaments, being exceptional only in that it had not
been called by a ruling sovereign. It made no abstract statements of
constitutional principle, or of the rights of the subject. The basis of
the settlement, the Bill of Rights, consisted of a set of specific provisions aimed at preventing any repetition of the policies by which
Charles, James and their ministers had endangered liberties (that is,
particular rights) and religion. This pragmatism is understandable.
General questions about the inherent rights of the monarchy and of
parliament had been exhaustively, acrimoniously and inconclusively
debated during the Exclusion Crisis. Renewal of these debates would
revive the deep and bitter divisions of that time, and shatter the
unity that was needed to defend the kingdom against James and his
patron Louis.

The first task was to settle the question of who should actually
reign. A few peers and bishops favoured the recall of James, but this
was impracticable since limits would have to be imposed on his royal
powers, and these he could not be expected to accept. This made
regency the conservative solution. For some, notably Bishop Turner
of Ely, it was intended as no more than a temporary device, to prove
to James that England could be governed without him, and so persuade him eventually to agree to return as a limited monarch. But
most of the tory party expected that the regency would have to last
for James's life. The scheme involved formidable difficulties. If
William became regent he would do so knowing that at some unpredictable date in the future he would have to step down. In any case
James was not likely to agree to any form of regency, and since he
was being backed by Louis it would be necessary for the regent to
fight James and Louis in James's own name—a position that would
not only be illogical, but would uncomfortably recall the Long
Parliament's stand of making war against Charles I in his own name.
The sole advantage of the regency solution was that it involved no
break in the legal continuity of the succession, but it was only just
defeated in the Lords. This was partly due to peers switching to the
alternative tory solution, sponsored by Danby, of putting Mary on

the throne as queen, with William acting as regent for her. There would be no infringement of the law of the succession; James was assumed to have deserted the kingdom, and the prince of Wales could be disregarded as an impostor. But in practical terms Mary would not accept what to her was the unnatural position of commanding her husband. William, even if he wielded effective power under Mary would lose this on her death, when Anne would succeed. He was strongly hostile to the idea, and favoured instead the radical whig proposal, for William to be king alone. Mary was willing to acquiesce, but Anne would never have accepted such an infringement of her rights, and it would not only have made her a rallying point for tory dissidents, but William would have found himself obliged to rely exclusively on whig support, as prisoner of one party. Despite Bentinck's advice, and whig pressure, this solution had to be rejected as unacceptably divisive.

The final settlement, of William and Mary as joint sovereigns with William exercising governmental powers, represented a constitutional monstrosity but it worked and had been made unavoidable by William's statement on 3 February that he would not be either regent or prince consort. This broke the deadlock created by the Lords' refusal to agree with the Commons' resolution that James had abdicated and that consequently that the throne was vacant. The other development that produced a solution was Anne's willingness to allow William to take precedence over her in the succession, but with the proviso that she and her children were to come before any children born to William by a second marriage, should he outlive Mary. This concession underlined the fact that the succession was being arbitrarily determined by parliament, although the detailed statutory delimitation reassured those who had feared that the Revolution would make the monarchy elective.

On 12 February the two houses of parliament agreed on the Declaration of Rights, the basis for the later bill, and on the next day William and Mary were offered the crown jointly. The Bill was finally passed on 16 December. Its justificatory preamble put the blame for misgovernment on James, whereas in his declaration before the invasion William had blamed only James's ministers. By initiating policies that broke his own laws, and failing to respect the constitution, James had in the view advocated by the whigs violated the original contract between the nation and its ruler, although the judges who were consulted proved to be unable to find any such contract. But although James had become a tyrant by accumulative misdeeds, there was no formal reduction in the powers of the monarchy. Only those powers which James had claimed without any basis in right were now stated to be illegal and unconstitutional—the suspending power, the dispensing power if used wholesale to invalidate statutes, the collection of taxes without parliamentary authorization, the revival of a prerogative court. Essentially the Bill of Rights was declaratory of ancient rights, which it re-established and secured; it did not create new rights.

Such was the continuing power of anti-popery that there was no opposition to the one clearly innovative portion of the bill, that restricted the monarchy. By experience, so it was claimed, the nation had found it inexpedient to have a papist sovereign. Any papist, or anyone married to one, was barred from the succession. This represented an extension to the monarchy itself of the principle underlying the Test Acts, and was a reversal of the European principle—*cuius regio eius religio* (the religion of the ruler determines that of his subjects)—so that in England the sovereign had to be of the same faith as the nation. As a result of this clause all James I's descendants in the Orléans line, and all but one branch of the Palatine family were barred.

The original drafts of the Bill of Rights contained provisions intended to redress outstanding grievances, both general and specific. There was insufficient parliamentary time to enact this package of reforms; many of the proposals were intrinsically difficult and complex, and some were controversial. The only appearance of these issues in the Bill was as statements of intent—that parliamentary elections ought to be free, as should debates and proceedings, that parliaments ought to be held frequently, juries ought to be duly impanelled, excessive bail should not be required or unusual punishments inflicted. There was no room in the final Bill for a long list of political safeguards that had been suggested—repealing the Militia Act of 1661, preventing overlong parliaments (like the Cavalier Parliament of 1661–79), securing corporations against *quo warranto* actions and restoring charters, prohibiting the buying and selling of offices, uniting all protestants 'in the matter of public worship as far as may be', regulating procedure in treason trials, instituting an independent judiciary and improving *habeas corpus* procedures. The Convention had time (and sufficient unity of purpose) to legislate on only a few subjects. An act changed the coronation oath to imply a contract, the sovereign having to swear to maintain 'the protestant reformed religion established by law', and to govern 'according to the statutes in parliament agreed on and the laws and customs of the same'. The Mutiny Act gave a statutory basis to army discipline, and was passed for one year only, a practice that was to continue. Proposals for a scheme of comprehension, to permit concessions that would allow presbyterians to re-enter the Church of England, eventually foundered, but a limited toleration or indulgence bill passed, exempting protestant dissenters from the penal laws, but not catholics (or deists and atheists). The oaths acknowledging William and Mary as king and queen were framed so as to accommodate those with constitutional scruples, who could not regard them as legitimate, but only as *de facto* rulers—the words 'rightful and lawful' were omitted.

The statutes passed in 1689 represented a lowest common denominator type of settlement. Few were fully satisfied, but it antagonized only an uninfluential and small minority of jacobites and non-jurors; the latter were a predominantly clerical body, men who were deprived of their livings for refusing to take the oaths but had little lay support. The Revolution Settlement was unspectacular and pragmatic, but it provided a basis for stable and generally acceptable government. Only James's own right, and that of his immediate family, was infringed and overthrown. However, the actual legislation of 1689 was incomplete, leaving many issues unresolved. The constitutional safeguards that had been suggested, but not enacted, were to provide the new country opposition with a programme for the remainder of the reign, and it was only with the Act of Settlement in 1701 that the legislative work initiated by the Convention Parliament was at last completed.

13 English Politics during the Nine Years War

Those who invited William to invade knew that they were committing England to participation in his life-long struggle to contain and reduce French power. But it is doubtful whether they had any real conception of what an inevitably prolonged war against France would entail. The war placed an almost unbearable strain on every branch of government, and on the economy; it was to accelerate long-term social trends towards a concentration of wealth and influence in a newly emerging oligarchy; and in the short run it led to a transformation of political alignments.

The changes produced by the Nine Years War were so important that they require clarification. William's preoccupation with diplomacy and the war, his absences overseas (1689 was the only complete year he spent in England) meant that he required ministers who could be relied upon to carry out the routine business of government. They had to accept responsibility and carry parliament for policies that were essentially the king's, and had often been decided without reference to them. Failures on their part to accept these tasks, or incompetence in carrying them out, caused William to make frequent and drastic ministerial changes. In 1689–90 he attempted to use a balanced administration of whigs, tories and independent politicians, but whig intransigence and irresponsibility made the experiment unworkable. Instead William had to rely on the tories, and especially on the experienced Carmarthen (the former Danby), but his absorption in the mechanical business of detailed political management and the incompetence with which a great deal of administration was performed (particularly in the admiralty) made this largely tory government obviously less serviceable to William than a newly available alternative. The Junto, a group of junior whig ministers, with Sunderland as an associate in the background, took on the almost superhuman tasks of financing the war during its last difficult years (1693–7), and of defending royal policies in both houses of parliament. Their cohesion and discipline made them the first real party administration, but could not enable them to survive the post-war reaction against abnormally high levels of taxation, and the maintenance of a large army. But although William substituted a much looser grouping of ministers, predominantly tory in political complexion, the approach of a new European war led him in 1701 to think of reinstating the more experienced and cohesive Junto.

The task of William's ministries was also made more difficult by the fluidity of party alignments and divisions. In 1689 the political nation was sharply and clearly divided between whig and tory, but this was on the basis of past controversies which were made less relevant by the emergence of new issues. By establishing a mixed administration of whigs and tories William initiated a process of regrouping. Both parties began to split into court and country sections; those who were not in office attacked their own nominal leaders as well as ministers from the other party, and found themselves working in cooperation with old enemies. The whigs were the more severely disrupted. Some radicals, like Ferguson 'the plotter' and their Scottish allies in the 'Club', were so disillusioned that they turned jacobite. More significantly the main body of country whigs were so alienated by what they considered to be the conscious and continual betrayal of whig principles by the Junto ministers and their readiness to use placemen as supporters that they parted company with them and moved closer to the country tories. The latter were equally hostile to corruption and self-aggrandizement on the part of their own, as well as whig, ministers, and especially those associated with Carmarthen's administration in 1690–93, but it was not until after its collapse that the full consequences of the war were experienced. It was the Junto that was identified with such unpopular policies as unprecedentedly heavy war taxation, the growth of government indebtedness and the maintenance of a large army; consequently the alienation of rank-and-file whigs from their leaders was deeper and more permanent than was the case with the tories. Furthermore, the central whig principle of commitment to the Revolution Settlement was far less politically advantageous than is generally assumed; it became less of a unifying factor as the jacobite menace rapidly faded, and it failed to counterbalance the damage done to the Junto by having constantly to advocate the unpopular policies which William and the war demanded. By contrast, the main tory characteristic of loyalty to the Church of England always acted as a factor uniting the court and country wings, and it also counteracted the effects of the ambivalent attitude of many tories to the Revolution Settlement; it was not until after 1710 that the potentially explosive issue of the Protestant Succession began to have a disruptive effect.

It would be difficult to overstate the severity of the effects of King William's war on every aspect of life. It posed a searching test of government and administration through requiring successive military as well as expensive naval campaigns; indeed the army and also the the diplomatic service were virtually creations of the war. Taxation rose to levels never equalled even during the Long Parliament and under Cromwell. Foreign trade was severely disrupted by systematic French privateering. At times the war seemed likely to go on for ever, with no prospect of a negotiated settlement. But despite almost universal inexperience of problems of such magnitude and complexity, the test was passed, and by 1697 France and the United Provinces were far more exhausted and almost demoralized. It can be said that the Nine Years War, far more than the political events of 1688–9, constitutes the really significant revolution of the late seventeenth century. Despite the country opposition's attempt during William's last years to put the clock back, this war permanently transformed England, equipping the country with the military, diplomatic and fiscal machinery, and generating the self-confidence, that were to enable it to expand and develop so spectacularly in the next century.

William had little option in 1689 but to appoint a mixed or broadly based administration, containing an approximately equal number of whigs and tories, reflecting the support that both parties had given him in the Revolution. He wished to avoid becoming the captive of either, and he already distrusted most partisan politicians. Some of his early moves betrayed inexperience and ignorance. On 15 March he made a proposal to repeal the Test Act for the benefit of the protestant dissenters, in the mistaken belief that they were as strong and influential as the Church of England; this move alarmed the tories, some of whom were already becoming cool towards him. Similarly William incorrectly thought that the whigs were significantly the strongest party (as they had been in 1679–81), believing also (from acquaintance with such radical exiles as Mordaunt, Wildman and Peyton, whom he had had to use) that they were really republican at heart, and would try to destroy or severely restrict the royal prerogative. These exiles were not representative whigs, and there was a real danger for William in becoming too closely associated with them. Eyebrows rose at Exeter in November 1688 at the sight of Peyton as a regimental commander; he had been expelled from the Commons in 1680 after being detected in an intrigue with James, and he had made himself distrusted while in exile. Wildman had been a Leveller representative at the Putney debates in 1647 and later a radical associate of Buckingham, but recently he had ratted on his promises to Monmouth in 1685; after the Revolution he stuffed his radical friends into offices and precipitated his dismissal by tampering with the mails. Mordaunt, later the 'great earl of Peterborough' of the campaigns in Spain after 1705, was politically ambitious but unbalanced; he later turned into the most extreme of tories. William therefore weighted some of his initial appointments in favour of the whigs: the treasury commission contained four whigs out of five, the admiralty three out of four. Danby as lord president balanced Halifax as lord privy seal. A tory peer, Nottingham, served as secretary with the whig figurehead, Shrewsbury. But as with the reformed 1679 privy council, a mixture of ministers divided by personal animosities and party differences only intensified factionalism. Quarrels damaged the king's service during the summer of 1689, when nearly all Ireland was lost to James.

William soon discovered serious weaknesses in every leading minister and politician. He faulted Danby for giving too much time and attention to mechanical parliamentary management and manipulative use of patronage, in which he had specialized in the 1670s. Halifax, in whom he confided and who could have become chief minister, lacked the political and personal stamina to endure virulent criticism, and his principled refusal as an advocate of trimming to construct a political following left him increasingly isolated. Shrewsbury, who was potentially the ablest of all, lacked determination. As early as August he asked leave to resign, displaying the deep-seated psychological reluctance to commit himself that was to result in prolonged retirements interrupting his career. The whigs were infuriated by the appointment of Godolphin as a treasury commissioner; William saw him as pre-eminently the man of business, and overlooked his long association with James, but he soon wished to resign. The 'high' tory leaders, Bath and Rochester, were blamed for Anne's coolness towards William and Mary; Marlborough and Godolphin were also discredited when this coolness later developed into outright hostility.

William's disillusionment with the whigs was even more profound, and stemmed largely from their irresponsible behaviour in the Convention, which impeded urgent business. The record of the Convention Parliament was impressively constructive down to the middle of May 1689, except over supply, where major issues were evaded by a series of stop-gap votes. After establishing the new government, the Convention passed the Mutiny Act (giving statutory sanction to military law), amended by statute the coronation oath so as to make explicit the sovereign's obligation to respect the law, and passed the Toleration Act in a restrictive form that reassured the tories and anglicans, while doing just enough to satisfy the protestant dissenters by giving them exemption from the penal laws. Satisfactory progress was also made on the Bill of Rights. These achievements made tory demands that the Convention should be dissolved, and a new parliament elected, look like self-seeking factionalism, but towards the end of the first session unfinished business began to accumulate; on 18 June thirty bills were pending. It was also ominous that only slow progress was being made with the most contentious issue, the proposed bill of indemnity and pardon.

The second session of the Convention, from October 1689 to January 1690, saw a succession of disorderly debates on this subject, which discredited the whigs in the eyes both of William and of the nation. Passions were heightened by bitter personal and political disputes, which prevented the early implementation of William's promise (following Charles's example in 1660) of a general pardon, excepting only James's most obnoxious collaborators. The whigs tried to extend the number of those who were to be excluded from pardon, so as to drive as many tories as possible out of office and political life; their method was by investigating alleged irregularities from Charles's last years (as well as James's reign), and by proposing to except from pardon entire categories of alleged instruments of royal absolutism. They made a sustained attempt also to fix local government in such a way as to give their partisans a permanent ascendancy in the corporations.

The vehicle for this attempt was the bill to restore municipal corporations. Recent changes had created complete legal and political confusion. The forfeiture or enforced surrender of charters in 1681–6, the regulations of 1687–8, the restoration of some old charters by James in October 1688, meant that there were often two rival charters in existence on which municipal elections were held, resulting in rival sets of officers denouncing each other as intruders and usurpers. What was at stake was nothing less than local primacy, superiority at the grass roots of politics, which would result in almost unassailable parliamentary majorities in future elections. The tories showed their hand in July, proposing that power to elect a new set of officers in restored corporations should be vested in those who had been members in 1675, a period of anglican domination; the survivors would be predominantly tory. The whigs at first attempted to obtain the repeal of the sacramental test for officers; this came to nothing, but in fact the test could be easily evaded by the device of occasional conformity. When the whigs counterattacked they intended to leave no similar loop-hole for their opponents. Taking advantage of a thin house after the short Christmas recess, on 2 January 1690 they amended the bill so as to disqualify from service for seven years all officers, aldermen and common councilmen who, with or without the consent of the body corporate, had assisted in the surrender or forfeiture of any charter—that is, those who had been active in 1681 6, almost all tories. Breach of this disqualification would be punished by being barred for life. The whigs blatantly rejected a proposal to extend this disqualification to disable anyone who had helped, or profited from, James's regulations of the corporations in 1687–8—simply because most of these beneficiaries had been rank-and-file whigs.

This attempt at political manipulation provoked a major clash, not only between whigs and tories, but also between the whigs and William. On 10 January, in a series of fiercely contested divisions the tories seized the initiative and eliminated all the whig amendments, and significantly most independent members seem to have supported them. The defeated whigs made it clear that their resentment would result in intensified obstructionism, including delaying vitally needed supply. On 21 January they blocked all progress on the indemnity bill. Exasperated, and also in order to scuttle a whig propaganda address asking him not to go to Ireland on campaign, William prorogued parliament on 27 January. On 6 February by dissolving the Convention, William undertook the first major political revolution (in the seventeenth-century sense of a general change) of the reign.

William's experiences with his whig ministers were equally unsatisfactory. The experiment of combining Godolphin in the treasury with four strongly partisan whigs—Mordaunt, Delamere, Capel and Hampden—did not work. Only the last showed any real aptitude for financial business, and proved to be the only whig survivor. Delamere was too conscious of his own political rectitude in what he soon came to detest as an allegedly corrupt court. In contrast Capel, as a willing newcomer to court jobbery, spent his energies on improving his own interests. Mordaunt, instead of building a useful connection with the monied interest in the City to obtain desperately needed loans—which was the main reason for his appointment—preferred to join with the opportunist Devonshire in encouraging the London radical whigs to petition for the dismissal of all tories from both central and local offices. The whig duke of Bolton, who may well have been mad, also affected popular politics, while Wildman (the old Leveller leader) abused his appointment as postmaster-general to tamper with the mails for personal and party purposes. Nor was the admiralty commission a success. Admiral Herbert suffered from the administrative incompetence of two vociferous whigs, Sacheverel and Lee, whose neglect of business hampered the provision of effective protection for merchant shipping, and seriously delayed the transport of forces to relieve Ulster.

More generally, the conduct of whig ministers and officers was indistinguishable in parliament from that of open opponents of the court; William was outraged by their indiscipline and factiousness, which he regarded as flagrant disloyalty of a kind that he had never encountered in Holland. Consequently he was certainly not prepared to accept the repeated whig argument that, because they alone were truly loyal to him and to the principles of the Revolution, they were entitled to monopolize office. In December 1689 the moderate Shrewsbury contended that most tories were still for James in their hearts and could never be relied on. Thomas Wharton the most aggressive of whigs, in a hectoring letter which William resented and never forgot, claimed that by employing evil ministers associated with the misgovernment of past reigns, William was ruining both himself and the kingdom. These 'flatterers, knaves and villains'—needless to say all tories—'the most obnoxious men of all England' must be dismissed wholesale as 'known enemies to the laws and government'. William was urged to unite with parliament: by this Wharton meant prolonging the life of the Convention which had made him king.

Wharton was asking William to place himself unreservedly in whig hands. Their selfishness and misbehaviour led the king to turn instead to the tories, even though many of the latter would accept him only as a *de facto* ruler. The crucial factor was the promise of steady parliamentary support from a now well organized tory party, centring on the Devil Tavern bloc of MPs. Paradoxically this bloc had been formed in March 1689 to prevent William making major concessions to the dissenters, but in January 1690, two days after the prorogation, a meeting of over 150 tory MPs promised votes of supply, if the Convention was dissolved and a new parliament called. The turn to the tories had a further advantage for the crown in that the new tory treasury commissioners, who replaced the whig ministers in mid-March, were more competent and far more successful in obtaining advances in London.

The general elections of 1690 had the effect of reducing the bitterness of party politics. The Convention had become polarized, with the Commons almost equally divided into two savagely hostile parties which were locked in constant combat. The elections reduced the number and influence of the extremists in both parties; forty-six out of the 150 tories who had voted against making William and Mary king and queen, and forty-three of the 146 whigs who had tried to rig the municipal corporations, failed to get re-elected. Many of the new members were not rigidly attached to either party, but were ready to decide on the merits of particular issues, and there was also a bloc of placemen who would support the administration, whatever its composition. Consequently this parliament (which continued until 1695) provided the basis of working majorities for two ministries of very different character and composition—for the first three years Carmarthen's predominantly tory administration, then after 1693 for the whig Junto.

During the summer of 1690 England was in greater danger of total defeat than at any other time in the whole series of wars against France that finally ended at Waterloo. The generally dismal experiences of the previous year had shown how ill-prepared were the army, navy and all branches of government for a major struggle against France. An avoidable political failure to gain control over Ireland at the start of 1689, when Tyrconnel and his largely catholic administration were demoralized by the Revolution in England and had hardly any trained troops, was followed by the remarkably rapid recovery of the kingdom by James. Landing on 12 March, within a month he controlled all Ireland except Londonderry and Enniskillen, and was in a position to start to give significant assistance to his adherents in the Scottish Highlands. The jacobite rising in Scotland was menacing for a time, but Dundee's death cancelled out his victory at Killiecrankie (27 July), a jacobite incursion into the Lowlands was repulsed at Dunkeld (31 August), and the clans then dispersed.

The Irish campaign exposed English weaknesses. Relief for the beleaguered protestants in Londonderry was tantalizingly delayed in May and June 1689 by poor communications, slow and bad intelligence, adverse winds and the poor organization of supplies, but a first attempt at relief in April had been turned back by the treachery of the governor, Lundy, and this provoked constant suspicions and repeated charges that all the mismanagement of the campaign was due to jacobitism rather than, as was clearly the case, to incompetence and inexperience. James's army had been for show, for parades, and badly prepared for war. A high proportion of its officers had been removed as potential jacobites, and their politically more reliable replacements had little or usually no regular army experience. Worse, many owed their appointments to patronage connections, lacked all aptitude and made little effort to master their new profession. Many of the rank and file were disaffected—in March there was a serious mutiny at Ipswich in regiments about to be transferred to the Low Countries—and those recruits who replaced the Irish soldiers were raw and untrained. It is not surprising that at first the Irish campaign went badly.

Schomberg (a veteran French general who emigrated as a Huguenot) crossed to Ulster with a large force in August 1689, but

lacked sufficient confidence in his men to strike at James's unimpressive Irish levies, whose limitations had been exposed by their
failure to take Londonderry during the summer. Schomberg's army
camped through the winter in weather wet even for Ireland; Dutch
and Huguenot regiments suffered discomfort, but the English regiments, largely neglected by their officers, without adequate clothing
or tents, badly fed and bundled in thousands into appallingly ill-
equipped hospitals, lost over half their men. Lazy contractors and
corrupt paymasters left the army to starve; parliament attacked
commissary Shales, vulnerable as a former servant of James, but
ignored the frauds perpetrated by the whig paymaster, Harbord. It
also showed its disinclination to accept responsibility in December
1689 when, after angry debates in which mismanagement and treachery had been vigorously denounced, William asked the Commons
to name persons who he would put into control of all provisioning,
and others to take an account of the numbers and state of the army.
The Commons declined to make any nominations, but asked
William to carry out an investigation; then the whigs tried to prevent him from going in person to command the campaign of 1690.

William's decision to risk his own invaluable life reflected his determination to finish off the jacobite threat from Ireland. The decisive battle of the Boyne (July) followed within a month of his
disembarkation, and although he had to abandon the siege of
Limerick, a brilliant combined operation suggested by Marlborough
captured the Munster ports of Cork and Kinsale (September), isolating the jacobites west of the Shannon and ensuring that the final
campaign of 1691 to take Limerick and Galway would be a
mopping-up operation.

While William and most of the army were in Ireland, the allied
fleet lost control of the Channel. The warning signs from the previous year's naval campaign had not been understood. In May 1689
Herbert, heavily outnumbered, had failed to prevent French rein-
forcements landing in Bantry Bay in Ireland. The main fleet was late
in putting to sea, while ships had also to be provided to escort con-
voys, transport Schomberg's army to Ulster and check privateers. In
1690 the new admiralty commission did not appreciate the need for
an early concentration of strength. Detached squadrons were sent to
escort merchantmen to the Straits of Gibraltar, to transport the new
queen of Spain to her impotent husband, and to escort William to
Ulster. By the time these ships returned, the decisive battle had been
fought—and lost. The French fleet under Tourville that entered the
Channel in June heavily out-numbered the English and Dutch force
under Herbert, created earl of Torrington the previous month. This
was not realized by the council in London, which now included

Torrington's professional rival Russell as well as the sole secretary of state, Nottingham (Shrewsbury having chosen this most critical time to resign), who distrusted the whig admiral. Ordered to fight, Torrington did so half-heartedly, failing to give all-out support to the Dutch squadron when it became heavily engaged and suffered severely. Following his original judgement he withdrew to the Downs, off the Kent coast. In theory, with a fleet in being, he could still deter the French from offensive action, but his ships were battered, and he was separated from the detached squadrons which were all to the westward, and could each have been intercepted and annihilated by a more inspired French commander than Tourville.

Fortunately for England the French strategy was defective: no real preparation had been made to exploit a major victory; no army had been provided for an invasion. Tourville shirked a full-scale assault on a defended port—Portsmouth, Plymouth or even Dartmouth—and after making a farcical raid on Teignmouth retired to Brest, with sickness depleting his crews and supplies running short. The French had squandered an opportunity for a decisive victory which was never to recur. An invading army would have been opposed by few regulars—1,000 cavalry and 5,000 foot—and it is doubtful whether the militia would have been effective against what was still the best army in Europe. However, thousands of militia turned out with enthusiasm; it was significant that at this time of crisis there was no sign of jacobite activity, but a genuine determination to resist the French, and a general contempt for James as their puppet. But there was a heated and political post-mortem on the failure of the fleet. Torrington was court-martialled but cleared of blame. This intensified factionalism within the navy and ensured that future reverses at sea would be followed by politically motivated attacks on the ministers and admirals responsible.

During the crisis of 1690 Carmarthen held the fort in England as Mary's chief adviser and the leading minister in the council of nine which governed while William was absent. When the king departed for Holland in January 1691 he was again left in charge, but this ministerial primacy was largely illusory. Carmarthen did not possess as much real power and influence as he had done in the 1670s, but he attracted the same unpopularity and hostility as in the past. He disagreed with William's concept of mixed administrations, but he was not consulted by William over the filling of the most important offices; in the spring of 1690 moderate whigs as well as tories were appointed to replace the whig radicals, and in the autumn Carmarthen had to accept Sidney as secretary of state and Godolphin's return as first treasury commissioner. These appointments were all the more damaging because Carmarthen's ministerial career had always been based on his skill and industry in dispensing political patronage. In a slightly contemptuous way, William left him only minor appointments. These were important in terms of parliamentary management, enabling Carmarthen to construct a bloc of over a hundred placemen, but it confirmed his reputation for manipulation and corruption. Repeating the techniques that he had pioneered during the 1670s, Carmarthen also systematically re-modelled local government, making sweeping changes in the lieu-tenancy and the commission of the peace. He worked closely with Compton, the bishop of London and still the most politically active of churchmen, who aspired to succeed to the see of Canterbury. Comp-ton's failure to become primate when Sancroft was deprived as a non-juror in February 1690 was a further blow to Carmarthen's prestige: it showed that he could not now effectively recover the role of cham-pion of the anglican church which he had formerly played with great success. Nottingham acted as patron of the moderate, latitudi-narian anglicans; his influence was not seriously diminished by the failure in 1689 of his comprehension schemes to widen the basis of the church, by granting concessions which would permit presby-terians to re-enter. Militant high churchmen looked to Rochester as their lay leader.

Carmarthen's greatest weakness was his failure to regain control over finance. William refused to give him the lord treasurership, preferring Godolphin as a more efficient administrator to either Carmarthen or his lieutenant, Lowther. Furthermore, he did not consult Carmarthen over the conduct of foreign policy or the war. Nevertheless, despite his lack of power Carmarthen incurred wide-spread hatred as a corrupt prime minister. His past reputation and current absorption in managerial politics contributed largely to the emergence of a loosely organized but vociferous country opposition. In many cases this opposition behaved irresponsibly and negatively, engaging excessively in personal attacks, and obstructing the prose-cution of the war. Its members, tories and whigs alike, justified their opposition by the belief that they were defending the principles of the constitution against the revival of tendencies that had already produced disaster in the 1670s. They suspected massive parliamen-tary corruption and official misappropriation, and were scandalized by the commonness of the 'skill of growing speedily rich at the public cost' in what came to be known as the Officers' Parliament. Carmarthen and Nottingham were accused of keeping William (when not abroad) in 'a box at Kensington'. It was asserted that power was being improperly concentrated in a cabinet-council, by-passing the legitimate body, the privy council. Mismanagement of the war was alleged, and whig members of the opposition attributed this to the jacobite sympathies of many ministers and officers, and urged that there should be a purge of all who were not prepared to pledge unconditional loyalty to William and Mary.

The country opposition was not wholly negative. As a result of the emergence of spokesmen with a whig background, especially Robert Harley and John Smith, new and constructive policies were advocated to complete the process of safeguarding constitutional liberties and parliamentary rights that had had to be left unfinished in 1689. Acting on the principle 'to get good laws in a good reign' (so vindicating their loyalty), these new leaders tried to enact reforming legislation which amounted virtually to a political programme. In 1690–92 the bills concerned relatively minor matters—to prevent false electoral returns, for the speedier determination of disputed elections, to establish judges' salaries. In the session of 1692–3 two more important and interrelated bills formed the subject of prolonged debate. A bill disabling office-holders and placemen from sitting in the Commons was passed there, but narrowly failed in the Lords (January 1693). Reintroduced in the next session, it passed both houses, with Lords' amendments to allow officers to be reelected, but was vetoed by William (January 1694). He also vetoed a bill to fix the life of parliament at exactly three years, no more or less (February 1693), and the court strenuously and successfully resisted a bill for biennial parliaments in November, and another triennial bill in December.

The triennial and place bills raised important long-term issues. The financial settlement of 1689, and the expense of the war, made it impossible for William and his ministers to think of ruling without parliament in the foreseeable future. But there was a counterbalancing danger. Expansion of the army and navy, the multiplication of offices concerned with the assessment and collection of taxes and the creation of new administrative offices made the country opposition fear that ministers would soon dispose of a permanent working majority of court dependants. This could be most easily achieved in a 'standing' parliament, as Danby had shown in the 1670s, and opposition MPs feared that the life of the existing, so-called Officers' Parliament would be prolonged until the war ended. They assumed that ministers, although able to manage and influence MPs in a long-lived parliament, lacked both the resources and organization to control or fix elections. Consequently, statutory provisions for frequent elections and for the elimination of placemen from the Commons, became the principal 'country' party objectives.

Country fears were partly justified. Ministers planned to retain the parliament elected in 1690 for the duration of the war—and no one could say how long that would be. This was not just because they had built up influence in both houses, but also because the financing of the war depended on the long-term credits that had been voted by this parliament, through anticipations of taxes voted for years ahead. A new parliament might fail to honour these votes, or amend them, creating a danger that the whole system of war finance would collapse. But the triennial bills would mean a major restriction on the royal prerogative, ending the king's discretionary power over the life of parliament. There would have to be annual sessions of a minimum duration. No parliament could last longer than three years; in the bill of February 1693 the Commons proposed that the king should not be able to dissolve before three years had elapsed. Naturally, William was bitterly opposed to these measures. However, because of their preoccupation with the intense and prolonged struggle to enact triennial proposals, the country MPs failed altogether to foresee the long-term effects which the Triennial Act (finally passed, and reluctantly accepted by William in December 1694) was likely to have. Frequent general elections, at least every three years, were intended to make MPs more responsive to their countries—'they are sure to be the true representatives of the people' said Harley—and to make systematic corrupting of MPs uneconomic or impracticable. In the long-term the Triennial Act worked to the disadvantage of the country opposition: frequent elections and short-lived parliaments hastened the trend towards oligarchical domination; only the comparatively wealthy could afford regular electioneering, and it became increasingly common for magnates to buy up controlling interests in constituencies, and to intervene annually in mayoral elections, rather than merely to intervene in parliamentary elections. Faced with the need to spend more, many gentry families had to abandon their parliamentary pretensions.

By December 1694, when the triennial bill passed and Mary died, the ministry had become predominantly whig. Carmarthen remained as a political passenger, clinging on to office but uninvolved in decision making. He was further compromised by the detection of dishonest practices on the part of close associates—Guy (treasury secretary) in February 1695, and then the sensational dismissal from the Speakership and expulsion from the Commons of Trevor (March) for having taken massive bribes to influence proceedings on the subject of the East India Company. The other tory leader, Nottingham, after surviving attacks in December 1692 for the failure to exploit the naval victory of La Hougue, was damaged by the loss of the large Mediterranean trade convoy in 1693. Furious whig attacks forced him to associate with tories (especially Rochester) who were completely unacceptable to William because of their criticisms and obstruction of his European policies. In November Nottingham was dismissed.

William hesitated before committing himself to a largely whig administration. He knew that the whigs wanted to monopolize governmental offices, both at court and in the localities. He hated some of their leaders, especially Wharton, as not only insensately ambitious and dictatorial, but for having further designs to encroach on the prerogative. They dispelled this fear, and now that the war was certain to continue for several years, William needed a much more coherent and disciplined ministry than Carmarthen could provide, with men willing to take responsibility for a series of frighteningly difficult political, administrative and financial tasks. The Junto whig leaders had demonstrated skill, industry and courage as junior ministers, but it is doubtful whether William would have decided to rely on them but for the advice which he received from Sunderland. It is an exaggeration to describe this period as a 'Sunderland era', but within a sphere largely restricted to the court and its relations with parliament, Sunderland was now acting as William's chief confidant, that is within those areas where his trusted Dutch friends were comparatively ignorant. William got disinterested advice, and the whigs were ready to use Sunderland as an intermediary, but they never trusted him.

The Junto was presided over by Shrewsbury, but he lacked the health and determination to give the king the service that would have been demanded of a chief minister. During his prolonged withdrawals or partial retirements the other Junto whigs acted as a group, without any individual emerging as pre-eminent. Somers as attorney-general had experience in parliamentary management, and as lord keeper he was to construct a durable reserve of whig strength in the Lords. Wharton's expertise lay in organizing elections and propaganda. Russell was the whig admiral while Charles Montagu, whose rise to prominence was the most meteoric of all, had the necessary ministerial talent to make use of those skilled in financial and fiscal matters, and to understand their political implications. In addition there were a number of able juniors (Trenchard, Smith, Rich for example) who accepted Junto leadership.

None of the Junto ministers (not even Somers) was quite in the front rank, and apart from Shrewsbury (briefly in 1714) none ever became chief minister. They were all brilliant seconds, but as a ministry they made a formidable combination through their unity and discipline, realism and ruthlessness. They needed these attributes, not only to initiate and pass through parliament the votes of supply on which credit for the war depended, but to hold firm to stringent fiscal policies despite clamours for a lessening of the immediate burden on the nation. The Junto inherited problems from the earlier use of short-term expedients, when ministers had weakly accepted the popular illusion that the war would be of relatively short duration. Short-term loans, and overestimates of the yield of taxes specified for their servicing and repayment, were recipes for eventual bankruptcy, but realistic remedial measures would sharply accentuate the strains caused to the economy by the war, and provoke widespread and genuine resentment. The objections that were raised to the act establishing the Bank of England (April 1694), which also raised a loan of £1,200,000, were to continue later and to inject a new issue into domestic politics. The Bank, by institutionalizing government creditors, gave them a secure and privileged status which was to continue after the end of the war. In political (if not financial) terms, it would restrict the treasury's freedom in bargaining by linking a particular group in the City with the administration. By guaranteeing government loans it would perpetuate a policy of unprecedentedly heavy governmental indebtedness, and so ensure that taxation would remain at levels higher than previously known.

This strengthening of the emergent 'monied interest' infuriated many of the gentry, whose views were forcefully represented by the country opposition. Their anger was intensified by the failure of the parallel project of a land bank, which was expected to enhance the value of landed property, in which the bank's funds were to be invested, and so offset in part the burden of the land tax. Although the failure of the land bank was due largely to the incompetence of its sponsors, who made mistakes in drafting the terms which were offered to the public, its collapse was blamed on obstruction by the ministry and the directors of the Bank of England, and indeed the latter believed that the land bank would make more difficult effective execution of their scheme of monetary reform.

This reform directly affected almost every individual in England, and in nearly all cases the short-term effects were disturbing and damaging. There had been a deterioration in both the quality and the quantity of the coinage since the Restoration. Popular opinion blamed clippers (or forgers) who tampered with coins, the unfavourable balance of trade with France which allegedly led to a massive outflow of coin and specie, and also large exports by the East India Company with which to buy oriental goods; after 1688, expenditure abroad on the army and subsidies to allies was added to the list of explanations. Prohibitions on the export of silver, the cessation of trade with France, and prosecutions of clippers had no perceptible effect, because the basic cause for the deficiency of the coinage was that silver was undervalued in relation to gold. The solution undertaken by the Junto ministry consisted of an enormously laborious and administratively complex operation of withdrawing the whole existing faulty silver currency, and a complete recoinage. It was also an act calling for extreme political courage and a high degree of perseverance. Montagu made the proposal at the beginning of the new parliament in November 1695, and pushed it through against considerable opposition. Clipped money was no longer legal tender. This greatly reduced the amount of coinage in circulation, and the general deflationary effects resulted in unemployment, dislocations of retail trading at the local levels, shortages of credit for industrial and commercial activity, and difficulties in paying taxes or repaying loans. For a short time there was widespread discontent and occasional, if rather aimless rioting. The Junto ignored all protests and would make no exceptions. They rejected insidious temptations of allowing loans to be made in the old currency, which should have been exchanged for new, or accepted in subscriptions to the land bank.

The recoinage provided a harsh, and ultimately successful solution to long-term structural problems, but it made the task of financing the war initially more difficult. Many and various expedients were attempted—taxes on salt, leather, windows, water-borne coal, additional impositions on wine, a quarterly poll—but the difficulties of raising further credit were even greater after the recoinage. In 1696 military operations were for a time actually hampered by the desperate state of government finances, and it was this fearsome responsibility of making it possible for the war to continue that 'educated' the Junto ministers and won them William's respect. In the ordeal of the last phase of the war the Junto came close to experiencing the almost continuous and intolerable strains, and fearlessness of unpopularity, that William had imposed on himself and his Dutch ministers since 1672.

The role of English ministers, generals and admirals in prosecuting the war was confined to supporting William and carrying out his commands. William made all the major decisions himself—deciding the dispositions of the army and fleet, preparing the Flanders campaigns, negotiating with the allies and arranging subsidies, and at the end bringing about the conclusion of the peace negotiations by direct personal intervention through Portland with a personal confidant of Louis.

Overall the war developed into a struggle of attrition, without any prospect of a decisive outcome. In 1692 the French repeated the English mistakes of two years earlier. They now had an army ready to invade and link up with jacobite insurgents who were overoptimistically reported to be prepared to raise a large army in England. Tourville was therefore instructed to take the offensive in the Channel despite a marked inferiority in numbers. These orders were based on the totally erroneous belief, derived from jacobite agents, that admiral Russell and many of his captains were disaffected, and would either refuse to fight or even defect to James and the French. The result was a crushing defeat for Tourville at Barfleur and La Hougue (May), and the effective end of any chance of a major French invasion—apart from the plan to throw an army into Kent in wintertime, if the assassination of William had been accomplished in February 1696. However, the aftermath of Russell's victory showed how limited were the offensive uses of naval supremacy. Projects for a major invasion of northern France came to nothing. Attacks on naval and privateering bases (notably on Brest in 1694) failed to do significant damage. Eventually, part of the fleet was sent to the Mediterranean, wintering in Spain in 1694–5, but its role was again essentially defensive, to prevent a French invasion of Catalonia.

The army's task was to contain French offensives into the Spanish Netherlands. At first this was an uphill struggle. Mons was lost in 1691, Namur in 1692, both reverses being primarily a result of the earlier appearance in the field of the French army, a result of its superior organization. The French had superiority in numbers also, which gave them the advantage in two fiercely contested and expensive, but inconclusive, set-piece battles, Steenkirk (1692) and Landen (1693). William's one great success came in 1695 when he mobilized all his resources to recapture Namur, but thereafter lack of money and credit restricted his operations. All combatants were feeling the strains of war, and after an appalling winter the year 1694 had already seen little military activity by either side; in 1696 near-bankruptcy faced William with the possibility that his army would have to be partly disbanded in the face of the enemy, and that his allies would for lack of subsidies follow Savoy's example and make peace separately with France. Furthermore, William was coming under increased pressure at home. By 1697, when the preliminary negotiations for peace threatened to become as interminable and inconclusive as military operations had been, a formidable and increasingly vocal country opposition was pressing for an early peace.

The Junto whigs recommended themselves to William by indicating that once the Triennial Act passed (December 1694), they did not intend to put further restrictions on the prerogative. For many rank-and-file whigs this was a betrayal of principle, confirming suspicions that all leaders and potential ministers would abandon their followers and their political ideals in return for office. Consequently, they responded when a new and independent group of party spokes-men, headed by Robert Harley and Paul Foley, proclaimed the need for further measures to safeguard individual and parliamentary rights and for continued vigilance against ministerial abuses of power. An effective country opposition began to develop as independent whigs and tories joined in pressing for significant political reforms. At first they persisted with bills to exclude placemen from parlia-ment (vetoed in February 1694, defeated in February 1695). Later, in a change of emphasis which reveals the character of the country opposition as essentially a gentry body, energies were concentrated on bills which would require all MPs to possess a qualification of landed property (£500 per annum for counties, £200 for boroughs), strengthen the law against electoral bribery, and confine candidacies to native-born subjects. The property qualification bill passed both houses in the 1695 session, but was vetoed by William; in the next session it passed the Commons but was lost in the Lords.

Harley introduced resolutions attempting to censure William and his advisers for these royal vetoes, but he was not dismayed when he was heavily defeated. These resolutions were a vindication of his sincerity, an indication to his followers that he was not interested in office or gaining the favour of the king. The resolutions were sup-ported by MPs who were always hostile to ministers, and often un-reasonably suspicious of any official or opposition move or proposal; they were usually fiercely independent and resentful of any attempt at direction, quick to flare up in opposition but intractable material for leaders to organize in pursuit of long-term political aims. Harley supplied what the opposition had tended to lack, a professional at-tention to parliamentary proceedings and business. He was able to use a newly developed parliamentary institution for this purpose, the committee for public accounts which had been established to in-spect and report on government expenditure and revenue. This committee's value as an instrument of political control was realized from 1691, when Harley was only a junior member, but after 1694 it became the engine of the country opposition in maintaining pressure on ministers and officials, enabling the opposition to initiate pro-posals and policies instead of merely reacting against ministerial moves. Members of the committee were paid salaries, but had no re-sponsibility except to the Commons. Consequently, during the 1690s they formed a kind of opposition front-bench group, and each for-mation of the committee by election, through a ballot of the Commons, became as much a trial of strength between the court and the country as the contest for the Speakership with which each new parliament began.

The Triennial Act provided for the dissolution of the Officers'

Parliament. In the new parliament of 1695–8 there was a further influx of new and uncommitted members. More than a hundred had not sat before, and most of them were ready to judge matters on their merits and to respond to intelligent leadership, whether from ministers or from the country spokesmen. They accepted the Junto case on the necessity for the recoinage bill, but in the early stages of this parliament it was Harley who got their general support, throwing the ministers on the defensive. He forced William to withdraw a lavish grant of lands to the Dutch favourite, Portland. A Trial of Treasons Act was passed that safeguarded the position of the individual but made it more difficult to obtain convictions. Experience of the failures of the admiralty to check French privateers led to a proposal (that narrowly failed) to establish a council of trade giving commissioners nominated by parliament (including MPs) control over the defence of merchant shipping (December 1695). By taking a firm but constructive line on major issues, Harley was able to counter the managerial techniques of the Junto ministers, and out-manoeuvre their spokesmen in the Commons. Sunderland, ever a weather-cock, began to move away from the ministers whom he had originally sponsored, and to ally with the country opposition. But the Junto was able to turn the tables on Harley, once they found an issue which they could exploit to divide the whig independents from the tories. Their success not only secured their own position in office, but postponed the fusion into a united and effective country opposition of its whig and tory sections.

On 24 February 1696 William informed parliament of the detection of a jacobite assassination plot against his life. Irrefutable evidence made it clear that a severe crisis had been narrowly averted, with a French army poised at Calais for an invasion during the confusion that William's death might be expected to cause, and the jacobites organized to assist them. The detection of this dangerous plot gave the Junto the opportunity to proclaim their own unconditional loyalty to William and the principles of the Revolution, and to smear as potentially disloyal or even as crypto-jacobites all those who had reservations and would go no further than accepting William as *de facto* ruler. In the past, such charges had failed to carry conviction because they had been made in general terms and not in relation to a real crisis or emergency. In 1690 a bill to impose abjuration of James's rights had been introduced rather too blatantly, to drive a wedge between tory ministers (especially Nottingham) and the country members. In 1694 the whigs sponsored a campaign by informers, the sham Lancashire Plot which evoked memories of Titus Oates, but their perjuries about alleged jacobites did not withstand examination. But in 1696 the country opposition contained

many members who were genuinely alarmed by William's revelations, to the point of being ready to follow the Junto lead.

Cleverly combining long-term measures for greater security
against the jacobite menace with proposals which would give them immediate party advantage, the Junto ministers acted swiftly. They
voted on 24 February to stand by the king and revenge his death on
all his enemies. A bill was passed for parliament to continue and not
be automatically dissolved after his death, and all commissions to
offices were to continue also for a limited period. But the key to
Junto exploitation of the assassination plot lay in the Association
which was resolved on the same day, which all MPS were to take. It
was cleverly drafted by Somers. Besides incorporating the resolutions
to stand by and revenge the king, to which few would object, the
Association also demanded recognition of William as 'rightful and
lawful king', something that many tories had consistently refused to
acknowledge. Subsequently this requirement was extended to all
office-holders, and all who refused to take the Association were disqualified from sitting in any future parliament. This threw the
country opposition into disarray; while whigs were generally prepared to subscribe the Association, Harley found many tories
unwilling—although eventually most agreed to do so. This division
gave the Junto managers the opportunities which they skilfully exploited to establish a clear parliamentary ascendancy.

The country opposition contained some individual MPS with
jacobite sympathies, but as a body and in principles it was not only
distinct from jacobitism, but represented popular opinions and
grievances in a way that the jacobites could not. James's agents rightly
reported widespread discontent among all sections of the nation, but
they were entirely wrong in claiming that the people were eager to
rise against their oppressors and to restore James in order to get
redress of their grievances. The jacobite case depended on the assertion that William's usurpation of James's rights would inevitably
lead, as had happened in the 1640s and 1650s, to the revolutionary
government lawlessly invading the rights of every other individual
and group, but this was falsified by experience. Only the non-jurors
suffered in this way; they were the high-church clergy who were
deprived for refusing to take the oaths to William and Mary. The
crucial difference from the arbitrary government of the Interregnum
was the central role that parliament now assumed in supporting, and
so controlling, the king and his ministers who could never think of
governing without its cooperation. But a restoration of James would
end this; it would mean the automatic repeal of all statutes passed
since 1688, including the Bill of Rights, and the return of a king who had
used the dispensing and suspending powers. It would mean trusting

a king who, unlike Charles in 1660, was not taking care to identify himself and his cause with the rule of constitutional legality.

The suspicions which James generated because of his catholicism
and his past record as sovereign were increased by his total dependence on France, and the inconsistency of his declarations. His
ministers at St Germain were bitterly divided between the compounders led by Middleton, who advocated giving promises to
protect the protestant religion and to accept certain constitutional
restrictions on the crown, and the militantly catholic non-
compounders who insisted that his restoration must be unconditional. James's declarations alternated between the two lines of
policy, between blustering threats of extensive and harsh punishments, and unconvincing efforts to conciliate. Only one jacobite
argument had any real impact on a war-weary nation, the claim
that Louis would never make peace until James was restored—so
that William's usurpation must perpetuate the war and its intolerable burdens. After the failure of the assassination plot in February
1696 this became a bogus argument; the ministers at St Germain
knew that Louis would make peace when he could, at the price of
sacrificing James's pretensions.

In practical terms the notion of a popular jacobite insurrection
was always wholly unreal. Effective leadership and efficient organization were equally lacking. James's hopes were pinned on either a
conquest by a French invasion, or on leading English politicians
deserting William in the same way as they had abandoned James in
1688. Jacobites interpreted the Revolution as being—like the civil
war in 1642 and Exclusion in 1679–81—the work of a small conspiratorial clique of ambitious politicians, cynically using and misleading
the credulous masses. They did not recognize a popular dimension
in any of these political crises, so jacobite agents were consistent
in concentrating on attempts to engineer a conspiracy and a
general act of desertion in reverse, getting promises to defect when a
crisis came or the French invaded. Great value was placed on promises or half-promises of future support which were obtained from
very prominent men—Shrewsbury, Godolphin, Marlborough,
Admiral Russell, Halifax and many others. But undoubtedly
William knew about these contacts, and connived at some, knowing
that they were merely insurances not pledges of active assistance.
None of these high-placed contacts made any move to honour promises, nor were there any signs of popular movements, when crises
did occur—in 1690 and 1692 with threats of a French invasion, or in
1696 with the assassination plot which technically James and Louis
may not have known about (that is in detail) but which they were
ready to exploit.

Jacobite plotting could never be ignored by the government, and a stream of jacobite propaganda (largely written by non-jurors) never ceased; but the politics of William's reign can be studied and understood without the necessity of giving more than a cursory examination to jacobitism. Its impact was negligible.

The Junto made thorough preparations, including consultative meetings involving a large group of influential MPs, for the parliamentary session of 1696–97. Their resolution and efficiency in management were demonstrated in the act of attainder which was pushed through against Sir John Fenwick, a jacobite implicated in the assassination plot. It was easy to pass an initial resolution against Fenwick (by 179 to 61), who prevaricated when questioned by the Commons and whose friends removed one of the necessary two witnesses against him. But it required discipline and political stamina to enact an attainder, by which Fenwick was put to death; in the Commons the majority sank to thirty-three, in the Lords to seven. It was equally important—and difficult—to maintain whig and ministerial unity on the measure, since Fenwick's selective charges of connections with the jacobites implicated some ministers, notably Shrewsbury and Russell, so that it would have been easy for envious colleagues to drive them from public life, but in the process wreck the ministry. Two whig leaders with radical connections, Devonshire and Monmouth, did try to make mischief but the Junto ministers resisted all temptations for personal advantage and emerged significantly stronger. An act was passed enlarging the Bank of England by a new subscription, and extended its privileges to 1710, whereas in contrast the land bank which Harley sponsored proved to be a total failure. In February 1697 the Junto captured control of the committee of public accounts, depriving Harley of his one institutional means of pressurizing the administration. The state of royal finances was no longer so critical as it had been in 1696, and now at last there was a prospect of peace.

During the late summer of 1696 informal peace negotiations began, but from the start the French indulged in delaying tactics and chicanery, aiming at splitting the allies and exposing William to charges by his own subjects that he did not genuinely want to end the war. The ministers were spectators, unable to influence developments and excluded from participation, but desperately anxious that peace should be concluded since the burden of explaining foreign policy when asking for supply fell on them. Their influence was sufficiently strong to obtain enough money to finance a defensive campaign in 1697, while formal negotiations continued, but after the conclusion of peace in October the position of the Junto ministry began to weaken.

With the coming of peace the Junto's services were no longer indispensable, and their insistent claims to a virtual monopoly of office began to antagonize William. He resented their treatment of Sunderland, who had been appointed lord chamberlain in April, both as a reward for his services as confidential adviser, and also as the senior politician who could free William from his dependence on the Junto. The latter had quickly appreciated the danger. They disliked being publicly linked with the most hated politician of the period, and they saw him as a mole undermining their own position. Disputes over appointments to minor offices soured relationships and confirmed the fact that Sunderland was trying to put together an alternative ministerial combination. This was such an extraordinarily heterogeneous group that it is difficult to see how they could have operated together—whigs of the Rose Club who were excluded from offices by the tightly organized and exclusive Junto, eccentric whig magnates with radical affiliations like Devonshire and Monmouth, opportunist tories led by Seymour who would do anything to gain office but could not be relied on thereafter, and Sunderland's own followers (Duncombe, Felton). But the Junto took no chances. They forced Sunderland out of office in December, and ruined Duncombe by exposing his corrupt practices, but as the Junto's predominance increased so their pretensions alienated William. He refused to contemplate Wharton, the symbol of Junto arrogance and belligerence, as secretary of state. Moreover, the behaviour of parliament during the 1697–8 session showed William that the effective influence of the Junto was declining.

After William opened with a calculatedly (and uncharacteristically) amiable speech, full of reassurances, it came as a shock when priority was given to discussion of supply by only three votes (156 to 153). On 11 December the court suffered an ominous defeat, on what was to emerge as the major issue over the next two years, when it was voted (by 185 to 148) that all land forces raised beyond the peacetime strength of 1680 should now be disbanded. This was followed by another country opposition offensive on an equally inflammatory subject, with calls for the resumption of grants of forfeited Irish lands. The increasing inability of the ministers to protect royal policies and prerogatives which William considered to be crucially important led the king to discard the Junto leaders and to return to his old preference for mixed or composite ministries. The return of peace was signalled by the emergence of a new set of issues, on which the capacity for service of the Junto was doubtful; not until the return of war clouds in 1701 did William look again to the whigs.

14 Foreign Policy, 1688–1714

American historians call the war of 1688–97 against France 'King William's War'. This is historically accurate because it really was his war in every sense. The inexperience of his English ministers, diplomats and officers obliged William to assume a dominant role, making all the crucial decisions himself. Working with a few Dutch advisers he also made the Peace of Rijswijk and negotiated the partition treaties without reference to his English ministers. The two old antagonists, William and Louis, acted as the arbiters of Europe, arranging and disposing of rulers and territories as if they were pieces on a chessboard. But the power of these two strange if temporary partners rested on very different political and ideological foundations, and they were actuated by fundamentally dissimilar principles. William consciously and consistently strove to maintain the 'liberties of Europe', which in practice meant freedom from French domination and dictation. This meant that William had to protect and further a very diverse collection of national, princely and sectional interests, many of which were actually or potentially conflicting. His most difficult task at all times was to preserve allied unity in the face of intimidatory French power and divisive diplomatic activity, but he was also faced with the problems involved in having to depend financially on the uncertain cooperation of representative institutions in England and the United Provinces. By contrast, Louis had no major allies in the 1690s to have to consider, and his absolute authority made it possible for him to mobilize and expend the resources of France, without having significantly to take into account the reactions of his subjects. When he repudiated the Partition Treaties, his decision to accept Carlos II's will and the Spanish inheritance was bound up with the principles of the *ancien régime* itself, indefeasible legitimacy and divine right.

William's death on the eve of the War of the Spanish Succession left Marlborough with the continuing task of containing and trying to reduce French predominance. An incomparably greater and more successful general, his victories restored a balance of power on the Continent. He also displayed the greatest skill as a diplomat, for example in dissuading Karl XII of Sweden from attacking the Habsburgs, and there could not be a greater contrast than that between the cooperation which he inspired between allied generals and diplomats, and the endless and bitter dissensions that wrecked the allied campaigns in Spain. Because he was constantly involved in high-level diplomatic business, Marlborough's enemies accused him of behaving like royalty, but in practice his powers and influence were far more restricted than William's. He could never impose his views and policies as the latter had done, and consequently Marlborough's achievement as the diplomatic guardian and director of the Grand Alliance was far less successful. William kept the alliance together in years of adversity; Marlborough's task was to reap the rewards of his military victories by imposing a peace that would satisfy all the principal allies. By missing the best opportunity in 1706, after Ramillies, Marlborough committed both England and the allies to a victorious but apparently endless war. Its indefinite prolongation became a principal reason for the ministerial revolution of 1710, and the new ministers were politically committed to bringing about a peace settlement. The way in which they imposed it on their reluctant allies in 1711–13 was as much a mark of English primacy as were Marlborough's victories. Acting in very much the same way as William in 1697–1700, the tory ministers joined with France in dictating to Europe, but at Utrecht (unlike Rijswijk) particular English interests were selfishly but energetically promoted.

William's control over English foreign policy was so complete that it can be described as a continuation and extension, using English resources, of the policies that he had been pursuing as *stadtholder* since 1672. This made William politically vulnerable. Jacobite propaganda immediately claimed that England was being exploited by her natural enemies, the Dutch. Leading politicians as well as backbench country MPs were naturally jealous of the virtually exclusive influence exerted by foreign advisers—Portland, Albemarle, Rochford, Dijkvelt, Athlone and Galway—and of the rewards which they received. In practical terms, however, William was obliged to rely on Dutch and Huguenot advisers and officers because English ministers, diplomats and soldiers lacked sufficient experience. Very few of the latter were willing and able to undertake the crushing weight of responsibility and business that William expected his servants to bear and Blathwayt, the secretary at war, was a rare exception. In the one area where England had experience and greater resources from the start—the navy and the war at sea—William logically assigned command to his English admirals, with the Dutch having to accept the same junior or subordinate position that the

English occupied in the conduct of diplomacy and European campaigns.

Despite their past hostility and the survival of xenophobic prejudices in England, which the tories were to exploit after 1710, there was a fundamental similarity of interests between England and the United Provinces. At least until William's victory at the Boyne (1690), and the failures of the French to invade in 1690 and 1692, the war was essentially a struggle to maintain English independence from the total French domination that a restoration of James would have involved. The country opposition would not acknowledge English dependence on Dutch assistance, but without Dutch regiments and allied contingents provided by the States General, it would have been much more difficult if not impossible to conquer Ireland in 1689–91. In Europe, Dutch diplomacy played an equally decisive role: it defeated Louis's attempts in the same years to disintegrate the alliance by arguing to its catholic members (notably Spain and the Emperor) that the Revolution in England and Ireland showed that William was conducting an anti-catholic war of religion from which they should dissociate themselves.

Yet once England, Scotland and Ireland had been secured, members of the country party in parliament suggested that for the remainder of the war England should restrict her contribution to the 10,000 men and thirty ships stipulated in the defensive treaties of 1677 and 1678 with the States General. A sizeable minority steadily opposed the raising and maintenance of an army of the size (around 60,000 men) that William insisted was essential. The country view was that England ought not to be a principal in the war, but only an auxiliary power, while English resources were used to mount a separate naval war against French trade and colonies. Such national selfishness would soon have been imitated by others of the allies. William did not exaggerate when he warned parliament that the eyes of Europe were fixed on its annual debates in which the size and cost of the next year's naval and military establishments were decided. Each session opened with a royal speech in which the progress of the war was reviewed, often (as in 1693) with candid admissions of reverses on land and at sea. William had to persuade a comparatively uninformed assembly of country gentlemen to finance a foreign policy of expensive commitments which few of them could understand fully, and to take account of their frequently irrelevant representations.

As in 1674–8, William's chief commitment was to the defence of the Spanish Netherlands, the key strategic area on which depended the security of both England and the United Provinces. It was there that the main French armies were deployed, but William conducted

a defensive war far more successfully than in the 1670s. He lost
Namur in 1692 but recaptured this major fortress in 1695. The
French claimed Steenkirk (1692) and Landen (1693) as victories,
but they failed to penetrate the barrier of allied fortresses despite
having a considerable superiority in numbers. This defence was
materially assisted by the English contribution, even though the newly
raised troops were at first badly officered and poorly organized.
However, the management of the English army involved William in
serious political complications. The officer corps was divided into
competing factions. Those who had defected from James during
the Revolution felt that their own professional advancement was
blocked by the preferential treatment being given to foreign officers and
to those English and Scots who (like Tollemache and Cutts) had been
in Dutch service before 1688. Marlborough was their most ambitious
and politically active spokesman, but when in 1692 he demanded
that neither foreign nor naturalized officers should command
English troops, he was dismissed, and allegations of jacobite associations kept him in disgrace until 1698 and out of a command until
1701. Other dissatisfied officers kept up a barrage of criticism in
parliament, formed a vocal section of the country opposition, and
built up a widely accepted picture of the army as a foreign-
dominated 'trade' with an interest in prolonging the war for its own
advantage.

The country opposition also constantly criticized the conduct of
the war at sea. William had obligations to Admiral Herbert, created
earl of Torrington, who commanded the invasion fleet in 1688, but
the state of the fleet which the latter inherited was such that he could
not prevent the French fleet convoying James and a French army to
Ireland in 1689, and in 1690 he was compelled against his better
judgement to engage a superior enemy force off Beachy Head. Had
the French been better prepared they could have exploited this
victory either by invading the south coast (defended mainly by militia)
or by preventing William returning from Ireland with part of his
army. Torrington was dismissed, but his successor Russell had the
advantage of a very thorough and expensive programme of naval
construction. This gave him a decisive margin of superiority in 1692
when Tourville, the French admiral, had orders to seek battle, after
which James was to invade with a French army. The French were
heavily defeated at Barfleur and La Hougue, but the summer's campaign became the subject of an embittered dispute between Russell
(supported by the whigs) and Nottingham, tory secretary of state
and virtually navy minister, which ended with the former resigning
his command (January 1693), and the latter losing influence on
naval affairs and, in November 1693, his office.

Underlying the intense personal competition for office, intertwined with the rivalry of whig and tory, this controversy centred on a major and perennial problem of all the wars against France. Barfleur–La Hougue was exceptional because the French chose to engage in a set-piece action. Subsequently the general French strategy was to rely on avoiding set-piece battles. Technically, the French lost command of the seas to the English, but contrary to expectations English naval supremacy exerted little influence on the course of the war. The offensive role of the navy was very limited. In 1692 it was planned to turn the enemy's flank by a 'descent', a major invasion of the provinces on the Channel coast. This was quickly found to be impracticable, and no such invasion was to be effected in any of the later wars (indeed not until 1944). For the remainder of the war the fleet protected England from threat of invasion, but it could do little to check the depredations of French privateers. The 1690s and 1700s were the golden age of the St Malo and Dunkirk corsairs, above all of Jean Bart and Duguay-Trouin, and the failure of the admiralty to take effective protective measures infuriated mercantile interests whose complaints were taken up by the country opposition.

While English merchant shipping was suffering unprecedentedly heavy losses, the effects of the allied blockade on France were disappointingly meagre. The Dutch became scapegoats for this failure, because their merchants continued to trade with the enemy. The other factor that reduced the effectiveness of the blockade was the need to avoid antagonizing the Danes and the Swedes who continued to trade with France, but also supplied mercenary contingents for William's army. Overall the war had extremely adverse effects on the trading community. Trade with the Mediterranean was suspended for three years, and then the large outward bound Smyrna convoy was partly destroyed, off Lagos in Portugal (1693). Trading posts in west Africa were ruined. The pressing of men for the navy left sufficient seamen for only a reduced number of ships in the distant trades to the colonies. The outflow of money for subsidies to the allies, and to maintain the army in Flanders, led to a deterioration in the exchange rates, and was blamed for the shortage of credit and the deficiencies in the coinage. There is no evidence to support the thesis that William's war was either encouraged by, or popular with, mercantile interests. Only those directly engaged in credit and financial operations, or in victualling and supplying the army and navy, had any interest in continuing the war.

By 1696 war weariness was almost universal. The government had the greatest difficulty in finding money to finance the campaign.

England, France and the United Provinces were all approaching an exhaustion of their resources. Nevertheless, there were formidable obstacles to be overcome in making peace. The Emperor, who was still concentrating largely on his separate war against the Turks, wished the war in the west to continue indefinitely. If Carlos II, whose health was crumbling, died while hostilities were still in progress this would mean that the Austrian branch would be well placed to take the entire Habsburg inheritance. The skill and unscrupulousness of French diplomacy posed the major difficulty in making peace. First in secret conversations in 1694–5 and then from May 1696 in preliminary negotiations to prepare for a formal peace congress, the French confused the issues, 'chicaning' in the contemporary usage, first making and then withdrawing proposals. This was particularly on the issue that most concerned William, his recognition by Louis as king of England and the withdrawal of support for the exiled James. Even when the conference opened the French refused to negotiate with the plenipotentiaries of an English usurper but addressed themselves to the Dutch. They also tried to detach the minor allies from William, whose bargaining position had already been weakened when Savoy made a separate peace in 1696. Louis had the advantage of knowing that English and Dutch opinion strongly favoured an early peace, and that any failure to achieve it would be reflected in intensified opposition in parliament and the States General. Moreover, as the conference began in May 1697 one of the allies was on the point of total collapse; the Spanish defences on the Catalan frontier broke and Barcelona was besieged.

William, in his eagerness to conclude an early peace, decided to by-pass the conference and reach a direct, personal understanding with Louis. This was achieved with surprising speed and ease, through unofficial discussions between Portland and Boufflers in July and August, so that peace could be concluded in September, with the Emperor reluctantly acceding in October. William obtained recognition from Louis, but the latter was not prepared to expel James from France. His prestige suffered enough at Rijswijk, by having to return most of his recent territorial gains. William was extremely dissatisfied by Louis's refusal, but the settlement achieved what he had always set himself to obtain, a real balance of power. The Rijswijk settlement was a necessary preliminary to the resolution—in advance of Carlos II's death—of the impending problems of the Spanish succession. William had to be satisfied with promises by Louis that he would not give James aid, and he went on to stake even more on French good faith in negotiating the Partition Treaties.

Louis's motives in negotiating the Partition Treaties are still a matter for speculation, but it is certain that William had no alternative. The English public, and even his chief ministers, were largely indifferent towards the threatening crisis in Europe. The enforced disbanding of all but 7,000 of the English standing army virtually disarmed William, making it impossible for him to exert direct pressure on Louis. The parliamentary attitude of suspicion and isolationism ruled out any initiation of policies that carried a risk of war. Only if Louis provoked English opinion by aggressive moves could parliament be expected to react and possibly give William the kind of financial support that an active and credible foreign policy required.

Unlike William, Louis possessed and cautiously followed a second line of policy that constituted a complete alternative to the negotiation and implementation of the Partition Treaties. After their defeats in the recent war, it was possible that the Spaniards would see in the succession of the Dauphin, or one of his sons, the only expedient by which the unity and integrity of the Spanish possessions could be preserved. The French ambassador in Madrid, Harcourt, worked systematically to build a party sympathetic to Bourbon claims, but this only began to produce results after the Partition Treaties had been concluded. The fact that Louis had an alternative option, and William did not, should not obscure the central point about the negotiations—the desperate anxiety of both kings to avoid another prolonged and destructive European war. Louis could not lightly engage in another war against virtually the whole Continent, and if he refused to negotiate at all the prospect was that all the allied powers would act together when Carlos died, being pledged by the terms of the Grand Alliance of 1689—but not explicitly by the renewal treaty of 1695—to support the Habsburg claim. Some gains might be made by France in a new war, but at an unacceptably high cost. It should be emphasized that in 1698–9, when the negotiations began, there was no prospect whatsoever of Louis asserting his full claims to the entire Habsburg inheritance. If he could expect only relatively minor gains, there was everything to be said for obtaining these by agreement rather than by war.

The determination of the Spanish succession would affect the whole balance of power in Europe. Louis could not permit the reconstitution of Charles v's empire by a new union between Madrid and Vienna. Similarly the other powers must insist on a separation of the French and Spanish crowns, but the valuation they placed on the component territories of the Spanish empire varied considerably. For the Dutch and the English the Spanish Netherlands were the key to their own security. The former already had garrisons in the chief fortresses, by agreement with the Spanish government. However, the

Emperor was comparatively uninterested in what was for him a remote area that was difficult to defend against French encroachments. Imperial aspirations were centred on Spain's possessions in
Italy, above all Milan. Naples and Sicily were commercially important for English and Dutch mercantile interests, who were afraid of
further French economic advances in Mediterranean trade. In addition, they were alarmed at recent evidence of French economic
penetration of the jealously preserved American possessions of Spain.
Existing commercial rights in Spain itself were also thought to be
imperilled.

The question of 'right' was thoroughly confused. Philip iv's two
daughters had both renounced theirs—Maria Theresa on marrying
Louis (although it was claimed that her renunciation was conditional on payment of her dowry, and this had never been made),
Margaret on marrying the Emperor Leopold. The two husbands
had compromised as early as 1668 with a secret partition treaty, and
set a precedent by proposing to dispose of the Spanish possessions
without any reference to its government or people, both of whom
were at all times firmly opposed to any form of partition.

Negotiations between Louis and William for the (first, secret)
Partition Treaty began in March 1698 and were successfully completed by October. The Dauphin was to be compensated with
Naples, Sicily and the Tuscan ports; the Emperor's younger son Karl
was to take Milan, but the remainder of the Spanish possessions was
to go to the third candidate, the young son of the Elector of Bavaria.
This arrangement would have satisfied all major parties, with the
important exception of the Emperor, but it was soon invalidated by
the death of the electoral prince (February 1699). The Second
Partition Treaty, provisionally agreed by Louis and William in June
(again without reference to the Emperor) but not formally approved
until March 1700, divided Spanish possessions between the two principal rivals. The Dauphin was to have Lorraine as well as Naples
and Sicily (the duke of Lorraine being compensated with Milan),
while the rest of empire was to go to Karl. Later, appreciating that
English and Dutch mercantile interests feared the commercial ascendancy that France might gain from the acquisition of Naples and
Sicily, William proposed an exchange by which the duke of Savoy
would take these territories, and in return France would incorporate
Savoy itself, but this was unlikely to be acceptable to the duke.

In contrast to the First Partition Treaty, the details of the Second
soon became known. This substantially reduced the chances of it
being implemented. The main objections came from Spain and the
Emperor. The territories in Italy allocated to the Dauphin were
precisely those which Leopold most particularly wanted, and in any

case he was not prepared to accept compromises arranged by others. When he approached Louis, the territories Leopold was ready to concede to France were those (the Spanish Netherlands and the Spanish Indies) which the maritime powers were least prepared to allow France to annex. Leopold was determined to back his claims with force; the Peace of Karlowitz had ended the Turkish war, freeing his attention and resources for use in Italy. Louis faced a war with Leopold, regardless of whether he tried to enforce the Partition Treaty or made a bid for the entire Spanish inheritance. The other insuperable objection to the Treaty arose from Spanish hostility to any form of partition. Although encouraged by the French, this spontaneous sentiment was finally embodied in the will that Carlos signed shortly before his death on 1 November 1700. By this will the entire inheritance was to go to the Dauphin's second son, Philip, but if he refused the bequest it was to go intact to the Emperor's younger son, Karl.

By accepting the will and repudiating the Partition Treaty Louis did not make a general European war inevitable. It was an appalling blow to William, who complained bitterly that he had been duped, but such was the gap between the king and his subjects that most English politicians positively welcomed Louis's decision. They believed that enforcement of the treaty would have involved war, whereas the acceptance of Philip as king by all Spanish territories seemed to show that any war would now be confined to Imperial attempts to invade northern Italy. This would not directly affect England at all. The country party concentrated on furious attacks against the secret diplomacy that had produced the Partition Treaties, and these culminated in the abortive impeachments of the ministers who, in the view of MPs, had supinely allowed William to commit England to a policy that had utterly failed, but which would have led—if the partition had been carried out—to French domination of the Mediterranean. But these furious country criticisms were rapidly overtaken by events. Without apparently considering possible English and Dutch reactions, Louis began quickly to extend and exploit French influence in Spanish territories. His moves could not be justified as defensive precautions against Imperial enmity, and they make sense only if Louis was right in fearing that sooner or later William would reconstruct the Grand Alliance and then attack France. On the other hand, Louis, while doing more than enough to alienate English and Dutch opinion, failed to take full advantage of his dominant position by assuming an offensive against the ill-prepared maritime states.

In February 1701 Louis used French troops to blockade the eight garrisons which the Dutch were occupying in the Spanish

Netherlands. The 15,000 troops were permitted to return to Dutch territory only in return for a formal recognition by the States General of Philip as king of Spain. In Germany the French broke up the unity that had existed since 1688; with Bavaria, Cologne and Liège as French allies, Dutch security was further threatened, and Habsburg influence reduced. Louis also had the right of Philip to succeed to the French throne registered by the Paris *parlement*. If Philip ever did succeed, he would hand Spain over to another Bourbon, but clearly the prospect of doing so would commit him and his heirs to eternal friendship with France, and they would always remain Frenchmen on the throne of Spain. French troops moved into Spanish territories. Their governors took orders from Versailles and ignored Habsburg claims. These developments made it easy for William to restore the alliance with the Emperor which Rijswijk and the Partition Treaties had fractured. The Grand Alliance of 27 August 1701 provided compensation for the Habsburgs, who were to have Naples, Sicily, Milan and the Spanish Netherlands, but not the Spanish crown itself. The Dutch were to get a strengthened barrier. Existing Dutch and English trading rights were to be confirmed, and any possessions in the Indies which they could seize might be annexed. All French trade to the Spanish Indies was to be prohibited, and the crowns of France and Spain were to be kept rigidly separate. Finally, the treaty provided that the alliance was to continue after the end of the war, in order to maintain a peace embodying these provisions.

During 1701 English opinion turned strongly against France as a result of moves by Louis, although the whigs probably hampered William by their popular agitation. This culminated in the Kentish petition which alleged that the tories were actively sabotaging an effective foreign policy. Whig activity created a danger that William would again become exclusively associated with one party. But fortunately for William, during the course of the year Louis managed to antagonize virtually every section of the nation. On 6/17 September James died, and Louis formally recognized his son as James III. This was a logical, indeed a necessary move, since James's right to the English throne was juristically and ideologically identical with that of Louis's son and grandson to the throne of Spain. Having (successfully) asserted the latter, Louis was bound to uphold the former. But in doing this Louis certainly did not intend to give him direct assistance to recover England, nor does he appear to have had any idea of how this recognition of the Pretender (an infringement of the spirit, if not the letter, of the Rijswijk Treaty) would help William in his management of English opinion—but that was a technique that Louis had never had to acquire or use. The effects were immediate.

William withdrew his ambassador. Exerting considerable pressure on the Emperor he obtained an additional clause to the Grand Alliance to protect the Protestant Succession in England, as it was now established by the Act of Settlement.

Louis also played into William's hands by policies of economic discrimination. The commercial concessions made to the Dutch at Rijswijk were repudiated within a year; progress in negotiations for a commercial agreement with England was blocked. In October 1701 crippling duties were imposed on those English exports to France that were allowed to continue, and customs officials were clearly acting under instructions in rigidly enforcing regulations, and using any pretexts to levy fines and confiscate ships and cargoes. Most ominous, however, was the eagerness with which French mercantile interests were preparing to take advantage of the new dynastic connection with Spain. Companies were formed to trade with the Indies and to contract for the *asiento*—the supply of slaves for the Spanish colonies—which was obtained in September 1701. Malouin ships were already opening up a new trade with the 'south seas', an evocative term for the west coast of South America, universally believed to be an area of great potential wealth. French ships were sent out with the annual *flota*, which supplied all the colonies with their imports. Spanish customs policy was aligned with French in what was obviously the start of a campaign to exclude English and Dutch competitors. The new duties placed on English exports to, and imports from, Spain itself were likely to have wide-ranging effects on the woollen industry. Colonial officials began to take preventive action against the illicit trade between the Caribbean colonies and Jamaica and Curaçao that had previously been tolerated. English merchants began to encounter official obstruction of their long-established trade with the Spanish Netherlands, where Philip's chief partisan, Bergeyck, was the proponent of protectionism.

These damaging consequences of French domination of the Spanish Empire made this war one in which economic and commercial considerations played a much larger part than had been the case with the Nine Years War. It had far more spontaneous and organized support. But this carried with it a difficulty for ministers, or as it turned out Marlborough, in the actual conduct of operations. Marlborough like William, his mentor, was committed to England taking a full part in the military campaigns on the Continent. The trading interests alienated by French discrimination, and the country party with whom they were associated, favoured an alternative strategy of naval and colonial warfare with the objective not only of maintaining existing rights but of making commercial and colonial gains that they had no intention of sharing with England's Dutch allies.

When war was declared on 4 May 1702 the allies' overall strategic position was far weaker than it had been in 1689–97. Louis was in effective possession of the entire Spanish empire, and in addition Philip had initially the loyalty of nearly all its inhabitants. France occupied the whole Spanish Netherlands, which the allies had fought so hard to preserve in 1674–8 and 1688–97. The Dutch barrier had disappeared. Imports of specie from the Spanish colonies in America restored French finances to a state of near-solvency in the earlier stages of the war. The French occupation of northern Italy, and their allies in Germany, separated the Emperor from his western allies. The Northern War against Sweden threatened to divert the attention and resources of the German princes, and gave Louis the opportunity to repeat Richelieu's coup of 1631 by trying to involve Karl XII in what would have been a damaging war against the Emperor. French diplomats were also active from as early as 1704 trying to persuade the so-called peace party in Holland to make a separate peace. Fear that the Dutch would respond to these approaches made Marlborough and Godolphin reject the 'blue water' strategy of naval and colonial warfare, advocated by Rochester and several of their tory colleagues in Anne's first ministry. The common cause (a phrase ministers used) demanded a concentration of effort in the Low Countries, to check the main French army and drive it from the Rhine and Maas, so safeguarding communications with the north German states.

As in the Nine Years War naval supremacy was established, but brought limited advantages. Mediterranean trade continued to move, the Imperial conquests of Naples and Sardinia were assisted and the allies were able to occupy Catalonia and Valencia. The capture of Gibraltar (1704) and Minorca (1708) gave the navy independent bases, and the French fleet ceased to be an effective force after the one (inconclusive) naval action (Malaga, 1704). But seapower by itself could not achieve decisive success, or prevent French privateers again inflicting heavy losses on merchant shipping. Insuperable logistical problems of victualling and refitting, together with weather hazards and the devastating yellow fever which was spreading epidemically during this decade, made substantial or permanent conquests in the western hemisphere unattainable. Navigational mistakes and bad planning wrecked the Quebec expedition of 1711. Occasional successes were achieved, such as Rooke's capture or destruction of the Spanish treasure fleet in Vigo (1702), but as in the previous war the navy's main service was to render impossible a major French invasion of any part of the British Isles, and to keep open the army's main supply lines.

The only way of restoring a balance of power in Europe was to defeat the main French armies. In 1702 and 1703 Marlborough, restrained by Dutch caution, fought a piecemeal war, consolidating the allied position inside the frontiers of the Spanish Netherlands and on the Rhine. But in 1704 the French threatened to deliver a knock-out blow by advancing down the Danube on Vienna. Inaction would leave the Emperor to his fate, but Marlborough was incurring great risks by his justly celebrated march across Germany. He had to overcome formidable logistical problems and he had to establish harmonious relations with Imperial generals who were unknown to him (he succeeded with Eugène, but not with the Margrave of Baden), and anything short of a decisive victory—which no one had obtained against a major French army since the 1630s—that would permit him to return with his army to the Low Countries, would leave the Dutch frighteningly vulnerable to invasion. The victory at Blenheim rewarded Marlborough's courage and skill to the full. It represented a turning point not just in the war but in European history; not until Napoleon would France again occupy such a dominant position. Although rather surprisingly Louis retained superiority in numbers until 1711, his army was thrown on to the defensive, deteriorated in quality and lost most of its self-confidence. In 1706 Marlborough's second great victory at Ramillies was followed by the rapid conquest of the larger part of the Spanish Netherlands, and Eugène ejected the French from northern Italy. In 1708 the French were again thoroughly beaten at Oudenarde, and Marlborough began dismantling their frontier defences by taking Lille. Until the last of his set-piece battles, Malplaquet (September 1709) which was really a French defensive success, Marlborough achieved a psychological as well as military ascendancy, which made him and his ministerial colleagues believe that this series of victories could be turned into a punitive peace in which the maximum allied objectives could be realized.

Not surprisingly, allied appetites and ambitions increased as French power waned. The original war aims had been limited —compensation for the Emperor, a barrier for the Dutch and recognition of the Protestant Succession in England. The first commitment to put the Habsburg candidate, Karl, on the Spanish throne came in the treaty of alliance with Portugal (1703), but this was far from an irrevocable undertaking; such a minor ally could easily be jettisoned—as was to happen in 1713–14. The decisive, indeed fatal, step was taken after the capture of Barcelona in October 1705 when the provinces of Catalonia, Aragon and part of Valencia rallied to Karl. The queen's speech in November stated that a true balance in Europe was impossible so long as France remained master of Spain. To place Karl on the Spanish throne involved conquering the heartland of the country, because the Castilian aristocracy and clergy stayed stubbornly attached to Philip. Furthermore, although Karl went to Barcelona personally, the resources of the Emperor were largely concentrated on the campaigns in Italy, which left the task of conquering Castile to the English, the Dutch, and the Portuguese for whose pay they were responsible. Madrid was temporarily occupied in 1706, but a severe defeat at Almanza in April 1707 meant that Spain, if it was to be conquered, would have to be won in Flanders, not in the peninsula. But this defeat did not deter the whigs, on whom Marlborough and Godolphin increasingly had to rely, formally committing England to a 'no peace without Spain' policy in December.

Allied differences and jealousies were a by-product of success. Their incessant disputes virtually ensured failure in the Spanish campaigns, and the attack on Toulon in 1707 failed because of suspicion between Savoy and the Imperial generals. Leopold concluded a local armistice with the French in Italy in March 1707, which permitted them to evacuate their forces and transfer them to other theatres of war. The allies also complained that he employed an unnecessarily high proportion of his resources in suppressing a stubborn rebellion in Hungary. More damaging were the differences that developed in the Spanish Netherlands after Ramillies in 1706, when each of the allies tried to cash in on success, and by their enmities and jealousies prevented the formation of a united front at the very time that a satisfactory peace could have been imposed on Louis. The Dutch acted to establish an expanded barrier, maintained by their control over local revenues, and they tried to obtain a privileged position for their traders. The Emperor offered the rich bait of the office of governor-general to Marlborough, in order to weaken the Dutch hold. Marlborough had to decline the offer, but his transparent reluctance to do so created an unfavourable impression at the Hague and at home.

The final blow to France came from the forces of nature, not the allies. Defeats in the field, mounting war taxation, and the consequential decay of trade and industry weakened national resources and morale, but the catastrophically severe winter of 1708–9 produced utter destitution and despair. French approaches for peace in 1705–8 had been tactical, intended to split the allies, and the Dutch had seemed to be the likeliest to make a separate peace. Louis had offered a renunciation by Philip of the Spanish throne, but he mischievously required compensation consisting of the valuable Italian lands which the Habsburgs already occupied. The variety of offers which Louis put forward, the rather dubious intermediaries whom he employed and the corrupt inducements that he offered to Dutch republicans kept alive the distrust that had been generated by his repudiation of the Partition Treaty and breaches of the Rijswijk undertakings. However, in 1709 Louis was desperately and genuinely anxious to conclude an early peace, and at almost any price, and he proved his seriousness of purpose by despatching Torcy, his foreign minister, to negotiate at the Hague in April.

By 1709 the Marlborough–Godolphin ministry had become dependent on whig support, and was committed to the 'no peace without Spain' policy. The terms which the Dutch demanded from Louis on behalf of the allies as a whole amounted virtually to capitulation. Philip must concede the entire Spanish inheritance to Karl, without any promise of compensation. An enlarged barrier (including French territories) was to be provided for both Savoy and the Dutch. Louis must recognize the Protestant Succession and expel James. A truce of two months would be agreed (to give Philip time to evacuate Spain), but only on condition that some key fortresses were handed over to the allies. If he refused to do so, then either the war would be resumed, or Louis must assume responsibility for forcing him to do so, that is by military means. It was this demand, in article 37, that Louis refused to accept. His refusal was interpreted as evidence of ineradicable insincerity. Fundamental distrust explains the severity of the demands which the allies put. They assumed that Philip was no more than a French puppet, who would abandon his kingdom on his grandfather's orders, but that Louis would pretend otherwise simply in order to buy time, so as to recover his strength for a renewal of the war. The allies feared that if peace was made with Louis alone, he would be able to send Philip clandestine help while the allies undertook the difficult task of expelling the latter from Castile. From the English viewpoint it was all too likely that most of the burden of a continuing war in Spain would fall on the English fleet, army and taxpayer. An enlarged barrier would have satisfied the Dutch, who were already defaulting on their quotas of men and ships and money to keep Portugal in the war. The Emperor had consistently failed to send adequate support to Karl, and relations between the Austrian and English generals and diplomats at Barcelona were poisonously bad. On the other hand England stood to gain significantly from Philip's expulsion; a secret commercial treaty with Karl (1708) conceded exclusive trading privileges in the Indies.

The breakdown of the 1709 peace negotiations meant that the Marlborough–Godolphin ministry now occupied a false, ultimately untenable, position. Louis had been effectively defeated and his power significantly reduced, but the publicly proclaimed war aim of obtaining the entire Spanish inheritance for Karl was unattainable. However, in the autumn the ministers pushed the Dutch into sharing the same position, by the Barrier Treaty negotiated by the whig Townshend. Both parties to the treaty displayed bad judgement. The English persisted in fearing that the Dutch might be persuaded to make a separate peace with France, so they were prepared to pay too high a price for a Dutch guarantee of the Protestant Succession. The Dutch were conceded a greatly improved barrier and considerable trading privileges which English competitors complained would virtually exclude them from markets in the southern Netherlands. In addition, the ministry gave even more widespread offence by agreeing that Dutch merchants would get an equal share in whatever commercial advantages were obtained in the Spanish colonies.

The Dutch government, badly served by Vrybergen, the ambassador in London, did not fully realize that they were tying themselves not just to England but to the whig party. This treaty ensured the failure of renewed peace negotiations at Geertruidenberg, from March to July 1710, when the Dutch adopted an intransigent line. This failure left the allies with the prospect of a never-ending war. Anne recalled Marlborough's confident promises in 1706 and 1708 that another year's campaign would produce a durable peace. Her belief that Marlborough and Godolphin were actually sabotaging all efforts to end the war, out of self-interest, made her listen sympathetically to Harley. Continued heavy war taxes, increasing government indebtedness, heavy maritime losses to French privateers and distortions caused to the economy by the war were generating almost universal war-weariness. The new administration formed by Harley, which came in during the summer of 1710, was obliged to satisfy this national demand for peace.

The tory thesis that governed the conduct of the new administration was that while Britain had gained only a general advantage—of lessening French power—each of the allies had also secured their own particular interests, as could be seen in the detailed demands made on their behalf in the negotiations of 1709. St John commented, 'our allies have always looked first at home' and it was high time for Britain to do the same. The recent failures to conclude peace were blamed on a combination of selfish individuals and parties—Marlborough, the largely whig officers in the army, the monied interest, financiers and contractors—with the equally self-interested allies who received British subsidies for fighting to achieve their own particular objectives. Britain was depicted as bearing the burden of the war, while the allies gained disproportionate advantages.

Although this was a simplified propaganda picture, the ministers had to reckon on allied obstruction of the difficult process of making peace. As early as July 1710 Vrybergen communicated to Anne the resolution of the States General against any dissolution of the whig-dominated parliament. The new ministers knew that they must act independently or all decisions would effectively be subject to allied vetoes. Harley, Shrewsbury and Dartmouth were determined to lead the allies, willingly or not, into a general peace. This involved taking unilateral action in preparing the ground for a peace conference, by secretly negotiating preliminaries with France, and in this process the negotiators certainly did not neglect to press particular British demands. But this display of national egoism did not mean, as it would have done if St John had had more to do with the negotiations, a ruthless betrayal of the allies and their interests. The tory government was not, like the States General in 1678, intent simply on getting an advantageous peace and leaving its allies to fend for themselves. Although Harley would not insist on France conceding the full allied claims which his predecessors had endorsed, and although he did not consult them or keep them informed regularly, he knew that the French would take every advantage of divisions among the allies.

These tory ministers who condemned their predecessors for having become the dupes of the allies were, with the exception of Jersey, wide awake to the danger of being duped by France. They knew that it was necessary to maintain pressure on Louis, and this was why Marlborough was not dismissed with Godolphin and the whigs but retained in command for the campaign of 1711. In the following year they insisted on the occupation of the key French fortress and naval base of Dunkirk so as to prevent Louis going back on earlier undertakings. Harley and Dartmouth were also alive to another danger, that the French would try to combine the peace negotiations with intrigues for a jacobite restoration. This would give them a hold over the English ministers, who could be blackmailed into accepting French demands.

Throughout the preliminary negotiations the tory ministers were subject to a barrage of whig propaganda, whose authors were kept supplied with information by allied diplomats in London. The latter regarded the preliminaries and the final treaty as a sell-out because they fell so far short of the demands that had been advanced in 1709–10. To this the tories answered that such harsh terms would have had to be enforced by continuing pressure on a resentful, revanchist France. An imposed peace, a *diktat*, would have required endless cooperation with predatory and selfish allies on their own terms, and would have necessitated the maintenance of an inflated standing army and a large fleet, continuing high taxation and a further growth of indebtedness. By contrast a freely negotiated treaty would be self-enforcing, and would restore Britain to happy independence from other nations.

The first tentative negotiations, the so-called Jersey phase, were conducted by Harley and Shrewsbury, using Lady Jersey's catholic chaplain Gaultier as intermediary. It was not until April 1711 that the cabinet (including St John) knew about these negotiations, or that the Dutch were informed. During this phase important working principles were established. In December 1710 it was agreed that Philip should keep the Spanish throne; the second evacuation of Madrid (November), followed by the defeat of Stanhope's army at Brihuega (December), made this an act of realism. The ministers quickly became confident. They rejected the first French draft of propositions, and easily detected and checked a French attempt to open up differences between the English and the Dutch. But when the latter were officially informed about the French offers (April 1711), and started to make difficulties, Harley excluded them from the further negotiations. In July Matthew Prior (a poet and secondary diplomat) was sent secretly to Paris with the British proposals. Those which related to allied interests—including the Dutch barrier and separation of the French and Spanish crowns—were generally acceptable, but the French thought the specifically British demands excessive. These included not only recognition of the Hanoverian succession and colonial concessions (Newfoundland and Hudson's Bay), but also extensive advantages at the expense of Spain. Gibraltar and Minorca, which Jersey had said would be returned, were to be annexed. The *asiento* contract was required. Free trade to Caribbean colonies was to be permitted, and guaranteed by the cession to Britain of four key ports. Clearly this penetration of the jealously preserved colonial monopoly was designed to give Britain a commercial ascendancy that would lead to the early subordination, and eventual annexation, of Spain's American possessions.

Prior was not authorized to negotiate, but merely to exchange proposals. In August he returned to London with a French diplomat, Mesnager; the preliminaries were agreed and signed on 27 September. Oxford (as Harley had become) limited his commercial demands on Spain and dropped the idea of annexations. The general articles agreed on were to serve as the basis for the full negotiations in a general peace conference, so they had to be drafted in a form that could be communicated to the allies. The Dutch accepted them for this purpose in November, but only after pressure had been exerted. They and still more the Emperor and the German princes could hardly be expected to acquiesce throughout in principles that were now being imposed on them. Publication of the preliminaries in the whig *Daily Courant* of 13 October, an act instigated by Gallas, the Imperial envoy, signalled the intention of the allies to wreck the peace policy in cooperation with the whigs and Nottingham who were joining in a determined fight to bring down Oxford's ministry.

The queen's speech at the opening of parliament in December dealt only with generalities—that a place and time had been fixed for a conference despite 'the arts of those who delight in war', adding unconvincingly that the allies (including the Dutch) had expressed their entire confidence in the ministry's proceedings. This display of what was anxiously interpreted by many tories as dangerous complacency was followed by an opposition offensive. In the upper house a proviso passed on 7 December, condemning any peace that left Spain and the colonies in Bourbon hands as neither safe nor honourable. Marlborough openly joined with the opposition at this stage, but it was totally routed. A similar vote was defeated in the Commons by 232 to 106. Oxford manufactured a ministerial majority in the Lords by the creation of twelve new peers. Even more important, he won public opinion for the peace. Swift's masterly pamphlet commissioned by the ministers, *Reflections on the Conduct of the Allies*, appeared on 27 November and sold enormously. Swift cleverly emphasized all the failings of the Dutch as allies, because he knew that these were far more familiar and resented than those of the much more culpable Imperialists, and because they were identified in the public's mind as associates of the whigs.

By withstanding what appeared to be allied blackmail, Oxford enhanced his reputation for true patriotism. To general applause he dismissed Marlborough, and when Eugène arrived in January 1712 to rally opinion for a continuation of the war, the ministers skilfully made use of him to denigrate Marlborough. Yet in the long term this triumph over the allies (which earned the ministers applause in Paris) contained the seeds of catastrophe for the tories. Among the foreign diplomats who supported the attacks on the preliminaries was Bothmer, envoy from the Elector of Hanover. He had been instructed by his master to seek Marlborough's advice, and this led him to share whig hostility to the ministry. But Bothmer had a further cause for disquiet. He feared that Louis, having defied Europe in keeping Philip on the throne of Spain, would now try to dispose of the British succession. In January these suspicions grew when St John laid the whig Barrier Treaty with the United Provinces before the Commons, so that it could be savagely criticized and then repudiated. Bothmer sought reassurances that his master would not suffer, and particularly that the Dutch guarantees of the Hanoverian succession would continue to be valid. St John sharply rebuked him for improperly intervening in parliamentary affairs, adding that George must learn to trust the queen (which meant her ministers). St John privately boasted that he had sent Bothmer a 'peppering answer', and that he despised him as a tool of the whigs.

This arrogance was almost suicidal. St John compounded the mistake which the new ministers had made from the beginning by underestimating the importance of managing Hanover. Their first special envoy, Rivers, a bluff but unintelligent soldier, made little impact in two missions in 1710 and 1711. On the first he had been authorized to offer George the post of commander-in-chief for the 1711 campaign in place of Marlborough. George had not responded, and in retrospect the offer appeared to be insincere. Certainly it was incompatible with the ministerial policy of winding down the war. George was among the princes who were infuriated by the restraining orders that were sent to Marlborough's successor, Ormonde, under which he unilaterally ceased operations and left the allies to face the French alone in the summer of 1712. This manoeuvre led to their defeat at Denain. Communication of the orders to the French was interpreted as evidence of collaboration between Louis and the ministers, which might continue after peace was established and include work for a jacobite restoration.

The Treaty of Utrecht, signed in April 1713 after fifteen months of negotiations, provides a classic example of what later diplomats would call *realpolitik*. Britain played the decisive role—this meant Oxford and Bolingbroke (formerly St John) in London, rather than Strafford and bishop Robinson, the plenipotentiaries at Utrecht. Bolingbroke would have made peace separately, but Oxford kept control in his own hands and appreciated the need to maintain a negotiating combination with the Dutch. But he was not prepared to work to achieve inflated Habsburg claims, and eventually the Emperor was left to negotiate his own peace (Rastadt, March 1714).

The Utrecht settlement proved to be satisfactory and durable because it reflected the realities of European power. England made colonial acquisitions—Newfoundland, Acadia, St Kitts, Gibraltar and Minorca. France kept the earlier territorial gains of Louis's reign, especially Lille and Strasbourg. The duke of Savoy acquired Sicily; the rest of Spain's Italian possessions went to the Emperor. The Dutch got an adequate barrier. These arrangements underlined the primacy of Britain and France. From an earlier position of minor importance (or none at all) Britain had now emerged as the new

great European power, acting as arbiter in conflicts and problems
that had previously stood well outside the range of her interest and
power.

Not surprisingly this new-found power and influence had an in-
toxicating effect on ambitious Englishmen, notably Marlborough
and Bolingbroke. The latter plunged with zest into high diplomacy.
He was flattered by the reception which he received on his visit to
Paris in August 1712. By 1713 he was thinking of a new diplomatic
revolution through alliances with France and Savoy. Absorbed by
great issues, Bolingbroke left detailed negotiating to inadequately
instructed and laxly supervised subordinates. This resulted in unnecessary ambiguities and difficulties in the treaties, for instance over
Newfoundland fishing rights. In the shorter term Bolingbroke's in-
attention to vital detail led to two extremely damaging political
reverses—the rejection of the commercial treaty with France (June
1713), and the early realization that the commercial treaty with
Spain was an abject failure and would have to be renegotiated.

These set-backs were serious because the tories had solicited and
won the support of the bulk of the commercial and mercantile interests (as distinct from the financial or monied) by their advocacy of
peace. They had promised that peace would be accompanied by
commercial treaties with France and Spain that would 'improve and
enlarge' trade. Encouragement of trade with France ran counter to
policies accepted and followed for half a century. Trade with France
had been regarded as prejudicial to sectional and national interests.
French tariffs excluded English exports and produced a consistently
unfavourable balance of trade. This was politically dangerous because the deficit had to be paid in coin and specie which Louis and
Colbert used to finance an aggressive foreign policy and the expansion of the French navy. Consequently the whigs discouraged trade
with France, which was prohibited from 1678 to 1681, and duties on
French goods had been raised to prohibitive levels in 1697–1702.
Bolingbroke attempted to reverse this policy. Without having full
supporting information, he assumed that an open trade with France
would be economically advantageous. His real purpose was party-
political advantage. Trade would consolidate the peace and facilitate the alliance that he was planning with France. As he wrote,
'nothing unites like interest, and when once our people have felt the
sweets of carrying on a trade to France, under reasonable regulations, the artifices of whiggism will have less effect amongst them'.
In addition, expansion of trade with France would weaken the
economic links between France and the Dutch, reducing the latter's
competitive abilities.

During the negotiation of the commercial treaty, the French in

fact cleverly played the Dutch against Britain. The basis was a return to the low French tariff of 1664 and (without using the term)
most favoured nation treatment for merchants of the two countries.
Early on the British negotiators agreed that the Dutch should not
enjoy the 1664 tariff on certain commodities, only to find later that
these exceptions would also apply to Britain. They included woollen
goods, sugar and tobacco and this seriously reduced the value of the
treaty. Those connected with trade in these excepted commodities,
and textiles were especially important, opposed the agreement.
There was also the issue of reciprocal dismantling of British tariffs on
French goods. The French insisted that these must be reduced to a
level equivalent to their 1664 tariff and suggested that the book of
rates would have to be revised by officials representing the two
governments—which would mean that bureaucrats of Louis XIV
would be carrying out governmental functions in Britain at the invitation of the queen's ministers. In addition to generalized fran-
cophobe agitation the proposals were violently assailed by the new
trades that had developed behind high tariffs—silk manufacture,
paper-making and the greatly expanded Portuguese trades.

The bill to give effect to the commercial clauses passed easily
through its preliminary stages. The court managers Davers and
Moore (an able but corrupt associate of Bolingbroke) became complacent. They were outmaneouvred by the whigs who inspired a
journalistic campaign against the treaty, to which the government
responded, notably with *Mercator: or Commerce Retrieved*, which was
partly Defoe's work. But they failed to match the whigs' organization
of petitions: over forty were presented to the Commons, all hostile to
the proposals, and these impressed some tory MPs, who faced a
general election later in the summer. When the commercial clauses
were narrowly defeated (18 June) by 194 to 185, over half the tory
defectors were men who had previously been loyal to the ministry.
The others were 'whimsicals', who were alarmed by Bolingbroke's
obvious wish to forge closer links with France, fearing that this
would endanger the Protestant Succession.

Coming a year later there was no excuse for the gross mishandling
of the Spanish commercial treaty. Oxford took no interest, beyond
furthering the interests of the South Seas Company that he had
sponsored. The preliminary treaty confirmed prewar trading rights
in Spain itself, but the later explanatory articles conceded higher
duties which merchants complained would make profitable trading
impossible. The explanation for this strange outcome is that Moore,
who conducted the negotiations, was receiving massive bribes from
Spain. He was also engaged in very dubious dealings, in partnership
with Bolingbroke and Lady Masham, so that when the whigs and

whimsicals got on to the trail in June 1714, Bolingbroke had to give him protection by proroguing parliament. But by then the tory attempt to represent themselves as champions of the mercantile interest, and the whigs as the puppets of oligarchical, capitalist big business, had collapsed. By accusing the tory ministry of betraying national interests in the commercial negotiations, the whigs rehabilitated themselves as true patriots.

The tory ministry had had no alternative but to conclude peace: by their denunciations of Godolphin, Marlborough, the whigs, and the allies, they had led their supporters to expect nothing less. But there was a price to pay. It was openly said at Hanover in 1713–14 that those who had made such an unsatisfactory peace would never be forgiven. This threat was politically all the more damaging because it did not mean proscription of all tories: Nottingham and the whimsicals would be exempt. Oxford was fully aware of the danger, but by 1714 he was too slow and irresolute to retrieve the position. In February Thomas Harley was sent to Hanover to ask the Elector what action he wanted the ministry to take, that is, an invitation to work through them. But Bolingbroke obtained Harley's recall as part of his campaign to undermine Oxford. He then used a memorandum presented in April by Schutz, George's envoy, asking Anne to invite the electoral prince to come over and reside in England as a kind of guardian of his father's rights, to deliver offensive rebukes to both George and his mother Sophia (Anne's actual heir) for intervening in English politics. These literally killed Sophia (8 June), but they also doomed the tory ministers as a whole. It was now generally believed that they were working for a jacobite restoration. Thomas Harley's designated successor Paget, a tory adherent of the Protestant Succession, refused to go to Hanover because he could get no clear instructions from the feuding ministers and, even more revealingly, because he could not satisfy himself that they genuinely favoured George's succession.

Bolingbroke's final overthrow of Oxford came too late to affect the issue, but it facilitated the successful whig campaign to smear the entire ministry and its associates with jacobitism. Paradoxically, the success of the peace negotiations led directly to the decline and collapse of the tory party. Denouncing their rivals' subservience to the allies, the tories had temporarily claimed to embody and represent the national interest. But their diplomatic collaboration with France in imposing peace, followed by Bolingbroke's indiscretions and association with extremists, seemed first to George, but in the end to the political nation generally, to threaten the Protestant Succession.

15 William's Last Years

Although the Nine Years War placed intolerable burdens on nation and government, its prosecution provided administrations and politics with a kind of stability by imposing a routine. William spent at least half each year abroad, engaged in diplomacy and commanding military operations. Parliament was not permitted to sit in his absence. Sessions were dominated by the attempts of ministers to obtain the votes of supply which the war required, while resisting the persistent efforts of the country opposition to reduce royal prerogatives and restrict ministerial influence by legislation. The end of the war in 1697 broke up this set pattern, and there then followed one of the most confused periods in English political history. There had been only two regular parliaments since William came to the throne—those elected in 1690 and 1695. Now there were four in as many years, with elections in the autumn of 1698, December 1700, November 1701 and July 1702, and these hotly contested elections revived political consciousness and heightened popular excitement.

Each of these elections was fought on different issues and under different conditions. In 1698 the country opposition profited from a strong reaction against the heavy war taxation with which the electors identified the Junto whigs. Subsequently the Junto ministers lost their offices, although this was not a direct consequence of the changes of parliamentary strength produced by the elections. The new country party virtually demanded a dissolution, and in the December 1700 elections they increased their strength. But a year later, with a new war fast approaching, William incurred country hostility by another dissolution and elections in November 1701, which were visibly intended to facilitate the return of the former Junto ministers into a new ministerial partnership with the king. However, the death of William, on 8 March 1702, destroyed this emerging re-establishment of the political pattern that had existed in the later stages of the previous war. Parliament by law had to be dissolved three months after Anne's accession, and in the July 1702 elections the new country party profited from the enthusiasm for new courses under the new sovereign, so that initially it dominated the new parliament that lasted until 1705.

During these confused years there were frequent ministerial changes, affecting every major office. These changes cannot all be related to the changes in strength of parties and groups produced by elections, nor did subsequent elections consistently confirm and consolidate ministerial changes, as was to be the case after 1714. Since there was no notion of collective responsibility, ministerial changes were always made piecemeal, with individuals resigning, being dismissed or appointed without these changes necessarily affecting their colleagues. In general it can be said that by the summer of 1700 the Junto had been replaced by a composite ministry of independent politicians, tories and courtiers, and professional administrators. In the winter of 1701–2 William was beginning to construct a new war administration; this would have included Marlborough (but not Godolphin), and places were being prepared for Junto leaders. It was the latter who suffered from Anne's accession, being excluded from the Marlborough–Godolphin ministry which took on the prosecution of the war. However, the new ministry was obliged to rely on tory colleagues who put a higher priority on achieving partisan objectives in domestic politics than on overcoming the grave problems which the war created. Consequently, although gradually, the chief ministers had to persuade the queen to discard such tories as Rochester and Seymour, and to reconstruct the ministry with the inclusion of a more constructive, but less influential, group of country politicians associated with Robert Harley.

In a third area, that of foreign affairs, changes were even more frequent and more disturbing in their consequences. William in 1697 resolved the difficulties of bringing the war to an end only by a personal negotiation, using Portland to establish direct contact with Louis. Both kings saw a continuation of these negotiations as the only way of preventing a new European war that could be precipitated at any time by the death of the ailing king of Spain. A secret partition treaty was concluded in September 1698, leaving most of the Spanish possessions to the least powerful claimant, the electoral prince of Bavaria. He inconsiderately died in January 1699, necessitating another round of secret negotiations, and a second partition treaty, signed in February 1700. In contrast to the first treaty, details of the Second Partition were soon generally known, and universally disliked in England. When Carlos II died in November he left a will bequeathing the entire Spanish empire to the French candidate, Philip, and when Louis accepted this will in preference to implementing the Partition Treaty, the reaction in England was at first cautiously favourable. William believed that France now occupied the dominant position in Europe that he had fought since 1672 to prevent, and that the liberties of Europe were endangered. But at first English and Dutch opinion prevented him from following policies that might lead to war. It needed a series of provocations by Louis, culminating in his recognition of James II's son as king of England in September 1701, to educate the nation in the need to resume what was at first essentially a defensive war to check and reduce French predominance.

Marlborough and Godolphin were the beneficiaries of this change in opinion, yet they had to struggle in order to achieve the freedom to act according to their judgement of the situation, both in Europe and at home. To say that the country party ruled in the years after 1697 is in a sense impossible, since most of its principles and attitudes were largely incompatible with effective government. Yet it was during this period of country dominance and weak, composite ministries that the most important of all issues—the succession—was finally resolved in the 1701 Act of Settlement. This act consolidated the constitutional safeguards contained in the Revolution Settlement, and provided the essential basis for a century of political stability.

The four parliamentary sessions of 1697–1701 and the waves of pamphleteering activity and popular agitation over their main issues completed the fusion of the former whig and tory sections of the opposition into what was now called the new country party. They were united in suspecting the principles and practices of the ministers, and thought that the abnormal circumstances of the war had been used as a cover for personal self-interest, attempted extensions of court influence, and even the subversion of parliamentary independence. William bitterly resented criticisms of his own integrity. He was driven to the edge of despair by the political defeats and personal humiliations of these years, but he contributed to his reverses by consistently refusing to act like a politician. Unlike Charles II during the Exclusion Crisis, he would not demean himself by cynically concealing his real intentions, making promises that he had no intention of keeping, flattering men whom he loathed and despised, and appealing to the nation. As always William lived by his motto, *je maintiendrai*, and indeed his unpopularity and vulnerability were the product of his life-long commitment to the task of containing and reducing the overmighty power and influence of France. It is not surprising, therefore, that there are suggestive similarities between the new country party and the republican party in Holland which had for decades opposed what it regarded as William's ruinously expensive and unnecessarily bellicose policies. Both parties claimed to represent the dominant social group or class—the gentry

in England, the urban patriciate in Holland. Both parties tried to
perpetuate their control over representative institutions by laying
down exclusive qualifications for membership: by limiting entry into
parliament, or the town governments, they could prevent William
installing his own dependants, and also eliminate or at least reduce
the opportunities for any exercise of popular pressure on the
legislature.

In seventeenth-century Dutch politics fear of the dynastic ambitions of the house of Orange had been centered specifically on the
large and cosmopolitan army that it had consistently worked to
maintain. In England standing armies were associated with continental absolutisms, but even more with Cromwell's tyranny and
the policies of James II. The Nine Years War necessitated the raising
of unprecedentedly large forces (over 60,000 men of whom two
thirds were foreigners), and the lack of experienced English officers
and regulars meant that, in addition to foreign regiments, many
hundreds of foreigners (especially Huguenots) had to be employed.
William knew that the peace achieved at Rijswijk in 1697 might
prove to be no more than a temporary truce, and he was concerned
to maintain his trained forces. With the increasing professionalization of warfare, effective forces could not be quickly improvised if
hostilities broke out, so that it was essential to retain trained, disciplined and well organized forces during time of peace.

Few Englishmen accepted, or were even aware of, these unpalatable facts. The pamphlets on the army issue which poured out in
great quantity during 1697 and 1698 mostly ignored contemporary
realities. A standing army was simplistically depicted as primarily an
instrument of tyranny, or at least as a direct threat to the balance of
the constitution. An army was seen as being intrinsically incompatible with a free parliament. Country party writers refused to accept the possibility that an army could be safely governed by statutory controls—such as the so-called annual Mutiny Acts, first passed
in 1689. Facile generalizations were offered to justify claims that
national security could by safeguarded by the navy and an improved, but still amateur and part-time, militia so that all standing
forces could be disbanded. Country party arguments were without exception fallacious and unrealistic, but they were very generally accepted; there is a striking resemblance between the passionate, genuine
and almost universal fears of standing armies that the country opposition reflected, and the equally irrational, emotive and deep-seated
fears of popery that the first whigs had embodied and exploited.

In 1697–8 fear and suspicion of the standing army brought together independent whigs and tories. Country whigs regarded their
former colleagues and associates who supported the court case for

retention of an army as renegades, betraying their principles in order
to cling on to office. Equally significantly, and to William's un-
measurable disgust, many of these whig ministers represented the
court case half-heartedly and ineffectively with the result that, under
Harley's skilled and far more energetic leadership, the country party
was able to seize and retain the initiative in parliament. During both
sessions there was in fact a sizeable bloc of MPS who could have been
mobilized to defeat some of the more extreme country demands, but
the Junto ministers failed to give a resolute lead, and by failing to
preserve the army they forfeited William's confidence.

Although it was known before parliament met in December 1697
that there would be strenuous opposition to the retention of a large
army, no detailed preparations seem to have been made. In his
speech (3 December) William played down the issue, mentioning no
figure but merely arguing that, 'for the present, England cannot be
safe without a land-force'. The court had not prepared an alternative to counter the motion made by Harley on 10 December, that
the forces should be reduced to the strength of 1680. This surrendered the initiative; the final resolution (11 January 1698) for a
reduction to 10,000 men went through without effective resistance.

In practice William delayed disbanding (in December 1698 he
still had 15,000 men in England and another 16,000 in Ireland), so
that the full onslaught on the army issue came in the session of
1698-9. On 17 December 1698 under Harley's leadership the
Commons resolved that all forces in England over and above 7,000
men should be immediately disbanded, and that only native-born
subjects should be continued in service. This time the ministers had
suggested an alternative strength of 10,000, which might have been
acceptable; but William would not allow such a low figure to be
offered. By this time he was so close to despair that he seriously
considered withdrawing from the conduct of government, retiring to
Holland, and leaving to parliament the nomination of commissioners
to act in his absence, whereas during his periodical absences abroad
the lords justices who acted for him were nominated by the king.
Some of his friends even spread the rumour, which historians have
taken too seriously, that he was considering abdication. In any case,
William's unconcealed disquiet had no effect. All his wishes were
ignored. In January 1699 the Dutch guards were specifically included in the forces that were to be removed from service, Harley
speciously quoting William's 1688 promise to dismiss his foreign
troops when they were no longer needed. Xenophobic parliamentary attacks on the employment of foreign officers and men received
rapturous popular applause, but deeply hurt William; he particularly resented having to discard homeless Huguenot refugees who

had served England well in Ireland and Flanders. But he had to
acquiesce and assented to the bill for disbanding on 1 February 1699
with no more than guarded reproaches, saying that he thought himself 'unkindly used' and warning that 'the nation is left too much
exposed'.

In the session of 1699–1700 William suffered an equally humiliating defeat on another major issue that inflamed both the country
party and public opinion outside Westminster—the resumption of
the grants that had been made to courtiers and officers of confiscated
Irish lands. This issue revived in a particularly acute form the antagonism between court and country, and put William in a completely
indefensible position. It represented a variation on a major political
theme in seventeenth-century Europe, where there had been many
examples of lands being resumed, and financial grants recovered,
from the associates or accomplices of corrupt but all-powerful ministers (Lerma and Olivares in Spain, Fouquet in France, the regents of
Karl xi's minority in Sweden). In England, however, it was not a
criminal minister but William himself who had made the grants.
Many had gone to Dutch and Huguenot courtiers and generals,
whose original appointments and continuing favour infuriated the
country opposition; the country spokesmen made grossly exaggerated estimates of how much money could be obtained from selling
lands that should be resumed to offset debts incurred during the war.

Harley and his associates in the country leadership behaved with
extreme ruthlessness during the struggle over Irish grants. Dissenting
members of a commission sent to inspect the situation in Ireland were
intimidated and refused payment of their full expenses. It was made
plain to William that any attempt in the Lords to introduce wrecking amendments to the resumption bill would be countered by refusal of all supply—which would mean forcing the disbandment of
those regiments that remained and the laying up of the fleet. Some
country MPs threatened impeachment of the main recipients of the
grants (William's Dutch favourites Albemarle and Portland, and his
former mistress, lady Orkney), and their vulnerability and unpopularity with all shades of opinion made William realize that he could
not defend them at the risk of virtually dissolving all government.
Eventually he not only had to assent to the bill (April 1700), but he
had to put pressure on a group of whig peers to refrain from making
mischief by holding it up in the upper house.

The proceedings in parliament and the excitement in the country
over these two issues confirmed and strengthened all the political
assumptions, principles and prejudices of the new country party. In
their own eyes they had succeeded in checking, but not eliminating,
foreign and corrupt elements at court which had manipulated the

government to serve their own selfish and alien interest. In 1698 the country party attacked those whom they accused of financial dishonesty, treasury officials associated with Sunderland (Duncombe) and Montagu (Burton and Knight). In 1701 the country turned against another conspicuously corrupt interest, the 'new' East India Company which had been sponsored by the Junto, and had just intervened in the general elections with massive bribery; several MPS connected with the company were expelled. In the same year a campaign was launched against partisan (and allegedly socially inadequate) JPS who had been installed by the whig Somers, and who were charged with instigating the wave of petitions which accused the Commons of lack of patriotism.

Backbench supporters of the country party became absorbed by the venomous personal attacks which were made against the Junto, culminating in the attempted impeachments of Portland, Orford, Somers and Halifax in April—June 1701, but the more constructive leaders also attempted to provide legislative remedies against what was conceived to be misgovernment. Bills were introduced to eliminate placemen from the Commons (February 1699), to regulate elections and impose a landed qualification on all MPS (April and December 1698, and February 1701) and to impose similar qualifications on all JPS (January 1700). Activating a clause in the supply act of 1694, commissioners concerned with the collection of certain fiscal duties were declared ineligible to sit as MPS. Where flagrantly corrupt electoral practices were detected (as in the December 1700 elections), those returned by bribery were barred from re-election to that parliament, and the constituencies involved were disfranchised for the session, by orders that no writ should be issued for a by-election.

The intransigence and vehemence of the country opposition during William's last years were a natural consequence of the disturbing and damaging effects that the Nine Years War had had on the life of the nation. Heavy taxation, the deflation caused by the recoinage, a run of bad harvests and dislocations of overseas trade had adversely affected the economic interests of the majority in the political nation who were engaged in agriculture or foreign trade. On the other hand, the task of financing the war had necessitated considerable extensions of governmental machinery, greatly increasing the number of personnel employed, especially in the assessment and collection of direct taxes and the administration (or extortion, in the popular view) of customs and excise. Favoured individuals prospered, ministerial patronage increased. More generally the landed gentry, whose interests were consciously and aggressively represented by the country party, were becoming uneasily aware that what would now be called long-term trends were operating to their disadvantage. They felt that they had to bear, through the land tax, a disproportionately heavy share of the financial burdens of the war. In contrast to the fiasco of the land bank, which might have enhanced land values, could be seen the emergence of a new rival social class—the capitalists of the 'monied interest'. Many gentry families were living beyond their means; most lacked the capital resources in liquid form to take advantage of the new opportunities for investment in the Bank of England and the 'new' East India Company (both statutory creations of the Junto ministers), or in real estate development, mining and improved estate management. Many gentry families were beginning to encounter increased electoral competition from new men as outsiders with money invaded their boroughs, either with spectacular bribery (as in the 1700 elections) or, more insidiously and effectively, by systematic purchases of property in parliamentary boroughs.

The politics of the half-century starting in 1673 can be interpreted as a long and ultimately unsuccessful defensive struggle on the part of the landed gentry to preserve and perpetuate their predominance. There was, however, a very important difference between the country party in the years after 1697, and the same party in the years of its decline after 1714. In the earlier period it possessed a consistent, responsible and organizationally resourceful leadership—provided by Robert Harley, Sir Christopher Musgrave and a group of younger men, including St John and Harcourt.

Harley's mastery of parliamentary procedure and organization, and the aggressiveness of his followers, enabled him to harass ministers over a period of years, but the country party had a long list of failures to achieve positive aims. The land bank had been unable to raise its capital, partly because of an incompetently drafted statute. An attempt to revert to farming of the excise, which would have cut ministerial patronage, came to nothing. Nothing was accomplished to give greater importance to the militia or to improve its efficiency. Early in 1697 the opposition lost control of the public accounts committee, the parliamentary machine which had enabled Harley to keep the ministers under constant pressure, when Montagu and the whigs of the Rose Tavern Club won the ballot to select its members. Harley's leadership maintained the morale of the country party, and reverses did not lead him to imitate Seymour and Howe by engaging in indiscriminate opposition, endless abuse of personalities and senseless obstruction. There was always a constructive element in Harley's politics: first as the most influential backbencher, then from 1701–4 as Speaker, he was always ready to consider cooperation with each successive ministry, particularly on supply matters. This led as early as 1699 to invitations to take office, but he preferred to retain his independence, acting as an unofficial adviser or consultant and in the process establishing a close relationship with Godolphin in 1700, and again after May 1702.

Unlike most of his country colleagues, Harley was fully aware of the dangers and complexities of the European situation, and at this time there were no ambiguities in his attitude over the succession issue, whereas the tory leader Rochester (and also Godolphin) were at least considering the possibility of an eventual succession by the jacobite prince of Wales. It was Harley's responsible leadership and unrivalled influence in the Commons that produced the Act of Settlement, required by the death of Anne's only surviving son, the duke of Gloucester, in July 1700. Despite the fact that political passions were running at an exceptionally fevered level over the attempted impeachment of the Junto leaders and the whig-sponsored Kentish petition, nothing was permitted to obstruct the passage of the Act, which received the royal assent on 12 June 1701. It was doubly a triumph for the country not only vindicating its loyalty to the principles of the Revolution, but also representing a comprehensive attempt to enact a series of clauses embodying country principles.

The object of the Act of Settlement was to complete work that the 1689 Bill of Rights had left unfinished, both in defining the succession and in securing liberties. The succession after Anne was to go to Sophia, daughter of Charles 1's sister Elizabeth, who headed the only protestant branch of the Palatine family and was mother to George, the newly created Elector of Hanover. This meant passing over male and senior branches of the Palatine family, and also the surviving daughter of Charles 1's daughter, Henrietta, all on account of their catholicism. The succession was made conditional (as it still is in 1978) on the Hanoverians remaining protestants, and refraining from following the general Stuart practice of marrying catholics.

The constitutional provisions did not formally embody the principle of a separation of governmental powers, but they were aimed at prohibiting recent innovative practices, by specifying how, and by whom, certain governmental functions were to be exercised. Judges were to hold office during their good behaviour, with secure salaries; this gave statutory force to what had been William's practice since 1689, the only novel feature being the provision of a procedure by which defective judges could be removed—by a joint address of the two houses of parliament. Another long-standing country demand was enacted in the clause (subsequently amended by the Regency Act, 1706) barring all holders of offices of places of profit under the crown from sitting in the Commons. Arising directly from the controversy over the Partition Treaties, and in a conscious attempt to reverse the trend towards cabinet government by a small inner group of ministers, the cabinet council, it was stipulated that all major decisions were to be made in the full privy council, with ministers establishing their responsibility by attaching their signatures to all resolutions which they sanctioned.

These provisions represented a codification of the country opposition programme which Harley had failed to accomplish earlier. The Commons was to be entirely cleansed of official members and influence to enable the house to bridle and supervise the executive; an independent Commons would have at its disposal the full range of institutional devices that Harley had established or planned, such as the public accounts committee, the council of trade, the commission of inquiry into Irish grants. Privy councillors in signing resolutions would never be able to forget their vulnerability to impeachment. On legal and constitutional questions the Commons could hope to work in cooperation with a judiciary that would have no careerist reason to fear and obey the crown and its legal officials. These provisions have generally been regarded as a deviation from the main stream of English constitutional development, and condemned as unworkable. But in fact Harley had shown since 1697 that a systematic policy could be based on them, and he had been acting in very much the same way as a modern majority leader does in the United States Senate or House of Representatives. Furthermore, these provisions need to be related to the methods of government that William had been using, and which had crumbled in failure with the collapse of the Junto, the disbanding of the army and the resumption of the Irish grants.

The provisions on the privy council and judges' tenure were not to come into effect until after Anne's death, when the throne would again have a foreign occupant. A whole set of clauses were effectively a condemnation of William's governmental methods, and were intended specifically to prevent his bad example being followed by a German sovereign. The latter would be barred from engaging England in war for the defence of his foreign dominions, unless parliament consented, thus raising what was to be a perennial eighteenth-century issue, that of the 'beggarly electorate'. Nor could a future sovereign employ even naturalized persons of foreign birth in any office, or give them titles and grants; Portland, Albemarle, Athlone and Galway were to have no German successors. The sovereign was even to be required to ask parliamentary permission to leave the British Isles, and he must be a communicant member of the Church of England. Finally in a postscript that looked back to

Danby's case in 1679, no royal pardon was to be pleaded in order to block an impeachment.

The Act of Settlement was passed during a period of weak composite ministries. The Junto ministers had been united in shouldering the prolonged burden of the war, but after 1697 they lost their determination and political stamina. Montagu and Orford resigned in May 1699. The former had been saddled with the heaviest burdens; as chancellor of the exchequer and treasury commissioner he had to finance the war, and as senior minister in the Commons he had led the court against an increasingly aggressive country opposition. His blatant careerism and unlovable sense of his own importance also made him the most vulnerable of the ministers. In contrast were Wharton's political belligerence and organizational flair, but the king was permanently antagonized by his unconcealed determination to achieve a monopoly of office for Junto supporters, and his vehement, almost bullying manner. In December 1697 William refused to appoint him secretary of state, preferring a bureaucrat and protégé of Sunderland, James Vernon. Only Somers among the Junto ministers was really congenial to William. As lord chancellor he led for the court in the upper house, where he had the advantage of a bloc of latitudinarian bishops, but he was quite ruthless in filling the commission of the peace with Junto supporters, dismissing those who were critical or unreliable, and he exploited his legal and ecclesiastical patronage with equal skill. Bad health and relatively humble social origins alone prevented him from emerging as chief minister.

The crumbling of the Junto's position began with the junior ministers' failure to give a resolute lead in the Commons, at a time when popular interest in the issues debated in parliament was running strongly. Court spokesmen were placed in the difficult position of arguing in favour of a hated and costly standing army, and defending land grants made to Dutch favourites, but they failed to do everything possible to rally the uncommitted, who preferred Harley's lead and deserted the Junto ministers once the latter came under sustained pressure. Junto ineptitude in the Commons also persuaded William that the ministry must be reconstructed; between Orford and Montagu's resignations in May 1699 and the dismissal of Somers in April 1700, he replaced almost all the Junto ministers. Their impeachments followed a year later, being voted by the Commons in April 1701, with the objective of making it impossible for William to re-employ them if, as was now increasingly likely, a new European war broke out.

The Junto and its supporters showed their political skill and resilience in defeating the impeachments. The articles concentrated on individual abuses of ministerial powers and on the former ministers' involvement in the unpopular and discredited Partition Treaties, but the specific charges were not well substantiated and would certainly be subjected to critical scrutiny by the peers. The Commons' managers anticipated defeat, and so refused to accept an early date for a trial, while scoring debating points over whether any accused peers should sit as judges in the trials of others. The controversy between the two houses ended in farce. Solemn trials of Somers and Orford were held (17, 23 June) in the absence of the Commons, and since no prosecution case was presented both men were acquitted. The Lords dismissed impeachments against Portland and Halifax (the former Montagu), because although articles had been voted for their impeachment, the Commons refused to exhibit them to the Lords and proceed with a prosecution.

The weakness of the composite ministries which succeeded the Junto gave Harley and the new country party a virtual veto on all major policy decisions. Two phases of ministerial reconstruction proved to be makeshifts. In May 1699 Jersey became a secretary of state, Pembroke took over as lord president, with Lonsdale as privy seal, followed by Bridgewater as first lord of the admiralty, and the naming of Tankerville as treasury commissioner. These appointments combined tories with whigs who were not closely associated with the Junto. They cooperated no better than in 1689 and formed a feeble administration of second raters. Under continuing pressure from the country, further changes had to be made. William had to overcome his distrust of high tories who were highly critical of his foreign policy, and accept their titular head Rochester as lord lieutenant of Ireland, with Hedges as secretary of state and Godolphin at the treasury, and also dissolve parliament in the autumn of 1700. But not surprisingly he did not see such a patchwork administration as being either willing or capable of helping him prosecute a new major war; however, William did not live long enough to reinstate the Junto, and those who did receive offices (Carlisle, Manchester and Wharton as lord lieutenant of Buckinghamshire) lost them on Anne's accession. Only lesser men—Boyle, Devonshire and Somerset—continued in office but, although again displaced, the Junto whigs had recovered their confidence, and were to survive the first four years of Anne's reign in opposition with their cohesion and morale unimpaired.

When the War of the Spanish Succession began it was Marlborough and Godolphin (dismissed by William in December 1701, but appointed lord treasurer by Anne) who experienced all the difficulties of working in harness with a heterogeneous ministry, composed of men closely associated with the country party. Men like Rochester and Seymour shared, and actually encouraged, attitudes towards foreign policy and any effective prosecution of a major war that were totally unrealistic. The country opposition had a long tradition of suspicion of royal initiatives in foreign policy that went back at least as far as the detected duplicities of Charles II. William confirmed their fears and suspicions by his secret diplomacy of 1697–1700, and they could justify their opposition by pointing to his abject failure. The two Partition Treaties had been negotiated without the knowledge or participation of any English ministers, who had given William a completely free hand. In the country view he had subordinated English maritime and commercial interests to diplomatic considerations, by conceding Naples and Sicily to Philip in the second treaty, and so establishing French predominance in the Mediterranean, and a contrast was made with the safeguards contained in the treaty for the particular interests of the major allies, the Dutch and the Emperor.

The same principle underlay the country party's objections to the war strategy that William initiated and Marlborough was to continue. Large scale participation in the land campaign in the Low Countries would ensure the permanent subordination of English interests to those of the allies. It would be ruinously expensive, and despite the subsidies that would have to be paid to minor allies, actual control over the conduct of the war would not be in English hands. The planning of operations, the formulation of diplomatic demands, and the conclusion of an eventual peace settlement would all depend on the goodwill and cooperation of the allies, and past experience combined with xenophobic prejudice taught the country to distrust all allies. Instead of continental warfare, England should in the country view concentrate on a maritime and colonial strategy in which national resources would be used to maximum advantage, and operations would be controlled by English ministers and officers. Only an auxiliary force should be assigned to operations in Europe.

William and then Marlborough had successively to convince parliament and nation that the strategy propounded by the country party critics was unrealistic. In the parliamentary session that began in February 1701 William reversed his previously secretive manner, carefully explaining his moves and intentions. As his messages were printed and published he was also informing and preparing the way for an appeal to public opinion. But his task was made more difficult by the activities of the Junto whigs, who organized a series of petitions accusing the country majority in the Commons of wilfully neglecting, or even betraying, the interests of national security. The

Kentish petition of May 1701, got up by Junto activists, led to fierce clashes at Westminster, and by combining denunciations of the Commons' failure to cooperate in supporting William's foreign policy with demands for the immediate dissolution of parliament, it provoked the country party into retaliatory action. In the short term the Commons imprisoned the petitioners, members of the grand jury for Kent. More significantly, the more extreme leaders of the country began to consider how to weaken the whigs by initiating legislative action against the dissenters, who were seen as the allies or auxiliaries of the Junto. The device for this purpose was the bill against occasional conformity, which would have prevented dissenters holding offices in corporations. This was introduced for the first time in the session of 1702–3, when the country majority in the Commons led by Bromley, Packington and Seymour showed that they would if necessary exploit the financial needs of the administration to try to get the measure enacted; in fact the whigs in the Lords got the house to insist on wrecking amendments. But the priority that the country party gave to domestic issues seen in a narrowly partisan manner, at a time (1702–4) when the war situation was critical, showed that William's attempt to educate English opinion in contemporary European realities had not been effective. Decades of ignorance and prejudice were not easily effaced. Marlborough and Godolphin were to discover that tories in the early difficult years, and whigs during the period of victories, were more concerned to use the war for their own party advantages than to give them the consistent and reliable support that they required to serve the national interest.

16 Godolphin, Marlborough and the War of the Spanish Succession

Politically Anne's reign fell into two distinct phases; during the first, from 1702 to 1710, the country was governed by the Marlborough–Godolphin ministry which successfully prosecuted the war against France, and brought about the union with Scotland. For the last four years of the reign, this government was replaced by the administration of Robert Harley who succeeded in concluding a comprehensive and durable peace settlement at Utrecht. Both these ministries, then, recorded remarkable achievements. They were far stronger and much more cohesive than their predecessors, the ministries that had served William III, but both ended in disastrous collapses. A detailed examination of the two great ministries makes it apparent that each was subject to almost continuous difficulties that put its survival in doubt, and that each was forced into positions and policies against the will of the leaders. Only if it is appreciated that both ministries had to operate under almost constant pressure from both the political parties, is it possible accurately to estimate the skill and resilience of the leaders.

The Marlborough–Godolphin ministry provided the indispensable political, administrative and above all financial support for the victorious conduct of the War of the Spanish Succession. Few, if any, later administrations have ever come near to equalling its triumphs. It transformed what was at first a desperately uncertain defensive struggle into a victorious war that established Britain as a major European power, and re-established a balance of power on the Continent. Careful administration of government finances enabled the country's economy to bear the strains of a decade of war, with far less damage and disruption than had been the case in the 1690s—or in contemporary France and the United Provinces. The passage of the Regency Act (1706) and the Union Treaty with Scotland (1707) virtually guaranteed that the Protestant Succession laid down in the Act of Settlement would take effect, without the kind of difficulties or uncertainties that the jacobites hoped to exploit.

These achievements of two successive sets of ministers were all the more remarkable because previously all major policy decisions had been made by William on his own; even the whig Junto ministers had only been his executants. Now, although Anne could never be ignored, it was her ministers who actually governed. Marlborough commanded the allied armies during each summer's campaign, and spent the autumn and early winter months negotiating with the allied diplomats and planning the next year's operations. He kept in touch with Godolphin throughout, so that on his annual return to England they could determine the strategy of the war, and prepare for the sessions of parliament that met during the winter months. Godolphin as lord treasurer had responsibilities that were as onerous and extensive as Marlborough's, although less spectacular. It was his primary task to obtain the financial supply and recruiting acts that the war effort required. He had also to raise and service loans on an unprecedented scale and to control vast and regular expenditure, including remittances to the allies and forces overseas, of a magnitude never previously known. Godolphin subjected himself to an almost intolerable weight of business, but of course there were important advantages to be derived from the close measure of control that he achieved over most areas of government. The extensions of government that the war necessitated gave him extended patronage powers of which he took full advantage. Down to 1708–9 he enjoyed the personal confidence and sympathy of the queen, helped by the friendship which both maintained (despite periodical strains) with the duchess of Marlborough.

Although Godolphin had overall responsibility for general political management and led personally in the Lords, no man alone could hope to deal effectively with so many and such complex sets of governmental and political duties, especially when subjected to unremitting and systematic pressures from the two parties. Specifically, Godolphin needed an efficient and entirely reliable lieutenant to manage the Commons, where whigs and tories were equally quick and ruthless to exploit the ministry's needs and weaknesses. The Junto had used a group of secondary politicians, who had lost control after 1697, so that on Anne's accession Godolphin found that predominant influence in the Commons was firmly in the hands of the Speaker, Robert Harley. From 1702 to 1705 as Speaker, and from 1704 as secretary of state until his fall in February 1708, Harley was the third figure in the ministry, almost but not quite an equal partner with Marlborough and Godolphin. He was at first concerned primarily with parliamentary management, but his industry and ambition soon led him to act and be accepted as a minister in his own right, involved in general policy and major decision-making. In one particularly important and sensitive area of business, the disposal of ecclesiastical patronage, Harley was pre-eminent, acting with archbishop Sharp (of York) as Anne's confidential advisers. Close contact and mutual trust resulted, the queen accepting his judgement and coming to realize how far Harley shared her own principles. This rapport between Anne and Harley was a formidable, although hidden, political asset—one that he would use after 1706 in a long-term plan of campaign to replace Godolphin as chief minister.

The rivalry between Godolphin and Harley, which came into the open when the latter made an unsuccessful bid for power in February 1708, and was resumed two years later when he dismantled the ministry, was not merely a personal struggle. The two rivals were actuated by fundamentally different principles in dealing with the central problem in domestic politics that confronted ministers—their relationship with the whig and tory parties. Naturally, Godolphin wanted as much freedom as possible from party pressures, and he set as his working principle 'a cautious and prudent management from parties'; but his own background was more administrative than political, and he had risen to the treasurership through long service and the personal favour of successive sovereigns. He did not possess the experience of political and especially parliamentary in-fighting that Harley had, and he lacked the taste and aptitude for the continuous application to the essential tasks of fixing individuals and groups, dealing and manoeuvring in tactical arrangements, that were necessary if the ministry were to retain its independence from the two parties. In any case, Godolphin had delegated the unpalatable business of management to Harley from the beginning of the ministry; to try to recall these duties would provoke Harley's immediate defection.

In contrast, Harley excelled at political intrigue and devious manoeuvres, and they were his *raison d'être*. Although in the end his reputation for skilful exploitation of men and situations became a liability, Harley was an instinctive political animal, almost infinitely capable of using, deceiving and misleading even the shrewdest rivals and colleagues. He did have one consistent principle that can be seen underlying his behaviour as a minister, both in 1702–8 and again in 1710–14: he always worked to achieve and maintain an administration that could operate independently, free from dictation by the parties and party leaders. Unlike Godolphin, he knew from experience how much labour and strain such an effort would require, but he was confident that he had almost unique qualifications to undertake such a task. It is misleading to call Harley a tory. He would work with men from either party, but they must come into service on the queen's terms (which in practice meant those of the chief ministers), and they must always be kept subordinate, in an essentially supportive role.

There were three distinct phases of party pressure on the Marlborough–Godolphin ministry. From 1702 to 1705 it came from the high tories, who tried to establish a total monopoly of office in the central government and in the localities. Not only did they give first priority to controversial issues, concentrating on the occasional conformity bill, but their view that England should either play the role of an auxiliary, not a principal, in the war, or alternatively devote most of her resources to a maritime and colonial strategy, threatened relations with the allies. Intransigent and independent tories within the ministry were discarded in 1703–4, and Harley's careful management paid off when, in November 1704, the tory enthusiasts' attempt to tack occasional conformity was decisively defeated. This success was partly due to the divisions within the tory ranks which Harley had carefully fostered; this meant that although whig votes were needed to help defeat the tory attempt at a tack, the ministry was not left obviously dependent on them.

This independence was weakened by the general elections of 1705, which considerably increased whig strength in the Commons and consequently the amount of leverage they could exert on the ministry. In the second phase, from 1705 to February 1708, Godolphin gradually gave way before whig pressure and Harley, knowing that the whigs were pressing for his dismissal, began to organize and intrigue on his own behalf. The failure of his attempted palace coup in February 1708 and the resignation with him of a group of junior ministers left Godolphin even more vulnerable to whig pressure. During the last phase from 1708 to 1710 the ministry was slowly overrun by the whigs who, for their own advantage, committed both it and the nation to an apparently indefinite prolongation of the war. But this third phase also saw Harley put together in opposition an alternative administration which could secure tory support, but was not dominated by, or confined to, the existing tory leadership. As the whigs drove Godolphin and Marlborough into compliance with their partisan and sectional demands, they alienated the queen, provoked the anglican clergy into furious political activity, and largely discredited the ministers in the eyes of the electorate and the nation at large.

While it would be wrong to attach party labels to ministries, the politics of Anne's reign cannot possibly be understood without constant reference to the division of the political nation into whig and tory on every issue of importance. One of the effects of the collapse of the Junto in the years after 1697, the whig agitation over foreign affairs in 1701, and the dissolution of November 1701 which was interpreted as a preliminary to the return of the Junto, was the recharging of the old divisions between whig and tory. The political world was again sharply divided into hostile parties, which superseded the far more loosely organized and flexible groups associated with the court and the country. Historians now generally recognize the reality and primary importance of parties and of the political warfare that raged between them throughout Anne's reign. This warfare and the very perceptible rise in the political temperature were directly connected with the controversies and passions generated during the five general elections of Anne's reign—in 1702, 1705, 1708, 1710 and 1713. Each of these elections provided the occasion for an intensification of the press and pamphlet propaganda campaigning that was now a regular feature of politics. However, no government actually fell as a direct result of defeat at a general election. On the other hand no ministry 'made' an election; results did not necessarily or automatically ratify or confirm changes that had already occurred within the ministry. Each election changed the political environment in which ministers had to operate, and the crucial point was not so much whether tories or whigs had made overall gains, but rather whether the extremist wings of committed men within both parties had increased their strength, and so would be in a better position to put pressure on their own leaders, and on the ministers.

Anne's accession arrested and reversed the political trend of William's last months that had worked in favour of the Junto whigs, whom he had regarded as certain to be more serviceable in war time than tory ministers. Anne's first ministry was predominantly tory, with Godolphin replacing Carlisle at the treasury, Nottingham and Hedges coming in as secretaries of state, while Rochester was continued as lord lieutenant of Ireland. Some extreme tories were admitted to the cabinet council—Seymour, Jersey and Normanby. In the next few years several of these men were to be seen to possess characteristics that impeded effective prosecution of the war, so retrospectively justifying William's preference for whig war ministers, but Anne's ministerial changes reflected her own preferences and associations. These tories were men who had sympathized with her during her conflicts with William. Rochester was her uncle, and he was at this time engaged in the filial duty of publishing the *History of the Rebellion* by his father, Clarendon, to which he attached a preface and dedications that had considerable effect as tory manifestos. Rochester developed the theme that contemporary events and parties closely resembled those of the 1640s, warning the queen that the whigs were the descendants of the rebels of Charles I's reign.

Rochester's appeal to loyalist sentiments was well timed; a genuine, spontaneous and widespread tory revival was touched off by Anne's accession. This was reflected in the 1702 elections. The last parliament of William's reign, which was evenly balanced in the Commons between whigs and tories, neither possessing a majority, was continued under an act of 1696 into the first weeks of the new reign, but it was prorogued at the end of May and dissolved in July. The new Commons that replaced it, and met at the end of October, contained about sixty additional tory MPs, and in general groups and interests associated with members of the new administration strengthened their representation. Successes in the elections boosted tory morale. Confident and aggressive, the leaders and the rank and file were united in their resolve to secure objectives which had been publicly announced during the elections; by comparison the war in Europe was a secondary matter.

The primary tory aim was to consolidate and perpetuate their own supremacy. This was understandable, since their interpretation of what had happened in the recent past gave them cause for disquiet. Parliamentary investigations had uncovered what the tories saw as corrupt and unconstitutional practices on the part of the Junto ministers; but obstruction on William's part, and obstinate opposition in the Lords by a whig majority that was itself the result of royal favour, had prevented effective prosecution of the alleged offenders. Although the king had been forced to discard the Junto ministers in 1699–1700, the tories had not been able to prevent him bringing some of them back in 1701–2. Consequently, it was not just factiousness or self-interest that led the tories to resurrect the public accounts committee and launch attacks on Halifax and Ranelagh (paymaster-general of the army, 1685–1702) for alleged misappropriation, to revive an agitation against William's land grants (English ones, this time), and to propose a fresh investigation of the whig Orford's navy accounts. The tories saw themselves as the sole authentic representatives of the landowning classes, freeholders as well as gentry, and as upholders of national and social unity and harmony. They genuinely despised their whig opponents as an artificial and unnatural combination of sectional interests. They feared and hated the whig leadership—a tight-knit group of ambitious oligarchs and ruthless careerists, who controlled and used dependent groups, office-holders, military and naval officers and, in the constituencies, the protestant dissenters.

The tories pressed from the beginning of the reign for the elimination of all whigs from positions of influence. One minister responded with vigour: Nathan Wright, lord keeper from 1700 to

1705, purged a great many whigs from the commission of the peace and, although only a mediocre lawyer, earned respect and applause from the party. In any case his purges were a form of tit for tat, intended to reverse the purges carried out in the late 1690s by Somers, who was equally unscrupulous and partisan in his manipulation of patronage, although he was far more creative and authoritative as a lawyer. However, the largest and most obvious class of whig dependants were the dissenters, and it was against them that the main weight of tory hostility was directed. The central political issue of 1702–4 was provided by the tory attempts to enact an occasional conformity bill. Whig-orientated historians have generally described this bill, and the agitation to pass it, as a tiresome irrelevance impeding the war effort, and as an example of tory factiousness. But from the contemporary tory angle it was absolutely crucial to pass the bill in order to preserve the established order, both in church and state, from whig subversion.

The most obvious characteristic of the tory revival of 1702 was the sentiment of vociferous loyalty to the church, which had been expressed during the elections through the emotive slogan of 'the church in danger'. Tories believed that Anne's accession provided an opportunity to reassert and re-establish in practical terms the supremacy of the Church of England. Occasional conformity was a term describing the technique used by dissenters to evade the requirements of the Test and Corporation Acts, that all office holders must take the anglican sacrament; after receiving the sacrament so as to qualify for office, occasional conformists then habitually attended dissenting services. Tories denounced this use of the sacrament for political convenience as a form of sacrilege, entirely in keeping with the deceitfulness and hypocrisy which their prejudices led them to believe were principal dissenting characteristics. There was also a major political objective involved: by eliminating dissenters from all offices the church would gain in security, and the strength of the whigs in the corporations would be substantially reduced.

All tories were united on the issue of occasional conformity. But the most fervent advocates of the bill were the underpaid and overtaxed parochial clergy, who felt isolated, and in need of protection against competition from dissenters, and who did not trust their latitudinarian (broad church, whig-aligned) bishops to defend the best interests of the church. Occasional conformity bills did not formally encroach on the religious toleration instituted by the Indulgence Act of 1689, but their intended effect would have been to reduce the independence and security of the dissenters very substantially. Deprived of the protection of friendly officials and magistrates in the localities, and especially the corporations, dissenters would be obliged to keep strictly within the law. They would become no more than an indulged minority, enjoying no rights as such, but being allowed certain exemptions from the laws. Dissenters would subsist by the grace and favour of the authorities, lay and clerical, and would be in no position to attempt independent activities, or to challenge the established order. This, tories alleged, was the legal position that the legislators of 1689 had intended in passing the Indulgence Act; the re-emergence of the dissenters as active competitors to the anglican church was said to have resulted from William's favour to them, whig connivance and self-interest, and the betrayal of their trust by latitudinarian, whig-aligned bishops.

For tory MPs the greatest attraction of the occasional conformity bills was that they promised, at a stroke, to undermine the popular basis of whig strength. At the grass-roots level of politics, whig dominance in many corporations depended on the association of whig politicians with long established municipal interests based on dissenting congregations and families and those sufficiently sympathetic to work with them. The bills would exclude all who at any time attended dissenting services from central and (what mattered far more) local offices. This would force men to choose either to stick to their religious faith, at the price of accepting exclusion from public life, or of deserting the dissenting churches. By conforming to the established church they would be separated from their closest associates. In either case, local whig interests would be dissolved, and more generally the whigs would suffer from being seen to be unable to protect their allies. In time the bills would produce not only perpetual tory predominance in the localities, but as a direct consequence a permanent majority in the Commons. Occasional conformity bills were also a form of revenge on earlier whig attempts to rig the electorate and exclude tory supporters from offices, as in the Association Act of 1696, and the recent Abjuration Act of 1702, passed by William on his deathbed, which excluded non-jurors (mostly potential tory auxiliaries in the constituencies) from all participation in politics.

Three occasional conformity bills were introduced. The first easily passed the Commons, but in the Lords the whigs just managed by two votes to insert amendments which they knew the Commons would not accept (February 1703). The second bill was defeated in the Lords by seventy-one to fifty-nine (December 1703). Marlborough and Godolphin found themselves obliged to vote for the bill, for fear of being accused of desertion, but they were not sorry to see it fail. This compliance with tory prejudices proved to have been wise; extremist proposals to hold up a new recruiting bill, or to tack occasional conformity to supply bills, received insufficient

support. But a more serious crisis developed over the third bill, introduced in November 1704. The majority for this bill in the
Commons was significantly smaller than on the two previous occasions, but its backbench sponsors were determined to override the
anticipated opposition of the Lords by tacking the bill to the land
tax. This threatened to imperil the next year's campaign; as Cutts, a
general and an MP commented, it would largely undo the effects of
that year's victory of Blenheim. Such intransigence forced the ministers to come into the open as enemies of the bill as well as the tack.
After intensive lobbying under Harley's direction, the tack was decisively defeated in the Commons by 251 to 134, and the occasional
conformity bill itself failed in the Lords by fifty-one to thirty-three.
While it would be true to say that support of the tack, rather than
that of the actual bill, was a mark of tory extremism, the struggle
over occasional conformity did contribute to a widening gap between high-church tories on the one hand, and Marlborough,
Godolphin, Harley and their associates.

The failures of three hard-pressed occasional conformity bills
brought the tories up against a long-standing and major disadvantage—the secure majority of whigs and ministerialists in the
Lords. Relations between the two houses were also aggravated by
the concurrent struggle over the case of the Aylesbury men (*Ashby* v.
White) which continued throughout Anne's first parliament. This
case contained major constitutional issues, but it was also concerned
with some crucial if sordid realities of electioneering practices.
Ashby, a pauper and instrument of Wharton the aggressive Junto
peer, was denied a vote at Aylesbury in the December 1700 election.
He was set up to sue White, the returning officer and an associate of
Wharton's tory opponents, at common law and got a verdict stating
that he possessed a vote. On appeal the Queen's Bench quashed this
judgement by three to one, the dissentient being Lord Chief Justice
Holt, but the Lords on a writ of error upheld Holt and the original
verdict by a party vote of fifty-five to sixteen—that is by a majority
of peers who were not legally qualified. The dispute flared up again
when, in November 1704, five more Aylesbury men sponsored by
Wharton brought similar actions. The Commons responded in
December by imprisoning them for breach of privilege and, recognizing that its jurisdiction in that area was unchallengeable, the
Queen's Bench rejected their application for writs of *habeas corpus*.
However, Wharton was determined to prolong the conflict, and by
bringing an appeal by writ of error to the Lords was trying to embroil the two houses in a fresh confrontation when parliament was
prorogued in March 1704. This caused both his action and the detentions to lapse.

The passions aroused by this case stemmed from the fear of the tory majority in the Commons that an attempt was being made to undermine their basic independence, since the Lords were trying to achieve a legal position which would enable them to determine at least partly the composition of the lower house. The Commons had for a century possessed the exclusive power to determine disputed election cases (which averaged some fifty in each new parliament), and invariably abused these powers for partisan purposes, but the danger in the case of the Aylesbury men came from the prospect that in future the bitter clashes that occurred within the Commons would extend to disputes between the two houses. Returning officers were frequently summoned to appear before the Commons or its committee of privileges and elections; if they were now to be similarly and simultaneously answerable in actions in the common law courts, the scene would be set for constant direct clashes between the Commons and the courts and judges and, if the latter were supported by the Lords, total deadlock would ensue. On the other hand, Ashby's case raised a genuine issue, of the rights of the individual voter, who in practice had no redress against the arbitrary and often scandalous decisions of the Commons which could deprive him of representation in parliament. The case of the Aylesbury men ended inconclusively, but it kept alive the mutual suspicion and hostility between the two houses, which had never really subsided since the abortive impeachments of the Junto ex-ministers in 1700–1701.

For most politicians in Anne's day (as now) the gratification of personal ambition in the struggle for offices and promotion was the chief concern of life. Godolphin faced an early challenge from the arrogant and presumptuous Rochester, who regarded himself as the principal tory leader and aimed at becoming lord treasurer again. Rochester was also violently hostile to Marlborough, trying first to prevent him being given command of the land forces, and then to reduce the number of men and the amount of money to be allocated to the army in the Low Countries. This fitted in with Rochester's vehement hostility to the Dutch, but although this recommended him to tory backbenchers, he showed little interest in actually participating in the business of government, at least until he was assured of political predominance. Fearing that his influence would be seriously disruptive, Marlborough and Godolphin managed to engineer his resignation by insisting that he must go to Ireland to take up his lord lieutenancy; Rochester's refusal to do so discredited him with his niece, the queen. Seymour was an equal embarrassment to the ministry which he nominally supported. An unrivalled master of parliamentary procedure, and a biting critic of ministerial incompetence and corruption, he was uncomfortable and unconstructive in office. Exasperated by his intrigues, Godolphin had him dismissed in April 1704, together with Normanby and Jersey, two other critics and self-important political lightweights. However, they were accompanied by a much more important figure in Nottingham, who regarded himself as Rochester's rival to the leadership of the tories and as Godolphin's successor. He demanded the dismissal of all surviving whig cabinet ministers and when this was refused he resigned, expecting that all dissident tories would rally to him.

These tory secessions would have left the ministry's position in a precarious state but for Harley, who lobbied tory MPs intensively. He and his associates filled the gaps left by the outgoing tory ministers, Harley replacing Nottingham as secretary in May 1704 and bringing into office with him some younger men of ability, including Henry St John and Mansell. But Harley had only limited success in reassuring the tory rank and file that the ministers were not deserting tory principles, and even before the 1705 elections whig votes were needed to defeat attacks on the ministry, as in January 1705 to reject a bill to exclude all place-holders from the Commons. The elections made the ministerial position more vulnerable by generating a great deal of bitter recrimination, especially over the recent attempted tack, which promised a continuation of party strife in the new house. By Godolphin's own later estimate this contained 190 tories, 160 whigs and 100 members at the queen's disposal. In theory this meant that provided the ministers could isolate the extremist wings of both parties, they would be able to rely on a composite, middle-ground majority. But from the start of the session, when a hotly contested election for Speaker showed how deep and bitter were the personal and political divisions, it became increasingly clear that in order to resist tory attacks the ministry was going to need whig support, and that for this a high price would be exacted.

During Anne's second parliament of 1705–8 great successes were achieved. In the war, Ramillies (1706) and Oudenarde (1708) secured the Spanish Netherlands and forced the French on the defensive. The Union was concluded with Scotland and the jacobite invasion of 1708 ended in a fiasco. But throughout its life the ministry found itself constantly harassed as the tories responded to irresponsible initiatives by Rochester and the other recently dismissed ministers. In December 1705 he raised the emotive issue of the 'church in danger'. The previous month he moved cynically for an invitation to be sent to the heiress to the throne, Sophia, to come to reside in England. Theoretically, the object was to secure the Protestant Succession, by avoiding a hiatus between Anne's death and the arrival of the new sovereign from Hanover, but the real aim was to set up a rival court and a reversionary interest, around which the tories would rally. The proposal put the ministers in a predicament. Anne detested the prospect of an expectant successor in London, but if the ministers pleased her by resisting Rochester's proposal they would become acutely vulnerable to whig charges that they were crypto-jacobites. It required a major political manoeuvre to overcome these difficulties; this was achieved by introducing and passing the Regency Act in 1706–7.

This important act virtually ensured that the Protestant Succession, as laid down in the Act of Settlement, would take effect without turmoil or disputes. It provided an insuperable obstacle to jacobite hopes and strategies, since if these were to have the slightest chance the Act would have to be repealed before Anne's death. As the purpose of such a move could hardly have been concealed, any such attempt lay outside the realm of practical politics. The Act prolonged for six months after Anne's death the existing privy council, the commissions of officers of state, and either an existing or the last parliament (even if it had been dissolved). The interim control of government, until the new sovereign arrived from Germany, was vested in the holders of seven great offices (the archbishop of Canterbury, the chancellor, lord treasurer, lord president, privy seal, lord high admiral and lord chief justice of the Queen's Bench), acting as lords justices in combination with other statesmen nominated in advance by the heir. The act laid on them, and on all holders of subordinate and local offices, the obligation to take the positive step of proclaiming the protestant successor immediately after the queen's death.

However, backbench members of both parties took advantage of the ministers' need to pass this act. In a revival of 'country' agitation, they pressed a so-called 'whimsical' clause; this would disqualify all but forty holders of offices from the parliament that was to continue after the queen's death, and from all subsequent parliaments. This clause was narrowly defeated only after an agreement had been struck with the whig leaders, which marked an increase in their influence over Godolphin. A compromise was reached on the actual bill; only the holders of new-created offices (and holders of some named offices, such as commissioners of prizes, the navy, army transport) were to be incapacitated from sitting in the Commons, and holders of positions of profit were to be capable of re-election after resigning their seats.

Sustained whig pressure on the ministry soon began to produce changes in its composition. In October 1705 Cowper replaced Wright, the tory activist, as lord keeper, and the duke of Newcastle

came in for Buckingham as privy seal. But neither of these new
ministers was sufficiently partisan to satisfy the Junto whig leaders,
who forced the issue in 1706 by insisting on the appointment as
secretary of state of their most aggressive and outspoken colleague,
Sunderland, although it was known that he was personally repugnant to the queen. Sunderland was deliberately chosen as a test case
because of his close relationship to Marlborough as son-in-law, who
would be obliged to press his merits, and in the belief that if he could
be forced into office the way would be clear for further appointments
until the administration was totally dominated by whigs.

Sunderland became secretary in December 1706, at the price of
antagonizing Anne. Her resentment was skilfully used by Harley,
who was becoming increasingly aware of his own vulnerability. He
had hoped that Godolphin would take initiatives to establish and
develop closer relations with the moderate whigs, while he did the
same with the moderate tories, so isolating both packs of extremist
party leaders. He knew that the whigs were starting to press for his
own dismissal, and although he had been able to defend himself, the
appointment of the most belligerent whig to such a key position as
secretary quickly antagonized moderate tories. Harley's first political
moves were defensive, but by the autumn of 1707 he was developing
a 'scheme' by which he would become chief minister in place of
Godolphin, while retaining Marlborough in command of the army.
He established a connection with a group of whig magnates
(Newcastle, Somerset and Devonshire), who were independent from,
and rather resentful of, the predominant influence within the party
of the Junto hatchet-men. Through St John and Harcourt he renewed attempts to reassure tory moderates, and the younger tory
MPs, but he had less success in this.

Harley's main asset, the queen's increasing confidence in his
judgement, came as an unpleasant surprise both to Godolphin and
to the whigs. It became apparent during the course of a prolonged
tussle during 1707 over the filling of vacant bishoprics. The whigs
extracted from the ministers a promise that two whig-aligned clergy-
men would be appointed to the sees of Exeter and Chester. When
there was no sign of the appointments being made, the whigs jumped
to the conclusion that Godolphin was playing them false. In fact,
Anne personally was the obstacle. Ever since 1702 she had employed
Harley and Sharp, the archbishop of York, as her advisers on ecclesiastical patronage matters, and they now encouraged her to resist
whig demands, and in August to nominate two tories, Blackall and
Dawes. It was Godolphin who felt the effects of whig fury, and came
to fear that the Junto leaders would make the forthcoming session of
parliament unmanageable. Living under almost intolerable pres-

sures, Godolphin became extremely suspicious of Harley's advice, although he accepted a compromise suggested by the latter on the bishoprics issue: in January 1708 a whig protégé, Trimnell, was appointed to Norwich as a counterbalance to the two tories. But Godolphin rejected Harley's repeated proposals (December 1707, January 1708) for a much more crucial political initiative, a reconstruction of the ministry in order to take in tory moderates and exclude the more extreme whigs. This would mean Sunderland's dismissal and war against the Junto leaders, but Godolphin also realized that it would leave him dependent on Harley and whatever support he could mobilize, and he began to suspect that ultimately Harley aspired to become lord treasurer.

Harley's scheme ended in total failure. His reputation for intrigue and deviousness frightened off possible associates, and he was obliged to unmask himself before he had completed all his preparations. Anne was ready to support him, but only a group of lieutenants—St John, Harcourt and Mansell—stood by him when the confrontation occurred on 8 February 1708. Godolphin and Marlborough threatened to resign, and boycotted a meeting of the cabinet council. Three days later Harley had to go, followed by his three associates. In the short run Godolphin's tenure of office was safeguarded, but the real victors were the Junto leaders on whom he was now dependent, although in terms of office they had to wait several months.

While the chief ministers were still united, they had negotiated the Union Treaty with Scotland (July 1706), and enacted the necessary legislation for the Union to come into being on 1 May 1707. In whig historical mythology the Union was natural, inevitable and beneficial in all its results, but now that it is being seriously challenged a different perspective is opening up on its character. It can be seen that from the Scottish angle the economic advantages of the Union were, and have always remained, the paramount consideration. On the other hand, in the eighteenth century English interests were exclusively political—at first to secure the Protestant Succession—for which the concession of free trade to Scottish merchants was an acceptable price to pay. But unlike the later union with Ireland (1800), this was a freely negotiated agreement, in which both parties were finally able to safeguard those interests which they particularly valued—but only, it must be added, after recklessly engaging in blackmail and brinkmanship in order to get their own way.

Although a freely negotiated union, it was one between grossly unequal kingdoms. Scotland was not only smaller in population and markedly poorer, but in the two decades after 1688 its economy was depressed almost to the point of causing national demoralization.

The traditional trades with France, Holland, Scandinavia and the Baltic, which had been declining over a long period, were dislocated by the wars against Louis xiv and the concurrent Great Northern War that started in 1700. Exports to England had been affected since soon after the Restoration by bans or tariffs on cattle, linen, salt and grain. Extremely primitive methods, the cultivation of marginal land and a general lack of working capital made Scottish agriculture frighteningly vulnerable to climatic adversities; the wet and cold years of the 1690s produced regional famines and the depopulation of some rural areas. Moreover, the one major attempt at a new economic development, the Company of Scotland Trading to Africa and the Indies (1695), whose capital had been raised in small sums from ordinary people throughout the country, collapsed after the failure of the attempt to establish a colony at Darien on the Isthmus of Panama.

The divisions in Scottish society were far more fundamental and structural than the English division between whig and tory. There were two separate nations. A tribal Highlands contained a militarized society, largely episcopalian or catholic in religion and predominantly jacobite in politics. It had virtually nothing in common with the Lowlands, where both peasantry and lairds were fiercely presbyterian, but they and the relatively small towns were still politically dependent on a small number of great aristocratic families—Hamilton, Queensberry, Argyll and Montrose. These magnates controlled the government of Scotland but largely from London where they competed for patronage and influence. Scotland was a badly governed country in two senses: the administration was weak and incompetent, and it was largely corrupt. But after 1689 there was an additional complication in that the one-chamber Scottish parliament became an independent force after the abolition of the Lords of the Articles, a committee of the Scottish privy council whose consent had been needed before legislation could be introduced. Possession of a legislative initiative, and exploitation of the financial needs of the administration, intoxicated some of the members. In the 1690s the Club of radicals, led by Montgomery, went so far as to try to put Scotland up to a kind of constitutional auction, evolving a fantastic scheme to restore James vii in return for large-scale concessions that would leave him only limited monarchical powers. The Scots parliaments of William's reign and 1703 both engaged in endless obstruction, embarrassing those who were saddled with the government. The latter's response was a general use of inducements for awkward politicians and the clients of the magnates and regular pensions for the jacobite clan chiefs.

A first set of negotiations for a union took place in 1702–3. Although eventually the English half-heartedly agreed to concede free trade under the Navigation Acts, no real progress was made. The majority in the new Scottish parliament elected in 1703 did not regard this offer as sincere, and also feared that as a price for a union the English tories would demand fundamental changes in the Scottish church, amounting to the destruction of presbyterianism. The ministry of Queensberry was weak. It could not prevent the passage in 1703 of the Act of Security, for which the opposition obtained the royal assent in the following year by withholding all grants of supply. The purpose of this act was to put intensified pressure on England, but it received support from a substantial jacobite and crypto-jacobite minority. They hoped that the act would poison relations between the two countries and produce a complete separation. They pinned their hopes on the provision that, if England had not made acceptable concessions to Scotland by the time that Anne died, the Scottish parliament was to choose a successor from those descended from the royal Stuarts, who must be a protestant (which in theory barred the Pretender, although this could be amended later). But he was explicitly not to be the same person as the successor named to the English throne by the Act of Settlement, which did not have any legal force in Scotland. Although this provision apparently encouraged the claims to the throne of the duke of Hamilton who was partly a Stuart, he would find it far more difficult to keep the Pretender out than would a Hanoverian sovereign controlling the resources of two kingdoms, whether united or governmentally separate. The second form of pressure on England was almost equally dangerous and mischievous. An act to improve and embody the militia involved arming the population of the border counties, as if war against England was envisaged.

The Westminster parliament responded by a similar use of blackmail. The so-called Aliens Act of March 1705, 'to prevent inconveniencies which may speedily happen if a nearer and more complete union be not made', empowered Anne as queen of England to name commissioners to negotiate a union, provided that the Scots did the same. But if the Act of Security was still in force at the end of 1705, all Scots would be declared aliens in England, incapable of owning and inheriting land, and imports of cattle, linen and coal from Scotland would be banned, as would exports of arms and horses. This exchange of damaging acts threatened not merely complete separation, but open war, between the two countries, which could only benefit France and the jacobites. In appreciating this danger, both parties came to their senses. They opened serious negotiations, and surprisingly it was quickly agreed that the aim should be a complete or 'incorporating' rather than a federal union. The threatening Aliens Act was repealed.

English and Scottish commissioners met in April 1706; by July they agreed on a treaty. At Westminster ratification was carried without too much difficulty, despite high tory attempts to create disquiet among the anglican clergy. In Edinburgh the crucial factor was that the presbyterians were satisfied by the guarantees to the Scottish church, which were written in as a fundamental and un-alterable condition of the Union. The perpetuation of the established presbyterian church, and the continuation of a separate system of Scottish law, meant the preservation of autonomy in those areas of life which most directly affected the individual, and also ensured that Scotsmen would continue to monopolize offices in the church and the law within what was henceforward technically 'North Britain', in addition to becoming eligible for appointment to offices in the United Kingdom administration.

Some personal bribery was needed to ease passage of the Union through the Edinburgh parliament, but all the economic clauses were really inducements. Free access to English colonies, trade and markets was the key advantage, but Scotland also benefited from the provisions on taxation. The obligation to pay only 2.5 per cent of the total land tax, and exemptions from stamped paper duties and the window tax, went beyond what was strictly justified by Scotland's relative poverty. A more immediate inducement came in the form of the 'Equivalent', the payment of £398,000 to discharge public debts, compensate for losses consequent on recoinage, and repay the lost capital of the Darien Company. English country MPs complained that there was a contradiction between this generous recognition of Scottish poverty, and what they saw as an excessively large repre-sentation for Scotland in the new parliament of the United Kingdom; there were to be forty-five MPs and sixteen peers, the latter to be elected before each parliament by the Scottish peers as a whole. They also suspected (and this has been borne out ever since) that these representatives were on the whole to provide ministers with docile and economical material for their managers in both houses.

The Union was not initially popular. There were violent mob protests in Edinburgh against its ratification, and a number of petitions that were a more authentic and accurate indication of opinion. Most of the general benefits were long-term; economic development came later in the century and the quality of adminis-tration only improved slowly. Similarly the political advantages were at first relatively limited. Political instability continued, but the jacobites were now far less well placed to exploit it. An attempt at a major jacobite invasion in March 1708 was a miserable fiasco, with little sign of mustering the support on which the Pretender and his French sponsors had banked. Jacobite agents eagerly but ineffectively tried to take advantage of any forms of popular discontent, such as arose when the tory government imposed export duties on linens (1711), granted toleration to the episcopalians and restored church patronage (1712), and antagonized the agricultural interest by the malt duties of 1713. But although discontent mounted to the point where a motion to consider a formal dissolution of the Union narrowly failed in the Lords in June of that year, it became apparent that economic advantages could be expected. It can be said that until the oil discoveries of the 1970s an independent Scotland remained a romantic fantasy, desirable in many ways because of English condescension and neglect by a government situated in remote London, but economically impracticable.

The whig leaders lost little time after the fall of Harley and the general elections of May 1708 before intensifying pressure on Godolphin and Marlborough. As whig influence increased, so the ministers' relations with Anne deteriorated. In the autumn of 1708 the whigs threatened to withhold or at least seriously delay supply, which could prejudice the next year's campaign. They also renewed attacks on mismanagement at the admiralty, which was nominally headed by Anne's husband, George. The queen made no secret of her displeasure, but her resistance to her ministers' advice to give way before whig pressure, in order to save her husband, collapsed when the latter died on 28 October. Her acquiescence, however, was purchased by an intensification of her coolness to the whig chiefs, and a growing dislike of Godolphin and Marlborough.

By 1709 the administration had become predominantly whig, isolating Godolphin, Marlborough and Queensberry. The four leading Junto leaders (Somers, Sunderland, Wharton and Orford) entered the cabinet council, together with Cowper and Devonshire. The last two had been more moderate and detached, but now that they were accompanied by party colleagues in the ministry they began to behave in a more obviously partisan way. Junior appointments were also filled with whigs (for instance Robert Walpole as secretary-at-war), and many placemen who had formerly depended on the lord treasurer began to align themselves with the whig ministers. Whig MPS also took control of key Commons committees, and their managers took full advantage of divisions among the tories to build up their influence in what Sunderland rightly called the most whig parliament since 1688. Only at court were the whigs less than dominant. Relations between Anne and the duchess of Marlborough deteriorated. Godolphin and the whigs became extremely alarmed at the apparent influence being exerted by a new favourite, Mrs Masham, a former protégée of the duchess of Marlborough. The ministers consistently exaggerated Mrs Masham's influence and her utility to Harley as a channel of communication with Anne, and they overreacted in January 1710 when they began to press for the removal of Mrs Masham and three other royal servants. But they hesitated to organize a Commons address when Anne indicated that she would show her dislike of the demand, since this would only publicize the coolness of relations between the queen and her ministers.

One principal reason for this coolness was Anne's conviction that her ministers were prolonging the war for personal and party reasons. Marlborough and Godolphin were formally committed by the Lords' resolution of December 1707 to the policy of 'no peace without Spain'. English conditions for peace were spelled out in detail in March 1709. The Spanish territories were to go in their entirety to the Habsburg candidate, the Dutch and Savoy must both receive effective barriers against France, and Louis must recognize the Protestant Succession and expel the Pretender from France. Such severe demands seemed not unreasonable during 1709, when France faced famine as well as military defeat, and Louis accepted (though his sincerity is questionable) all the 'preliminary' articles in May, except the thirty-seventh, which obliged him to expel his grandson, Philip, from Spain. Subsequently the negotiations broke down. They were renewed by the Dutch, acting on behalf of the other allies, at Geertuidenberg in March 1710, and there was still a possibility that an early peace would be made. But the nation, as well as the queen, was becoming increasingly war-weary, and Harley throughout 1709 was busy creating the impression that Marlborough and Godolphin were deliberately obstructing the conclusion of peace. However, this subject was not the one that eventually proved fatal to the ministry. Its fall was precipitated by its mismanagement of the Sacheverell impeachment, which gave credibility to the tory cry that the church was in danger. It was not until after the change of ministry that the war in Spain was lost (November 1710, the evacuation of Madrid; December, defeat at Brihuega). Moreover, it was Godolphin, the chief minister responsible for managing domestic politics, not Marlborough who was mainly associated with the conduct and continuation of the war, who became the immediate victim of the ministerial changes.

The Sacheverell impeachment introduced to politics a new popular dimension of involvement and excitement that had been absent (except during general elections) since the beginning of the reign. It provoked the most serious riots of the period, in London, and a countrywide reaction against the ministry resulted in the 1710 elections, which produced the most considerable swing of opinion of any during the reign. The crucial part played by religious fervour in

this transformation of politics needs explanation. Most of the anglican clergy were already roused by the cry of 'the church in danger'.
Alienated from the bishops, whom they distrusted as latitudinarians
and friends of the whigs, the parochial clergy resented the virtual
immunity from ecclesiastical discipline and clerical control which
the dissenters enjoyed. They blamed the growth of atheism and immorality on this reduction in their own powers and prestige. But if
the clergy were already mainly vociferous tories, the laity were far
less involved and excited until the prosecution of Sacheverell extended to many sections of opinion the feelings of insecurity and anxiety
that had already affected the clergy. It is therefore not surprising
that the reaction which followed took on strongly negative forms;
although many of the high-church leaders had constructive
aims—ultimately the complete restoration of a full partnership between the established church and the state the immediate effects
were to stoke up passions and prejudices. Anglican militancy was
exploited to destroy the Godolphin ministry, and the crippling attacks on the dissenters which followed the change of ministry were
intended to strike at the basis of whig electoral support.

The ability of the high-church clergy to influence public opinion
was already causing alarm to Godolphin and his whig colleagues,
who genuinely feared that many of them were not merely irresponsible trouble-makers, but were secretly working for a jacobite restoration. In 1709 high-church clergy and tory journalists were very
successful in whipping up popular xenophobia against the 'poor
Palatines', German protestant refugees who entered the country in
large numbers under the Naturalization Act passed by the whigs. In
any case the latter tended to be anticlerical, but constant sniping at
their lack of personal and political integrity incensed many whigs,
while Godolphin, as a member of a formerly conspicuously loyal
anglican family, was extremely sensitive to such attacks. It was in
the hope of silencing clerical expositions of the theme, that the church
was in danger, that the ministers decided to make a test case out of
a 5 November sermon preached at St Paul's before the lord mayor,
by the most exhibitionist of high-churchmen, Henry Sacheverell.

Sacheverell in this sermon denounced 'false brethren' in church
and state, obviously meaning the bishops and the queen's ministers,
and in vilifying the dissenters he obliquely attacked the principle
and practice of religious toleration. What made him even more vulnerable to charges of sedition was Sacheverell's denial that the subject had any right to resist an unjust ruler. This could be construed
as not only a reflection on the legality of the Revolution of 1688, but
(at the least) as an argument for passive acceptance of a jacobite
restoration. The impeachment was intended as a show-trial to

assert Revolution principles and vindicate religious toleration, and
to fix on the high-church clerics and their tory associates the charge
of crypto-jacobitism. It was impossible not to take some action.
Sacheverell consciously sought the maximum publicity for his views,
flaunting a challenge which the ministers could not ignore. By the
end of 1709 well over 60,000 copies of the sermon had been sold,
with an openly inflammatory dedication added, to underline the
arguments which had already caused resentment among the ministers. Impeachment was resolved by the Commons on 14 December,
but procedural miscalculations led to serious delays; the trial did not
begin until 27 February 1710, and then the prosecution was committed to a full-scale impeachment that would require at least three
weeks, rather than a summary hearing at the bar of the Lords as had
originally been intended.

Sacheverell cleverly exploited these delays to turn public opinion in
his favour. He posed as the victim of party persecution, helped by
the fact that all the managers of the prosecution were whigs, including Dolben, son of an archbishop, but hated as a renegade careerist.
Technically they made out their case, showing that under all
Sacheverell's verbiage there had been a seditious purpose. But the
defence counsel succeeded in identifying his case with that of the
'poor oppressed clergy' as a whole, and persuaded several peers that
the severe punishment called for by the prosecution would be politically unwise and divisive. The ministry won only a hollow victory.
Sacheverell was found guilty by an unexpectedly narrow majority of
sixty-nine to fifty-two, but this erosion of the whig majority in the
Lords was even more clearly demonstrated by the derisorily lenient
sentence imposed (21 March)—no imprisonment or fine, but only a
three year suspension from preaching. The rapturous, almost hysterical, welcome that Sacheverell subsequently received, first in London
and then on a series of provincial tours, underlined the fact that he
was the real victor.

The impeachment exposed the domination of the ministry by the
whigs, although in fact Godolphin had been strongly in favour of
bringing the prosecution. It was generally believed that the whigs
had manufactured a case against the most conspicuous anglican
preacher of the time, in an effort to put the clergy as a whole into a state
of complete dependence on the administration. It was another stage
in their apparent attempt to consolidate and perpetuate their hold
on office. It tended to confirm their identification with the enemies
of the church. In 1709 there had been reports that they intended to
press the ministry into repealing the Test Act provisions that barred
their dissenting allies from holding offices. Moreover, the dispropor-
tion between the vast expenditure of time and energy on the trial of

Sacheverell, and the real importance of the man (a vain, showy and shallow orator) underlined the party character of the case. By their conduct of the prosecution the whigs dramatized the fact that they really were acting as a party, that is as a combination or confederacy of separatist interests; their use of governmental powers for selfish, factional purposes aggrieved those whose interests did not coincide with those of the whigs—the gentry as well as the clergy, the merchants who wanted an early end to the war, and those in the towns who resented the favour shown to the dissenters at their own expense. The Sacheverell case seemed to show that there was nothing that the whigs would not do in order to extend and defend their near-monopoly of power and office.

The resolute defence offered by Sacheverell's tory counsel, the manifest public reaction in his favour and the lenience of the Lords, all greatly encouraged the tories. The failure of the impeachment to impress or intimidate led directly to the emergence of a reunited and effective opposition under Harley. Although he had nothing but contempt for Sacheverell's extremism, Harley now re-established a working alliance with the tories, whose leaders had previously failed, or refused, to give him their confidence. During the summer months of 1710 he was engaged in a double task: he was putting together a combination that could serve as an alternative administration, and simultaneously distracting, dividing and finally dismantling the Godolphin ministry.

Even more important than the unpopularity of the ministry, Harley had the queen's trust and confidence. Anne, who shared Harley's dislike of Sacheverell, was looking for liberation from her existing ministers whom she resented as tyrants. She had refused to give way on Mrs Masham in January, and her former affection for the duchess of Marlborough had been replaced by open hatred; the two women met for the last time in April. She would have preferred Harley to Godolphin in 1708, and she was now ready to give him full support for a complete ministerial revolution. On his side Harley had the advantage of experience; he had failed in 1708 partly because he had been forced to act before he was ready, but in 1710 he took his time, thoroughly preparing every move, keeping his intentions concealed and making very effective use of divisions and hesitations among his opponents. He was greatly assisted by his nominal superior, Shrewsbury, who had recently returned from retirement in Italy, and became lord chamberlain in April. Shrewsbury was content to let Harley make all the major decisions and moves, but his support meant that Harley did not have to concede the highest offices or predominant influence to the tory chiefs, Rochester and Nottingham, who would never have allowed a junior politician to dictate to them. Secondly, Harley detached Somerset and Newcastle from their association with the whigs, but he also created further options by secretly negotiating with some of the whig leaders; thus he hinted to Somers and Cowper that he would like to retain them in office, and he continued a long-established intrigue with the most easily detached of the whigs, Halifax.

It is difficult to say whether these were serious offers, or simply deceitful manoeuvres, but they certainly had their intended effect in creating divisions and mutual distrust among the whig leaders. Consequently, there was no resolute or united reaction from them when Harley struck his first decisive blow on 14 June, with Sunderland's dismissal as secretary and replacement by the tory Dartmouth. This dismissal, like his entry into the ministry in 1706, was both symbolic and crucial. Sunderland's whig colleagues could have forced the issue by resigning en bloc, as Harley's lieutenants had done in 1708. They chose inactivity. Marlborough suspected that Anne and Harley were waiting for a pretext to discard him, and he knew that Harley was actively intriguing with a group of disaffected generals in his army. Marlborough by this conduct showed that he would hang on to office for as long as possible, and at all costs; he could be kept on until the time was opportune for his dismissal. More creditably, both Marlborough and Harley knew that his resignation or dismissal would encourage the French, disrupt the summer campaign, and might even lead the Dutch to make a separate peace. Godolphin was complacent, believing himself to be indispensable, assuming that no one else could manage the finances. Other whigs rationalized their passivity by condemning Sunderland's intransigence, and by vainly hoping that Shrewsbury could be detached from his understanding with Harley. There was consequently no reaction when Godolphin was dismissed (8 August), but Harley still had the most difficult of all decisions to make—when to dissolve the whig-dominated parliament. He could not afford to antagonize the tories, who were pressing for an early dissolution, but when this was done on 21 September it soon became evident that Harley's room for manoeuvre would be severely restricted in the future. The elections returned so large a tory majority that he was in danger of becoming as much their captive as Godolphin had been of the whigs. Secondly, it was all very well for Harley to conceal his actions and intentions while he was engaged in undermining Godolphin and the whigs, but he persisted in keeping his own supporters and associates mystified and uncertain after this had been accomplished. Harley's behaviour created a distrust which his subsequent actions were never entirely to dissipate.

17 The Tory Ministry 1710–14

Although it would be dangerous to press the parallels too far, there are suggestive resemblances between the strange, lingering death of the first tory party in the early eighteenth century and that of liberal England in the twentieth. In both cases rapid decline followed soon after an electoral triumph of the first magnitude, and developed during the period of a particularly brilliant administration as deep, underlying weaknesses began to have an effect. After 1710 the tories occupied an apparently impregnable position. Marlborough, Godolphin and the whigs had antagonized Anne and most of the political nation. Overwhelming tory victories in the elections of 1710 and 1713 seemed to confirm the claim that while the whigs were an artificial combination of minority interests, the tories represented a natural majority of those with political rights. The new tory administration satisfied the most urgent national demand, achieving a satisfactory and popular peace settlement at Utrecht after successfully completing long, complex and difficult negotiations. Harley administered government finances efficiently, and the peace brought about not only a welcome reduction in the level of taxes but more generally an appreciable economic recovery after two decades of consuming war. The large and aggressive tory majority trampled on the whigs in the Commons. By an astonishing coup at the end of 1711—the mass creation of peers, something no other ministry has ever dared to undertake—the permanent whig majority in the Lords was overcome.

Yet by the time that Anne died, on 1 August 1714, the administration was already disintegrating and the tory party was dividing into irreconcilable factions. During the last months of the reign, the leading ministers destroyed each other by undermining faith in their integrity and judgement. In particular they aroused so much distrust on the central issue of the Protestant Succession that the myth could be fixed on the tories as a whole, that it had been intended to restore the Pretender. George was confirmed in his belief that only whigs could really be trusted. Bewildered by their leaders' behaviour, divided and left without direction, the tories were left in a state in

which they could offer little effective resistance in the first months of
George's reign, when the whigs systematically used legislation, partisan investigations into past ministerial activities, selective intimidation and a brilliant propaganda campaign to ensure their own
perpetual supremacy. They panicked Bolingbroke and Ormonde
into joining the jacobite cause, so condemning all their associates
and putting the tories as a whole into a position of permanent inferiority and exclusion from office.

In a wider perspective the tory failure was even more fundamental. Apart from the peace, they achieved nothing lasting. In 1710
tory leaders promised a new restoration—of harmony and cooperation between an honest, frugal administration and a 'country' majority in parliament composed of independent representatives. But
after 1713 the very large tory majority quickly fragmented into hostile factions, many peers and MPs allowed themselves to be seduced
by offers of offices, and large scale corruption was beginning to become evident among ministers. This reappearance of all the familiar
political vices made nonsense of the tory claim that they would restore government to its former, customary state of relying on the
natural rulers of the country, the landed gentry. The tories failed to
fulfil their promises that they would effect an improvement in the
quality of administration and a reduction in its quantity, by eliminating the influence of the parasitical and corrupting monied interest and dismantling the system of enlarged patronage constructed
during the war. The tory pose as protectors of the interests of the
commercial and mercantile classes was also exposed as a mere political manoeuvre by the ineptitude with which the commercial treaties
with France and Spain were handled.

There was a similar failure of a parallel attempt to restore the old
order (perhaps counter-revolution is too general a term) in religious,
intellectual and moral affairs. The tory revival of 1710 was inseparably accompanied by an anglican attempt to reintroduce a full
integration of church and state, to uncover and check undesirable
and subversive influences, and reverse recent trends. By 1714 this
attempt had already failed, even before George's accession strengthened the forces opposed to it.

The author of the ministerial revolution of 1710 was Robert
Harley, the most adept and devious of contemporary politicians,
who began (as in his unsuccessful attempt in 1708) with a palace
coup. Although she had not maintained regular, direct contact, Anne
had never ceased to trust Harley. He alone could satisfactorily replace
Godolphin in all his multifarious duties, and guarantee against
the substitution of the existing whig-dominated administration

with one controlled by the equally unacceptable extremists of the tory party. These high-flyers would certainly repeat their arrogant attempts to dictate to the queen (as in 1702–4), and their inexperience, xenophobia and indiscipline could rapidly produce a breakdown of government finances, and a collapse of the alliance against France which could enable Louis to recover his old strength and influence. Harley enjoyed Anne's personal favour, ensured by the links maintained by Mrs Masham, but it was the queen's recognition of his indispensability for the effective continuation of government, above all in the financial field, that led her to prefer him as chief minister, rather than the more senior and prestigious rival tory chiefs, Rochester and Nottingham.

Harley displayed great skill during the ministerial changes in keeping control in his own hands. First he played on the divisions within the Godolphin–Marlborough ministry, making offers of continued employment to some of its members; these were not so much moderates, but simply those whom he thought it would be easiest to detach. Of those whom he approached, Cowper eventually refused to continue as chancellor, but Marlborough was desperately anxious to retain his command, even though Godolphin, his great friend and close associate, was the principal casualty (dismissed 8 August). Some minor whigs were allowed to carry on, for example Robert Walpole as treasurer of the navy, so confusing the adherents of the old ministry and rendering out of the question any possibility of their chiefs maintaining party unity. Harley was greatly assisted by the failure of these whig chiefs even to consider resigning en bloc; instead each minister waited until the time was ripe for his dismissal.

Harley valued the support of independent politicians. He retained Somerset and Newcastle, magnates who had been only loosely associated with the Godolphin ministry, and he welcomed men whom Godolphin and Marlborough had snubbed or excluded from influence, particularly in the army (Argyll, Rivers and Peterborough). His principal aim was to prevent the partisan tories dictating the composition of the ministry, because this would reduce his own influence and would be greatly resented by Anne. In the early stages Harley cleverly used Shrewsbury, who was appointed lord chamberlain in April 1710. The latter had the requisite status and prestige but (as Harley well knew) neither the commitment nor the political and physical stamina to act as chief minister for long. Acting in combination with Shrewsbury, Harley had no difficulty in neutralizing Rochester, who accepted the honorific post of lord president and proved to be a surprisingly congenial colleague, and in excluding Nottingham altogether. As Harley's colleague, Rochester behaved constructively and responsibly, acting in the role of an elder statesman until his death in 1711, but Harley saw that Nottingham, who personified partisan passions, would never accept a subordinate role. Nottingham would have immediately launched impeachments of the dismissed ministers, starting with Sunderland; this would not only have had the backbench tories in full cry against their old enemies but would almost certainly have revived the deadlock of 1701 between the Lords and Commons.

When the ministerial changes were complete Harley acted as chief minister, although formally he was only chancellor of the exchequer, then a comparatively minor office, under Poulett as first commissioner of the treasury. His main tactical problem was the timing of the dissolution of parliament and general elections. He used the threat of dissolution to intimidate some whigs and win others over, but he probably delayed it too long, since when the returns came in the tory majority was rather too large for his comfort, and too many of the MPs were new, hot and not very amendable to management and guidance. But in constructing the ministry, Harley made only one major mistake. During the period when he was rightly keeping his intentions secret, and mystifying both whigs and tories, Harley inexcusably slighted his old associates and lieutenants, Harcourt and St John, who had loyally resigned with him in 1708. He kept them unrewarded until September, leading them to fear that they would be ignored, or at best offered contemptuously humble appointments, and although both eventually received high office, Harcourt as lord keeper, St John as secretary of state, they never entirely trusted Harley thereafter. This insensitive behaviour was symptomatic of a weakness that was to become increasingly damaging. Harley was in his element during the ministerial changes of the summer of 1710, manoeuvring and intriguing, deceiving and misleading opponents, gratifying or disappointing aspirants for office, but his secretive methods confirmed his reputation for deviousness and untrustworthiness. Unfortunately, his complete success strengthened Harley's tendency to concentrate exclusively on short-term tactical politics; once the basics of peace with France had been agreed, he increasingly evaded making difficult decisions and postponed even the discussion of urgent business.

However in 1710–11 Harley was faced with major problems which he could not postpone. The most critical was finance for the war. Four whig-aligned directors of the Bank of England, in a personal interview, had tried to persuade Anne not to dismiss Godolphin, by threatening to withold loans (June 1710), and Harley had to resist tory pressure for a clean sweep of all whig office-holders, for fear that this would result in the ruin of government credit. The whigs and their associates in the City underestimated Harley's skill, and the extent of his contacts among financiers. He was able to construct and use an alternative group of bankers, whose loans and advances improved his bargaining position with the Bank, and he found himself able to finance the campaign of 1711 and to continue remittances to support forces abroad without having to employ the services of the small whig oligarchy headed by Sir Henry Furnese. However, Harley's subsequent attempt to push tory candidates in elections for the boards of the Bank and the East India Company failed; as an alternative, in effect a tory rival to these institutions, the new South Seas Company was established by statute in 1711. Its directors were appointed by the crown—nine out of thirty were politicians—and the new company was to assume the servicing of the unfunded part of government debt, in return for hypothetical concessions in trade with the Spanish colonies. But politically significant relief from the burden of war taxation and mounting debt could be obtained only by ending the war.

Harley initiated the first secret moves for peace with France as early as August 1710, that is before he assumed office or entered the cabinet council. Acting in partnership with Shrewsbury he entrusted the handling of negotiations to Jersey, a former ambassador to France, whose catholic wife's chaplain, Gaultier, acted as go-between. Jersey was to prove a bad choice; from the start he gratuitously connected the secret negotiations for peace with talk of jacobite restoration. Characteristically, Harley kept these negotiations secret from the cabinet until April 1711; this widened the rift that was developing with St John, who began to thrust himself forward, trying to take control of the peace negotiations and resenting the overall control that Harley insisted on retaining. In October 1711 preliminaries of peace were agreed with France, but the final settlement depended on a further diplomatic process of imposing the agreed terms on the allies, whose diplomatic representatives in London were to act during the crisis of 1711–12 as auxiliaries of the whigs.

In 1710–11 Harley did not wish to have to depend exclusively for support on one organized section of opinion. During both the construction of his ministry and his first year as chief minister, Harley consciously tried to make use of moderate and minor whigs, independent magnates, and the bloc of permanent court dependants. He intended to use them as a counterweight to the pressure that could be exerted by the enthusiastic but inexperienced tory backbenchers. This was not a new problem for Harley; indeed, it was his political instinct and parliamentary flair that had made the country party so effective in the late 1690s, and from 1702 to 1708 he had undertaken the same task of moderating country party passions on behalf of the Marlborough–Godolphin ministry. However, his task in 1710–11 was intrinsically far more difficult. The expansion of governmental patronage by Godolphin and its exploitation to build a formidable parliamentary interest, the knowledge that vast profits were being made out of the war by associates of the ministers, and the increasingly sophisticated and expensive electoral techniques which were now being used regularly—and which they could not match—all incensed the tory squirearchy. The tories believed that only corruption and manipulation had enabled the ministers and the whigs to dominate the parliament of 1708–10, and they were determined to make any repetition impossible. Harley's wish to base his ministry on a 'broad bottom' aroused their suspicions; as a first step they demanded a clean sweep of all whigs, from local as well as central governmental offices. The majority of tory members did not regard themselves as beholden in any way to the ministry; they triumphed in the 1710 elections thanks to their own efforts and resources, and owed little if anything to ministerial assistance or influence. Furthermore, they had already declared themselves, with remarkable unity on essential points, in the popular addresses to the queen which had been organized in the counties from April 1710 onwards.

During 1710–11 this problem of how to control tory enthusiasm was made much more difficult by its organization and institutionalization through the October Club. This originated in November 1710, when parliament first met, in meetings of independent members and particularly those who had not sat before. It quickly developed into an extemely influential and even powerful pressure group. At the time of its maximum influence, early in 1711, it comprised 160 MPs, nearly one third of the Commons but, although they were inexperienced, their social homogeneity and the similarity of their political prejudices and attitudes made them extremely effective. Overwhelmingly they were country gentry; the Club included half the members for the prestigious county seats, but only six for ports or major urban centres. Their initial cohesion was such that the Club did not require formal leadership: decisions taken at the regular weekly meetings were accepted as binding on all, including for a time those who argued against them. Usually the October Club is described as extremist, and its behaviour certainly created major difficulties for the new ministry and its parliamentary managers, but it should be emphasized that its principles and prejudices were those which the 'country' had always tried to assert, albeit far less effectively.

The October Club members initiated a mass of legislation in the sessions of 1710–11 and 1711–12 that amounted to an attempt at a

new act of restoration, or even counter-revolution, intended to
reverse all those developments that were undermining the predominance of the landed gentry. They repeated perennial country
demands: bills were introduced to end bribery and corruption in
elections, to limit further the number of officers and placemen in
the Commons, to investigate all grants made by the crown since 1689
(either so as to resume them, or to impose a heavy tax on them).
Other investigations were actually launched against alleged breaches
of trust by associates of the late ministry, in victualling, guards' pay,
remittances sent overseas for the maintenance of the armed forces
and navy debts. A new public accounts committee, largely composed of October MPs, was to scrutinize all accounts in order to
substantiate charges that Godolphin and the treasury officials had
been guilty of wilful neglect. Great play was made of its wildly exaggerated conclusion that no less than £35 million was not accounted
for (April 1711). In May an address was voted which denounced the
entire system of government credit that had developed during the
two wars with France. The charge was that this system undermined
effective parliamentary control over finance. Parliament could not
disown obligations incurred by ministers without specific authorization, or the whole system of credit would be affected. Furthermore, ministers could expend money raised by loans according to
their own judgement, without the kind of restrictions that were
imposed when the Commons passed supply bills.

Not surprisingly the October Club tried to legislate to ensure that
gentry interests were supreme. It initiated bills to impose landed
qualifications for both MPs and JPs, and to prohibit the practice of
creating 'faggot' votes in constituencies by fraudulent conveyances
of property—a technique that was being used by magnates and
wealthier landowners at the expense of both freeholders and the
smaller gentry. The October Club's hopes of carrying a programme of
legislation in cooperation with the lower house of Convocation
largely failed to materialize, but a start was made by voting money for
new churches, and reviving an occasional conformity bill. Given the
strength of anglican sentiment in the country and on the backbenches,
Harley could not discourage these initiatives, but the free rein employed by the ministers encouraged what was virtually a backbench
rebellion in March and April 1711 by the October Club. Taking
advantage of Harley's absence—he was severely wounded on 8
March by Guiscard, a French spy, whom he was interrogating—and
St John's negligence, tory MPs impeded supply, rejecting a proposed
leather duty. On his return in late April Harley displayed his skill as
a manager in reasserting control. Although he actually suspected St
John of conniving at these October Club moves, Harley took no

action against him; dismissal would have equipped the zealots with a destructive leader. Many of the leading October MPs were actually rewarded, and muzzled, by being offered honorific or profitable, but not particularly influential, offices—the time-honoured way of splitting any hostile group or faction. These appointments outraged the more intransigent and honest members of the Club, who regarded those who accepted them as renegades to country principles. Harley was also helped by the progress of the negotiations for peace, which held out the prospect of a substantial cut in taxes.

Harley led the ministry during this first phase while occupying the then comparatively humble office of chancellor of the exchequer. His ennoblement on 24 May 1711 as earl of Oxford, and his appointment five days later as lord treasurer, sealed his position as chief minister. However, he had still to meet a dangerous challenge from Nottingham, the tory dissident whom he had deliberately excluded from the ministry in 1710, who now combined incongruously with the whigs against the ministry. At first Oxford alarmed his colleagues and supporters by remaining apparently inactive and irresolute, but in reality he was playing a deep game. He knew he possessed Anne's continuing support. He was confident that the hostile alliance, being based on an attempt to block an almost universally desired peace, was only momentarily dangerous. The agreement between Nottingham and the whigs was tactical and blatantly cynical on the part of the latter. Nottingham had earlier followed a diametrically opposite line, encouraging the October Club in its attacks on the very men, the former whig ministers and Marlborough, with whom he was now allying. He had denounced Oxford's policies for their moderation. Now he hoped to seduce the October Club MPs by sponsoring a new occasional conformity bill, symbolizing militant and authoritarian anglicanism; but simultaneously he got the whigs to renounce their principles and tradition as the friends of the dissenters, by agreeing to support this measure in return for assistance in defeating approval of the peace. Unable to resist the temptation, the whig leaders eagerly complied, and began to draft schemes for a new ministry with Somers as chief minister and Walpole as secretary.

In the Commons the whigs and Nottingham's associates were easily defeated, by 232 to 106, but in the Lords there was a majority of one for a motion condemning any peace that left Spain and the West Indies in Philip's hands (7 December 1711). The upper house had been a whig stronghold since the early 1690s, but Oxford was unperturbed by the prospect of a confrontation between the houses. On 31 December the creation of twelve new peers was announced, and on the same day Marlborough was dismissed from his offices. These moves destroyed the last obstacles to the conclusion of peace. Public opinion had already been prepared, by the publication of Swift's most immediately influential pamphlet, *Reflections on the Conduct of the Allies* (27 November), and by the expulsion of the Imperial envoy, Gallas, for prematurely publishing the terms of the preliminaries (to a peace treaty) in the whig press.

The peace conference opened at Utrecht in January 1712, and although difficulties remained and French sincerity was constantly in doubt, the basic principles had already been agreed with France. At home Oxford dealt severely with his defeated opponents. Somerset was dismissed for joining with Nottingham, although Anne's favour protected his duchess, who retained her household office and was to be blamed by the tory ministers whenever the queen gave them less than full support. Robert Walpole, the most aggressive of the younger whigs, was expelled from the Commons in January, declared incapable of re-election (March), and imprisoned on a charge of corruption. A tory address denouncing abuses of the liberty of the press, organized in January, was followed by prosecutions against whig journalists. In April the imposition of a new stamp duty was designed to price newspapers out of a mass market. But the prime target was Marlborough. Tory propagandists, headed by Swift, publicized and exploited his insatiable appetite for money as well as offices, and the unattractive miserliness that blemished his heroic character. Marlborough was particularly vulnerable for having tolerated financial malpractices by many of his closest associates. In December 1711 charges were formulated by the public accounts committee to destroy his reputation and eliminate him from active politics; these referred to the army bread contract, and alleged misappropriation of funds for intelligence, but there were additional charges in reserve. Threat of prosecution was more effective than an actual impeachment. Marlborough lapsed into inactivity, and in November 1712 went into voluntary exile.

Oxford had retained Marlborough in command for the 1711 campaign because it was necessary to maintain pressure on France during the negotiation of the preliminaries. During 1712 the ministerial task was different—to impose the terms agreed with France on the allies. This involved secret collaboration with the nominal enemy to prevent the allies upsetting the balance of military power and relighting the war. Marlborough's successor in Flanders, the popular tory magnate Ormonde, was issued with orders restraining him from undertaking offensive action (May), and to obstruct operations by the allies. As a result the British forces separated from the allies in July, and those contingents which were maintained by British subsidies had their pay cut off when they opted to remain under Eugène's command. By these actions the ministers sabotaged the allied offensive, which was repulsed by the French at Denain, and compelled the Dutch to realize that there was now no alternative to peace. This was power-politics of the roughest sort. Villars the French general was informed of each move, but public opinion in England had been skilfully inflamed against the past behaviour of the allies. Papers relating to the 1709 Barrier Treaty, which had been negotiated by the whig Townshend, were put before the Commons, examined, and denounced. Both the Dutch and the Imperialists were accused of having failed to honour their treaty obligations to provide men and ships. Unilateral British action was justified by the argument that the former ministers had conceded most of the particular objectives of the allies, and that it was now time for Britain to follow this example.

The tory pursuit of policies of national self-interest, and their willingness to coerce the allies, were extremely popular. Parliamentary attacks on the restraining orders were crushingly defeated. However, this line of policy, while extraordinarily successful in the short-term, proved to be dangerous and indeed fatal to the ministry in the longer term. Among the allies who were deserted and humiliated in 1712 was the Elector of Hanover, who was confirmed in his suspicions that the tory ministers were crypto-jacobites. As his coldness became apparent, many of the ministers began to lose their nerve. When the queen's health deteriorated they faced the possibility that their secret collaboration with the French generals and ministers would be used as a basis for charges of treason. Although possessed of current power, they became frightened men when they looked into a dark future; not surprisingly Oxford took to drink, and there is a perceptible air of hysteria or panic in the actions and misjudgements of some of his colleagues, notably Bolingbroke. Furthermore, expectations of material advantage from the peace were disappointed. Negligence, incompetence and corruption on the part of those entrusted with the commercial negotiations provoked opposition and, ominously, a new split within the tory majority. The clauses of the Utrecht Treaty that dealt with commercial matters required statutory provision, but the bill was rejected (June 1713) by 194 to 185 after the Commons had received a stream of whig-organized representations from merchants, companies and trades. More than seventy identifiable tories voted against the proposals, most of whom had previously been loyal to the ministry but feared in an election year that public opinion and important interests were being ignored by their superiors. The articles negotiated by Moore and Gilligan (associates of Bolingbroke who had probably been receiving bribes) to govern trade with Spain were to prove equally unsatisfactory, and by the summer of 1714 it could be seen that they would have to be renegotiated.

The tories achieved sweeping successes in the general elections of 1713. These concealed their internal weaknesses and divisions, and apparently confirmed the tory view that with the coming of peace, and after being deprived of any share of government patronage, the whigs would gradually fade into a permanently powerless minority. An overwhelming parliamentary majority allowed Oxford to relax his efforts; he was entirely content with a situation in which he could freely follow his political philosophy of forming no long-term plans or schemes but making use of incidents and developments as they occurred. He kept up secret contacts with some of the less aggressive whig leaders, particularly Cowper and Halifax, but generally he became increasingly lethargic, frequently postponing decisions and neglecting business. His inertia roused Bolingbroke who, in advocating a much more positive line, now began to challenge Oxford's position as chief minister. His hostility was partly personal: he never forgave Oxford for hesitating before appointing him secretary in 1710, and excluding him from the first phase of the peace negotiations. Bolingbroke felt humiliated when in July 1712 he failed to get an earldom and the garter; a mere viscountcy he characteristically interpreted as a snub. But the representations which he made in July 1713 were designed to attract wide support within the tory ranks. Bolingbroke complained to Oxford that friends of the ministry were receiving neither encouragement nor direction, and that some dependants were not even receiving their salaries. He argued that a firm lead must be given, and urged that all those who would not accept it must be dismissed and treated as opponents, including those who had recently voted against the commercial clauses of the French treaty. Bolingbroke was in too much of a hurry, and overplaying his hand. He was responsible for mishandling both the negotiating of the commercial clauses and their passage through parliament, where he had not anticipated serious opposition. He made no secret of wishing to include among the dismissals several of Oxford's most loyal colleagues, in particular Dartmouth. Bolingbroke's frequent indiscretions and rackety private life (no other aspirant for top office has, yet, openly enjoyed nude orgies in London parks) alienated Anne and older politicians. Incautious political behaviour during a diplomatic visit to Paris in August 1712 enabled the whigs to charge him with considering a jacobite restoration.

Bolingbroke's ambition and flamboyance divided the tory rank and file, as well as his ministerial colleagues. He was only partly successful in his bid for the support of the enthusiasts. Most of the

October Club MPS looked to him for a more dynamic lead than was being provided by Oxford, but by the summer of 1713 the Club had itself split. It was weakened by the secession of the simon-pure March Club, members who renounced any intention of taking office, fearing that many of their former friends were really only careerists and would shed their principles in return for office. Bolingbroke's apparent, or alleged, flirtations with the idea of at least considering the possibility of a jacobite restoration also tended to strengthen the other principal tory faction, the whimsicals led by Sir Thomas Hanmer, who pledged themselves to assuring the Protestant Succession at all costs.

Oxford responded to Bolingbroke's pressure by a tactically astute ministerial reshuffle (August 1713). He promoted two of the ministers whom Bolingbroke had tried to dislodge: Dartmouth became privy seal, Bromley replacing him as secretary. Hanmer, the leader of the whimsicals and wrecker of the commercial clauses, was to succeed the latter as Speaker, while Mar would as third secretary keep control of Scottish affairs out of Bolingbroke's hands. But after checkmating Bolingbroke, Oxford then lapsed into virtually complete inactivity. Superficially, his reserved inaction during the succeeding months resembled the deep, secretive games that he had played in the past—for instance in 1707–8, 1710 and December 1711—but in reality Oxford now had no sense of purpose, and increasingly lost touch with even those ministers who were still well disposed towards him. They complained that he would neither delegate nor undertake business himself. He allowed affairs to drift, and seems to have been fuddled with drink for much of the time. Parliament was elected in August and September 1713, but it was not convoked until the following February. It is hard to avoid the conclusion that Oxford was hanging on to office quite consciously for the purpose of depriving Bolingbroke of the freedom to act.

Despite Anne's serious illness in December 1713, no one seems to have realized quite how precious was the time that Bolingbroke was losing. He did at least have a coherent political strategy, although a risky one. First, he deliberately focused attention on the issue of religion, knowing that all tory groups and factions could be united in support of aggressive policies directed against the whigs' dissenting allies. The Schism Act was passed (June 1714), which made the dissenting academies (their secondary schools) illegal, and it was intended to follow this by legislation disfranchising dissenters as parliamentary electors. This would have been a body blow to the whigs in the popular constituencies; in those with a corporation franchise they had already been severely weakened by the Occasional Conformity Act. Bolingbroke also advanced his interest at court, winning over Lady Masham, the queen's favourite, who had previously worked solely for Oxford and with great effect. He also made a start in remodelling the army, installing his own connections and clients, a move that was denounced by whigs and whimsicals as giving key posts to crypto-jacobites.

In reality, and contrary to the impression created by his flight to join the Pretender in 1715, Bolingbroke did not have any plan or commitment in favour of a jacobite restoration. Like many of their contemporaries (including Marlborough), both Oxford and Bolingbroke had in the past given the Pretender vague personal promises of service, but they were in no way committed as ministers to him. Intermittent contacts and discussions which had taken place while the peace preliminaries were being negotiated produced nothing definite or practical. An air of unreality surrounded all the initiatives and suggestions made by the Pretender in 1712–14. He was pinning his hopes on an impossible strategy: first Anne should be given the power to nominate her successor, and then she would willingly name her half-brother for conscience sake, to make up for her usurpation and her action against her father in 1688. James took no account of the likely attitudes of the nation, or of the constitutional difficulties. He does not seem to have realized how difficult it would be for the ministers to declare themselves openly by proposing the repeal of the Act of Settlement and the Regency Act that ensured enforcement of the Protestant Succession. Even more obtusely, James obstinately rejected almost universal advice that he must declare himself a protestant if he was to have any hope of restoration. It was this refusal to listen to advice that led Oxford and Bolingbroke to conclude (independently) in February or March 1714 that there was no prospect of managing James, but that the succession of Sophia or George must be accepted as inevitable. The former was a somewhat erratic octogenarian, who died in June, but in the latter the ministers faced the prospect of a sovereign closely associated with their deadliest enemies—Marlborough and the whig chiefs.

The tory ministry had grossly mismanaged George. The abandonment of the allies during the 1712 campaign, and the curt termination of subsidies to Hanover, had antagonized George who, down to the end of 1713 when Anne's health began to crack up, placed more stress on improving his position in Germany than on the longer-term but, in his mind, slightly problematical prospect of the British succession. Not only did the ministers make no serious attempt to gain George's confidence, but they also irrevocably alienated George's key advisers on English affairs and policy, his secretary Robethon and the diplomat Bothmer. Robethon, Huguenot émigré and formerly William's private secretary, was passionately committed to the Protestant Succession, and deeply suspected the tories. Most unwisely St John decided as early as January 1711 not to establish a continuous and confidential correspondence with Robethon, although the latter drafted George's English correspondence and memoranda and in effect formulated his policies. Bothmer served as envoy in London in 1711–12, then represented Hanover at the Utrecht peace conference and returned to London again in June 1714. On both his visits to England he showed that he trusted only the whigs. He worked closely with the whig leaders, especially in November and December 1711 when he collaborated in Nottingham's attack on the Preliminaries. He was formally rebuked for doing so by the ministers, but they made no effort to counter the obviously hostile advice which he was feeding to his master. Bothmer was told that the best guarantee of the Protestant Succession was the 'good inclination' of queen, ministers and parliament, but nothing was done to substantiate the claim that the ministry was well disposed to George. Indeed tory attacks on the whig Barrier Treaty, which included provision for Dutch assistance to secure the Protestant Succession, deepened his suspicions.

In 1714 Oxford's line had not changed. He continued to ask George to trust the ministry and renounce the whigs. In February Thomas Harley was sent to Hanover to say that the ministers were ready to enact better guarantees for the succession, but left it to George to suggest what these should be, provided that they were not contrary to the queen's honour. Nor must they be communicated to the whigs, for if they were involved any proposals would become a party matter. George replied with specific suggestions. He asked the ministers to use pressure to get James, who had had to leave France under the Utrecht Treaty, removed from Lorraine to Italy. Sophia should be given a public pension as successor. For practical as well as symbolic reasons one of the electoral family should be invited to reside in London as a watchdog. In fact Oxford did nothing in reply to these proposals, and his inaction led to a sharp conflict with the new Hanoverian envoy Schutz in April. The latter, acting on instructions from Sophia who was making trouble, but nevertheless in the spirit of George's recent proposals, demanded a writ of summons to enable the Elector's eldest son, the future prince of Wales and George II, to take his seat in the Lords. Nothing could be more repugnant to Anne, who had never been prepared to tolerate an expectant representative of her heirs at court. Moreover Schutz orchestrated his demand with whig claims that the Protestant Succession was in danger under the existing ministry. A furious offensive was mounted in both houses of parliament, and although the whig motions were defeated it was by ominously smaller majorities;

in the Lords by only seventy-six to sixty-four, in the Commons by 256 to 208. Schutz was expelled, and Bolingbroke understandably but unwisely sent sharp remonstrative letters to George and Sophia, the latter dying almost immediately after receiving hers.

Inactive and irresolute, Oxford made no serious attempt to restore friendly relations. He selected one of his friends, a committed tory partisan of the Hanoverian succession, Lord Paget, to go on a special mission to George, but Paget first delayed and finally refused to leave (May), because he realized that the ministry was fundamentally divided on the issue of the succession as on every other topic, and that the assurances he was to convey might be insincere. Oxford was warned by Cowper, the former whig chancellor, that he could establish his own sincerity only by ejecting from what was still nominally his ministry all those who were unreliable on the issue of the succession, but by May 1714 this was no longer possible. By unreliable men, Cowper meant Bolingbroke and his associates, but in these early summer months the latter had neither time nor energy to devote to the succession question. All his attention was given to breaking Oxford. Bolingbroke's priority was to displace Oxford as the queen's trusted minister, install a new ministry of his own choice, and then build up an impregnable interest by filling all governmental posts with his own partisans. This would include those offices whose holders would be *ex officio* lords justices or regents in the event of Anne's death, in fulfilment of the Regency Act. Once Bolingbroke's supporters were entrenched in office, George would have to come to terms with him in order to ensure an orderly take-over of the kingdom. But while he was relentlessly pressurizing Anne, Bolingbroke had simultaneously to fight a defensive campaign in parliament, where he had to try to prevent the widening divisions among the tories from undermining his plans.

Bolingbroke once revealingly compared his own difficult and often precarious position with that of French ministers, who had the advantage of serving a single master and of knowing that their service would be rewarded. Such security was unrealizable in England; in practice it was only by party organization that he could retain and use power. During 1714 Bolingbroke started using the word junto to describe his aspiration of a tory party leadership and a ministry as cohesive and disciplined as that of the whigs. This would have been difficult to achieve at any time with a party consisting mainly of fiercely independent country gentlemen who resented direction and would resist dictation. But in the summer of 1714 the tories were divided on all basic issues except that of the schism bill. Bolingbroke had to manage some eighty to a hundred crypto-jacobites or fellow-travellers who would accept a jacobite restoration if it was effected by others. He also needed the support of a smaller but determined body of whimsicals or Hanoverian tories, whose distrust of his intentions on the succession could only be dispelled by moves or statements that would alienate those who favoured James. Furthermore, Bolingbroke would have to eliminate Oxford's lieutenants from office, but the removal of Bromley and Dartmouth would add to the disquiet of the whimsicals, and the men being considered as their replacements did not constitute an impressive or reassuring collection. Several were barely concealed jacobites (especially the high-church bishop Atterbury) and they were generally inexperienced; backbenchers like Campion, Strangeways, Packington and Stonehouse were aggressive men in the Commons, but it is difficult to see them constructively carrying the weight of administration. Finally, Bolingbroke numbered among his associates several dubious political adventurers whom he had to defend. On 9 July he was obliged to prorogue parliament in order to suppress an investigation of the most prominent, Moore, the commissioner of trade, who had taken bribes from the Spanish government. Indeed profits from one of his corrupt schemes were promised to Bolingbroke himself, and he had used them to win over Lady Masham and induce her to desert Oxford.

During the summer months of 1714 Bolingbroke concentrated on destroying Oxford's position, but this was only the first, if crucial, step in his plans, and he had no assurance that he would be able to succeed as first minister. Bolingbroke and his lieutenants were not proving to be very effective in managing the Commons. In the Lords Oxford still had substantial support, the tory bishops were suspicious of Atterbury, who became bishop of Rochester in 1713, and of his sponsor Bolingbroke, and the whigs were still a substantial force. Even at court, where by July Lady Masham had transferred her invaluable services from Oxford to Bolingbroke, the latter had still to dislodge prominent men and women who distrusted him. He had to decide what attitude to adopt towards Shrewsbury, who had been used by the tories as titular chief during the ministerial changes of 1710. Latterly in exile as lord lieutenant in Dublin, he still retained considerable prestige and direct influence over Anne. Shrewsbury disliked Bolingbroke, but it is difficult to see how a durable administration could have been formed against his wishes, or even without his participation.

In the event, of course, Bolingbroke lacked the time to do more than force Oxford's dismissal from a harassed Anne (27 July). Two days later the queen fell critically ill. The meeting of the privy council on 30 July attended, on Bothmer's advice, by Argyll and Somerset, former whig ministers who had never been dismissed as

councillors but had not attended meetings for some years, recommended Shrewsbury's nomination as the last lord treasurer in British
history. On that day and the next, with Bolingbroke having no option but to cooperate as secretary, the council issued all the orders
necessary to ensure the undisputed proclamation of George 1 when
Anne died on 1 August.

The classic historical view has been that the collapse of the tories
in and after 1714 and the subsequent triumph of the whigs were
inevitable because the latter represented the national interest. It is
crystal clear that a large majority of all classes favoured the
Protestant Succession, and feared that a jacobite restoration would
mean the reintroduction of absolutism and catholicism. But although the whigs took their stand on what they called Revolution
principles, their ascendancy after 1714 was due primarily to their
technical superiority as a political party. The elections of Anne's
reign showed that the whigs represented only a minority of the
political nation, and this was conspicuously so among the gentry and
parochial clergy. But unlike the tories in their years of adversity after
1714, the whigs in opposition after 1710 were industrious in elections
and by-elections, regular in attendance at Westminster, and remarkably consistent in voting in divisions. They showed themselves to be
as resilient, aggressive and united in defensive opposition as they had
been when forcing themselves on the Godolphin administration in
1706–8. They kept up pressure on the tory ministry both at
Westminster and in the country, issuing a stream of propaganda and
missing no opportunity to aggravate and exploit divisions among the
tory factions. By the summer of 1714 the whigs had gone far to
undermine the confidence of many of their opponents. Some junior
ministers were frightened by threats of future partisan retribution;
they got no reassurance from a virtually paralytic Oxford, and could
not bring themselves to trust Bolingbroke.

Although the whigs still had a great deal to do to consolidate their
position after George's accession, they had the advantages of being
united, systematic and disciplined. Their experience in opposition
had educated them in the techniques which they would use after
1714 to ensure that the tories would be made permanently impotent.
They persuaded George to discard the Hanoverian tories as soon as
they had served their purpose, extended the life of parliament by the
Septennial Act, and strengthened the law by the Riot Act. The
whigs successfully combined short-term tactical skill with an appreciation of long-term considerations that Oxford never possessed,
while Bolingbroke behaved in 1713–14 like a political adventurer
concerned only with the pursuit of power and personal wealth.

There is little evidence that at the time he gave serious thought to the fundamental problems that would have to be overcome if the tories were to be entrenched in power and their ideal realized, of an England ruled by its gentry. Admittedly, Bolingbroke did not have the necessary time to organize the tories, but he also lacked the solid reputation to inspire conservatives into an active and effective defence of their influence, interest and principles against a thrusting party that represented sectional, minority interests. Much later Bolingbroke painted a flattering self-portrait of himself as the thoughtful champion of traditional values, but he did not act any such part in 1713–14. He associated with natural extremists like Atterbury. His skills were most strikingly displayed in the purely destructive campaign of political in-fighting which ended in his destruction of his colleague, Oxford. He seems to have considered the possibility of creating divisions within the whig ranks but, quite apart from the unexpectedly early death of the queen, circumstances were against him. The whig leaders could match him in political resourcefulness and ruthlessness, but above all they had the advantage of defending the principles of the Revolution which united the party, and by their consistent advocacy of the Protestant Succession they could make an appeal to those who stood outside the party and had earlier regarded the whigs with distrust.

18 Conclusion

The changes and developments that occurred in England between 1658 and 1714 can be seen most clearly when set in a European context. Commonwealth England made an impression as a new great power, whose military and naval strength few states could ignore, but its domestic politics were unintelligible to foreigners, and the meteoric career of Oliver Cromwell was universally misinterpreted. Few Europeans understood the part played in his life by religious faith. The catholic half of Europe accepted an interpretation (popularized by Père d'Orleans) of English politics for the century down to 1688; they saw the continuous turbulence and endemic rebelliousness of Englishmen as the inevitable product of protestant schism and heresy, and believed that domestic peace and order could never exist until catholicism was restored and England conformed to the rules and principles of good government as practised in the France of Louis xiv. The main characteristics of English cultural life, when they were noticed at all, were rated as aberrations—the vigorous but uncouth and savage Shakespeare, the hybrid architectural styles employed—while the English language was little known, and acquired mainly for utilitarian commercial reasons by Dutchmen.

In 1714 Britain was making a major impact on Europe in virtually all spheres of life. It was not just a question of Marlborough's decisive military victories, although these made the most striking impression, or of two decades of naval supremacy and the joint dictation (with France) of peace in 1711–13. By the end of Anne's reign, England had become the pre-eminent commercial and colonial power eclipsing the Dutch, and London had superseded Amsterdam as the centre not only of European but of world trade, although not yet as a financial centre. More surprisingly, England had begun to exercise a major cultural influence on Europe, for the first time since the spread of the Arthurian legend. It was not Augustan literature that ended England's cultural and intellectual isolation, but the unparalleled development of science and philosophy in late-Stuart England, and their recognition by a newly emerging international community of scholars and intellectuals, the 'republic of letters' which Englishmen and refugees from Europe living in England did much to create.

The appearance of a whole constellation of great original thinkers—Newton, Locke, Wren, Boyle and Ray to name but a few—cannot easily be explained, but they lived and worked for most of their productive careers in a more favourable environment than could be found elsewhere in Europe. Locke suffered for his political association with Shaftesbury, but it is significant that the scientific processes of investigation and experimentation, and the discussion and publication of hypotheses and new theories met with less misunderstanding, obstruction and bigoted opposition than in any other European country. Much of the interest shown in science by educated Englishmen was undiscriminating and naive, but a whole generation of scientists knew, and were not afraid to know, that they were exploring entirely new regions of knowledge and thought. The widespread interest in science represented a conscious turning away from the largely theological concerns of the previous generation of thinkers, which had become sterile and exhausted and repulsive through endless polemical controversies.

The interest in scientific inquiry and its achievements that gave late-Stuart England its distinctive reputation is indicative of several characteristics of what we call the modern, that is our, world. First, it was secular. Although English scientists, unlike the *philosophes* of eighteenth-century France, were confident that science would reinforce, not undermine, revealed religion, it nevertheless diminished the place of theology in intellectual life. Secondly it was self-consciously modern. The authoritative systems of knowledge being disproved were not only medieval in origin, but were derived from classical antiquity. Now, as Sprat claimed, modern man was daily surpassing the ancients, and there was no apparent limit ahead to the advance of knowledge. Furthermore, the acceptance of new ideas and theories by the educated, the virtual absence of widespread and popular prejudice and bigotry, was a sign of a capacity to adapt to change, to see in changes what was to emerge as a theory of progress. This was of vital importance to a society like England's in 1714, on the eve of a transformation of a kind that had never happened before in Europe.

The rate of change in many areas of national life was perceptibly quickening in the years after the Revolution of 1688. There was not, as in the 1640s, a cataclysmic collapse of the established order, no repetition of the melodrama of a world turned upside down by zealots and iconoclasts, but England after 1688 was entering the early stages of the processes of transformation that were to produce the first 'modern' society in Europe. The continuing expansion of London, already the largest European city, the growth of the west coast ports engaged in colonial trade, the development of the coal mining areas, improvements in internal communications, technological innovations in textile manufacture and metal working, the spread of new and specialized methods in farming, were not only producing a new England but were setting in motion dynamic economic and social forces that would produce further irreversible changes.

The role of the state was to permit or, as in the case of the Navigation Act and the bounties on the export of grain, to facilitate these changes. They were not the result of state intervention; although James II proposed to organize commerce he did practically nothing to initiate the kind of mercantilist policies that Colbert had enforced in France. Moreover, those who possessed political power failed when they tried to use legislative means to limit and restrict the effects of social and economic changes on political life. The landed gentry and anglican clergy who felt that their supremacy was threatened justified their actions by invoking the principle of restoration. They sought to re-establish securely and permanently the bases of order, stability and harmony, not only in 1659–60 but again after the collapse of the Cabal's policies in 1673–4 and the defeat of Exclusion in 1681. Similarly the country opposition participants in the Revolution of 1688 and the victorious tory partisans in 1710–14 believed that they could legislate to reverse recent policies and trends that were undermining their own position.

The main challenge to the supremacy of the gentry and clergy did not come from below, from their social inferiors in the form of popular radicalism. It came from two successive artificial or synthetic ruling groups—first, the republican combination of careerist army officers, military politicians, Rumpers and puritan clergy whose power crumbled so easily in 1659–60; secondly, James II's court was a similarly composite grouping of catholics, dissenters and former whigs, Irish and Scots. Both these ruling cliques collapsed ignominiously, the first at the Restoration and the second at the Revolution, because of their artificial character and narrow base of support. But in the long term the gentry and clergy were unable to deny a share of power and influence to much more formidable rivals, the new elements that were being enriched and expanded by social development and economic diversification and expansion. Of these the new monied interest was the most conspicuous and thrusting, and therefore the most unpopular. Bolingbroke and the tories in 1711–14 failed to impose effective legislative obstacles to their entry into the ruling and leading section of the political nation. Had the

tory attempt succeeded for any length of time, this would have produced a critical state of tension with (as in late eighteenth-century
France) political power and social status being monopolized by a
class that was losing its economic predominance as the economy
became increasingly diversified. Similarly, if James II had succeeded
in his policies, or been restored by a French invasion in the 1690s, it
is difficult to see how a general and destructive revolution could
have been long postponed.

Although there were many imperfections in both government and
society in 1714, and by modern standards most people lived on the
edge of poverty or destitution, there was a self-confidence and resilience in the nation that had been missing in 1658. England was a
divided society, but adversary politics provided a safety valve for
tensions and discontents. The division between whig and tory canal-
ized and gave expression to discontents and passions that had earlier
taken forms that endangered the stability and survival of the regime,
both republican and that of the restored monarchy. In all European
monarchies there was a permanent and direct confrontation between
the mass of the subjects and their ruler, who regarded himself as
responsible only to God. In England the lesson of 1688, enshrined in
what were known as Revolution principles, was that government
must take into account (and be sensitive to changes in) the interests
of the nation.

Bibliography

The purpose of this bibliographical essay is mainly to survey recently published work on the period, and to indicate reasonably accessible specialist studies which can be used to go more deeply into major topics than is possible in this volume.

Abbreviations

BIHR	*Bulletin of the Institute of Historical Research*
EcHR	*Economic History Review*
EHR	*English Historical Review*
HJ	*Historical Journal*
JBS	*Journal of British Studies*
PP	*Past and Present*
TRHS	*Transactions of the Royal Historical Society*

1 Bibliographies

The best bibliography covering the whole period is the new edition by M. F. Keeler, *Bibliography of British History: Stuart Period, 1603–1714* (Oxford 1970), which supersedes the first edition by Godfrey Davies (1928). Also useful are C. L. Grose, *A Select Bibliography of British History, 1660–1760* (Chicago, 1967), and the volume in the current series being published by the Conference on British Studies, W. L. Sachse, *Restoration England, 1660–1689* (Cambridge, 1971). See also G. R. Elton, *Modern Historians on British History, 1485–1945* (London, 1970) and C. H. Carter, *The Western European Powers, 1500–1700* (London, 1970).

2 General

No student of the period can ignore two great historical classics: T. B. Macaulay, *The History of England from the Accession of James II* (first published in 1849–61, best edition is by C. H. Firth, London, 1913–15). See also Firth's *Commentary on Macaulay's History* (London,

1938). The second is Clarendon, *History of the Rebellion* (Oxford, always in print and may it continue to be so), together with *The Life
... being a Continuation of the History* (Oxford, 1857). Almost to be
included in the same category is G. Burnet, *History of My Own Time*
(best edition is that by O. Airy, Oxford 1897–1900) because, like
Clarendon, he wrote from the inside of politics, and displays an
understanding of major historical movements that excuses frequent
carelessness and errors. H. C. Foxcroft's *Supplement to Burnet's History*
(Oxford, 1902) is a useful corrective in this respect.

Of modern surveys D. Ogg, *England in the Reign of Charles II* (revised edition, Oxford, 1956) and *England in the Reigns of James II and
William III* (Oxford, 1955) are the outstanding products of a long
life's scholarship. C. Hill, *The Century of Revolution* (Edinburgh, 1961)
gives an interesting but arguable interpretation, by a leading
scholar of the early Stuart period. G. E. Aylmer, *The Struggle for the
Constitution* (London, 1963) is a useful introductory survey. G. N.
Clark, *The Later Stuarts* (1934, latest edition Oxford, 1955) is beginning to show signs of age, as is G. M. Trevelyan, *England under
Queen Anne* (3 vols, London,1945–6). M. Ashley, *England in the
Seventeenth Century* (Harmondsworth, 1954) can be used as a brief
introduction, but now stands in need of revision. J. P. Kenyon, *The
Stuarts* (London, 1958) maintains a hostile attitude towards its subject. G. Davies, *The Restoration of Charles II* (San Marino, Cal., 1955)
is far too detailed and descriptive; there is a much more succinct
account at the end of I. Roots, *The Great Rebellion* (London, 1966).
The two volumes in the *New Cambridge Modern History*, V *The
Ascendancy of France, 1648–88* (edited by F. L. Carsten, Cambridge,
1961), and VI *The Rise of Great Britain and Russia, 1688–1715/25*
(edited by J. S. Bromley, Cambridge, 1970) are generally very useful.

There are three good collections of documents: the most comprehensive, with an excellent commentary, is A. Browning's volume
VIII (London, 1966) in the English Historical Documents series,
covering the period 1660–1714. The two relevant volumes in the
Cambridge series are perhaps more manageable: J. P. Kenyon, *The
Stuart Constitution* (Cambridge, 1966) and E. N. Williams, *The
Eighteenth Century Constitution* (Cambridge, 1960). W. C. Costin and J.
S. Watson, *The Law and Working of the Constitution I* (London, 1952)
has an illuminating selection of documents, but without commentary. On a narrower front, G. S. Holmes and W. A. Speck, *The
Divided Society: Parties and Politics in England, 1694–1716* (London,
1967) is a model of how selected documents can be presented.

Among the vast collections of original source material in print the
following are both important and not too difficult to obtain: the
Bath, Portland, Ormonde, Finch, Downshire, Leyborne-Popham,

House of Lords, and Dartmouth volumes published by the Historical Manuscripts Commission. The main collections of correspondence are: Sir John Dalrymple, *Memoirs of Great Britain and Ireland* (2 vols, London, 1771–3); P. Grimblot, *Letters of William III and Louis XIV* (2 vols, London, 1848); G. P. R. James, *Letters illustrative of the Reign of William III* (3 vols, London, 1841); W. Coxe, *Private and Original Correspondence of . . . Shrewsbury* (London, 1821) and *Memoirs of the Duke of Marlborough* (3 vols, London, 1818–19); H. L. Snyder, *The Marlborough–Godolphin Correspondence* (3 vols, Oxford, 1975); G. Parke, *Letters and Correspondence of Bolingbroke* (London, 1798).

There are four main collections of parliamentary debates that are easier to find and far easier to use than the typographically repulsive *Parliamentary History*: A. Grey, *Debates of the House of Commons from . . . 1667 to . . . 1694* (10 vols, London, 1763); H. Horwitz (ed.), *The Parliamentary Diary of Narcissus Luttrell, 1691–1693* (Oxford, 1972); C. Robbins (ed.), *The Diary of John Milward* (Cambridge, 1938); B. D. Henning (ed.), *The Parliamentary Diary of Sir Edward Dering, 1670–73* (New Haven, 1940). The widest selection of pamphlets is to be found in the Somers' Tracts—*A Collection of Scarce and Valuable Tracts* (London, 1809–15) edited by Sir Walter Scott.

3 Political

After a long period of neglect, a great deal has been published in the last two decades, and a group of these studies represents a new interpretation of late seventeenth-century politics. The way was led by J. H. Plumb, *The Growth of Political Stability in England, 1675–1725* (London, 1967), with which should be read his article, 'The Growth of the Electorate in England from 1600 to 1715', *PP* 45 (1969). The other major studies are: H. Horwitz, *Parliament, Policy and Politics in the Reign of William III* (Manchester, 1977); G. Holmes, *British Politics in the Age of Anne* (London, 1967); W. A. Speck, *Tory and Whig* (London, 1970); B. W. Hill, *The Growth of Parliamentary Parties, 1698–1742* (London, 1976); J. R. Jones, *The First Whigs* (London, 1970); J. R. Western, *Monarchy and Revolution* (London, 1972). They add up to a refutation of the attempt by R. Walcott in his *English Politics in the early Eighteenth Century* (Oxford, 1956) to demonstrate that politics were similar in their operation to the system described by Sir Lewis Namier in *The Structure of Politics at the Accession of George III* (London, 1965); this (in my view, unfounded) assumption colours Walcott's bibliographical essays, 'The Later Stuarts (1660–1714)', *American Historical Review* LXVIII (1962); *The Tudor–Stuart period of English History* (New York, 1964) a pamphlet issued by the Service Center for Teachers of History; and 'The Idea of Party in the Writing of Later Stuart History', *JBS* I (1962). In sharp contrast is the interpretation by K. Feiling, whose *History of the Tory Party, 1640–1714* has like an old madeira matured with the years—it was published as far back as 1924 (Oxford). A. Browning, 'Parties and Party Organization in the Reign of Charles II', *TRHS*, 4th series, xxx (1948) has also stood the test of work done since then.

Monographs on the period 1660–88 include D. T. Witcombe, *Charles II and the Cavalier House of Commons, 1663–74* (Manchester, 1966); M. Lee *The Cabal* (Urbana, 1965); K. H. D. Haley, *William of Orange and the English Opposition, 1672–74* (Oxford, 1953); J. P. Kenyon's *The Popish Plot* (London, 1972) supersedes the older book of the same title by J. Pollock (1903, 1944). J. Miller, *Popery and Politics in England, 1660–1688* (Cambridge, 1973) is a superb study of a wider subject than the title suggests—that of the catholic factor through the whole century. On Exclusion, besides my own *The First Whigs*, there is a useful examination of the pamphlet material that was published during the crisis in F. S. Ronalds, *The Attempted Whig Revolution of 1678–81* (Urbana, 1937); this should be read in conjunction with O. W. Furley, 'The Whig Exclusionists: Pamphlet Literature in the Exclusion Campaign', *Cambridge Historical Journal* XIII (1957). There are several not entirely satisfactory studies of the Monmouth Rebellion: C. Chenevix Trench, *The Western Rising* (London, 1969); W. R. Emerson, *Monmouth's Rebellion* (New Haven, 1951); B. D. Little, *The Monmouth Episode* (London, 1956), and in B. Bevan, *James, Duke of Monmouth* (London, 1973). The latest, and best, study is P. Earle, *Monmouth's Rebels* (London, 1977).

Omitting articles that have subsequently been incorporated in monographs or extended studies, the following cover important topics, or aspects of major topics: A. H. Woolrych, 'The Good Old Cause and the Fall of the Protectorate' and C. Roberts, 'The Impeachment of the Earl of Clarendon', both in *Cambridge Historical Journal* XIII (1957); J. H. Sacret, 'The Restoration Government and Municipal Corporations', *EHR* xxxxv (1930); J. Walker, 'The Censorship of the Press during the Reign of Charles II', *History* , new series, xxxiii (1950) and 'The English Exiles in Holland during the Reigns of Charles II and James II', *TRHS*, 4th series, xxx (1948); A. Browning and D. J. Milne, 'An Exclusion Division List', *BIHR* xxiii (1950); D. J. Milne, 'Results of the Rye House Plot', *TRHS*, 5th series I (1951); E. S. De Beer, 'The House of Lords in the Parliament of 1680', *BIHR* xx (1943–5); J. R. Jones, 'Political Groups and Tactics in the Convention of 1660', *HJ* vi (1963) and 'Restoration Election Petitions', *Durham University Journal* LIII (1961); H. A. Nutting, 'The Most Wholesome Law—the Habeas Corpus

Act of 1679', *American Historical Review* LXV (1960); D. Allen, 'Political Clubs in Restoration London', *HJ* XIX (1976); M. Priestley, 'London Merchants and Opposition Politics in Charles II's Reign', *BIHR* XXIX (1956).

The Revolution of 1688 has emerged as a controversial topic in recent years, though this is no thanks to the careless and tendentious study, containing a conspiracy theory, of L. Pinkham, *William III and the Respectable Revolution* (Cambridge, Mass., 1954); J. P. Kenyon, *The Nobility in the Revolution of 1688* (Hull, 1963) sketched a neo-feudalist thesis; J. Carswell, *The Descent on England* (London, 1969) set the Revolution in its European context; M. Ashley, *The Glorious Revolution of 1688* (London, 1966) gives a narrative account; S. E. Prall, *The Bloodless Revolution: England, 1688* and J. R. Jones, *The Revolution of 1688 in England* (London), both appeared in 1972. A recent study of the Revolution in a locality breaks new ground: D. H. Hosford, *Nottingham, Nobles and the North* (Hamden, Conn., 1976). See also R. J. Frankle, 'The Formulation of the Declaration of Rights', *HJ* XVII (1974); H. Horwitz, 'Parliament and the Glorious Revolution', *BIHR* XXXXVII (1974); W. L. Sachse, 'The Mob and the Revolution of 1688', *JBS* IV (1964); R. Beddard, 'The Guildhall Declaration of 11 December 1688', *HJ* XI (1968).

Apart from H. Horwitz's major study, *Parliament, Policy and Politics in the reign of William III* (Manchester, 1977), to be read with his 'Parties, Connections and Parliamentary Politics, 1689–1714', *JBS* VI (1966), and the concise and informative essays in G. Holmes, *Britain after the Glorious Revolution* (London, 1969), less has been published on the very complex politics of William's reign than on the preceding and following periods. D. Rubini, *Court and Country, 1688–1702* (London, 1967) is useful for reference, but his thesis is not entirely convincing; see also his 'Politics and the Battle for the Banks, 1688–97', *EHR* LXXXV (1970). J. A. Downie has emphasized the important role played in the reign by 'The Committee of Public Accounts and the Formation of the Country Party', *EHR* LXXXXI (1976). G. H. Jones, *The Mainstream of Jacobitism* (Cambridge, Mass., 1954) supersedes earlier studies. The disbanding crisis is dealt with in L. G. Schwoerer, *No Standing Armies* (Baltimore, 1974).

Apart from biographies, specialized studies on Anne's reign include G. Holmes, *The Trial of Dr Sacheverell* [London, 1973); J. O. Richards, *Party Propaganda under Queen Anne* (Athens, Ga., 1972); L. W. Hanson, *Government and the Press, 1695–1763* (London, 1967); G. V. Bennet, *The Tory Crisis in Church and State* (Oxford, 1975). There are many excellent new articles: G. V. Bennet, 'Robert Harley, the Godolphin Ministry and the Bishoprics Crisis of 1707', *EHR* LXXXII (1967); in the same number there is also H. T. Dickinson, 'The Poor

Palatines and the Parties'; G. Holmes and W. A. Speck, 'The Fall of Harley in 1708 Reconsidered', *EHR* LXXX (1965); H. L. Snyder, 'Godolphin and Harley: A Study of their Partnership in Politics', *Huntington Library Quarterly* XXX (1967) and 'The Defeat of the Occasional Conformity Bill and the Tack', *BIHR* XXXXI (1968); P. Rogers, 'Swift and Bolingbroke on Faction', *JBS* IX (1970); E. G. Cruickshanks, 'The Tories and the Succession to the Crown in the 1714 Parliament', *BIHR* XXXXVI (1973); W. A. Speck, 'Political Propaganda in Augustan England', *TRHS*, 5th series XXII (1972); E. Gregg, 'Was Queen Anne a Jacobite?', *History* LVII (1972).

4 Biographies

All rulers except Richard Cromwell have attracted new biographers: for his life there is only the thin R. W. Ramsey *Richard Cromwell* (London, 1935), but then there is little to say about him. A. Bryant's revisionist or apologetical *King Charles II* was reissued in 1955 (London) in revised form. M. Ashley, *Charles II: the Man and the Statesman* (London, 1971) and F. C. Turner, *James II* (London, 1950) provide straightforward accounts, but are superseded by John Miller, *James II: a study in kingship* (Hooe, 1978). S. B. Baxter, *William III* (London, 1966) is superior to the more general H. and B. van der Zee, *William and Mary* (London, 1973); D. Ogg, *William III* (London, 1956) is concise and sympathetic. D. Green, *Queen Anne* (London, 1970), give an understanding portrait; her half-brother the Pretender awaits convincing treatment.

Pre-eminent among biographies, both because of the importance of the subject and the excellence of the study are: A. Browning, *Thomas Osborne, Earl of Danby* (3 vols, Glasgow, 1944–51); K. H. D. Haley, *The First Earl of Shaftesbury* (Oxford, 1968); J. P. Kenyon, *Robert Spencer, Earl of Sunderland* (London, 1958) and H. T. Dickinson, *Bolingbroke* (London, 1970). R. L. Ollard, *Pepys: a Biography* (London, 1974) is a most useful companion to the monumental and superb edition by R. C. Latham and W. Matthews of Samuel Pepys's *Diary* (11 vols, London, 1970–83). The older study by A. Bryant, *Samuel Pepys* (3 vols: *The Man in the Making*; *The Years of Peril*; *The Saviour of the Navy*; Cambridge 1933–8) can also be strongly recommended.

Frankly disappointing are both recent studies of Robert Harley: E. Hamilton, *The Backstairs Dragon* (London, 1969) and A. McInnes, *Robert Harley, Puritan Politician* (London, 1970) and also T. Lever, *Godolphin: his Life and Times* (London, 1952) and two lives of Shrewsbury: T. C. Nicholson and A. S. Turberville, *Charles, Duke of Shrewsbury* (Cambridge, 1930) and D. H. Somerville, *The King of*

Hearts (London, 1962). W. L. Sachse, *Lord Somers: a Political Portrait* (Manchester, 1975) gets as near to his subject as perhaps is possible, but we are really no closer to understanding him. H. Horwitz, *Revolution Politics: the Career of the Second Earl of Nottingham* (Cambridge, 1968) and G. H. Jones, *Charles Middleton* (Chicago, 1968) are both excellent, especially in relating their subjects to the developments on which they had a great deal of influence. Of older biographies, W. S. Churchill, *Marlborough: his Life and Times* (2 volume edition, London, 1958–63) does now seem to be grandiloquently overwritten; C. H. Hartmann, *Clifford of the Cabal* (London, 1937) is based on original material; H. C. Foxcroft, *A Character of the Trimmer* (Cambridge, 1946) is a condensed, but still sweetened, version of her two-volume *Life and Letters of Sir George Savile, First Marquis of Halifax* (London, 1898). T. H. Lister, *Life and Administration of Edward, First Earl of Clarendon* (3 vols, London, 1837–8) is still valuable because of the selection of correspondence which it contains.

There is need of a new biography to replace V. Barbour, *Henry Bennet, Earl of Arlington* (Washington, 1914) and there are, rather surprisingly, no biographies of Rochester, the third Earl of Sunderland, Charles Montagu Earl of Halifax, Sir William Coventry, Charles Fleetwood and Sir Arthur Hesilrige. New studies are needed of Lambert, Clarendon, Buckingham, Jeffreys, Tyrconnel, Portland, Peterborough, Shrewsbury, Harley, Wharton, Godolphin and Lowndes.

5 Foreign relations, the navy and the army

Introductory sketches are G. M. D. Howat, *Stuart and Cromwellian Foreign Policy* (London, 1974); P. Langford, *Modern British Foreign Policy: the Eighteenth Century* (London, 1976); J. R. Jones, *Britain and Europe in the Seventeenth Century* (London, 1966); D. B. Horn, *Great Britain and Europe in the Eighteenth Century* (Oxford, 1967). There are invaluable essays in *William III and Louis XIV* (Liverpool, 1968), edited by R. Hatton and J. S. Bromley. K. Feiling, *British Foreign Policy, 1660–1672* (London, 1930) is perhaps too detailed and allusive, and C. Wilson, *Profit and Power* (London, 1957), while excellent on the First and Second Dutch Wars, inexplicably fails to deal with the Third. On the latter, see C. R. Boxer, 'Some Second Thoughts on the Third Anglo-Dutch War', *TRHS*, 5th series, xix (1969).

Monographs include P. S. Lachs, *The Diplomatic Corps under Charles II and James II* (New Brunswick, N.J., 1965); A. D. Francis, *The Methuens and Portugal* (Cambridge, 1966); D. Coombs, *The Conduct of the Dutch* (The Hague, 1958); M. A. Thompson, *The Secretaries of*

State, 1681–1782 (Oxford, 1932); C. H. Hartmann, *Charles II and Madame* (London, 1934). Of the innumerable articles some may be picked out for the new light that they throw on familiar subjects: B. W. Hill, 'Oxford, Bolingbroke and the Peace of Utrecht', *HJ* xvi (1973); D. McKay, 'Bolingbroke, Oxford and the Defence of the Utrecht Settlement in Southern Europe', *EHR* lxxxvi (1971); A. D. Francis, 'The Grand Alliance in 1698', *HJ* x (1967); G. N. Clark, 'The Character of the Nine Years War', *Cambridge Historical Journal* xi (1954); J. R. Jones, 'English Attitudes to Europe in the Seventeenth Century' in *Britain and the Netherlands in Europe and Asia*, edited by J. S. Bromley and E. H. Kossmann (London, 1968); R. A. Stradling, 'Spanish Conspiracy in England, 1661–63', *EHR* lxxxvii (1972).

There is no comprehensive study of the navy of the Restoration, although there are two stimulating chapters in P. M. Kennedy, *The Rise and Fall of British Naval Mastery* (London, 1976) which supersede the section in M. Lewis, *The History of the British Navy* (Harmondsworth, 1957). For the post-Revolutionary period administration is admirably treated in J. Ehrman, *The Navy in the War of William III* (Cambridge, 1953). J. H. Owen, *War at Sea under Queen Anne* (Cambridge, 1938) deals mainly with the operational side. For a good general survey see C. Barnett, *Britain and Her Army, 1509–1970* (London, 1970), and in two shorter periods, J. Childs, *The Army of Charles II* (London, 1976) and R. E. Scouller, *The Armies of Queen Anne* (Oxford, 1966).

6 Religious and intellectual

Essential reading are the two superb studies by N. Sykes, *Church and State in England in the Eighteenth Century* (London, 1934) and *From Sheldon to Secker: Aspects of English Church History, 1660–1768* (Cambridge, 1959). An excellent overall survey is G. R. Cragg, *The Church and the Age of Reason, 1648–1789* (Harmondsworth, 1960); he has also written two more specialized studies, *From Puritanism to the Age of Reason* (Cambridge, 1950) and *Puritanism in the Period of the Great Persecution* (Cambridge, 1957). Another aspect of dissent is treated in D. R. Lacey, *Dissent and Parliamentary Politics in England, 1661–1689* (New Brunswick, N. J., 1969). See also the essays in *From Uniformity to Unity, 1662–1962* (London, 1962) edited by G. F. Nuttall and O. Chadwick. There is a new life of Sheldon by V. D. Sutch, *Gilbert Sheldon* (The Hague, 1973) but for his work at the Restoration R. S. Bosher, *The Making of the Restoration Settlement* (London, 1951) is indispensable. For the other side see G. R. Abernathy, 'The English Presbyterians and the Stuart Restoration, 1648–1663',

Transactions of the American Philosophical Society LV (Philadelphia, 1965). R. A. Beddard, 'The Commission for Ecclesiastical Promotions, 1681–84', *HJ* x (1967) is an appetizing hors d'oeuvres for what should be a definitive study of the church under Sancroft. For the later period see G. Every, *The High Church Party, 1688–1718* (London, 1956); G. M. Straka, *Anglican Reaction to the Revolution of 1688* (Madison, 1962); F. James, 'The Bishops in Politics, 1688–1714' in *Conflicts in Stuart England* edited by W. A. Aiken (New York, 1960); G. V. Bennet, 'King William and the Episcopate' in *Essays in Modern English Church History* (London, 1966) edited by himself and J. D. Walsh; A. Whiteman, 'The Re-establishment of the Church of England, 1660–63', *TRHS*, 5th series, v (1955).

It is not possible here to survey the abundant literature on the developments in science and philosophy, but as an introduction mention can be made of a few titles: A. R. Hall, *From Galileo to Newton, 1630–1720* (London, 1963), *The Scientific Revolution* (London, 1956) and his current publication of Henry Oldenburg's *Correspondence* (Madison); R. S. Westfall, *Science and Religion in Seventeenth-century England* (New Haven, 1958) deals with their interaction. H. Hartley has edited a collection of essays on *The Royal Society: its Origins and Founders* (London, 1960).

7 Administration and finance

The outstanding study of recent years is C. D. Chandaman, *The English Public Revenue, 1660–1688* (Oxford, 1975), exhaustive and definitive. When someone else has spent thirty years of his life as profitably on expenditure we shall understand Restoration finances as a whole. For the later period there is another excellent study, P. G. M. Dickson, *The Financial Revolution in England* (London, 1967). See also S. B. Baxter, *The Development of the Treasury, 1660–1702* (London, 1957) and H. Roseveare, *The Treasury: The Evolution of a British Institution* (London, 1969): also an article by E. A. Reitan, 'From Revenue to Civil List, 1689–1702', *HJ* XIII (1970). W. R. Ward, *The English Land Tax in the Eighteenth Century* (Oxford, 1953) and E. Hughes, *Studies in Administration and Finance* (Manchester, 1934) are still the most useful studies on administrative developments; see also G. A. Jacobsen, *William Blathwayt* (New Haven, 1932) which is far more than a biography of one of the first bureaucrats. For government at the highest level, see J. H. Plumb, 'The Organization of the Cabinet in the Reign of Queen Anne', *TRHS*, 5th series, VII (1957), and J. Carter, 'Cabinet Records for the Reign of William III', *EHR* LXXVIII (1963). In the background to the life and work of ministers lurked the threat of impeachment; see the excellent monograph by

C. Roberts, *The Growth of Responsible Government in Stuart England* (Cambridge, 1966).

On the law see M. Landon, *The Triumph of the Lawyers* (University, Al., 1970); A. F. Havighurst, 'The Judiciary and Politics in the Reign of Charles II', *Law Quarterly Review* 66 (1950) and 'James II and the twelve Men in Scarlet', *ibid.* 69 (1953). For a different view see G. W. Keeton, 'The Judiciary and the Constitutional Struggle', *Journal of the Society of Public Teachers of Law* VII (1962), and *Lord Chancellor Jeffreys and the Stuart Cause* (London, 1965).

8 Scotland

The Union obviously looms large in general histories and has attracted more attention as the issue of devolution or national independence has become a practical one. General histories are G. Donaldson, *Scotland, James V to James VII* (Edinburgh, 1965); W. Ferguson, *Scotland, 1689 to the Present* (Edinburgh, 1968); T. C. Smout, *A History of the Scottish People* (London, 1969). I. B. Cowan, *The Scottish Covenanters, 1660–1688* (London, 1976) describes the period of political instability from the point of view of those resisting episcopacy and government. On the Union see G. S. Pryde, *The Treaty of Union of Scotland and England* (London, 1950); the essays in T. I Rae, *The Union of 1707: its Impact on Scotland* (Glasgow, 1974).

9 Ireland

There is a new general account in *A New History of Ireland* III, *Early Modern Ireland, 1534–1691* (Oxford, 1976). J. G. Sims has written two excellent monographs, *Jacobite Ireland, 1689–91* (London, 1969) and *The Williamite Confiscation in Ireland, 1690–1703* (London, 1956).

10 Addenda

Publications that have appeared since this book's original printing include Antonia Fraser, *King Charles II* (London, 1979) and, a much briefer and more penetrating study, *The Image of the King: Charles I and Charles II* (London, 1979) by Richard Ollard. A more specialized subject receives excellent treatment by Lionel K. J. Glassey, *Politics and the Appointment of Justices of the Peace, 1675–1720* (Oxford, 1979).

Index

Aachen, Treaty of, 103, 169
Abjuration Act (1702), 323
Absalom and Achitophel, 3, 221
Absolutism, notions of, 2, 3, 20, 46, 57, 105–6, 110, 131, 141, 163, 164–5, 178–9, 209, 217
Addison, Joseph, 23
Africa: royal company, 77, 99, 106; company of Scotland trading to, 330, 332
Albemarle, duke of, *see* Monk
Albemarle, earl of, *see* Keppel
Alibone, Sir Richard, 240
Aliens Act (1705), 331–2
Allin, Sir Thomas, 101
Almanza, 292
Amsterdam, 77, 357
Anne: characteristics, 12, 317; as heir, 13; death of son, 310; relations with confidants, 21; with William, 259; with duchess of Marlborough, 333, 337; with Marlborough and Godolphin 334, 340; with Harley, 328–9, 337–8, 340–41, 346; with the church, 48; dislikes Sacheverell, 337; initial appointments, 303, 313, 320; and the succession, 253, 327, 352; declining health, 350; pressurized by Bolingbroke, 353; death, 355; mentioned, 7, 23, 31, 79, 84, 316, 333
Annesley, Arthur, 130, 138, 156
Appleby, 35
Argyll, earl and duke of, *see* Campbell
Arlington, earl of, *see* Bennet
Armstrong, Sir Thomas, 211, 224
Army: as an issue, 2, 7, 15, 41, 62–3; and Rump, 121–4; and Monk, 113–15, 125–7, 128–9; Danby's, 194–5; James II's, 230, 245, 247–8, 249–50; and Mutiny act, 254, 259; William's 263–4, 272, 281–2; disbanded, 284–5, 305–7; Marlborough's, 314, 351
Arton, Willem, 108
Arundell of Wardour, Lord, 104, 169
Ashby v. *White* (Aylesbury men), 324–5
Ashley, Lord, *see* Cooper
Asiento, 296, 299
Association (1696), 274–5, 323
Athlone, earl of, *see* Ginkel
Atterbury, Francis, 354, 356

Baber, Sir John, 142
Bank of England, 43, 49, 65, 66, 68, 76, 91, 270, 277, 309, 342–3
Bantam, 112
Barfleur–La Hougue, 268, 282, 283
Barrier Treaty (1709), 294, 297, 348, 352
Barrillon, Paul, 199, 237
Bart, Jean, 283
Barwick, John, 136

Bath, earl of, *see* Grenville
Bavaria: as French ally, 288; electoral prince, 286, 303
Baxter, Richard, 148, 152
Beachy Head, 265, 282
Bedloe, William, 199
Bellasis, John, Lord, 64
Bellings, Sir Richard, 142
Bennet, Thomas, earl of Arlington: career, 18, 155; secretary, 51, 156; negotiates Triple Alliance, 102–3, 104; and Dover Treaty, 104–5, 169–70, 172–3; mission to Holland, 107–8; and Clarendon, 142, 155; as manager, 155, 158; and Buckingham, 167; his caution, 172; opposes Danby, 181; attacked, 183–4; loses secretaryship, 185
Bentham, Jeremy, 81
Bentinck, Willem, earl of Portland, 21, 246, 253, 271, 274, 280, 284, 303, 307, 308, 311, 313
Bergeyck, Count, 289
Berkeley, Charles, earl of Falmouth, 21, 99, 156
Bertie, Charles, 50, 192, 204
Bishoprics, value of, 31, 89
Blackall, Offspring, 328
Blathwayt, William, 57, 280
Blenheim, 291, 324
Bolingbroke, Viscount, *see* St John
Bolron, Robert, 199
Bolton, duke of, *see* Pawlett
Bombay, 98
Booth, Sir George, 121, 122, 131
Booth, Henry, Baron Delamere, 10, 229, 261
Bordeaux, Antoine de, 114
Bothmer, J. G. von, 23, 297–8, 351–2, 354
Boyle, Henry, 313
Boyle, Robert, 358
Boyne, battle, 264, 281
Brandenburg–Prussia, 46, 102, 164, 165
Breda: Declaration from, 132, 136, 150, 157, 175; Treaty of, 102
Brent, Robert, 243
Bridgeman, Sir Orlando, 47, 133, 173
Bristol, 77, 215, 219, 229
Bristol, earl of, *see* Digby
Bromley, William, 28, 68, 315, 350
Bunyan, John, 153
Burton, Bartholomew, 308
Butler, James, first duke of Ormonde, 114, 158–9, 161, 181
Butler, James, second duke of Ormonde, 298, 339, 347

Cabal ministry: composition, 166–7; and French

Index